Empires to Nations:

Expansion in America, 1713–1824

Europe and the World
in the Age of Expansion

edited by Boyd C. Shafer

EMPIRES TO NATIONS

Expansion in America,

1713–1824

by
MAX SAVELLE

UNIVERSITY OF MINNESOTA PRESS □ MINNEAPOLIS

Library of Congress Catalog Card Number: 74-78995

ISBN 0-8166-0709-5

Europe and the World
in the Age of Expansion

For

Jean

the beloved partner

Editor's Foreword

The expansion of Europe since the thirteenth century has had profound influences on peoples throughout the world. Encircling the globe, the expansion changed men's lives and goals and became one of the decisive movements in the history of mankind.

This series of ten volumes explores the nature and impact of the expansion. It attempts not so much to go over once more the familiar themes of "Gold, Glory, and the Gospel," as to describe, on the basis of new questions and interpretations, what appears to have happened insofar as modern historical scholarship can determine.

No work or works on so large a topic can include everything that happened or be definitive. This series, as it proceeds, emphasizes the discoveries, the explorations, and the territorial expansion of Europeans, the relationships between the colonized and the colonizers, the effects of the expansion on Asians, Africans, Americans, Indians, and the various "islanders," the emergence into nationhood and world history of many peoples that Europeans had known little or nothing about, and, to a lesser extent, the effects of the expansion on Europe.

The use of the word *discoveries*, of course, reveals European (and American) provincialism. The "new" lands were undiscovered only in the sense that they were unknown to Europeans. Peoples with developed cultures and civilizations already had long inhabited most of the huge areas to which Europeans sailed and over which they came to exercise their power and influence. Nevertheless, the political, economic, and

ix

social expansion that came with and after the discoveries affected the daily lives, the modes of producing and sharing, the ways of governing, the customs, and the values of peoples everywhere. Whatever their state of development, the expansion also brought, as is well known, tensions, conflicts, and much injustice. Perhaps most important in our own times, it led throughout the developing world to the rise of nationalism, to reform and revolt, and to demands (now largely realized) for national self-determination.

The early volumes in the series, naturally, stress the discoveries and explorations. The later emphasize the growing commercial and political involvements, the founding of new or different societies in the "new" worlds, the emergence of different varieties of nations and states in the often old and established societies of Asia, Africa, and the Americas, and the changes in the governmental structures and responsibilities of the European imperial nations.

The practices, ideas, and values the Europeans introduced continue, in differing ways and differing environments, not only to exist but to have consequences. But in the territorial sense the age of European expansion is over. Therefore the sponsors of this undertaking believe this is a propitious time to prepare and publish this multivolumed study. The era now appears in new perspective and new and more objective statements can be made about it. At the same time, its realities are still with us and we may now be able to understand intangibles that in the future could be overlooked.

The works in process, even though they number ten, cover only what the authors (and editors) consider to be important aspects of the expansion. Each of the authors had to confront vast masses of material and make choices in what he should include. Inevitably, subjects and details are omitted that some readers will think should have been covered. Inevitably, too, readers will note some duplication. This arises in large part because each author has been free, within the general themes of the series, to write his own book on the geographical area and chronological period allotted to him. Each author, as might be expected, has believed it necessary to give attention to the background of his topic and has also looked a bit ahead; hence he has touched upon the time periods of the immediately preceding and following volumes. This means that each of the studies can be read independently, without constant reference to the others. The books are being published as they are completed and will not appear in their originally planned order.

The authors have generally followed a pattern for spelling, capitalization, and other details of style set by the University of Minnesota Press in the interests of consistency and clarity. In accordance with the wishes of the Press and current usage, and after prolonged discussion, we have used the word *black* instead of *Negro* (except in quotations). For the most part American usages in spelling have been observed. The last is sometimes difficult for historians who must be concerned with the different spellings, especially of place names and proper nouns, at different times and in different languages. To help readers the authors have, in consequence, at times added the original (or the present) spelling of a name when identification might otherwise be difficult.

The discussions that led to this series began in 1964 during meetings of the Advisory Committee of the James Ford Bell Library at the University of Minnesota, a library particularly interested in exploration and discovery. Members of the university's Department of History and the University of Minnesota Press, and others, including the present editor, joined in the discussions. Then, after the promise of generous subsidies from the Bell Foundation of Minneapolis and the Hill Family Foundation of St. Paul, the project began to take form under the editorship of the distinguished historian Herbert Heaton. An Advisory Council of six scholars was appointed as the work began. Professor Heaton, who had agreed to serve as editor for three years, did most of the early planning and selected three authors. Professor Boyd C. Shafer of Macalester College (now at the University of Arizona) succeeded him in 1967. He selected eight authors and did further planning. He has been in constant touch with all the authors, doing preliminary editing in consultation with them, reading their drafts, and making suggestions. The Press editors, as is usual at the University of Minnesota Press, have made valuable contributions at all stages. Between Professor Shafer and the authors — from England, Canada, New Zealand, and the United States — there have been voluminous and amicable as well as critical exchanges. But it must be repeated, each author has been free to write his own work within the general scope of the series.

Max Savelle, the author of this book, volume V in the series, is a specialist in eighteenth-century American history. With his doctorate from Columbia University, he has taught at Columbia, Stanford, and the University of Washington, and is now, after retirement from Washington, at the University of Illinois at Chicago Circle. Under various sponsorships he has studied and lectured in France, Spain, and Chile. He is the author of several works on colonial America and American diplomacy, including *Seeds of Liberty: The Genesis of the American Mind.*

About this volume in our series he writes, "It is my desire to have the reader see America [the two continents and the islands] whole (with all its diversities)," and he thinks of his book as a "case study in the *process of history* in the formation of new societies and nations."

Boyd C. Shafer

University of Arizona

Preface

In the broadest historical sense, the outpouring of Europeans that subdued and occupied the American continent was a single event. It was participated in, to be sure, by men of many nationalities — Portuguese, Spanish, French, English, Dutch, Italian, Danish, Swedish, Prussian, and others. But the movement was one. In one fashion or another all the Europeans who were involved in the occupation of America had many things in common: they were all Christians; they all spoke European variants of the great family of Indo-European languages; many were motivated by the new mercantilistic capitalism; in some way each group was composed of agents of one or another of the newly emerged, integral monarchical states and the European states system; all were members of a western European culture that was highly institutionalized and self-conscious, possessed of the most sophisticated and effective technological instruments of war yet developed. The methods of conquest and colonization were basically similar in all the national penetrations of the new continent; in this great movement the common characteristics of a *European* culture were transplanted to America. The expansion of Europe was one phenomenon, much as the Crusades were one; the conquest and colonization of America constituted a segment of a still larger whole, the expansion of European civilization throughout the world.

Many historians have recognized the basic unity of the expansion of European civilization into America. Several have written the early history of America in the context of this overall concept. This was typically true of such eighteenth-century historians as the Abbé Raynal. In modern times, Herbert E. Bolton formulated the unitary thesis of the history of America in his *History of the Americas* (1928) and, most particularly, in his presidential address to the American Historical Association in December 1932.[1] Others, in Latin America, such as Carlos Pereyra, Eugenio Pereira Salas, and Leopoldo Zea, have contributed to the historiography of America as a whole.

But since the eighteenth century the dominant tendency in the historiography of America has been to treat the histories of the various parts of America separately. Says Silvio Zavala of Mexico, one of the outstanding contemporary historians of America,

The departures from Europe, at more or less proximate intervals, of various peoples who created the world of the American colonizations . . . have customarily been studied, since the historiography of the Enlightenment, nationally or fragmentarily. . . . It is true that . . . the life of the transatlantic provinces has been little studied in its particular position in the totality of Western Civilization, and this has made it difficult to perceive the generality of certain phenomena, the significance of comparative studies, and the importance of the relations among colonial empires themselves.

Whence it has resulted that the habit of seeing the totality of the European colonizing expansion as well as its multiple results within the framework of the American hemisphere has been lost, to the prejudice of a true understanding of modern history and of American history in the colonial period.[2]

Or, as the late Carlton J. H. Hayes stated the principle, quoting Ross Hoffman,

Every state of the North and South American continents originated from Western European Christendom which Voltaire, in the age before the independence movements, characterized so well as a "great republic." Englishmen, Frenchmen, Spaniards, Portuguese, Dutchmen and Danes in the early modern centuries made the Atlantic Ocean the inland sea of Western Civilization; they made it an historical and geographical extension of the Mediterranean. . . . Many of these early-forged bonds still span the Atlantic, and the spread of British, French, and American ideals

[1] Herbert E. Bolton, "The Epic of Greater America," *American Historical Review*, 38(no. 2):448–474 (April 1933). This problem is ably and penetratingly discussed in Lewis Hanke, *Do the Americans Have a Common History? A Critique of the Bolton Theory* (New York: Alfred A. Knopf, 1964).

[2] Silvio Zavala, *El mundo americano en la época colonial*, 2 vols. (Mexico: Editorial Porrua, 1967), I, xv.

of liberty and constitutional government has made this oceanic region the citadel of what today is rather loosely called Democracy.[3]

At the same time, within the overall unity of western European civilization there were numerous diversities. Although all the Europeans were Christians, mostly Roman Catholic, the English, Dutch, Swedish, and Danish colonizers were Protestants. Although all spoke one or another variant of the European family of Indo-European languages, these national languages were different from each other. Although every political system represented in the European occupation of America was a variant form of the modern integral state, each differed in some detail from all the others. There was a sharp and striking contrast between the British form of limited constitutional monarchy and the Dutch republican forms, on the one side, and the quasi-absolute monarchical forms of the French, the Spanish, and the Portuguese systems on the other, all of which were extended to America. Although by the sixteenth and seventeenth centuries the economic institutions and mores of most of the western European states were basically capitalistic, the economies of France and the Iberian countries were still characterized, even at the end of the eighteenth century, by many conventions and practices that derived from economic feudalism; these were also transported to, and planted in, America.

Furthermore, each of the Euroamerican empires was part of a larger, worldwide whole. Lusoamerica was a segment of a global Portuguese empire; Hispanoamerica was part of a world empire that included, outside of Europe and the Mediterranean, territories in Africa and Asia (the Philippines) as well as America; Francoamerica was made up of two segments (North America and the French West Indies) of an empire that included vast territories in Africa and India; the British empire and the Dutch empire both included huge areas in Africa and Asia.

In each of these empires there was one national language, one generally integrated system of government, one generally integrated economic administration held together by the ideology of a national brand of mercantilism, one uniform — or nearly uniform (except the English) — system of religion.

These differences among the Euroamerican empires originated in

[3] Quoted by Carlton J. H. Hayes, "The American Frontier — Frontier of What?" *American Historical Review*, 51:207–208 (1946).

Europe, and they were extended to America right from the beginning of conquest and colonization. Thus, the history of the overseas expansion of European civilization must be written both as a great expansive movement of many people constituting a conglomerate whole and bound together by many powerful common elements and as a congeries of separate national movements that differed in many ways, though never very profoundly, from one another. These unities and these diversities all characterized the expansion of Europe even before it "hauled up the anchor" in Europe itself.

This great expansive movement of Europeans engulfed America, then, already characterized both by many dominant major unities and by numerous minor diversities. Once the swarm of Europeans had settled in America, new unities and new diversities were generated by the American experience to make an already complex European phenomenon a yet more complex American one — to make a highly conglomerate old historical movement a yet more conglomerate American growth.

The upshot of all this is that the history of the American hemisphere, especially in the eighteenth century, is a complex history of many unities and many diversities. Some of these were inherent in the expansion of Europe when it started; others (of both kinds) were created by the growth of societies in America after the Europeans arrived.

Within the intricate network of circumstances that constitute the historiographical problem, the history of America during the eighteenth century emerges as a chapter — a highly complex chapter — in the drama of expansion in this hemisphere. The "name of the game" is people — human beings — struggling to survive and find the good life in the American environment. If, within that broad spectrum, there is any major theme in the eighteenth century that dominates all others, it is the theme of the formation, the maturity, and the achievement of independence of a congeries of new societies, that is, new nations. It is, indeed, a history *e pluribus unum*.

This book is concerned with the history of the ongoing expansion of Euroamerican civilization in the eighteenth century. It must of necessity see that history from three perspectives. First, it must comprehend the totality of the expansion of Europe, especially the two-way relationship between America and Europe. Second, it must see the internal history of the American continent as a whole, both in its unities and in its diversities. Third, it must recognize the histories of the particular regional societies that would eventually become, as the eighteenth century wore into the nineteenth, the nations of the American hemisphere. It is primarily a history of America, but, as a chapter in the history of the expansion of Europe, it must also take note of the reflex impact of the overseas experiences on the internal life of Europe itself: economic, political, international, religious, cultural, and ideological.

It is with pleasure and a deep sense of gratitude that I acknowledge my indebtedness to the Newberry Library of Chicago, which honored me by an appointment to a Senior Fellowship of the Library, and where most of the work for this book was done, and also to its director, Dr. Lawrence W. Towner, and its never-failing staff. I am also indebted to the Library of the University of Washington in Seattle for much help and many services. I am especially grateful to Professor Robert Conrad of the University of Illinois, Chicago, who read the manuscript in its entirety and made many helpful suggestions for its improvement. I am deeply indebted, also, to the editor of this series, Professor Boyd C. Shafer, of the University of Arizona, for his careful reading of the manuscript, for his many helpful suggestions, and, above all, for his patient and scholarly exchange of ideas toward making this a worthwhile contribution to the history of the world and of the Western Hemisphere. Finally, I should like to express my gratitude to the copy editors of the University of Minnesota Press for their superb editorial assistance in the preparation of the manuscript of this book for the press.

M. S.

University of Illinois at Chicago Circle
June 1, 1973

Contents

List of Illustrations

List of Maps

Empires to Nations:

Expansion in America, 1713–1824

Introduction

By the end of the seventeenth century the expansion of European civilization had reached most of the major land masses of the world. Yet at the time of the Peace of Utrecht (1713), European man's geographic knowledge of the earth was still far from complete. The interiors of Africa and the American continent were largely unknown; Australia, Australasia, the Arctic area, and Antarctica were hardly dreamed of, despite the epoch-making voyage of Magellan and El Cano in 1519–22.

During the eighteenth century most of the blank spaces on the map of America were filled in. Also in the course of that century, the small nuclei of Euroamerican society that had been founded in the sixteenth and seventeenth centuries grew until, along the coasts of the continent at least, they were almost coterminous with one another. Increasingly, they became rivals, as between national imperial entities, for the further occupation, possession, and exploitation of the hemisphere.

The population of Euroamerica, at the beginning of the century a conglomerate of Amerinds and their Portuguese, Spanish, Dutch, Swedish, Danish, English, and French masters, had by the end of the 1700s become vastly more numerous and diversified. Millions of blacks from Africa had been imported into the colonies to add another non-European ethnic ingredient to the population of the hemisphere. Above all, the Europeans had intermingled with the Amerinds and the blacks to produce numerous ethnic minorities of mestizos and mulattoes. Europeans and creoles, pure-blooded descendants of the original European colo-

3

nists, still dominated the economic, political, religious, and intellectual life as well as the social realities of these Euroamerican societies, but the masses of the people were neither genetically nor culturally wholly European. They were predominantly American, especially biologically. Probably the greatest and most significant characteristic of American society lay in the fact that, conglomerate though it was, it was so clearly and remarkably different from the society of Europe. This highly essential difference had arisen not in Europe but in the nature and the processes of experience in America itself.

In similar vein, by the end of the eighteenth century the peoples of America no longer felt the pull of cultural or emotional ties with their mother countries sufficiently powerful to bind them inseparably to their metropolises. The Amerinds, blacks, mestizos, and mulattoes never had been aware of such ties in the first place. Now, the cultural and emotional ties of the Americans, even of the creoles, had matured to the point where their supreme loyalties were no longer to their mother countries but to the regions in which they had been born.

Just as the changing nature of the population of America had given it a character that was profoundly different from that of the society of Europe, so the experiences of the Americans in America itself had also created certain "unities" within the hemisphere that defied imperial boundaries. Thus, for example, in the area of politics the creation of many colonies under the rule of a single king and governed by a single royal council was a bond of unity that grew out of the experience itself. The international (that is, intercolonial) commerce that developed into a vast interimperial network of commercial relationships in the eighteenth century was a powerful bond that drew the colonies of all nations toward the formation of a North Atlantic economic community largely independent of exclusive, mercantilistic, national-imperial economic blocks. Nothing illustrates this fact more clearly than the network of international relationships represented by the Atlantic slave trade, or even the vast network of "illicit" commercial relationships that transcended interimperial boundaries almost with impunity. Slavery itself was an international phenomenon expanded and intensified by the conditions of the New World — a continental institution that had little relation to national or imperial boundaries. The presence of Amerind societies on the continent, from one end of it to the other, was a common condition whose roots and whose very being were peculiar to America. The creation of a line of Christian missions from Hudson Bay to Patagonia — French, Spanish, Portuguese (to say nothing of the missionary efforts carried on in a much less planned and formal way by the English and the Dutch) — was a sort of international crusade, governed in a general way from one center in Rome, that arose peculiarly and exclusively out of the American frontier experience, with only remote antecedents in Europe.

In the same historical process, if the New World experience had created new continental unities of effort and of institutions, it had also created new diversities. Thus, under the stress of experience in differing environments, the French in Canada created one regional life-style while those who went to the Caribbean created another. The Portuguese who settled in northeastern Brazil created one life-style while those in Minas Gerais, São Paulo, or Rio Grande do Sul developed life-styles that were sharply different from one another; the Spaniards who went to the Rio de la Plata created a life-style that was markedly different from those of Peru and Mexico; and the Englishmen who settled in the British West Indies evolved a life-style that was notably different from that of Puritan New England.

These internal differences can be attributed chiefly, if not entirely, to the struggle of Euroamericans of the same nationalities to adapt their new societies to, and to find the good life in, differing environments. These regional adaptations and consequent cultural variations do not necessarily mean, however, that the history of each region must be treated separately. Some of these regional differences eventuated in new societies; others did not. Canada and the French West Indies became separate nations, as did Mexico, Venezuela, Peru, Argentina, and Chile. But while the continental colonies of Angloamerica separated nationally from the British West Indies, New England and the southern colonies on the continent held together (at the price of a disastrous intersectional civil war later, to be sure). And the three or four regional cultures of Brazil stayed united even though powerful social, economic, and political forces worked for centuries to separate them.

Not only that: in each of these segments, whether they separated or remained united, there had appeared by the last quarter of the eighteenth century a cultural life and a regional self-consciousness that made it, psychologically at least, an embryo nation. Although not all of them separated to become de facto nations, most of these self-conscious regional societies did break off not only from Europe but from the others to form new nations.

Thus, it may be said that the most characteristic historical process at work in the American hemisphere in the eighteenth century, though it was not always apparent to contemporaries, was the process of nation building. The century ended with the independence movement well under way; it would culminate with the independence of Brazil in 1824.

Economically the natural penchant of the colonies was also toward self-sufficiency and even freedom of commerce rather than toward the rigid prohibitory or regulatory systems of imperial mercantilisms. So long as a mother country provided a monopoly market for its colonies' exports and a viable source of the manufactures needed by the colonies, the mercantilistic system operated, by and large, successfully. But as soon as the colonies learned that they could sell their products more profitably and buy their imports at better prices outside the national monopolies, they flouted the monopolies and rationalized their violations by espousing the elementary ideas and the practices of free trade. Benjamin Franklin, the great Angloamerican "creole," was probably the most outstanding exponent of this fact, yet there were many others.

Indeed, the sheer magnitude of the interimperial (that is, intercolonial) commerce, licit and illicit, that flourished in the eighteenth century despite the efforts of the metropolises to control or suppress it is clear and conclusive evidence that economic "expansion" in the hemisphere really meant economic growth — growth of production and exchange — which, by its very nature, simply could not and would not be contained within the old mercantilistic frameworks.

Expansion, then, in America was chiefly inward, not outward. Not only did political expansion mean the steady enlargement of the territorial areas and the numbers of people ruled by colonial and imperial governments; it also meant a steadily ongoing refinement of political institutions, coupled with a continuing growth of political "know-how" among the Americans themselves. In the English and French colonies (especially those in the West Indies) this process was marked by the development and the increasing power of colonial representative bodies. The process was not as dramatic in the Portuguese and Spanish colonies, but even in those empires the imperial administrative reforms of the third quarter of the eighteenth century had a tendency, despite their intended centralization of imperial control, to stimulate the political consciousness of the colonials and to stir in them an impulse toward autonomy.

One of the most striking aspects of the history of the expansion of Europe in America in the eighteenth century was the intensification of the complexity of the diplomatic history of the continent and the impact of that on the development of international law. Whereas before the eighteenth century the overseas colonies, in the eyes of the chancelleries of Europe, were hardly more than pawns on the international chessboard, by the latter part of the seventeenth century and increasingly in the eighteenth the colonies were regarded as integral parts of the European-centered empires, not lightly to be alienated and very much worth fighting for.

Even before the Peace of Utrecht, the overseas European possessions and their problems had already had a powerful impact on the evolution of international law. Such international principles as, for example, the doctrine of the freedom of the seas, spheres of colonial influence, effective occupation, and the rights of neutrals had been derived in large part from problems arising out of the contacts and conflicts of the expanding European empires as they rubbed against each other in the course of their expansion.

Now, in the eighteenth century, the practice of diplomacy pertaining to the colonies was a large and significant part of the work of all the chancelleries of western Europe. Much of the diplomacy involved in the major peace settlements of the eighteenth century was concerned with problems related to overseas empires. Indeed, most of the wars fought by the European states in the eighteenth century were directed, in part at least, toward the rectification or the maintenance of the colonial balance of power.

During this same period, as the colonial societies matured, they discovered international objectives and interests of their own that at times did not coincide with those of their mother countries, although they usually did. For example, the interests of Angloamericans, Brazilians, and Argentines in seizing the territories of rival empires usually corresponded to those of the mother countries and demanded their support. On the other hand, the so-called "illicit" trade among the colonies of all the Euroamerican empires ran directly counter to international agreements made in Europe to stop such trade. Often, too, the colonies criticized or resented the willingness of the mother countries to swap lands in America. Another clear example of the conflict of international interests between colonies and mother countries appeared in the effort of Spain and Portugal to dispose of the Jesuit missionary territories in South America, an effort which caused the Amerinds, sponsored by the Jesuits, to fight both mother countries.

In short, the colonies, as they grew, were developing international objectives of their own. These, in general, were likely to center on the colonial greed for land — whether Indian or Euroamerican — freedom of commerce, and isolation from European wars.

In intellectual and religious life, "expansion" meant hybridization, secularization, and "enlightenment." To be sure, there were many more "Christians" in America at the end of the eighteenth century than there had been at the beginning. But the Christian religion in America, by the end of the century, had absorbed, in many regions of the hemisphere, powerful non-Christian elements of belief and of ritual derived from the Amerinds and the Africans. At the same time, in many areas, especially in Angloamerica, the religious impacts of the eighteenth-century Enlightenment had watered down the traditional Christianities of both medieval Catholicism and modern Protestantism to the point where many of the ancient doctrines were drastically modified or, in the name of rationalism, discarded altogether. "Expansion" in religion signified, then, not only an increase in numbers, but also a steady increase in sophistication, hybridization, and modernization.

In the overall perspective of the expansion of Euroamerican civilization in America in the eighteenth century, perhaps the most significant development was the emergence of some twenty new nations. The eighteenth century was the century of the birth of nations and the emergence of nationalism. This was as true of America as it was of Europe: perhaps more true of America, in fact, since the new societies formed in the amalgamation of European culture with Amerind and African cultures were less retarded in their flowering than were those of Europe by the cultural, social, and intellectual ideas, emotions, and institutions carried over from the feudal era.

It is clear, in any case, that the new nations were not really just children of Europe. Their deepest roots were in America, some running far back into the pre-Columbian past, some springing from the experiences of the Amerinds, the Europeans, and the blacks in this hemisphere after the arrival of the Europeans. Therefore, national cultures that appeared in the hemisphere — the national-cultural groupings that became the new American states — in the long run and in the most essential ways were American, not European.

CHAPTER 1

The Completion of the European Occupation of the American Continent

Territorial Distribution of the Euroamerican Colonial Empires, 1713

The Peace of Utrecht, which brought to an end the War of the Spanish Succession in 1713, was one of the great mileposts in the international history of the American hemisphere. Representing a stunning victory for England and its allies against the forces aligned with France and Louis XIV, it provided for territorial changes that were surprisingly small. Hudson Bay was recognized, once and for all, as belonging to England; Acadia, or Nova Scotia, "with its ancient boundaries" (nobody knew what they were), was ceded to England by France; the island of St. Christopher in the West Indies, hitherto shared by France and England, was now given over in its entirety to England. The Portuguese Colonia do Sacramento, on the eastern shore of the estuary of the Rio de la Plata opposite Buenos Aires, which had been seized by the Spaniards in the course of the war, was restored to Portugal. Otherwise, the territorial pattern of the colonial empires established in the American hemisphere in the sixteenth and seventeenth centuries remained essentially unchanged.[1]

The Peace of Utrecht left Portugal in possession of Brazil. The exact boundaries of this vast empire were not precisely known, but they were generally regarded as extending from the Rio de la Plata in the south to well beyond the Amazon River in the north and westward to the

[1] See volume IV of this series.

Andes or to the eastern boundary of Peru. Its capital until 1763 was Bahia, and the governor of Bahia was referred to as the viceroy of Brazil; however, not until the capital of the colony was moved to Rio de Janeiro in 1763 did the viceroy really become a significant official, a real vicegerent of the king, with corresponding power.

Spain remained in possession of its American empire in much the same form as it had had since the other colonizing powers, England, France, and Holland, had occupied parts of the hemisphere for themselves. Spain still held Florida and the viceroyalty of New Spain (Mexico), which stretched from the western borders of French Louisiana (wherever they were) southward to the Isthmus of Panama. The viceroyalty of New Granada (established in 1717), whose capital was Bogotá, covered the northern segment of the continent of South America and included what are today Colombia and Venezuela; the viceroyalty of Peru, centered in Lima, comprised the massif of the Andes and the coastal area as far south as modern Chile; the region of the Rio de la Plata was at this time also a part of the viceroyalty of Peru, but it had its own governor and *audiencia*, established in 1661. The viceroyalty of La Plata, centered in Buenos Aires and including modern Argentina, Paraguay, and Uruguay, was not created until 1776.

France continued to possess Canada, which stretched an unknown, undefined, and unexplored distance toward the western parts of North America, as well as the entire Mississippi Valley, still also claimed by Spain. Into this area French settlements were just now pushing, from Detroit, on the Great Lakes, into the Illinois country, and southward to Mobile and Biloxi on the Gulf of Mexico; New Orleans was to be founded in 1718. In the Caribbean area France had firmly established colonies in Martinique, Guadeloupe, and western Santo Domingo and held vague and debatable claims to such other islands as Dominica and St. Lucia.

The English empire in America consisted of about twenty-five separate colonies, stretching from Hudson Bay to the northern coast of South America. These included Newfoundland, Acadia, twelve so-called "continental colonies" on the eastern seaboard of the continent of North America (Georgia was added in 1733, twenty years after the Peace of Utrecht; Nova Scotia was founded as a separate colony in 1749), a number of islands in the West Indies, the most important of which were Jamaica, Barbados, and St. Christopher, the Bahamas, and the Bermudas, together with indefinite claims to several disputed islands in the Caribbean area and to certain other areas in the Orinoco delta. Nowhere, if Hudson Bay be excepted, did England possess any territory in the interior of the American continent. All the British colonies faced upon the Atlantic or its subsidiary basins.

The Dutch, who had once held extensive colonies in America, including much of northeastern Brazil, now found themselves in possession of only a few small colonies in the Caribbean area, Surinam, Curaçao, and St. Eustatius, whose greatest significance lay in their importance as bases for commerce, mostly illicit (that is, contrary to Spanish or French law), with the Spanish colonies carried on by English, Dutch, and French interlopers.

The Danes remained in possession of St. John and St. Thomas, the chief of the group of islands known as the Virgins.

Rounding Out the Geographic Knowledge of the Continent

The boundaries of the Euroamerican empires were far from fixed. This was not because they were deliberately left open but, rather, simply because the makers of the Peace of Utrecht knew so very little — in some parts of the continent, next to nothing — about the geography of the areas involved. As a matter of fact, there was no discernible desire to close the frontiers anywhere: the expansion of European control was still going on and it continued, in a sort of continuing race for first occupation, throughout the eighteenth century.

At the beginning of the century, then, large areas of the American continent were still unknown to Europeans. That part of North America west of Hudson Bay and the Great Lakes and north of the areas in the southwestern plains and along the Pacific Coast explored by the Spaniards in the sixteenth century had never been visited by white men. In South America the enormous region in the upper valleys of the Amazon and the São Francisco, constituting in area almost one-third of the territory of South America, remained unexplored. Apart from the voyages of Orellana and Aguirre in the sixteenth century down the great river from Peru, no significant effort had been made before about 1700 to explore, much less to exploit, these vast basins. They continued to be, in 1700, an unknown wilderness.

All the old motives for expansion in the American continent remained, however, in the minds of the expansionists in the mother countries as well as in those of the entrepreneurs in the already settled areas and centers of capital along the coast. There was a continuing capitalistic interest in finding new mines, exploiting the fisheries, prosecuting the skin and fur trade with the Indians, and establishing missions for the advancement of the Christian faith. There was still, in North America, a desire to find a short route to the Far East. There was still — in a more intensified and articulate form than ever — a nationalistic sense of *la gloire* among Americans and American officials such as the Marquis de la Galissonière, governor of French Canada about the middle of the century, the conviction that the flags of their nations must fly over ever-increasing extents of American territory, no matter how useless these areas might be. Back in Europe, besides the drive for commercial expansion, there was a belief among imperial statesmen that the balance of power in Europe depended in large measure upon a real or imagined balance of power among the colonial empires. It seemed to follow, therefore, that the greater the expanse and the wealth of the national overseas empire in America or elsewhere, the greater would be the power and the influence of the mother country in Europe.

In North America the fur traders, the voyageurs, ever in search of sources for valuable pelts, about the beginning of the century drove westward into the Great Plains and established among the Plains Indians bases from which other explorers could operate. In 1690 and 1691, for example, Henry Kelsey, traveling for the Hudson's Bay Company, reached Lake Winnipeg; he then ascended the Saskatchewan and established a base in the neighborhood of Lake Winnepegosis.

The Missouri River was thought to provide a gateway to the Pacific, and there exist unsubstantiated reports of many voyageurs who, after 1700, traveled up that valley. But the Foxes and the Sioux Indians, living west of Lake Michigan, constituted a barrier. After the Peace of Utrecht, as the supply of furs around the Great Lakes — particularly in the region south of them — decreased, the French, especially, were forced to look farther west for pelts. In 1717, Zacharie Robutel, Sieur de la Nouë, went westward as far as Rainy Lake, and in 1720–23 Pierre François Xavier de Charlevoix traversed the entire French Mississippi band of territory from north to south and urged the desirability of exploring farther westward to the western sea (the Pacific). From this time on there took place in France and in Canada a fervid discussion of routes, possibilities, and prospects for the opening of the North American West. The most important figure to emerge from this interest in the opening of the west was Pierre Gaultier de Varennes, Sieur de la Vérendrye. Hearing vaguely of the great lakes and rivers of the western Canadian plain, he secured the backing of a group of Montreal merchants for a monopoly of the far western fur trade, which received the approval of (but no subsidy from) the crown. The crown's endorsement required that La Vérendrye and his sons continue the search for the western ocean. They made a genuine effort to succeed in this objective, but they were basically fur traders, not explorers, and the expansion of European and American knowledge about North America must be understood as growing principally out of that activity — coupled with France's rivalry with the English and its desire to exclude them from the interior of the continent.

Between 1731 and 1749 La Vérendrye and his sons explored a vast area of the western plains toward the Rockies, although they never reached the mountains. In the course of his exploring and fur trading, La Vérendrye built a number of forts, on the Lake of the Woods, on Lake Winnipeg, at Portage-la-Prairie, on the Assiniboine, and, perhaps, on Lake Manitoba and the upper Missouri. He also had trouble with the Indians. In 1736 the Sioux fell upon one of his parties, numbering about twenty-five men, and massacred them all, including one of his sons.

La Vérendrye eventually reached the upper waters of the Missouri River and, possibly, those of the Saskatchewan. On the Missouri he met the Mandan Indians, whom he had been led to believe were white men, and later they told him of contacts they had had through other Indians with the Spaniards in the southwest, presumably at Santa Fe. To his great sorrow he learned from them and from the Indians on the Saskatchewan that the distance between him and the Pacific was undoubtedly so immense that it would be impossible for him to reach the coast. However, he and his party continued to explore and probably saw the Black Hills of South Dakota.

Meanwhile the English, under the auspices of the Hudson's Bay Company, undertook the exploration of the western Canadian plains farther north. In 1719 the company sent out Captain James Knight to search along the northwestern shores of Hudson Bay for a river that was reputed

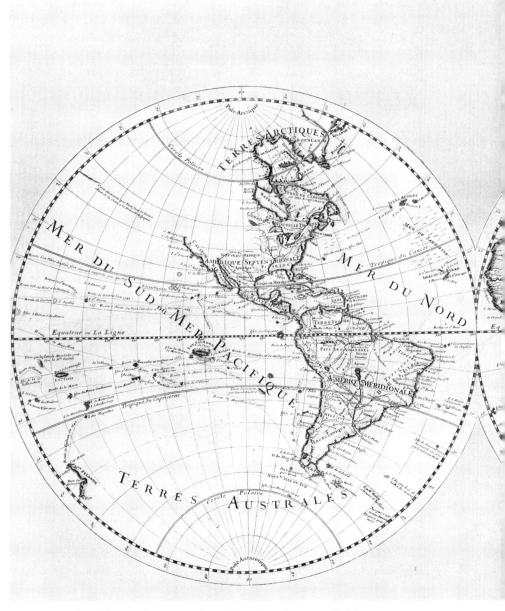

The Western Hemisphere about 1700. From Guillaume Delisle,
Mappe-Monde . . . (Paris: G. Delisle, 1700). Courtesy of
The Newberry Library, Chicago.

among the Indians to have copper and gold along its shores; but the expedition was cast away on Marble Island. Whether because of the French competition represented by La Vérendrye or because of the publication in 1744 by Arthur Dobbs, a critic of the Hudson's Bay Company, of an Indian account of the lands to the west of Hudson Bay, the company sponsored an expedition by Anthony Henday (1754–55) which actually reached the foothills of the Rocky Mountains west and south of the Saskatchewan River. In 1769 Samuel Hearne set out from Fort Prince of Wales (built in 1751) on Churchill Bay to find the legendary Coppermine River and to search for the Northwest Passage. He made a series of expeditions into the badlands northwest of the bay and eventually reached the Coppermine and Great Slave Lake. Hearne's explorations revealed that this vast stretch of land was useless and, more significantly, that the continent was huge: Hearne once more and forever dispelled the hope that an easy passage lay across it to the Pacific.

During this same period, the outlines of the western shore of the continent were being revealed by the Russians and the Spaniards. The Russian interest in North America may be said to have stemmed from Peter the Great's encouragement of science and scientists and his own interest in knowing whether Russia and Asia were connected by some sort of land bridge. In 1720 Peter sent two explorers to find out, but they did not get beyond the Kurile Islands. Then, in 1725, he commissioned Vitus Bering, Martin Spanberg, and Alexander Chirikof to pursue the search further. They actually set out in 1728. Their first expedition failed to disclose any significant information, but Bering started out again in 1733, accompanied by the French cartographer J. N. Delisle. After a long delay at Kamchatka, Bering reached the coast of North America in 1741. Although he himself died of scurvy, his lieutenants and the crews of his ships reported one of the world's greatest herds of fur-bearing seals and sea-otter. Russian fur hunters rushed into the Alaskan islands from about 1743 onward and proceeded south along the Alaskan coast. Other European hunters heard of the fabulous Alaskan hunting grounds and swarmed in, while reports from the hitherto unexplored area prompted France, Spain, Holland, and England to send out exploring expeditions which became the bases for rival claims to the territories of the area.

By about 1744 the Russians had built a line of forts and trading stations as far south as Fort Ross, just north of San Francisco Bay in modern

California. On the basis of the doctrine of "effective occupation," the Russian claim to the new lands was more clearly established than that of any other nation. That, however, did not deter the others from moving into the same territory. The Spaniards, indeed, had already spied out parts of the northern Pacific coasts in a series of expeditions in the sixteenth and seventeenth centuries, the most significant of which was that of Sebastián Vizcaíno, which had reached approximately latitude 42° (northern California) in 1603. But Spanish interest had lagged until news of the Russian discoveries reached Spain about the middle of the eighteenth century. Even then, the advent of the Seven Years War prevented any Spanish explorations until after 1763. At last, in 1765, King Carlos III charged José Gálvez, whom he made *visitador general* of Mexico, with the task of countering the Russian expansion.

Using the already established Jesuit missions in Lower California as his base, in 1769 Gálvez sent out five expeditions, three by sea and two by land, to establish Spanish hegemony in what is now California before the Russians got there. The land expeditions, commanded by Gaspar de Portolá, made contact with the seaborne expeditions at San Diego in the summer of 1769. Portolá then pushed on to Monterey, and from there he journeyed north and discovered the great bay of San Francisco, which he reached late in October 1769. In May of 1770, the Spaniards staked their claim to the coast this far north by building a fort at the mouth of the bay.

Once the land route to the San Francisco Bay and the outlines of the coast were known, the Spaniards proceeded to occupy the newfound territory by establishing between 1769 and 1775 a line of missions from the formerly Jesuit missions of Lower California up through California to San Francisco itself. Father Francisco Garces and Father Junípero Serra, both Franciscans, were largely responsible for the founding of these missions. (The Jesuits had been expelled from the Spanish empire, including Spanish America, in 1767.) Then, in 1775, the Spaniards established a real colony at San Francisco. The race to forestall the Russians, at least as far north as the San Francisco Bay, had been won.

The Spaniards went even farther north; about 1785 they fortified Nootka Sound on Vancouver Island. Their claim to territory so far north, however, could not be sustained, and they had to content themselves with the area of actual settlements south of the San Francisco Bay. In fact, the northwestern shores were already lost to them, for those coasts were now penetrated from three directions: from Canada overland and from the United States and England by sea.

In Canada, the years following the Peace of Paris of 1763 were marked by the arrival of English, Scottish, and American fur traders and by a bitter competition which arose between them and the old French traders of Montreal, typified by the new Northwest Company on the one side and the Hudson's Bay Company on the other. In the course of the competition, the traders of both companies traversed, mapped, and established trading posts in most of the areas of the Canadian western plains; and out of it there emerged a number of remarkable explorers, the most notable of whom were Peter Pond and Alexander MacKenzie. Pond explored Lake Athabaska in 1778. Some ten years later Alexander MacKenzie of the Hudson's Bay Company, having heard of the rich harvests of furs being reaped by the Russians and of the explorations of Captain Cook, went out to search for the river that was reputed to flow from the Canadian plains into the Pacific in the Russian zone. He discovered the river that bears his name and explored and mapped it to its mouth, but he was deeply disappointed to find that it debouched into the Arctic Ocean and not the Pacific. Not one to be daunted, he started another expedition up the Peace River toward the Rockies in 1791. Although he discovered the upper part of the Fraser River, he decided to go overland to the Pacific instead of descending the river. On July 22, 1793, he stood on the shore of Dean Channel in what is now British Columbia where he beheld the Pacific Ocean, thereby becoming the first white man to cross the North American continent by land and finally dispelling the old dream of easy access to Asia by either that route or the illusory Northwest Passage.

MacKenzie was followed by Simon Fraser, who, traveling for the Northwest Company, in 1807 and 1808 descended the Fraser River almost to its mouth. Four years later David Thompson of the Hudson's Bay Company explored and mapped the Columbia. Meanwhile, Captain James Cook, traveling for the English government and the British Royal Society, had continued the expansion of geographic knowledge in a spectacular series of voyages which took him into the South Pacific, Australia, and the Antarctic. On his last voyage (1776) he explored the coasts of Alaska. George Vancouver, one of his lieutenants, continued Cook's exploration of the western shores of North America and, just a few weeks before

MacKenzie arrived in July 1793, he explored the shores of the "Inside Passage" between the Canadian mainland and Vancouver Island. The voyages of Cook and Vancouver, coupled with those of MacKenzie, Fraser, and Thompson, provided a strong base for England's claim to all the Pacific coast between the Russians in Alaska and the Spaniards in California.

In the United States, the golden vision of the fur harvest to be gathered on the northwestern shores of America was heralded by John Ledyard of Connecticut, who had sailed with Cook on his last voyage. Ledyard never succeeded in gaining financial support for an expedition, although he does seem to have aroused the interest of Thomas Jefferson. With the publication of Cook's narratives, other Americans took up the idea of exploration, and in 1787 a group of Boston merchants organized an expedition of two ships — the *Columbia*, captained by John Kendrick, and the *Lady Washington*, commanded by Robert Gray — to try out the northwest fur trade with China. The expedition was fabulously successful, and when Gray went back in 1792 he discovered the mouth of the Columbia River. This trade, with its base at the mouth of the Columbia, became the foundation of the United States' claim to the Washington coast — the same coast then being claimed by England.

A few years later, after Thomas Jefferson became president of the United States in 1801, he purchased the vast trans-Mississippi territory called Louisiana from Napoleon and proposed to Congress an appropriation that would provide for the scientific exploration of the Missouri River and the route by way of that river to the Pacific. His request, actually made before the purchase of Louisiana, resulted in the organization of the famous expedition led by Meriwether Lewis and William Clark, which ascended the Missouri, crossed the Continental Divide, and descended the Snake and Columbia rivers to the Pacific.

The Lewis and Clark expedition, as is well known, was eminently successful. It left St. Louis on May 14, 1804, and arrived, after an heroic series of adventures, at the mouth of the Columbia on November 15, 1805. Following this came the founding of Astoria in 1811 and the development of trade that gave rise to a rather intense competition with the Hudson's Bay Company, which had built a post at Fort Vancouver, also on the Columbia. The entire continent of North America was now explored and fairly adequately mapped. Four nations claimed the northwestern parts of it, but the final division into accepted Spanish, Russian, English, and United States spheres belongs to a later period of history.[2] The earliest European occupation of South America, unlike that of North America, had involved both eastern and western shores of the continent right from the beginning. Thus, as of about 1700 the entire coastline was well known; the great unknown area was the inland center of the continent. In the course of the eighteenth century this immense core was explored and to a large degree occupied.

It may be said that there were two methods by which the interior of South America came to be known. The first was the establishment by the Portuguese and Spanish Jesuits of missions among the Indians deep in the interior. The other was the expansion of exploitation, whether in cattle raising, mining, or other ways of economic penetration. In both cases, clear and accurate geographic knowledge derived from what José Honório Rodrigues calls "a frontier in motion."[3]

In the course of the establishment of a chain of Jesuit missions along the upper reaches of the Paraguay River and its tributaries, for example, that area was explored and accurately mapped in the first half of the eighteenth century. On the other hand, the opening and the exploration of the great central massif of Brazil, the so-called *mato grosso*, begun in the seventeenth century by the *bandeiras* — halfbreed (Indian and white) bands of slave hunters among the Indians — entered a new phase in 1734 with the discovery of gold in that region by Antonio Fernandez de Abreu. This discovery was followed by a "gold rush" of vast proportions, which resulted in the settlement of large areas along the interior rivers. One of Abreu's lieutenants went on to explore the valley of the Madeira River, one of the major tributaries of the Amazon. In 1742, Manuel Felix, a Portuguese, succeeded in navigating and exploring the system of the Amazon from west to east, fortunately obtaining aid and sustenance from the Jesuit missions already founded among the Moxo Indians.

The exploration and penetration of the interior basin of the Amazon by the Portuguese and the establishment of a line of missions by Spanish Jesuits in the upper valley of the Paraguay brought the Portuguese and the Spaniards into contact and inevitably presented the necessity for

[2] See volume VI of this series.

[3] José Honório Rodrigues, *Brasil: Periódo colonial*, in Silvio Zavala, gen. ed., *Programa de historia de América* (Mexico: Instituto Panamericano de Geografía e Historia, 1953), II, chapter 11.

defining the boundary between them. The accession of Ferdinand VI, whose queen was a Portuguese princess, to the Spanish throne in 1746 made a joint effort relatively easy, and an agreement for the settlement of their American disputes was arrived at in the famous Treaty of Madrid of 1750. According to this treaty, the boundary ran from the coast of Brazil south of the new colony of Rio Grande do Sul inland along a series of rivers and ridges northeast to the Amazon. Two joint commissions were provided for in the treaty to survey the line, but they were never actually activated.

The chief reason for this was that the proposed transfer to Portuguese rule of certain Spanish Jesuit missions among the Guarani Indians in the upper Uruguay River region precipitated an Indian uprising that forestalled the transfer. Other difficulties between the two countries in South America also had arisen in the meantime, and the treaty was allowed to lapse. Not until 1777 was a new treaty made at San Ildefonso in Spain; this time the boundary and the areas it traversed were actually explored by a joint Hispano-Portuguese commission created under the Treaty of San Ildefonso. The new boundary ran in a zigzag fashion from the Atlantic Ocean south of Rio Grande do Sul to the Madeira River; Don Felix de Azara, the leading spirit in the survey, took advantage of his position as a commissioner to explore and map the upper waters of the Paraguay Valley. He also wrote a series of descriptions of the flora and fauna of the area. Later he extended his exploration and his work in natural history to the pampas of Argentina.

Meanwhile, the Portuguese missions had penetrated the wilderness northward from the Amazon toward the Orinoco, and knowledge of the nature of this vast wilderness was provided both by the missionaries and by the parties of slave hunters, or northern *bandeirantes*, operating out of Bahia. Formal exploring expeditions led by Nicolas Rodriguez and Antonio Santos in 1775 and 1780 added to the public knowledge of this area.

Apart from the work of the explorers and surveyors, much of the exploration and description of the vast interior of South America was done by scientists. For example, the Paris Academy sent an expedition (which will be described later) to Peru in 1735 under the leadership of Charles Marie de la Condamine to measure the length of a degree of longitude on the equator. This expedition contributed to European knowledge a vast amount of data about the geography, the flora, and the fauna of the Andean tableland. La Condamine himself returned to Europe by descending the Amazon to the Atlantic and taking a ship from there. Louis Godin, a member of his party, also returned to Europe by way of the great river; the narrative of the sufferings of Godin and his wife on this expedition constitutes one of the great personal epics in the history of discovery. Scientific exploration of the continent was completed by the famous German naturalist Alexander von Humboldt, whose studies, made in the last decade of the eighteenth century and the first decade of the nineteenth, have remained the great classics of scientific exploration and description of northern South America to this day.

Conclusion

By the end of the eighteenth century, then, the main outlines of the geography of the American continent were fairly well known and its division among the imperial colonial powers of Europe was roughly defined, despite the fact that many areas were still the subject of international dispute. But the explorational phase of the expansion of Europe did not stop there. It continued in the work of those explorers who traveled to the Pacific by way of the Strait of Magellan, the most notable of whom were Louis Antoine de Bougainville, who explored the South Sea islands on his way around the world in 1766–69, and Captain James Cook, who, after mapping parts of the eastern coasts of North America, was commissioned by the English government to observe the transit of Venus from Tahiti in 1769. Cook made three voyages altogether, in the course of which he explored Antarctica, New Zealand, Australia, Alaska, and Hawaii.

The end of the eighteenth century thus marked the end of the era of exploration which was such an essential part of the expansion of Europe. Indeed, the eighteenth-century phase of the "Age of Exploration" was already highly colored and influenced by the interests of science rather than by the more materialistic objectives of its earlier phases. From this time onward, the study of the earth and its life-forms was increasingly done more in the interests of science than of commerce, or even of exploration for its own sake.

By the end of the eighteenth century, too, most of the boundaries between the Euroamerican empires were more clearly known, though not actually surveyed. Parts of two of the former empires (the United

States and Haiti) had broken away and had become independent states. They would shortly be followed by the other new societies on the continent, and disputed boundaries, such as those between the United States and Canada and between the United States and Mexico, would be exactly defined, step by step, during the nineteenth century. The boundaries of the old empires would become the basic boundaries between the new American states. This fact is a sort of monument to the accurate extension of the geographic knowledge of the hemisphere. The continent, in the knowledge of the world, had been "rounded out"; with the advancement of geographic knowledge went the final territorial definition of the Euroamerican empires. In a certain sense, the close of the eighteenth century may be said to have been both an end and a beginning: it was the end of the colonial era in the history of the geographic aspect of the expansion of Europe in the American hemisphere; it was the beginning of internal expansions and regional differentiations that would culminate in the emergence, shortly before and after 1800, of the modern American nations.

CHAPTER 2

The Political Structures
of the Euroamerican Empires

General Characteristics

In the political administration of their American empires the European colonizing states tended to extend and to reproduce in the colonies their own political institutions. In the era of colonization (1492–1648) they had been monarchies (the Netherlands, which achieved de facto independence from Spain about 1588, was a federative republic), and the ultimate political sovereign of every empire, except that of the Dutch, had been the king of the mother country in that empire.

Thus in theory — that is, in the theory of the statesmen who administered them in Europe and who governed them locally under instructions from the metropolises — all the colonies in each empire were extensions of the mother country. These imperial or colonial territories (again with the exception of the Dutch) did not belong to the people of the mother country, however: they were new and personal territories or kingdoms or demesnes of the king, and the governing of these overseas kingdoms was the king's personal responsibility. To be sure, each ruler had delegated much of his authority either to private citizens, as in the case of the *capitanías* in Brazil, the *latifúndia* of Hispanoamerica, the *seigneuries* of Canada, the proprietary provinces of Angloamerica, and the patroonships of the Dutch colonies, all of which were essentially feudal in nature, or to great corporate companies of private merchants, as in the case of the English Virginia Company, the Dutch West India Com-

24

pany, and the French Compagnie des Indes Occidentales. Yet in every instance the monarch had retained his ultimate sovereignty: the final ownership of the colonial lands and the highest authority over the peoples in them — in other words, sovereignty — resided in the crown of the empire and not in the people of the mother country. These basic assumptions prevailed throughout the eighteenth century, although the king's authority — or in the case of the Dutch colonies, that of the Dutch West India Company — was still far from being fully effective in the colonies.

In the Portuguese, Spanish, and French empires, as of about 1700, imperial administration was retained directly in the hands of the crown itself, operating through a royal council or ministry. The affairs of the Portuguese empire were managed by the Conselho Ultramarino, or Overseas Council, sitting in Lisbon; those of the Spanish empire were directed by the Real y Supremo Consejo de las Indias, usually shortened to Consejo de Indias, or Council of the Indies, sitting in Seville; those of the French empire were administered, from the reign of Louis XIV onward, by the Ministère de la Marine, or Ministry of Maritime Affairs, functioning, with regard to the colonies, through a *commis*, or subminister. In the case of the Danish colonial empire, a system very similar to the French was in force.

In England, the king's Privy Council administered British imperial affairs in the name of the king. But since the English rulers during the era of first colonization had deputed much of their authority to the original proprietors to whom they had granted these colonial portions of their domains, the proprietors, whether private individuals or commercial companies, had countenanced, even encouraged, the invention and development of representative institutions which bore a vague resemblance to, but little real identity with, the parliamentary institutions of England itself. Thus, throughout the entire British empire in America there existed at the beginning of the eighteenth century a functioning structure of representative political institutions that made the British empire unique among the European empires in the hemisphere.

The Dutch system of imperial administration had begun in a manner similar to that of the British system. The Dutch West India Company, chartered by the States-General in 1621, had founded the Dutch colonies in America and had administered them until the reorganization of the company in 1670. Thereafter, through much of the eighteenth century, the Dutch West India Company by and large controlled the American colonies, more or less in collaboration with the States-General, private interests, and the city of Amsterdam.

It should be noted that since the Dutch Company had been chartered by the States-General of the Netherlands, the colonies did, in theory, belong to the nation, whereas all the early charters issued for the formation of English colonies were grants of royal domains by the crown. Only in the cases of Georgia (1732) and Nova Scotia (1749) were English colonies created by Parliament. This fact in itself, coupled with the steady increase of involvement of Parliament in colonial affairs, reflects the shift in emphasis in British political affairs from a dominance of the crown in England to the dominance of Parliament that had taken place with the Glorious Revolution.

At the beginning of the eighteenth century, then, the monarchical institutions established in the colonies earlier (again excepting the Netherlands colonies) were still in force. Furthermore, the eighteenth century was marked by efforts of the central governments generally to liquidate the old feudal or quasi-autonomous corporate administrations in the interest of strengthening the authority of the central sovereignty.

The colonies, as colonies, were thought of by the statesmen as originally having been economic enterprises, extensions of the mother country, and created for its benefit.[1] The basic ideology underlying the political administration of the colonies was still mercantilism, and it remained so through most of the eighteenth century. At its best, the mercantilism of the mid-eighteenth century saw the Euroamerican empires as federative, regionally specialized economic entities; this sort of concept underlay their political administration.

As the eighteenth century wore on, however, and the population, extent, and international political importance of the colonies steadily increased, the European statesmen adopted a new concept, that of "the empire" as an integral political unit, composed of both mother country and colonies as well as the different kingdoms or divisions within the "realm" immediately presided over by the king. Thus the French Academicians, in their *Dictionnaire* of 1718, explained that the word *empire* "is used with regard to all the lands which are under the rule

[1] See below, chapter 3.

of a single great king, as 'The French Empire.' "[2] After the union of
England with Scotland (1707), the term *British empire* was used to
describe the entirety of the British possessions everywhere, ruled over
by the English king. After the middle of the century, many statesmen
began to think of the national empires as wholes. These empires were
federative in their de facto existence, with the king of each ruling over
a congeries of kingdoms, provinces, and colonies. But the concept of
the whole "confederation" as a unit was growing, and it would not be
long before the imperial entity would come to be thought of, with reason,
as a "nation." This meant, in the last analysis, that the "empire" was
now beginning to be envisaged as an integral body of *people*, and only
incidentally as a confederation of political entities.

It was entirely in accord with the mood of his time, therefore, that
Benjamin Franklin, in discussing the Seven Years War in 1760, said,
"Our North American colonies are to be considered as the *frontier of
the British empire on that side. . . .* [The conquest of Canada] will not
be a conquest for them [the colonies], nor gratify any vain ambition
of theirs. It will be a conquest for the whole and all our people will,
in the increase of trade and the ease of taxes, find the advantage of
it. . . . If ever there was a *national war*, this is truly such a one: a
war in which the interest of the *whole* nation is directly and fundamentally
concerned."[3] In one form or another the concept of the British empire
as an integral whole was shared by such English statesmen as the Earl
of Halifax, Edmund Burke, the Earl of Mansfield, William Blackstone,
and William Pitt. In the other empires closely similar ideas, based upon
the concept of the integral empire centered in a strong imperial
monarchy, were held by such statesmen as the Marquis of Pombal in
Portugal, the Count of Aranda in Spain, and Moreau de St. Méry in
France. The concept found ultimate expression in the French empire
during the French Revolution, when, in 1789, deputies from the Caribbean colonies were admitted to the Estates-General and when, in 1791,
the Constituent Assembly declared the colonies to be "an integral part
of the Empire." Thus, under the Colonial Statute of June 15, 1791, France
assimilated the colonies completely into the metropolis; under this statute

[2] Quoted by Richard Koebner, *Empire* (Cambridge: At the University Press, 1961), p.
60.
[3] Benjamin Franklin, *The Papers of Benjamin Franklin*, ed. L. W. Labaree et al., 15
vols. to date (New Haven, Conn.: Yale University Press, 1959–), IX, 74–75.

the colonies sent deputies to the Assembly in France, but for local affairs the colonial assemblies were to a great extent politically sovereign.

By contrast, one of the most significant developments in the history of the theory and practice of empires during the eighteenth century was the appearance among the Americans of an ideology — or a set of ideologies — that rationalized their desire for large measures of political autonomy. This urge for political autonomy manifested itself most strongly and most distinctly in the Angloamerican empire and most weakly in the Portuguese, but it existed in all of them. It grew out of the impulse of the American-born "creole" leaders to govern themselves and out of their growing resentment of the rule and the attitudes of the European-born officials sent over to govern them. Expressed most clearly in Angloamerica in the writings of such political thinkers as Benjamin Franklin and Richard Bland, it everywhere envisioned a sort of imperial federalism which, without destroying the new concept of the imperial "nation," would have left a high degree of autonomous political authority — even internal "sovereignty" — in the hands of the provincials themselves, a sort of federalism which was actually effectuated in the Francoamerican empire during the French Revolution and was finally accepted in the British empire after the British North America Act of 1867.

During the second half of the eighteenth century, the statesmen of Portugal, Spain, France, and England extensively reformed the administrative systems of their respective empires. The overall objectives of these reforms were largely economic and fiscal, although significant political reforms were also adopted. These political measures centered on the mother country's desire to strengthen its political authority and control in the colonies. But the reforms aroused the resentment and, eventually, the active resistance of the Americans. In the British and Spanish empires the effort to increase the power of the monarchy was met with rebellion, which ultimately led to the independence of the major parts of those empires. In the French empire the result was an effective integration of a federal sort; in the Portuguese empire the desire for political autonomy was gratified when the imperial government itself moved to Brazil in 1808.

The Americans' naturalistic, "anticolonial" impulse to govern themselves brought them increasingly into conflict with the political theories and policies of the mother countries; it would eventually, in one way or another, gain for nearly all of them — except the Dutch and the French colonies and Spanish Cuba and Puerto Rico — complete independence in the half century between 1775 and 1825.

The Euroamerican Empires

Portuguese Imperial Administration of Brazil

Theoretically Brazil was the private property of the king, or, rather, a new and separate kingdom that did not in any way belong to Portugal itself or to its people. The king administered this kingdom through the Overseas Council, except that ecclesiastical concerns were managed separately by the church hierarchy — although, even here, church affairs were scrutinized by the Overseas Council.

The Overseas Council nominated the civil governors, captains general, viceroys, and minor officials of the kingdom of Brazil — all, of course, with the approval of the king. The council also decreed taxes for the colony and made laws of a general nature relating to such matters as property, the regulation of commerce, judicial administration, and immigration. Its chief concern, however, was the proper control of political administration and international relations involving the colonies, and broad questions of policy regarding the encouragement of Brazilian industry and agriculture, such as the cultivation of sugar or tobacco.

In Brazil itself the most important agents of the crown were the captains general or the governors of the provinces. The governor of the most important province, Bahia, was often spoken of as the viceroy, a title which in fact he did possess. But it was not until 1763, when the government of Brazil was moved to Rio de Janeiro, that this official became a viceroy in the full sense of the word. Before 1763 he was little more than a *primus inter pares*, the first in precedence among equal provincial governors.

The captains general and the governors of provinces were the personal representatives, or vicegerents, of the king. They were appointed by him and they received their instructions, actually written by the Overseas Council, from him. They had no representative institutions to contend with except for the town councils, now relatively decadent, which will be discussed below.

In practice, before 1763 each provincial governor dealt directly with the Overseas Council; he enjoyed a considerable amount of leeway, in administering his province, with the result that a strong "federalist" mood developed in interprovincial relations which was rooted in this aspect of the colonial experience — a "federalist" mood not unlike that which characterized the British colonies in North America.

Local subdivisions of the provinces were usually presided over by officials known as *capitães mors* (subordinate captains), who were responsible to the provincial governors. Every town had a town council, known as the *senado da câmara*, which usually included one judge and two *vereadors* who were selected by the local aristocracy, composed of the great *crioulhos*, or creoles, generally of pure Portuguese blood. These councils had a high degree of local authority and autonomy. They were empowered to levy local taxes, to provide sanitation and police protection, to fix wages and prices, and to appoint minor officials and check their behavior. They were relatively close to the people, and their semielective nature made them a voice of public opinion. By the eighteenth century, however, they had deteriorated through corruption and had fallen, in large measure, under the control of the provincial governors.

Except for the *senados da câmara*, therefore, the administrative system of the Lusoamerican empire was a pyramidal one, with the apex of the pyramid — the sovereign — in Lisbon.

In 1750 Sebastião José de Carvalho e Melo, who became the Marquis of Pombal in 1770, came into power as Portugal's chief minister. A man of the Enlightenment and a reformer devoted to the principle of a powerful, enlightened monarchy, Carvalho instituted a series of political and economic reforms calculated to strengthen the monarchy, to centralize imperial administration in the king (that is, the king's minister), and to restore the national independence and sovereignty of Portugal and its empire in the area of international affairs, particularly against the domination of England.

Carvalho succeeded in reducing the formerly all-powerful Overseas Council to the status of a rubber stamp and he himself assumed practically dictatorial powers, in colonial affairs as well as in the government of Portugal. In Brazil he extinguished all the old feudal *capitanías* except one, which expired in 1791, and made them provinces governed by the crown. He reorganized the courts and the fiscal administration in the colony, while instituting extensive economic reforms. His most significant political reform was the creation of the viceroyalty of all Brazil by the transference of the so-called viceroyalty of Bahia to Rio de Janeiro in 1763 and by the appointment of Luís de Almeida, Marquis of Lavradio, as viceroy in 1769.

The viceroy, as constituted in the person of Lavradio, was the personal deputy of the king of Portugal. He was, in effect, a sovereign ruler with almost absolute power: his sole responsibility was to the king; he was answerable only to the king or the king's minister. Below the viceroy in the chain of command there were, in 1772, nine provincial captaincies general and nine subordinate captaincies. These subdivisions of Brazil had long enjoyed a high degree of local autonomy. Now, under Lavradio and Pombal, the captains-general were brought rather severely into line with the centralized royal authority: they were made more directly and effectively responsible to the viceroy, as he himself was directly responsible to the king. Nevertheless, there persisted in the system a strong sense of localism, or federalism, which recognized the differences among provinces and, in a limited and somewhat personal or even "feudal" way, the aspirations of the provinces for political autonomy.

The Hispanoamerican Empire

In the Spanish empire, New Spain, Peru, New Granada, and, later, Rio de la Plata were assumed to be new and distinct *reinos* (kingdoms) of the king, governed by him directly. The Council of the Indies was thus a sort of royal council that assisted the king in the governing of his American kingdoms. Somewhat illogically, perhaps, this council did not assist the king with one American kingdom only, but with all of them.

The Council of the Indies was composed of a president, who was rather like a prime minister for the Indies, and eight "chancellors," all of aristocratic families, with a large bureaucratic staff of attorneys, clerks, secretaries, geographers, accountants, and others. It was a hard-working body, and it had, in the name of the king, supreme legislative and executive authority over every colony in America. It nominated all, or nearly all, imperial officials going to the Indies, and it enacted all general legislation for the colonies, including social legislation, taxation, import and export duties, the regulation of trade, and the treatment of the Indians. (The direct administration of the commerce of the Indies was in the hands of the Casa de Contratación in Cádiz.) Moreover, since the kings of Spain had been granted summary powers in ecclesiastical affairs in America by the popes, the Council of the Indies was also in effect the ultimate authority in matters pertaining to religion and the church in the colonies. Thus the council screened all ecclesiastical officials going to America, although they were nominated by the ecclesiastical hierarchy, the chief member of which for America was the archbishop of Seville. The council even scrutinized and passed upon papal and other church laws relevant to the colonies, reserving unto itself the right to veto any of them so far as America was concerned. Finally, the Council of the Indies was a sort of supreme court for the entire colonial empire, where appeals might be heard from the *audiencias* or other courts in the colonies. In exceptional cases, especially those involving issues in international law, it could also assume original jurisdiction.

Under the Council of the Indies, then, the entire Spanish empire in America was governed by one single executive, legislative, judicial, and ecclesiastical authority. Its seat was at the center of the empire, and its laws, rulings, and decisions, as well as its instructions to imperial officials in the colonies, applied to the entire colonial empire — except, of course, in special local cases, of which there were many. It was strictly a hierarchical system of government, rigorously authoritarian and systematically unitary, with no trace of representative institutions or of institutional provisions that would allow the people to place checks upon or criticize the government, with the one exception that in the *cabildos*, or town councils, of the chief cities there was a surprising amount of freedom of dissent on local issues. Unquestionably, the government of the Spanish empire was the most rigidly centralized and unified of all the Euroamerican empires. It should be added that it may also have been the most corrupt.

Under the king and the Council of the Indies, the highest administrative official in each of the *reinos* in America was the viceroy. In a very real sense he was the personal representative and a true vicegerent of the king of Spain. He was always a Spaniard, usually of the highest nobility. In addition to being the living symbol of the majesty, the power, and the glory of the crown of Spain, he was the *reino*'s chief executive, military commander in chief, and ceremonial head of state. He was also the president of the *audiencia* of his capital city and, effectively, the supreme secular authority in church affairs and in matters concerning the Indians. A viceroy's term of office was normally three years, although it could be extended. At the end of it, he had to submit to a thorough investigation of his regime by representatives of the Council of the Indies.

In every *reino* there were a number of captaincies general, each one presided over by a captain general, who held his authority from and was responsible to the viceroy. The captaincy general was essentially a military district, although the authority of the captain general covered many other matters, political, economic, and social; indeed, the captain general might exercise a high degree of administrative independence and usually did.

A smaller administrative unit within the *reino* was the *provincia*, or province, ruled over by a provincial governor. Such provinces were subdivisions of captaincies general, and their governors were under the supervision of the captains general. They, too, enjoyed a relatively large measure of independence and might become arbitrary and dictatorial petty tyrants.

In addition there were in every *reino* a number of *audiencias*, or judicial districts, each presided over by a court, also called an *audiencia*. This court was composed of four to six *oidores*, or judges, with a bureaucratic staff of attorneys, clerks, secretaries, guards, and chaplains. But it was not only a court, for it also sat as a governmental board that had a hand in the administration of political affairs. Indeed, some of the *audiencias*, such as those of Santo Domingo, Santiago de Chile, or Buenos Aires, all of which were far from their viceroys' capital cities, performed active and extensive administrative functions.

Below the *audiencia* court in every *audiencia* district there were local courts of many kinds — church courts, military courts, labor courts, courts for Indian affairs — from which appeals might be taken up to the *audiencia*. From the *audiencia* itself appeals could be taken, in important cases, to the Council of the Indies. The *audiencia* district did not coincide with the administrative area of the captaincy general.

Finally, a very significant institution in the local administration of the Spanish empire was the government of the important towns, which was centered in the *cabildo*, or town council. Although they had originally been composed of popularly elected members and had enjoyed a high degree of autonomy, by 1700 their autonomy, authority, and relatively representative nature had been severely reduced. *Corregidores* (mayors or supervisors) appointed by the crown had become a part of town govern-ment, and their chief purpose was to prevent the *cabildos* from exceed-ing their authority.

Even so the *regidores*, or members of the *cabildo*, of which there might be from six to twelve, exercised a considerable measure of local governmental authority. Almost always *criollos* (creoles of pure Spanish blood but born in America), they met in the town hall, also called the *cabildo*.[4] Acting as an administrative body, they regulated markets, sanitation, police, taxation, local courts, hospitals, and schools, although the latter two were usually regarded as functions of the church. No longer popularly elected, the *cabildo* was now a type of "closed corporation" that perpetuated itself by electing its own members or securing their appointment from the *corregidor* (membership was sometimes purchased, too). And yet, because the *cabildos* were composed of *criollos* and served in real but varying degrees as forums for public debate and even dissent against the vast body of officials made up of *peninsulares*, or Spaniards from Spain, they had become the only spokesmen of the Americans against the mother country. The time would come, as the mood of revolution swept over all of America, when the *cabildos* would become the focuses of revolutionary thinking and action.

In the second half of the eighteenth century the administration of the Spanish empire underwent a series of reforms both economic[5] and political. As in the other major empires, the political reforms were meant to increase the power of the king and to bring about a greater effective-ness in the royal administration of the *reinos*. Thus, the powers of the Council of the Indies were substantially reduced and were assumed by the king's ministers.

The new viceroyalty of New Granada had been created in 1717, was soon abolished, but reestablished in 1739; the Rio de la Plata area was constituted a viceroyalty in 1776. Between 1764 and 1790, the imperial government set up in America new administrative districts called *inten-dencias*, each one presided over by an intendant. The chief function of the *intendencias* was fiscal in that they were intended to make the collection of the king's revenues a more efficient process; they also had many other responsibilities in political, economic, and judicial affairs.

[4] For the origins and early history of the *cabildo*, as of all the other institutions of Spanish imperial administration, see volume IV of this series.
[5] For a discussion of the economic reforms, see below, chapter 4.

In practice they assumed many of the duties formerly performed by the viceroys; the power of the viceroys was correspondingly reduced, and the intendants, although of lesser stature than the viceroys in matters of protocol, became rivals of the viceroys, the governors, and even the *cabildos* in the execution of political power.

At the same time, the laws governing the colonies were revised to assure more extensive uniformity and centralization. Elaborate efforts were made, especially after 1763, to strengthen the military defenses of the empire. But the colonies were required to pay part of the expenses involved through increased taxes imposed by the imperial government; these new taxes aroused a great deal of discontent among the Hispanoamericans.

These imperial reforms, and others, were associated with the names of such statesmen as the Count of Aranda and José Gálvez. They represented a new imperial theory, which conceived of the empire as a federation of kingdoms presided over by a powerful monarch. Aranda even went so far as to propose that the four *reinos* be made full kingdoms, each ruled by a member of the royal family. On the whole, the political reforms, coupled with the economic reforms, did have the effect of centralizing the empire more than ever, even though, in the economic realm, the old exclusive, monopolistic, mercantilistic imperial policies were considerably relaxed.

The Francoamerican Empire

The basic theory underlying the development and administration of the Francoamerican empire in the eighteenth century was essentially similar to that of the Lusoamerican and Hispanoamerican empires. The territory acquired by the French explorers and colonists was assumed to be a private domain of the king. The king had deputed much of the power of government and exploitation to private companies, such as the Company of the One Hundred Associates (1627) and the Company of the West Indies (1664), but Louis XIV had rearrogated to himself the powers of government and the close regulation of trade, although the actual conduct of commerce and the profits therefrom were left largely in the hands of private entrepreneurs. During the heyday of Louis's reign, the details of imperial government were left in the hands of Louis's great mercantilist minister Jean Baptiste Colbert, who set up the machinery of imperial administration in his own ministry. After Louis's death, the administration of the empire was effectuated by the ministre de la marine (minister of maritime affairs), who was advised by his ministerial council, the Council of Marine Affairs. The actual administration of the colonies, however, was in the hands of a *commis*, or commissioner for the colonies, who, in view of the growing autonomy of the islands and despite the constant pressure of the economic vested interests of the metropolis, was required to govern the islands with a high degree of tact and diplomacy. Such administrators were Armand de la Porte, who was colonial commissioner from 1738 to 1758, and the *Martiniquais* Jean Dubuc, who initiated a series of significant economic reforms in the Caribbean empire after 1765.

In the government of Canada, the local administration was controlled by three colonial officials, the governor, the intendant, and the bishop of Quebec, while fundamental laws, regulations, instructions for the governors, and other administrative measures originated in the Ministry of Maritime Affairs.

Under this system, the governor, as the personal representative of the king, took precedence over the others. He was the embodiment of the majesty of the throne and the principal figure in the pageantry of government, of which there was much even in this crude frontier community. He was the military commander, and he conducted relations with the Indians and the English colonies in New England and New York.

On the other hand, the intendant, whose functions were patterned after those of the intendants in France, was concerned with more mundane matters, such as landholding, roads and bridges, and, most important of all, the supervision and regulation of trade.

The bishop of Quebec was an ecclesiastical official appointed by the Roman Catholic church of France. In general, no bishop could be appointed to Quebec who did not have the approval of the king; nevertheless, that did not prevent the bishop from occasionally challenging or quarreling with both the intendant and the governor. For his authority was great: not only did he rule the priests and the religious affairs of the colony; his jurisdiction also extended over such matters as matrimony, morals, and the sale of liquor to the Indians. The missions to the Indians, however, were administered by the regular orders, the Sulpicians, the Dominicans, and, most significantly, the Jesuits. These regular orders, with their own hierarchical chains of command directly from Rome by way of Paris, did not always see eye-to-eye with the bishop and the secular clergy.

There was little or nothing of representative government in Canada, except for the town councils of Quebec, Three Rivers, and Montreal, which bore a certain resemblance to the *cabildos* and the *senados da câmara* of the Hispanoamerican and Lusoamerican towns. For the town councils of Canada were a kind of "closed corporation," the members of which were elected by the businessmen of the towns. As was true of their Latin-American counterparts, they enjoyed considerable autonomy in local affairs.

In 1763 Canada was ceded to England by the Treaty of Paris; thereafter, its history became identified with that of the British empire.

In the French West Indies the general pattern of government was at first similar to that of Canada. But the island colonies were distinguished, in the eighteenth century, by colonial councils that had considerable power and became significant sounding boards for colonial opinion. Gradually they assumed many of the political functions of genuine local governments. These councils, called "superior councils," had originated as local courts; appeals could be made from their decisions to the king's Council of State. Over time their functions were expanded: they supervised the financial affairs of their colonies; in the promulgation of laws sent over by the Ministry of the Marine they eventually assumed the power of the Parlement of Paris to refuse to register such laws; and they found it possible to exercise embarrassing pressures upon governors or intendants who failed to win their approval. Their membership was composed of rich and distinguished members of the planter aristocracy; they thought of themselves, however, as representing not only their own class, but the lesser planters and the *petits blancs* (the "little" people among the whites) as well. They did, indeed, in matters of colonial interest, have the support of the white lower classes.

Thus, in a century during which metropolitan France was ruled by a system of near-absolutism, the island colonies (Martinique, Saint-Domingue, Guadeloupe) were governed by "representative" councils whose wishes even the king had to respect. The French empire, such as it was, was a sort of de facto federation. Even so, these "representative" institutions in the island colonies did not fail to arouse the fear of the monarchs — a fear expressed by Louis XV himself when he wrote, in a clairvoyant mood, "Let us take care that in our efforts to make our Islands flourish we may not give them the means one day, and perhaps soon, to separate themselves from France, for that will one day happen in all that part of the world."[6]

In the diminished Francoamerican empire (after the Peace of Paris in 1763), as in the other Euroamerican empires, a series of highly significant political and economic reforms was put into effect in the second half of the eighteenth century. The colonies had fallen, during the earlier wars, under a high degree of domination by the military establishment — an establishment, by the way, that was controlled directly from France and which stood as a parallel and rival power to the superior councils. These military regimes had reduced, flouted, or ignored the superior councils, to the great dismay and resentment of the creole planters. The result of this antagonism, essentially a conflict between creoles and continental Frenchmen, was a number of uprisings and near-revolts that greatly disturbed the internal peace and prosperity of both the islands and the mother country.

It was in large measure as a result of this situation that, in 1758 during the regime of the new minister of the marine Nicolas René Berryer, the Commission for Colonial Legislation was created in the king's Supreme Council of State, thereby effectively removing the function of political legislation from the Council of the Marine. For the next thirty years this commission supervised the political evolution of the island colonies. (Economic affairs remained generally under the jurisdiction of the Ministry of the Marine.) In 1759, a new set of councils, called "chambers of agriculture," was introduced in the islands; though chiefly economic in nature and devoted to agriculture and commerce, they did have considerable political influence. These new chambers had the power to address the king on all the affairs of their colonies; even more important, they were empowered to send their own deputies to represent them at the court at Versailles. It was as one of the deputies of the Martinique Agricultural Council that Jean Dubuc first attracted attention.

Jean Dubuc, a native of Martinique, was probably the first creole to become a European minister charged with the administration of the

<hr>

[6] Quoted in Joannes Tramond, "Les Antilles après le Traité d'Utrecht," in Gabriel Hanotaux and Alfred Martineau, eds., *Histoire des colonies françaises et de l'expansion de la France dans le monde*, 6 vols. (Paris: Société de l'Histoire Nationale, 1929–34), vol. I: *L'Amérique*, 464.

affairs of the American colonies of any European power. As a "delegate," or agent, of Martinique at the court of Louis XV, he was "discovered" by the Duke of Choiseul who, in 1764, made him a "first commissioner" in the Ministry of Maritime Affairs in charge of the colonies. Although a representative of the autonomy-minded groups in the islands, he nevertheless realized the extent of the colonies' dependence on the mother country. Since the political affairs relative to the colonies had been placed under the direction of the new commissioner for colonial legislation, Dubuc's duties were chiefly economic in nature; yet by writing a large number of pamphlets and other works he was able to promote in France a sympathetic attitude toward colonial political aspirations.[7]

The occupation of the French Windward Islands (Martinique and Guadeloupe) by the British armies during the Seven Years War had retarded the effectuation of Berryer's reforms. But the liberal administration of the British military government, influenced, as it was, by the British assumption of the principles of representative government, actually resulted in strengthening the autonomist sentiment among the people of the occupied islands. Thus, when the French reestablished their authority over the islands after the Peace of Paris, Martinique and Guadeloupe both continued to have representative assemblies, each with its own "deputy" at Versailles, even though the government of the Windward Islands as a group was reinstituted.

During the War for United States Independence,[8] the Caribbean area again became a major theater of operations, especially naval. The war resulted, by and large, in a victory for France: at its end, France retained its former islands, including St. Lucia, and added Tobago to its domain; England's title to Dominica, Grenada and the Grenadines, Montserrat and Nevis was reconfirmed.

The political institutions in the French islands did not change significantly in the period between 1783 and 1789. The tradition and the practice of representative government were already strong, and when the French Revolution began in 1789 the French Caribbean colonies were well prepared to assume the responsibilities of colonial political autonomy. Out of this colonial political milieu appeared another one of the famous French creole colonial administrators, Moreau de St. Méry, who assumed a place among the great eighteenth-century ideologues

---

[7] For Dubuc's economic reforms see below, chapter 4.
[8] See below, chapter 8.

on colonial affairs with the publication of his monumental *Lois et constitutions des Îles françaises d'Amerique sous le Vent* (six volumes) between 1784 and 1789.

In 1760 Berryer had sent M. de Clugny as an intendant to Saint-Domingue with instructions to break, if possible, the domination of the military. A long step in that direction was taken in an ordinance promulgated in the name of the king in March 1763, and Clugny called into being in the colony the "National Assembly" by joining the two older councils for the purpose of approving the increase in taxes demanded by the king. After Clugny returned to France to be succeeded by the Comte d'Estaing, there occurred a reaction and a revival of the power of the military, with the result that the island was torn by internal strife between the military and the autonomists, whose chief complaint was that they were being taxed without their consent. The military won out, eventually, and continued to control the island until the coming of the Revolution in France in 1789. The "national assemblies" continued to meet, but their function was reduced to that of registering the decrees of the military governors. The old Superior Council and the old Agricultural Council also met separately and became sounding boards for the growing "autonomist" sentiment that the military was unable to suppress. All the councils were largely ineffective, and whatever significance they had was derived from their character as voices of public opinion. This public opinion, however, was moving steadily in the direction of autonomy, even independence — a sentiment temporarily mollified by the policies of the French government during the Revolution, as will be noted later.

The British Empire

In underlying theory and in visible institutions the administration of the Angloamerican empire bore a fundamental similarity to those of the Portuguese, Spanish, and French empires. Theoretically the land explored by John Cabot, Sir Francis Drake, and their successors had belonged to the king, and grants to the Virginia Company, Lord Baltimore, Sir William Alexander, the Earl of Carlisle, the Council for New England, and the Massachusetts Bay Company had been made in the exercise of the king's prerogative of granting fiefs out of the crown's royal demesnes. The ultimate sovereign authority over these grants was exercised by the king's Privy Council. In principle, Parliament might legislate for England and for the broad imperial affairs of the empire, especially commerce, but in the seventeenth century it did not legislate for the internal affairs of any of these colonial fiefs. The most notable examples of this exclusion from parliamentary rule were the proprietary colonies, but the same exclusion was claimed by all the colonies at one time or another, and by the eighteenth century almost all the colonies had their own representative assemblies or parliaments, theoretically under the direct sovereignty of the king, not Parliament.

It is to be noted that the British Privy Council constituted the executive arm of the British imperial government and that its authority, exercised through a congeries of committees, embraced the empire in its totality, from the British Isles to the king's dominions overseas. Under the Privy Council, most colonial policy was actually determined by the Lords Commissioners for Trade and Plantations (the Board of Trade), organized in 1696. But the Board of Trade had no executive or administrative power; its functions were advisory only; actual executive action was taken by the appropriate members or committees of the Privy Council.

On the other hand, Parliament performed the legislative function involved in effectuating, controlling, and regulating the economic activity of the empire. And where the commercial activities of the colonies were concerned, as well as their intercolonial and intraimperial industrial relationships, Parliament passed a great series of acts called the Navigation Laws and the Acts of Trade, the chief objectives of which were the maintenance of England's monopoly of the economic benefits of colonial trade, the exclusion of foreigners, and the prevention of colonial competition with the mother country.

Under the original colonial grants, the British colonies in America enjoyed a far more extensive autonomy than did those of any other Euroamerican empire. By the beginning of the eighteenth century almost all the British colonies in America had devised for themselves quasi-autonomous governments, in some cases as adaptations of the governments of commercial companies, in others as adaptations made in response to the demands of the settlers for representative institutions. These governments were built upon the basis of territorial representation; legislative, executive, and judicial powers were all fairly clearly defined and were centered in the legislature, the governor, and the colonial council or supreme court. Furthermore, the legislatures in the colonies thought of themselves as little parliaments, with all the rights and privileges of Parliament in England.

By the second quarter of the century, all but four of the English colonies in America were colonies of the "royal" type; each of these had a governor appointed by the crown and a bicameral legislature made up of a lower house elected by the property owners and an upper house composed of Americans appointed by the crown. Each had a court system, patterned roughly after the English system and headed by the council. Of the other four, two, Pennsylvania and Maryland, were proprietary colonies, the governors of which were appointed by private businessmen in England (the descendants of the original grantees). Generally speaking, however, the administration of these colonies was quite similar to that of the royal colonies.

The remaining two colonies, Rhode Island and Connecticut, were "corporate" in political organization; that is to say, their governments, originally patterned after commercial companies, were still organized along corporate lines, with assemblies representing, and elected by, the towns (themselves organized as "corporations"). These assemblies elected both the members of the councils of the two colonies and their governors. Nowhere, in all the imperial world of America, were governments of colonies so directly and completely responsible to the people of the colonies as these two.

Local government in every British-American colony was organized and administered along English lines: the county, constituting the unit of local administration, was more or less subdivided into parishes or townships, though these were not exactly equivalent to the corresponding English forms.

Although the basic theory underlying the constitution of the Angloamerican empire was fundamentally the same as that of the Portuguese, Spanish, and French empires, it is apparent that in actual administration the British imperial institutions presented a dramatic and profound contrast with those of the other empires. Indeed, nowhere is this contrast more clearly seen than in the steadily rising conflict that took place in the British colonies between the provincial forces advocating colonial autonomy that were institutionalized in the colonial assemblies and the imperial institutions symbolized by the colonial governors. The chief theme in the political history of the Angloamerican empire in the eighteenth century is, in fact, this conflict between the increasing demand for colonial autonomy and the mounting assertion of imperial authority.

Thus, after 1696 Parliament extended its legislative power to pass laws affecting internal affairs in the colonies. In 1699 it passed the so-called Woolens Act, limiting the manufacture and transshipment of woolen cloth; in 1708 it passed the Colonial Coins Act; in 1710 it established the post office in the colonies; in 1740 it extended the "Bubble Act" (which prohibited the formation of corporations without Parliament's consent) to Massachusetts; in 1750 it passed the Iron Act, limiting the manufacture of hardware; in 1751 it passed the Colonial Currency Act, which prohibited the New England colonies from enacting laws making their provincial currencies legal tender. By the middle of the century Parliament had extended its power to legislate on the internal matters of the colonies; it specifically asserted this authority in the so-called Declaratory Act of 1765. It was indeed the growing extension of Parliament's power to legislate for the colonies "in all matters whatsoever" that aroused the colonies to resist violently this "new" power after 1763 and eventually to secede from the British empire.

There was a good deal of theorizing about these questions bearing upon the relationships and the distribution of political authority in the British empire, some of it rather confused, on both sides of the Atlantic in the mid-eighteenth century. In 1751, for example, Archibald Kennedy, an English customs official in New York, could still argue that the colonies were part of the king's domain, like the islands of Jersey and Guernsey in the English Channel, and that their assemblies were but local assemblies permitted by the condescension of the king and not true parliaments at all. In 1759 the Earl of Granville insisted to Franklin that the Privy Council was the true and only legislative body for the colonies; as late as 1772 the Privy Council, entirely on its own, had completed arrangements to set up west of the Alleghenies a new colony, Vandalia, which would be carved out of the new domains the crown had acquired by the Treaty of Paris in 1763. Against this "Privy Council" theory, William Blackstone, the Earl of Mansfield, and others argued that the power of Parliament was supreme everywhere in the empire, which these theorists conceived of as an integral and indivisible entity. It was in defense of this position, eventually, that England sought to suppress colonial dissent, even ultimately by force of arms.

For the British statesmen, as for the theorists of the other Euroamerican empires, there could be only one sovereignty in any imperial body, and for the British empire that sovereignty was vested in the "King, Lords, and Commons" in England; where else could it possibly reside?

Colonial theorists, on the other hand, deriving their theory of the empire from the colonial experience and from the fact that the empire was in all reality clearly a federative one, formulated the "federal" theory of the empire. Richard Bland, Benjamin Franklin, James Wilson, and others explained the fact, as they saw it, that every self-governing colony was sovereign within its own boundaries. Parliament was sovereign, to be sure, in matters pertaining to the "general welfare," intercolonial relations, and foreign affairs. But each colonial society, formed on the basis of a social compact, was internally sovereign. Its autonomy was exercised by its own representative assembly, or parliament; within the colony the English Parliament had no dominion whatever.

This theory of divided sovereignty within the empire was new, and it was the first clear statement of a way of thinking that was gestating in all the Euroamerican empires.

The Dutch-American Empire

The Dutch empire in America had been founded, exploited, and governed by the Dutch West India Company, organized in 1621.[9] It was a privately owned empire, although the company's stock was widely distributed among the merchant-oligarchs of the seven provinces of the Netherlands and its affairs were closely scrutinized by the States-General, of which many of the company's stockholders were members. The company was reorganized in 1670, but it never recovered its original strength and power. It remained, nevertheless, not only a great commercial corporation but, in its relations with the colonies, a great governmental institution as well. Its governing body, called the "Nineteen Lords," was a board of directors, or council, drawn from the towns and provinces that participated in the company; this board made all the laws, appointed the governors, and performed the functions of a supreme court for every colony it controlled. Since the company was always closely associated with the States-General, that body occasionally exerted its influence on

[9] See volume IV of this series. See also Charles de Lannoy and Herman Van der Linden, *Histoire de l'expansion coloniale des peuples européens*, vol. II: *Néerlande et Danemark* (Brussels: Lamartine, 1911), pp. 184ff; Charles R. Boxer, *The Dutch Seaborne Empire 1600–1800* (New York: Alfred A. Knopf, 1965), *passim*.

the company. In most cases, however, it was the other way around, and the company told the States-General what to do in matters of colonial policy or international relations. The States-General was associated with the "Nineteen"; it was not their master. Indeed, the "Nineteen" were in a very real sense "vassals exercising the greater part of the sovereign rights" of the nation in the colonies. This state of affairs lasted until 1790 when the company went bankrupt. Thereafter the colonies were administered by the States-General and state officials replaced the old company officials in the colonies; very often they were the same men. Colonial affairs were referred to a new "Council of the Colonies" in the States-General.

In the actual administration of the colonies, the government of the separate colonies was delegated to the cities in the Netherlands that were represented on the board of the "Nineteen Lords," but the "Nineteen" determined the general policies to be followed. For example, Zeeland administered the Windward Islands; Amsterdam managed the affairs of Curaçao; Surinam was administered by the "Society of Surinam," a conglomerate group representing public and private interests; after 1773 St. Eustatius, St. Martin, and Saba were administered by the Chamber of the Meuse. This unique form of colonial administration reflected the federal form of the government of the Netherlands.

The colonial governments were almost entirely in the hands of officials of the company. Curiously, the Dutch colonies more clearly illustrated the old mercantilist concept of colonies as "distant factories of the mother country" than did those of any other nation. There was also little of the colonial demand for political autonomy that characterized the political evolution of the other major empires. And yet, toward the end of the century, several of the colonies began to resist the political administration of a private company; after the English occupation in 1782–83, the colonists in Essequibo resisted the return of the colony to the private company and begged the States-General to assume the government. In Curaçao in the years following the War of United States Independence, the bourgeois militia, all white, was the center and voice of colonial resentment against the company. The last decade of the company's existence was marked by constant violence between the company and the colonists in nearly all the colonies. The company itself was completely hostile to autonomy; the colonial drive was inspired and encouraged by the example and influence of the English, not the company. The important fact is that even in the Dutch colonies, so long acquiescent under arbitrary company rule, the stirrings of autonomy finally manifested themselves.

Conclusion

It is clear that the expansion of European civilization to America had created in the Western Hemisphere, by the eighteenth century, a number of colonial empires that were similar in their basic political patterns but which differed widely in their detailed institutional administrations. In theory each empire was a single unit, administered from Europe. From the Europeans' point of view, the overseas segments of these empires existed for the benefit of the mother countries and must be and remain subservient to the metropolises. From about the middle of the eighteenth century onward, however, a new concept of these empires was emerging — a concept that saw them as entities, to be sure, but also as de facto federal empires ruled over by strong monarchies in which the colonies were coming to occupy a position of much greater recognition and status than that of mere "factories-at-a-distance." Many European thinkers were beginning to rationalize the federal nature of the empires; their theory of imperial federalism was made more explicit by certain Angloamerican and Francoamerican colonials.

It is also apparent that, in the course of their development, the colonies had grown politically, as well as economically and socially, along lines different from those of the mother countries. American institutions, in one way or another, were different from those of the mother countries and had diverged from the plans envisaged by the statesmen of the mother countries. American concepts and philosophies of government differed too from those of European statesmen. In all the empires autonomist impulses of various intensities were gestating. Presently these impulses would lead, with only a relatively few exceptions, not to autonomy, since they were resisted by the mother countries, but to independence and the creation of new states.

CHAPTER 3

International Aspects of the American Economy

The expansion of Europe had been, from the first, primarily a vast, composite economic phenomenon. The colonization of America by Europeans was basically a set of economic enterprises, formally undertaken for the sake of economic profit. There had been other motives, to be sure — religious, nationalistic, scientific — but the economic impulse was the most powerful. The European colonies in America, therefore, must be regarded as originally and fundamentally economic ventures that were in the long run successful;[1] yet these economic ventures, again in the long run, tended to become autonomous.

The prevailing opinion relative to overseas colonies among European statesmen and political philosophers of the early eighteenth century was still based upon the idea that the overseas colonies had been founded for economic reasons and that they now existed, in the last analysis, for the economic benefit of the mother country. It followed from this that the administration of, and the profits from, the economic activities of the colonies should be, in the case of each empire, a monopoly enjoyed by the mother country. "Very rightly so," said Montesquieu in *The Spirit of the Laws*, "because the whole aim of the establishment [of the colonies] was to expand commerce, not to build up a city or a new empire."[2] This basic set of ideas, which added up to a strictly and

[1] See volume IV of this series.
[2] Quoted by Richard Koebner, *Empire* (Cambridge: At the University Press, 1961), p. 91.

47

exclusively nationalistic "political economy," was also an international phenomenon in the sense that it was shared by the theorists and statesmen of all the imperial nations of western Europe. This same concept, of which the distinguished exponent in France had been Jean Baptiste Colbert, was adopted with little variation by Jerónimo Uztáriz in Spain, Joshua Gee and Chambers's *Cyclopedia* in England, and Véron de Forbonnais, writing in the *Encyclopédie* in France. Only the Dutch, who lived by commerce itself rather than by their colonies, were relatively free of the rigid mercantilist ideology; even they, however, were highly nationalistic in the administration of the economic life of their empire within the context of their international commerce.

In general, the statesmen of the great imperial states held to the belief that a nation's wealth and, therefore, a nation's ultimate might in the international balance of power depended upon a favorable balance in its international commerce; this favorable balance, in turn, depended in large measure upon the profitableness of the nation's colonial empire.

This meant that the economic life of all the Euroamerican empires was administered, in theory if not always in practice, according to this internationally held ideology or "political economy." Each empire was administered as a tightly closed national economic monopoly; since the colonies existed for the benefit of the mother country and since their international status and prosperity as well as that of their mother country depended upon the prosperity of the colonies, it was assumed that the productivity and commerce of the colonies must be closely regulated by the mother country.

In practice the mercantilistic outlook meant, as has been noted, that each empire had a control agency located in the imperial metropolis whose duty it was to supervise or to manage the colonial economy. In the case of Portugal this function was performed chiefly by the Conselho Ultramarino, or Overseas Council. The trade of the Spanish colonies was conducted exclusively through the Casa de Contratación, or House of Trade, while laws controlling agricultural production, mining, labor, and similar matters were made by the Council of the Indies. In England, oversight of the colonial economy was left in the hands of the Lords Commissioners for Trade and Plantations, although actual legislation was a function of Parliament and actual administration was a function of the Privy Council. In France, imperial economic affairs were supervised by the Ministry of Marine Affairs, but the actual conduct of the trade and production of the empire was directed by private individuals and companies. The economic life of the Dutch-American empire was still, theoretically at least, a monopoly of the Dutch West India Company, even though the company was closely controlled by the States-General.

The Portuguese, Spanish, French, and Dutch supervisory bodies had the power of making colonial regulations that had the force of law. The English Board of Trade, however, was a purely advisory body which passed its recommendations on to the Privy Council for executive action or to Parliament for legislation.

The economic life and activities of the new American societies were thus still bound, at the turn of the eighteenth century, by the rigid legal structure of the mercantilistic imperial monopolies established from the beginning of colonization.[3] But these mercantilistic nationalistic monopolies were now starting to break down. Despite all the efforts of the mother countries to be exclusive, the amount of international and interimperial exchange was growing apace, and no intraimperial law could be wholly effective in interimperial economic relationships: economic self-interest, especially in the colonies, was stronger than intraimperial law.

The North Atlantic had become a great economic community. By the end of the seventeenth century a large network of international exchanges had been established. As Bernard Bailyn puts it, "The result was a network of trading routes woven by the enterprises of merchants, shipmasters, and colonists representing all the leading mercantile nations of western Europe."[4] And, it should be added, of America.

As part of the evolution of the great Atlantic economic community there also developed a new economic theory, the theory of freedom of commerce — the antithesis of mercantilism. Thus, even though Montesquieu, Chambers, Voltaire, the Earl of Halifax, and others still clung to the theory of mercantilism, and even though imperial economic practices continued to follow, at least until mid-century, an overall pattern of mercantilistic laws and regulations, such economic thinkers as François Quesnay, Robert Jacques Turgot, and the other physiocrats in France, and Adam Smith, David Hume, and Benjamin Franklin in England and its colonies did not hesitate to formulate the new theory of freedom

---

[3] See volume IV of this series.
[4] Bernard Bailyn, "Communications and Trade: The Atlantic in the Seventeenth Century," *Journal of Economic History*, 13:379 (1953).

of commerce. At the most, the theory indicated that a revolution in economic and imperialist thinking was at hand. And with the theory came imperial reforms in the second half of the century that clearly moved away from the old concept toward a de facto application of the new.

Thus, the most outstanding general characteristics of the economic history of the American hemisphere during the eighteenth century were the weakening of the fabrics of the old monopolies and the decline of both the effectiveness and the idea of mercantilism in the face of the new, more positive theory and practice of freedom of international trade. In the colonies themselves, the century was marked by a steady growth of actual international and interimperial economic exchanges which defied the old mercantilistic systems and, most notable of all, by the emergence of the widespread demand for an increase in the degree of economic autonomy and self-direction that the colonies might enjoy. This tendency contributed, eventually and powerfully, to the growth of the sentiment of nationalism, to the impulses that lay at the base of the independence movement, and to the final achievement of independence, economic as well as political, throughout the continent.

Production

Agriculture

The great bulk of the commodities produced in the American hemisphere for international distribution was agricultural, and the most important agricultural industries producing for the international market were those devoted to the production of sugar, tobacco, indigo, rice, and wheat and other grains.

Sugar. At the beginning of the eighteenth century the cultivation of sugar was the largest single productive industry in the American hemisphere. Sugar production was one of the great international plantation industries. Sugar plantations of the same general type were the producing units in the British, French, Spanish, Dutch, and Danish West Indies and in the northeastern sections of Brazil centering around Pernambuco (modern Recife) and San Salvador (modern Bahia). The cultivation of sugar was also introduced into French Louisiana about the middle of the century.

The sugar plantation was a sort of agrarian factory that extracted the sugar from the sugarcane, crystallized it, and then marketed it. On each plantation, besides the fields where the sugarcane was grown, there were such technological devices as the cane press for squeezing the juice from the cane, boiling pans for extracting the water, and other utensils for precipitating the sugar. Since molasses and rum were very valuable by-products of the industry, the plantation would often have sedimentation tanks or other implements for purifying the molasses and stills for the distillation of rum from the "megass" or "bagasse," the mash remaining after the cane had been squeezed.

The methods were much the same everywhere. The labor of planting, cultivating, weeding, and harvesting the cane was performed by black slaves. The cane mill was a relatively simple device consisting of two intermeshing corrugated metal cylinders, one of which was turned by a mule, often from New England, or by the slaves themselves. Tending the fires under the boiling pans or the stills was also done by the slaves under the supervision of the one or more white overseers on each plantation. (In some areas, such as in Mexico, the labor was performed by free Indians. This was an exception to the general pattern, however.)

The quantity of sugar produced in the Euroamerican colonies was enormous: the island of Santo Domingo alone was estimated, as of about the end of the eighteenth century, to have produced over fifty million pounds of sugar each year. In the period between 1698 and 1791, the export of sugar from the British West Indies to England (exclusive of that shipped to the continental colonies) amounted to some 4,750,000 tons. In the same period, the total production of the French West Indies was about 5,250,000 tons.[5]

At the beginning of the century most of the sugar was shipped as brown, or "muscovado," sugar, since there were few refineries in the American hemisphere capable of performing the "highly specialized art" of refining brown sugar into white. At first, the great international refining centers were Lisbon, Marseilles, and Amsterdam; by the middle of the eighteenth century important refineries had opened in Hamburg and London in Europe and in Boston and Providence in Angloamerica.

The crude sugar was shipped in tubs, or casks; the molasses and rum were shipped in barrels. The work of assembling the casks and loading

[5] Noel Deerr, *The History of Sugar*, 2 vols. (London: Chapman and Hall, 1949–50), II, 424.

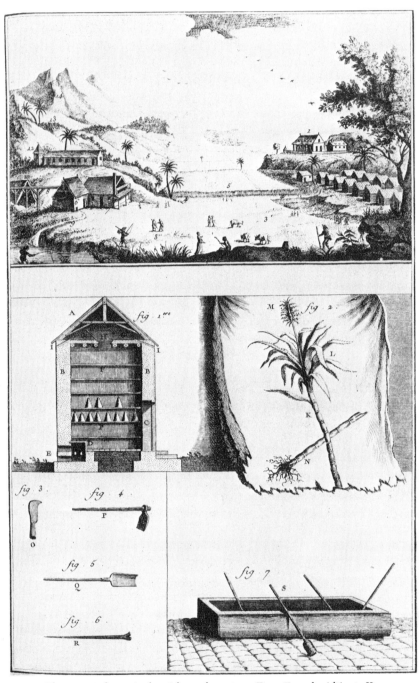

The sugar industry in the eighteenth century. From *Encyclopédié*, pt. II,
Oeconomie rustique: Sucrerie, plate I. Courtesy of the University
of Washington Library.

them was generally performed by blacks, although the actual carpentry involved might be done by white men.

Once produced and packed, the products of the sugar plantations were loaded on shipboard, either at the nearest point or at the very front door of the plantation if it was located on the banks of a navigable river, and were carried to the chief ports of the metropolis. From there they were distributed throughout the mother country or reshipped to some other foreign market. This market, too, was rapidly expanding, since it was during the seventeenth and eighteenth centuries that sugar became a staple item in the diet of Europeans.

Although sugar was the chief commodity produced by this international industry, its by-products, molasses and rum, were also of great international significance. For molasses, in addition to being widely used as a cheap sweetener, was also the base from which rum was made; and rum, in addition to being the "poor man's intoxicant" all over the Atlantic community, was also the chief commodity traded by Europeans and North Americans to the African chieftains in exchange for "black ivory," that is, black slaves.

Tobacco. A plant indigenous to America, tobacco had become by the eighteenth century another highly important commodity in the international economic network of the North Atlantic community. It, too, was produced on plantations, in Virginia, Mexico, the British, French, and Dutch colonies of the Caribbean area, Brazil, and other places. Everywhere the methods of planting, collecting, harvesting, and marketing were much the same; almost everywhere the productivity of the tobacco plantations was made possible by the use of black slaves.

The production of tobacco, as that of sugar, required much hard — and cheap — labor. Tobacco was an annual plant; the seedling plants, germinated in flats, had to be set out in rows or hills, the growing plants had to be weeded, and the stalks had to be stripped of the less flavorful leaves. At harvest, the leaves were removed from the stalks and then split off their stems, dried, or cured, sorted, and packed into great 500-pound casks or smaller "rolls," as in Brazil. The tobacco was transported by ship to the metropolis, where it was redistributed to the markets of Europe. Some of it, especially that from Brazil, went into the African slave trade.

The amount of tobacco produced in America in the eighteenth century was enormous; it, too, became one of the major items of international trade.

The tobacco industry in the eighteenth century. From *Encyclopédié*, pt. II,
Oeconomie rustique: Fabrique du tabac, plate I. Courtesy of the
University of Washington Library.

Indigo. Much used as a blueing and as a dye in the textile industries of western Europe, indigo was another important international commodity produced by American agriculture. It grew in commercial quantities in South Carolina, Georgia, the British, French, Spanish, and Dutch West Indies, Guatemala, and Brazil.

The raw base of this product was the leaves of a small plant, from which was drawn by infusion the plant's peculiar coloring matter. This matter, when cured, was dried into cakes and shipped in this form. The whole process involved difficult, back-breaking, stinking work; throughout the indigo-producing areas this task was performed by black slaves.

Like sugar and tobacco, indigo had an international market; it was shipped to London, Lisbon, Cádiz, Paris, or Amsterdam, and thence reshipped to other markets.

Rice. The methods of producing rice, an internationally distributed plantation product, varied little from empire to empire. It was cultivated in South Carolina, the West Indies, Brazil, Peru, and elsewhere.

The rice grain, the fruit of the rice plant or grass, had to be grown in fields or paddies that could be flooded during the growing season. Again, the hard labor required was universally done by black slaves.

Rice, which was a popular food all over Europe but particularly in the Mediterranean countries, was described by one contemporary as being "restorative, nourishing, and sweetening; it conglutinates the humours, and is useful in fluxes of the belly; it purifies the mass of blood, and stops hemorrhages. It is used either in ptisans [decoctions] or food."[6]

About the middle of the eighteenth century it was estimated that South Carolina alone shipped 50,000 barrels of rice per year to England; much of it was then reshipped to the markets of continental Europe.

Grain. Yet another agricultural product of America of great importance in international trade was grain — wheat, oats, Indian corn, and others. These grains were grown in sufficient quantities for export in the northern English colonies, Mexico, Peru, Chile, the Rio de la Plata region, and Venezuela. Because these grains are grown in cool climates and on lands at some altitude above sea level, they were not typically a plantation

[6] Savary, *The Universal Dictionary of Trade and Commerce*, trans. from the French and expanded by Malachy Postlethwayt, 2 vols. in 4 (2nd ed.; London, 1757), II, pt. 2, p. 612.

The cattlemen's frontier in western Brazil, early nineteenth century.
From Johann M. Rugendas, *Viagem pitoresca através do Brasil* (São Paulo:
Livraria Martins, 1940), plate 2/19. Courtesy of the
University of Washington Library.

product, but rather a product of relatively small, self-sufficient farms, operated by free white or, sometimes, free Indian labor.

A great deal of wheat was traded intercolonially, especially between foodstuffs-producing areas and such staple-producing regions as the West Indies. Flour, milled in the large towns along the seacoast, also became a major commodity in international commerce.

Cattle. Closely related to the agricultural productivity of the continent was the cattle industry. This industry, likewise international in scope, had become by the eighteenth century a highly important element in the economic life of the hemisphere. There were active cattle-raising areas in Mexico, Argentina, Brazil, Angloamerica, and Venezuela. The major products of this industry were beef, hides, horses, tallow, and mules. The methods used were roughly similar in all the cattle-raising areas. The labor force was not generally composed of black slaves, however, although many blacks were used in the industry in Latin America. On the other hand, cattle raising produced new social types such as the *llanero* of Venezuela, the gaucho of Argentina, and the cowboy of the North American west, and typical cattlemen's subcultures, each with its own mores, traditions of horsemanship, vocabulary, and costumes.

The Extractive Industries

A major part of the productive activity of America was made up of extractive industries — fisheries, forest industries, fur trading, and mining.

Fisheries. One of the most truly international industries in the American hemisphere in the eighteenth century was commercial fishing. This industry developed in several natural areas, the largest of which lay in the relatively shallow waters off Newfoundland, Canada, and New England. There the ships of many nations congregated to reap the harvest of the sea — codfish, mackerel, haddock, etc. The chief national groups of fishermen in this area were the French and the British (English and Angloamericans); the competition and contacts between these groups played their part in the great rivalry of the two empires around the world.

As an extractive enterprise the fisheries involved the catching of the myriads of fish that inhabited the waters off the eastern coasts of North America and the drying of those fish on the neighboring shores of Newfoundland or Nova Scotia. The fish were packed in salt or brine — thereby introducing salt as a highly precious commodity in international economic relations — and brought back to the metropolises of New England, England, France, Portugal, and the Basque provinces in Spain, whence they flowed into the channels of North Atlantic commerce.

Another important aspect of the fishing industry was whaling. There was a large field for whale fisheries off the southern coast of Greenland and another off the southeastern shores of Brazil. The Brazilian viceroy Lavradio, recognizing the potential economic value of this activity, even went so far as to encourage New England whalers to teach Brazilians the techniques of the business; but he was careful to prevent them from using this as a cover-up for smuggling. Presently Bahia became an important whaling port, although it suffered from the competition of the Yankee whalers from New England.

Forest industries. There were many forms of the forest industries. In Canada and the northern parts of Angloamerica the cutting of logs for

lumber or as masts and spars for ships was an industry of major significance. The forests of the southern parts of Angloamerica were sources
for naval stores — pitch, tar, turpentine, etc. Along the coasts of Central
America and Brazil there were important settlements devoted to the
cutting and shipping of Brazilwood, which was used in western Europe
for dyeing. In tropical America, too — Central America, the Caribbean,
Venezuela, Brazil — branches of this activity were devoted to the cutting
and shipping of mahogany, a fine hardwood that came to be widely used
for furniture in the eighteenth century.

The fur trade. A different type of "forest industry," though one which
was actually more trade than industry, was the skin-and-fur trade carried
on with the Indians of the American interior. Furs, in an age when
the heating of houses was only just beginning to be a practice, were
in great demand in western Europe, and the forests of America were
scoured to satisfy this demand.

Thus the Hudson's Bay Company took many shiploads of fur from
the Hudson Bay area each year, and the French in Canada shipped
large quantities of furs from Montreal. Albany and New York, until the
end of the eighteenth century, were the major emporiums for furs in
Angloamerica, although there was also considerable trade out of
Philadelphia. In the southern continental colonies of Angloamerica an
enormous quantity of deerskins moved to Europe by way of Charleston
and Savannah. In South America there was little or no traffic in the
skins of wild animals. By the nineteenth century, in fact, such productivity of furs or deerskins as had existed had almost disappeared.

Late in the eighteenth century the Russians discovered the fabulously
profitable fur-bearing herds of seals, sea otter, and sea lions on the northwest coasts of North America, and the hunting of these animals attracted
French, Canadian, English, and American seal hunters as well as Russians. The sealing industry became a highly international business that
gave rise to international competition and conflict.

Mining. The most dramatic, romantic, and fabled — as well as the
most tragic — extractive industry in America was, of course, mining.

It was the mining of precious metals in America that had originally
attracted the hordes of Iberians to the hemisphere, and these mines,
especially those of Mexico and Peru, had produced the gold and silver
upon which the power of the Spanish empire had been largely built.
The original mines of Mexico and Peru had reached their peak by the

eighteenth century, but the century witnessed the opening of gold and diamond mines in Brazil, the significant development of iron mining in Pennsylvania, and the exploitation of gems, especially emeralds, in Colombia.

In North America and Mexico the mines were operated largely by free white or Indian labor, although there was some employment of slaves, too. In Brazil, the mines were worked almost exclusively by black slave labor.

The mining products of America, like all the products of America, were of extreme importance in the international economy of the North Atlantic community. The iron of Angloamerica was shipped to England, where it was manufactured into hardware and then reshipped out of England to the European market or back to America, either to the Angloamerican colonies, Brazil, or Hispanoamerica. The precious metals of Hispanoamerica and Brazil, together with the diamonds of Brazil, flowed back to the trading centers of the mother countries whence they were shipped out to France, England, or Holland to equalize the unfavorable balance of trade between the Iberians and those countries.

Manufactures

The economy of the American hemisphere in the eighteenth century was, of course, predominantly agrarian; there were relatively few manufactures. Yet there were, especially in Angloamerica, a number of manufacturing enterprises that were of significance in the colonial economy.

There were many silversmiths as well as furniture makers in all the colonies up and down the hemisphere. Iron foundries were to be found in Angloamerica. Sugar mills and distilleries operated in all the regions where sugar was produced and sawmills were active in all the areas of the forest industry. In Angloamerica, in particular, shipbuilding had become a basic business, and ships built in New England were sold in England and elsewhere around the Atlantic basin.

Because most of the manufactures were for home consumption, little remained for export. Besides, the mercantilistic laws of the mother countries were calculated to retard or suppress the competition of the colonial manufacturers with those of the mother countries.

With the passing of the years, the amount of manufacturing increased everywhere. The two reasons for this were the scientific improvement in technological processes and the impact of the Industrial Revolution.

The influence of both was universal, but the Industrial Revolution, which had its first extraordinary development in England, leaped over the Atlantic to take root first in Angloamerica during and after the American Revolution and then, gradually, in other parts of the hemisphere. Such things as the building of spinning and weaving mills, patterned after those in England, and the invention of the steamboat and the cotton gin marked the Industrial Revolution's remarkable progress. Even so, it would be a long time yet before the Americans in any part of the hemisphere would produce manufactured goods to export.

It can be concluded, then, that the productivity of America, vast and varied and enormously valuable as it was, was a productivity of crude or partly refined raw materials. As yet, in the economic expansion of Europe, the function of America was to furnish Europe and Africa with raw materials that they could not produce for themselves.

But the European market for American products was practically unlimited; the sale of American products in that market netted fabulous profits for Americans and provided the economic foundation for the phenomenal expansion of capital wealth almost everywhere in the hemisphere. Much of the productivity was of an international nature in that the basic industries overlapped intercolonial and interimperial boundaries and the commodities produced were distributed in a truly international market. Much the same methods of production were employed everywhere, regardless of international boundaries; much the same labor institutions prevailed in all the colonies; and the basic commodities were likely to find their markets outside the empires that produced them. A beaver skin brought to England from the shores of Hudson Bay might be manufactured into a hat there and eventually sold in Buenos Aires. Sugar produced in Bahia might go first to Lisbon, then to England, then to a market in Norway. The economic "colonialisms" or "regionalisms" that were growing in the colonies were to a great extent internationally oriented, since they largely originated from the impulse of the colonies to be free to sell and to buy where it was to their "enlightened economic self-interest" to do so.

Commerce

The European colonization of America had been a part of the so-called commercial revolution, or the overseas expansion of European commerce, the first phases of which had taken place in the fifteenth, six-teenth, and seventeenth centuries. By the eighteenth century the Atlan-tic Ocean had become, in effect, commercially a European-American lake, with a constant movement of commercial ships east and west, north and south, and in triangular patterns over its waters. Basically, this com-merce rested upon the exchange of American products for European goods. But it included much more than that, for a large segment of the Atlantic commerce was made up of the international slave trade between Africa and America and the exchange of products among Euroamerican empires.

The trunk lines of this network of commercial relationships in the Atlantic were, of course, the lines of exchange between the Euroamerican colonies and their mother countries. But the most striking aspect of these intraimperial trades was their ultimately international, or interimperial, nature. Brazil traded with other countries besides Portugal; Peru's silver did not go only to Spain, Canada's furs to France, Virginia's tobacco to England, or Curaçao's sugar to Holland.

Much of what Brazil transported to Portugal — most of it, actually — was reshipped out of Portugal to northern countries, especially Eng-land, thus becoming part of a complex international trade. Only a small fraction of Peru's bullion remained in Spain: most of it was shipped to France, England, or Holland to pay for the manufactured goods needed in the colonies, as already noted. Much of the expansion of England's capital wealth was built from the profits derived from the reshipment of Virginia tobacco, Carolina rice, or Jamaican sugar to the countries of continental Europe. Holland reexported the majority of its West Indian products, along with those of the East Indies, to continental markets, the Mediterranean, America, and Africa. Dutch ships were the freight carriers par excellence of the eighteenth century. For not only did the Dutch reap a rich harvest from the freight charges on goods carried for other countries, but they were also, above all, seafaring traders, bear-ing goods from one non-Dutch country to another and selling them there, taking in return the products of the second to sell in the markets of a third.

England's trade with its American colonies multiplied five times between 1700 and 1770; from one-sixth to one-quarter of its seaborne commerce before the American Revolution was derived from the col-onies. France's colonial commerce increased tenfold between 1715 and

1787; much of it was with the French sugar islands; a substantial part of the imports to France from the Caribbean were reexported.

Not only had the expansion of European commerce to America enriched Europe and introduced to Europeans a host of new commodities and luxuries, even a higher standard of living. But as Voltaire commented in the third quarter of the eighteenth century, the expansion of Europe, the greatest event in the history of the world, had also brought the peoples of Europe knowledge of the rest of the world. They had come to feel new needs, which had revolutionized European commerce. To be sure, he said, there were many things that Europe had brought to America, such as horses, wheat, and refined sugar. But America had sent to Europe cochineal, indigo, tobacco, cocoa, vanilla, ornamental woods, and medicines such as quinine — "placed by nature in the mountains of Peru while she placed [malaria] fever in the other parts of the world." "It is certain," he continued, "that America today [ca. 1770] provides many things for the comfort and pleasure of the most humble citizen of Europe." And the Europeans, he concluded, can no longer do without them.[7]

On the other hand, the growth of the colonies had created a market for European goods that was of incalculable value to the mother countries. It is certain, as Adam Smith said, that the enormously multiplied wealth of eighteenth-century Europe was derived from commerce, much of which rested, in the last analysis, upon the economic expansion of the colonies.

Thus, in building up a new set of productive "factories" and markets for European goods, the expansion of Europe had generated a whole new Atlantic economy, a network of commercial exchange between America, Africa, and Europe, and a vast increase in the total capital wealth (gross economic product) of the Atlantic community as a whole. Above all, it had revolutionized the material way of life of the Europeans themselves.

The Slave Trade

One of the most extensive — and profitable — of the international trades of the Atlantic basin was the importation of black slaves from Africa to the American colonies.

[7] Voltaire, *Essai sur les moeurs et de l'esprit des nations, Oeuvres complètes de Voltaire,* ed. Louis E. D. Moland. 52 vols. (Paris, 1877–85, vols. XI, XII, XIII), XII, 38.

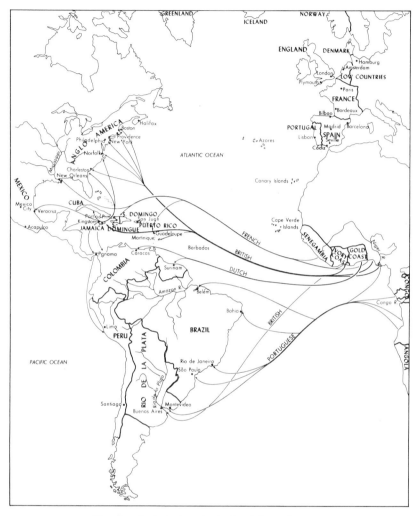

The slave trade to America in the eighteenth century

Both Indian and black slavery existed in all the colonial areas, as has been noted; on the whole, black slavery was more efficient and more durable than Indian slavery. In any case, slavery flourished especially in the plantation areas; black slaves provided the principal labor force in the production of most of the staples that were the foundations of the phenomenal expansion of capital wealth in America in the eighteenth century.

The slaves were generally collected by black slave hunters in Africa and then were bought by the Portuguese, French, Dutch, English, and Angloamerican slave traders who dealt with black potentates along the African coast.

For Portuguese traders, following the principle of national monopoly, the chief market for the blacks was Brazil. French slavers took most of their cargoes to French colonies. The British Royal African Company owned a monopoly of the British slave trade, but it issued licenses to other companies, particularly Angloamerican slave traders whose businesses were located in Rhode Island and Massachusetts.

Since Spain had no possessions in "black" Africa from which to draw black slaves, it was compelled to depend upon other nations. Thus, in a number of *asientos*, or royal contracts, companies of various nationalities had been authorized to take slaves to the Spanish colonies. During the War of the Spanish Succession, the *asiento* was given to a French company. When that war ended, the *asiento* was given to the English South Sea Company as a subsidiary part of the Peace of Utrecht. But this privilege was abused, and it opened the way for a vast amount of illicit trading not only by the company but by other Englishmen and Angloamericans as well. This clandestine trade resulted in a long series of diplomatic and armed conflicts between England and Spain. The South Sea Company probably made much more money out of the *asiento* and the illegal trade associated with it than the company ever admitted, and it persistently refused to give an accounting of its activities to the king of Spain, who was a partner in the enterprise, as provided by the treaty of 1713. Because of the abuses that arose under it, and the claims and counterclaims of England and Spain because of it, the English *asiento* was terminated by mutual consent in 1750.

Taken as a whole, the black slave trade was probably responsible for the forced immigration of as many as five million Africans into the American hemisphere in the eighteenth century. The religious, cultural, sociological, and biological results of this forced immigration were profound; they will be discussed elsewhere. As an economic phenomenon, the slave trade provided an indispensable labor force for the most important American productive industries and a base, therefore, for the commerce, the expansion of capital wealth, and the profitableness of the major part of the hemisphere.

The slave trade. Landing black slaves at a port in Brazil, early nineteenth century. From Johann M. Rugendas, *Viagem pitoresca através do Brasil*, plate 4/2. Courtesy of the University of Washington Library.

Interimperial Trade

In addition to the "trunk" trades of the Euroamerican colonies with their mother countries and the international extensions of these trades, there was a great and growing trade among the colonies themselves, much of it carried on in violation of the policies and the instructions of the imperial governments. The trade of the Angloamerican merchants of British New England and the middle colonies with the French, Spanish, and Portuguese colonies, while not prohibited by British imperial law, did violate the monopolistic laws of the other mother countries concerned. In general, however, this so-called clandestine or illicit trade was welcomed by the inhabitants of the colonies involved. In some cases, indeed, the inhabitants could not have subsisted without it.

A highly important segment of this intercolonial trade was that between the English continental colonies and the French, Dutch, and Spanish colonies of the Caribbean area; this exchange grew significantly during the eighteenth century. Thus, when the prices of sugar and molasses in the British West Indies went up and the British supply did not meet the continental demand, the Yankees turned to French Saint-Domingue, Martinique, and Guadeloupe, where they traded fish, barrels, mules, and farm products for French sugar, molasses, and non-English rum, all of which were cheaper in the French colonies than in the British islands.

The Yankees also sailed to the Dutch colonies, Curaçao, St. Eustatius, and Surinam, on similar errands. They went as well to the Spanish colonies on the mainland of South America and Central America — at considerable risk because of the Spanish *guarda costas* — where they diversified their cargoes with hides, dyewoods, and Spanish money for the New England market. Both English and Yankee ships visited Brazil.

The Dutch traders were, if anything, more enterprising than the English and the Yankees. The ubiquitous Dutchmen visited all the empires, with little regard for the prohibitive laws against such visits, and sold manufactured goods in return for the various sorts of commodities offered by the Americans. These were taken to Holland, chiefly to the city of Amsterdam, whence they were distributed throughout northern Europe. When the Dutch were not journeying to prohibited colonial ports, they were welcoming the ships of the other empires in their own ports in Surinam, Curaçao, and St. Eustatius, which thus became free ports for international trade of all kinds, visited legally or illegally by the ships of all the Atlantic nations.

The capital upon which the economic activity of America in the seventeenth century had been built had originally been European; it was still predominantly European in the eighteenth century. But as the capital wealth of the colonies had expanded, substantial funds had accumulated in the hands of merchants in the American cities, and these colonial entrepreneurs underwrote much of the economic activity of the hemisphere, especially that of an internal or intercolonial sort.

Thus a merchant capitalist of Buenos Aires, Rio de Janeiro, Santa Cruz, Kingston, Philadelphia, New York, or Boston would generally underwrite the extension of agricultural cultivation in his colony. But as the owner of ships, cargoes, wharves, and warehouses, he would also be fully capable of mounting commercial ventures into other parts of America, Africa, the Mediterranean, or continental Europe.

Such unfavorable balances of trade as those between Spain and Portugal and their foreign correspondents were in large part paid in bullion. In most cases, however, trade balances were liquidated with commodities. By the eighteenth century an elaborate international and intraimperial system of credit exchange had evolved that reduced a large part of the accounting for goods and services to certain accepted forms of documents, such as "bills of exchange," with the result that, in these avenues of economic exchange, relatively little bullion actually changed hands. For example, within the British empire a merchant of Boston who sold a shipment of fish in Barbados might readily take in payment a bill of exchange — a sort of draft — drawn by his Barbados correspondent upon a merchant-banker of London; similar arrangements existed in all the colonial empires.

There was a comparable mechanism for international exchange; a Dutch merchant selling a cargo of hardware in St. Eustatius to an American ship captain from Philadelphia might gladly take in payment a bill of exchange on the Philadelphia merchant's factor in London. Many merchants and companies, in fact, had their own branch offices or favored agents in foreign countries, with the result that a genuine international network of financial agencies and quasi-banking establishments existed through which the Atlantic community's economic interchanges might be conducted by the use of negotiable paper rather than bullion.

In other words, the economic activities of the Western world were already being conducted by means of a system of paper credit. Unfavorable balances, of course, still had to be paid by commodities or coin, but even in this segment of the economy the growth of capital wealth in any given area might well be essentially a form of wealth represented by an expanded credit balance.

As the eighteenth century wore on, it became increasingly apparent both to the statesmen-managers and to the colonies themselves that the seamless, exclusive fabrics of mercantilism were not working, indeed, that they could not work, because the now overwhelmingly international nature of actual economic life made imperative certain relaxations of the rigors of the mercantilistic system and imperial economic administration. The new experiences had produced a set of new ideas: these ideas rather rapidly were incorporated into reforms in all the empires — reforms that moved steadily and ineluctably, if not fully consciously, in the direction of freedom of trade.

CHAPTER 4

The Economies of the Euroamerican Empires

If it be true that the grand, overall pattern of American economic life in the eighteenth century was increasingly an international network which overlapped intercolonial, interimperial, and even intercontinental boundaries, it is also true that, within that macro-pattern, each Euroamerican empire had an economic model of its own, a micro-pattern, that was marked by certain institutions, ideas, and practices characteristic of, and peculiar to, itself.

Each of the colonial empires was conceived of and administered, in theory at least, as a closed, exclusive economic unit, operated primarily for the benefit of the mother country and the colonies to the near exclusion of foreigners from other empires. The empires thought of themselves, especially the statesmen who managed them, as independent rivals and always as potential enemies. In practice, each empire had a central control agency located in the imperial metropolis whose duty it was to supervise or to manage the colonial economy, as already noted. The Portuguese, Spanish, and French supervisory bodies had the power of making regulations that had the force of law. The English Board of Trade was a purely advisory body, which passed on its recommendations to Parliament for the making of law or to the Privy Council for executive action. The economic life of the Dutch-American empire was still, theoretically, a monopoly of the Dutch West India Company, but the affairs of the company were subject to scrutiny and regulation directly by the States-General of the Netherlands.

Institutionally, then, the economic life of every Euroamerican empire was centralized in administrative agencies seated in the mother countries in Europe. In theory, despite the de facto growth of freedom of interimperial exchange, the economic aspect of the expansion of Europe was still managed by European governmental agencies; in practice, there was a close operational relationship between these official, political, or quasi-political institutions and the private capitalists who still conducted the day-by-day economic activities relating to the colonies.

Brazil

The great axis of the economic life of the Portuguese colonial empire was Lisbon, and the management of that economy was centralized in the hands of the Conselho Ultramarino. For Lusoamerica, economic laws, commercial regulations, taxes, import and export duties — in short, every conceivable facet of economic control, except for certain unimportant aspects of economic administration left in the hands of local colonial officials — was exercised by this council. In accord with the accepted precepts of mercantilism, Brazil was a closed economic sphere, a Portuguese monopoly, and trade with the colony, legally at least, was conducted entirely within the framework of this monopoly.

The British, however, had succeeded in getting a predominant share of this lucrative commerce. By the Treaty of Westminster (1656) Oliver Cromwell had been granted certain privileges for English merchants, including that of sending English vessels to accompany the Brazil convoys and even to trade with Brazil on condition that the British ships touch at Portuguese ports on the outward and the return voyages. These privileges were extended in the Treaty of Alliance of 1668, and in 1703 John Methuen negotiated a treaty for England which tied the two empires together under very favorable terms for both. Portugal agreed to admit English woolen cloth free of duty, thereby giving a great fillip to the badly sagging English woolen industry, in return for which England agreed to admit Portuguese wines at a preferential rate of import duties as compared with wines imported from France, thereby giving an equally great fillip to an equally flagging Portuguese wine industry. The effect of this exchange of commercial favors was to open to England, via Lisbon, the gateway to the Portuguese colonies, especially Brazil, and a vast market for English woolens. Along with the woolens went many other

English products, a considerable part of which was paid for in Brazilian gold. In effect, by this treaty Brazil's economy was to a considerable measure placed under British hegemony — a condition that lasted for the better part of a century.

Production

As in all the Euroamerican empires in the eighteenth century, the phenomenal expansion of capital wealth in Brazil derived from the production of raw materials. In the older provinces of Bahia, with its chief port of São Salvador, and Pernambuco, whose main port was Recife, the basic staples were sugar and, in the eighteenth century, tobacco. In this sense, the vast sugar plantations and the smaller tobacco plantations were rather like agrarian factories, and the major (but not the exclusive) business of the ports was the exportation of these commodities and the importation of European-manufactured goods needed on the plantations.

The production of sugar in Brazil was immense: the harvest of 1725–26 yielded some 12,000 or 13,000 chests of sugar which were shipped to Portugal and thence to other parts of Europe. In 1748 the colony exported approximately 17,000 chests. Supplementary to the production of sugar was that of rum and sugarcane brandy, commodities that were exceedingly important in the slave trade.

Brazilian tobacco, reputed to be the finest in the world, was a highly profitable crop that became an essential item in the Brazilian export trade. The tobacco was shipped not only to Europe by way of Lisbon and to Africa as one of the commodities offered in the slave trade, but also to India, and even as far as China, in the East India ships that touched at Brazilian ports en route to Asia. About mid-century the colony was exporting some 25,000 rolls — perhaps 200,000 *arrobas* (an *arroba* was a unit of weight of from twenty-five to thirty-two pounds) — of tobacco, chiefly from Bahia and Alagoas.

Another very important crop was cotton, a fiber used in cloth manufacture, which began in the eighteenth century to replace wool as the Western world's most widely used textile. This revolution was brought about by the technological improvements developed in the eighteenth century in Europe, especially England.

Cotton fiber had been known for a long time, of course, and the chief supply had come from the Orient. But with the vast expansion of the demand in England that resulted from the invention of the power loom by Cartwright in 1787, the Oriental sources could not supply the need and England turned to Brazil. This gave a powerful impetus to the Brazilian cotton culture; cotton, for a time, was reported to be more valuable than even sugar or tobacco. Brazil exported some 38,000 bags of cotton in 1789; this amount rose to 55,000 bags in 1791.

In the interior Brazilian provinces cattle raising had now become a major industry. This business, while scattered over the interior parts of the whole country, had its chief centers in three major regions: the northern *sertões*, or hinterlands, along the upper São Francisco and the Parnaíba rivers, generally inland from Bahia; the southern plains of the broad Minas Gerais region, the chief city of which was São Paulo (in what is today the province of São Paulo); and the steppe country inland from Rio Grande do Sul and extending to the Rio de la Plata.

Basically, the purpose of cattle raising was to provide meat for the cities and plantations along the coast. Large herds of cattle were driven many miles from the great ranches of the hinterlands to the cities and plantations of the eastern seaboard. As a business, therefore, cattle raising was predominantly internal to the colony. Life on the ranches was similar to that on the cattle-raising ranches in other parts of the continent: the cattle were allowed to roam widely in broad areas of grazing land until ready for market; they were supervised and rounded up by a motley crew of free labor composed of blacks, mulattoes, Indians, and mestizos, called *vaqueiros*, that is, cowboys; the immense ranches were owned and managed by wealthy landowners who grazed their cattle in the almost limitless expanses of unpossessed virgin land.

The cattle-raising industry was not confined, however, to its internal functions, for it produced a number of significant commodities for export. Brazilian dried meat, for example, in an age when there was no such thing as refrigeration, was an essential food for sailors long at sea; hides, as a commodity for export to the European leather tanneries, were even more important; tallow, used in making candles and the manufacture of cordage, was another valuable by-product. Furthermore, the industry produced many horses and mules, indispensable in preindustrial transportation; at the turn of the century it is estimated that Rio Grande do Sul exported from 12,000 to 15,000 mules per year. Sheep, too, were important; their wool was widely used in the manufacture of the ponchos worn by the cowboys and the working classes of the cities. (Most of

The mining frontier. Gold mining at Itacolomi, Brazil, early nineteenth century.
From Johann M. Rugendas, *Viagem pitoresca através do Brasil*, plate 3/22.
Courtesy of the University of Washington Library.

the finer woolens for more expensive clothing came of course from
England.)

Toward the end of the seventeenth century gold was discovered in
the interior of Brazil; from Bahia, Pernambuco, and Rio de Janeiro people
came in search for gold in numbers comparable to those involved in

the rushes that had occurred earlier in Mexico and Peru and those that would take place later in other parts of the continent. This rush created a "mining frontier" that eventually became the region of Minas Gerais.

Other discoveries of gold followed, with the result that the total gold income of King José V (1706–50) has been estimated at some $50 million. Diamonds were also discovered at this time, and José V's royal income from diamonds is estimated to have been some $16 million.

Commerce

Brazil's expanding capital wealth was based on a magnificent productivity of agricultural, pastoral, and mineral crude materials. Its exports consisted of a great variety of profitable commodities from its plantations, ranches, and mines — sugar and rum, tobacco, cotton, hides, gold, silver, and diamonds. Until 1765 the bulk of these products was shipped to Portugal in fleets that sailed under convoy from Brazil's chief ports of Rio de Janeiro, Recife, São Luís de Maranhão, and Belém (Pará). The fleet from Rio in 1753 was reported to have carried gold, silver, diamonds, and other commodities worth a total of £ 15 million. Brazil was, indeed, a "milch cow" for Portugal and its kings.

Most of the commodities shipped from Brazil to Portugal were reexported to the other countries of western Europe, France, Holland, the Germanies, the countries of the Mediterranean, and, most especially, England. It is probable that over half of these reexports went to England, which was closely bound to the Portuguese economy in many ways. David MacPherson, in his encyclopedic *Annals of Commerce* published in 1805, estimated that in 1768 (to take a fairly typical year) England imported from Portugal commodities worth £ 391,502.[1] Among these were gold, silver, and diamonds, hides, brazilwood, cocoa, cotton, and whalebone, all from Brazil. Of the total English imports from Portugal probably two-thirds came from the colony of Brazil.

On the other hand, Brazil was almost completely dependent upon Europe for manufactured goods. These, of course, came largely from Portugal, which manufactured next to nothing but imported the goods destined for Brazil from the other countries of Europe, chiefly, again, England. MacPherson reported that in 1768 England exported to Portugal goods valued at £ 711,908. These included English woolens, linens,

---

[1] David MacPherson, *Annals of Commerce* . . . (London, 1805), III, 486.

hats (some of them made of beaver skins from North America), hardware of many sorts, lead, watches, arms and military equipment, cordage, etc. Most of these commodities were then sent to Brazil.[2]

Outside of these official exchanges there flourished in Brazil a great contraband trade. British ships, from both Britain and Angloamerica, did a prospering business in the colony. As has been noted, the Treaty of Westminster of 1654 had permitted English ships to go to Brazil provided they stopped at Portuguese ports on their way to and from America. Many of the ships followed this directive, but a great and increasing number simply ignored it. In 1794 it was estimated that in fifteen months thirty-five foreign ships, mostly English, had docked in Rio de Janeiro. But other nationalities also participated, the chief among them being the Dutch and the French. Many of the small ports along the coast were visited by these free traders; they did a thriving business, to the satisfaction of the Brazilians and the prosperity of both Brazil and the *contrabandistas*.

Economic Reforms

In the middle decades of the eighteenth century two major changes in the Brazilian economy took place. The first was the extraordinary effort of Portugal's chief minister Carvalho, later the Marquis of Pombal, to break the British hold upon the economy of the Portuguese empire. "The English," he said, "came to Lisbon to monopolize even the commerce of Brazil. The entire cargo of the vessels that were sent thither, and consequently the riches that were returned in exchange, belonged to them. . . . These foreigners, after having acquired immense fortunes, disappeared on a sudden, carrying with them the riches of the country."[3] Because of this conviction Carvalho took several steps to exclude the English and to concentrate the trade of Brazil in the hands of Portuguese merchants.

To begin with, Carvalho, although not technically the colonial secretary, reduced the Overseas Council to the status of a rubber stamp for his own ideas. He then proceeded to make a number of political reforms in the colony, while he turned his attention to the imperial

[2] *Ibid.*
[3] Quoted by Alan K. Manchester, *British Preeminence in Brazil* . . . (Chapel Hill: University of North Carolina Press, 1933), p. 39.

economy. In 1751 he established royal boards of inspectors to scrutinize the exports of the leading Brazilian ports; in 1755 he organized the government-sponsored General Company of Grand Pará and Maranhão to monopolize the commerce of those areas; four years later he created a similar company, the General Company for the Commerce of Pernambuco and Paraíba, for the sugar-producing area of the northeast. Then, in 1765, the convoy system of fleets from Brazil to Portugal was abolished in order to facilitate the movement of ships to and from the colony.

In the interior of the colony, Carvalho did away with the capitation tax on slaves in the mines and decreed that the "royal fifth" (the crown's share of the products of the mines) should be collected by a group of royal officers called intendants. He also created, in 1771, a royal control of diamond mining in Minas Gerais; under this administration private production might continue, but it was closely supervised by the crown officials. Finally, Carvalho reorganized the entire fiscal system of the colony.

The second major change in the Brazilian economy involved a series of deliberate efforts by the government to expand the productivity of the colony, acting through the office of Viceroy Lavradio, who governed Brazil from 1768 to 1779.

Lavradio himself took an active part in the economic development of the colony and initiated many programs for the diversification and improvement of its productivity. Supported by the interest of the crown, he expanded the areas devoted to the cultivation of tobacco and encouraged the intensification of the cultivation of wheat and rice. To stimulate the production of wheat, he prevailed upon Pombal to send over some grinding stones for flour mills, along with millers who knew how to build the mills and operate them. He was so successful in the promotion of the rice culture that the colony was able to supply the mother country, and Portugal, to stimulate colonial production, prohibited the importation of foreign (including Angloamerican) rice in 1781.

The viceroy also encouraged the cultivation of cotton in the south, already an important export commodity in the north, but without immediate success. Another crop he fostered was hemp, which was used in the manufacture of cordage and was of vital importance in the Portuguese navy and merchant marine, but this experiment failed, too. However, Lavradio was responsible for the successful beginning of the cultivation of coffee and indigo, which presently became principal items of Brazilian exportation. Coffee, in fact, eventually surpassed all other agricultural commodities in importance in the Brazilian economy.

Finally, it should be noted that the Marquis of Lavradio promoted the scientific — or quasi-scientific — study of economic problems by intellectual societies. The first of these was the Scientific Society, organized in 1772, which met in the viceroy's palace in Rio de Janeiro. Similar to the Societies of Friends of the Country that were springing up in Spanish America and the philosophical societies and societies for agriculture and the useful arts in Angloamerica, this example of the Enlightenment's exploration of practical scientific subjects interested itself in all the branches of science, including botany, medicine, physics, geography, and agriculture. But the Scientific Society was composed almost exclusively of Portuguese-born dilettantes, and, because of the prohibition of printing presses in Brazil, its members could not publish their findings. As a result, it had little impact on the practical economic life of the colony. It seems to have disappeared after Lavradio returned to Portugal in 1779. However, similar societies appeared later in the century.[4]

The Pombal-Lavradio economic reforms were fundamentally mercantilistic in conception and execution, and had as their objective the promotion of the economic welfare of the whole empire. Yet their overall result was a tightening of the control of the metropolis over the economy of the colony. In the last analysis, they exemplified the mercantilism of benevolent, enlightened despots.

But mercantilism, in the Portuguese empire as in the other Euroamerican empires, was weakening. Not only were the economic theories of the European economists leaning toward a philosophy of freedom of trade, but the American colonies, including Brazil, were slowly but surely moving toward a greater consciousness of the fact that their economic interests were not always identical with those of the mother country. This new awareness suggested, if it did not demand, that the colonies should be allowed an increasing degree of autonomy in the management of their economic affairs.

It was in the last two decades of the eighteenth century and the first decade of the nineteenth that the ideas of freer commercial relationships spread throughout America, including Brazil. The application of these

[4] See below, chapter 8.

ideas was hastened by the outbreak of the French Revolution and the ensuing Napoleonic wars. When the Portuguese court emigrated to Brazil in 1807–8, one of the first acts of Prince Regent João da Braganza was to open the Brazilian ports to the ships of all nations. Since England was blockading the continent of Europe, the only important fleets to benefit from this proposal were those of England and the United States, especially those of England. Indeed, the historically favored position of England in Brazil's commerce was reaffirmed in 1810 by a treaty of reciprocity.

A review of the economic development of Brazil in the eighteenth century reveals one outstanding fact: the reality of the phenomenal expansion of its capital wealth. The expansion of Europe was still going on, in a sense, in the internal and external expansion of the colony's economy; in another sense, however, it was no longer the expansion of Europe — it was the expansion of Brazil as a segment in the expansion of America as a whole.

Hispanoamerica

The economic life of the Spanish empire in the eighteenth century was controlled by the Casa de Contratación in Seville (it was moved to Cádiz in 1717). Overall imperial policies and laws, to be sure, were formulated by the all-powerful Council of the Indies, but the actual exporting and importing of goods and the dispatching and admitting of ships and cargoes were administered by the Casa.[5]

The theory behind the economic life of the empire was, of course, mercantilism. The colonies, under imperial law, were absolutely closed to non-Spaniards. Englishmen, Frenchmen, Genoese, Dutchmen, and others might come to Seville (later Cádiz) to deliver goods destined for the colonies or to transship goods from America destined for their own countries, but they had to do their business through the Casa and in Spain: they could not legally go to the colonies or trade with them directly.

The trade of Europe with the Spanish colonies through the Casa was indeed enormous. By the eighteenth century Hispanoamerica had become a huge market for European goods, most of which passed through Cádiz on their way to America. Furthermore, since Spain itself produced

[5] See volume IV of this series.

few of the manufactured goods needed in the colonies, it had to purchase those commodities in northern Europe, which meant that a very high proportion of the wealth that came to Cádiz from America, whether in the form of silver and gold, hides, dyewood, sugar, or tobacco, literally passed through Spain to find its way to France, England, Holland, or some other European industrial country. For the rest, the monarchs and the bureaucrats of Spain, careless or ignorant of the nature or the value of the wealth that came into the country, squandered much of it on dynastic wars, ostentatious living, and power struggles both inside and outside the country. For all these reasons, it could be said — and often was — that the country in the world with the greatest national income was the poorest nation among them all. The most striking fact regarding Hispanoamerica was that the colonial economy was an integral part of the whole empire, the central economic administration of which was fixed in Spain.

Production

The Spanish colonies in America enjoyed a variety of climates, terrains, and natural wealth. In the Caribbean area, for example, the economic productivity of the Spanish colonies was very much like that of their French, English, and Dutch neighbors. Mexico, most famous for its production of silver, was also endowed with fine soils for growing maize and wheat and with ideal areas for the grazing industries and the production of cattle, sheep, and horses.[6] In the northern parts of South America there was a good deal of mining, and increasing use of the forests, and, in the *llanos* (plains) of Venezuela, a thriving cattle industry. Peru, also famous for its silver mines, especially those at Potosí, was half semidesert (west of the Andes) and half tropical (in the upper Amazon valley east of the Andes). The valley of the Rio de la Plata and the pampas to the west of it became the locations of what was probably the most successful cattle-raising industry in the hemisphere.

The major agricultural product was sugar, which was grown especially on the great plantations of the Spanish Caribbean colonies, but Mexico and Central America also exported silk, cocoa, tobacco, indigo, cochineal, and cotton.

During the eighteenth century mining all over Hispanoamerica continued to be an integral part of the total economy, and production was

[6] It was through Mexico that the horse was first introduced into North America.

improved and expanded by the introduction of new technical methods. In general subsoil wealth belonged to the state, but the mines were operated by private operators under license from the king, who always reserved the "royal fifth" for himself and imposed a whole series of taxes and imposts. In some areas the mining was done by black slaves, but in Mexico and most other areas the mines were operated by "free" Indian labor.

The fact that the importance of mining was beginning to decline by the end of the eighteenth century stimulated an interest in technological improvements; mining was one of the divisions of economic activity most affected by the application of science to technology.

Commerce

As has been mentioned, the entire legal foreign trade of His-panoamerica was channeled through the Casa de Contratación. The two-way flow of goods between America and Europe generally followed the sea route that reached from the mouth of the Guadalquivir River in Spain to the Caribbean area, following the easterly trade winds by way of the Canaries and back to Europe by way of Havana, the Gulf Stream, and the northern westerlies past the Azores. Goods going out to America were loaded in two fleets, one, called the *flota*, which sailed under convoy for Vera Cruz in Mexico, and the other, called the *galeones*, destined for Puerto Bello on the Isthmus of Panama with a stop at Cartagena. Most of the goods for Puerto Bello went overland to Panama and the Pacific side of the isthmus and thence by sea to Lima, Peru. American commodities exported to Spain moved from Peru along the reverse route to Panama and Puerto Bello, where products from the Caribbean colonies were also collected for the return voyage of the *galeones*, while com-modities from Mexico and Manila were sent to Vera Cruz for the return voyage of the *flota*. The two returning fleets joined each other at Havana, whence they sailed together in a convoyed *flota* that followed the north-ern route eastward. Smaller groups of ships that constituted fragments of the great fleets served off-the-route colonies such as the Rio de la Plata.

The cargoes of the outgoing vessels were composed of European goods, largely manufactures, from France, Holland, Italy, England, and other countries. After arriving at the major ports in America, they were dis-tributed to the other colonies by local American shippers. Return goods, including gold and silver, were sent first to Cádiz and then to the other European nations. The trading nations of Europe were competitors for shares of this immense international exchange at Cádiz. France, while the Bourbons occupied the Spanish throne, was the largest single beneficiary of the system. The balance of exchange, on the whole, was more favorable to Europe than to America, but it was actually the other European nations, not Spain, that reaped the profits from it. This meant that the balance of trade between the colonies and Spain was unfavorable to the colonies; they made it up handsomely, however, in other ways, as will be noted.

By the eighteenth century the *flota* convoy system was already in decline; so much so that between 1706 and 1776 only twenty *flotas* sailed from Spain to America. The reasons for this decline were many. In the first place, the system was clumsy and inefficient: the final delivery of European goods at their destinations in America involved many handlings and cumulative costs; the operations of the fleets were constantly and drastically hampered by recurrent warfare. Spain sought to improve the system by organizing a group of monopolistic companies to carry on the commerce with specific parts of the empire and by permitting an increase in the number of *registros* (private Spanish ships trading under license). Most of all, competition from the direct trade of the *contrabandistas*, who could deliver goods more efficiently and much more cheaply, cut deeply into the business of the official system. The convoy system was suspended for a number of years and then revived in 1756; it was finally abandoned altogether in 1789.

Since Spain had no African colonies of its own, it was compelled to compromise its great mercantilistic system in order to procure slaves for its colonies. As already noted, the Spanish kings were forced to grant *asientos*, or contracts, to foreign slave traders — Dutch, Portuguese, or French — which gave them the right to ship African slaves to Hispanoamerica. After the Peace of Utrecht, an *asiento* was awarded to the English South Sea Company (in which the king of Spain was a partner) that permitted the company to deliver 4800 black slaves to America each year in return for American products, which were then taken back to England. The company was also allowed to send one 500-ton merchant ship each year to the fair at Puerto Bello, where it might sell its British goods and take on a cargo of American products.

The English *asiento* was not a success, however; its business was interrupted time and again by war, and its profits were reduced by the competition of Angloamerican, Dutch, French, and Portuguese *contrabandistas*. Actually, only four "annual ships" ever sailed. The *asiento* was terminated by mutual consent in the Anglo-Spanish Treaty of Madrid of 1750.

In an effort to shore up its decaying colonial commercial system Spain organized monopolistic commercial companies composed of private capitalists. The first and most famous of these, established in 1728, was the Royal Guipuzcoan Company of Caracas, or the Caracas Company, which was given a monopoly of the trade on the Venezuelan coast. Others were the Galicia Company, for trade with Campeche on the coast of New Spain, the Havana Company, and the Barcelona-Catalan Company for trade with Hispañola and Puerto Rico.

All these companies were unsuccessful, except the Caracas Company, which lasted until 1784. This company wrested control of the cacao trade from the Dutch interlopers, introduced the cultivation of cotton and indigo, and expanded that of tobacco in the lands of the Spanish Main. These commodities, along with dyewoods and hides, earned the company a good profit and also brought prosperity to the colony. But even the Caracas Company finally succumbed, partly because of losing favor with the crown and of the growing popularity of free-trade ideas among the imperial statesmen and the application of those ideas in the opening to Spanish competitors of commercial areas formerly served by the company, partly because of foreign competition, but especially because of the antagonism of the Venezuelan people, who were aroused by the company's arbitrary and often unscrupulous impositions and exploitations. Numerous charges against the company were reported by José de Abalos, the intendant of Venezuela, and many others, voicing the discontent of the people held under by the monopoly, and one by one the privileges of the company were taken away. The final blow came with the paralysis of trade caused by Spain's entry into the War of United States Independence in 1779. Because the establishment elsewhere of partial free trade had been successful, it was now extended to Venezuela. Under these circumstances the Caracas Company could not survive, and it was liquidated in 1784.

The old mercantilistic system had, indeed, almost reached its end.

One of the major factors contributing to its failure was the de facto growth of an increasingly flourishing contraband commerce — a universal activity that was, in fact, a genuine form of free trade.

The greatest agents of the "new freedom" were the Dutch, who, because of the happy proximity of their colonies, especially Curaçao and St. Eustatius, to the Spanish colonies in the Caribbean and on the mainland of South and Central America, found it easy in their small, swift ships to evade the Spanish *guarda costas* or to outwit or bribe Spanish officials. The Dutch, furthermore, made the most of the fact that many of the Spanish colonials, frustrated and overcharged by the cumbersome official systems of convoys or monopolistic companies, actually welcomed the Dutch (and other) interlopers who came to them directly and sold more cheaply and bought at higher prices than did their Spanish compatriots.

But the Dutch were not the only ones. The English, whether from England, the British West Indies, or the continental Angloamerican colonies, also did a thriving business. Bringing in manufactured goods, textiles, fish, and other foodstuffs, they took in return hides, indigo, cochineal, dyewoods, mahogany and, most precious of all, Spanish gold and silver in the form of hard money. They often ran afoul of the Spanish *guarda costas*, even far outside Spanish territorial waters, and on such occasions England found itself in the unaccustomed position of defending the freedom of the seas. Despite all such risks, the profits from the clandestine trade still exceeded the losses.

Although there was some French smuggling of goods into Spanish America, this illegal commerce was centered in the French Caribbean colonies; metropolitan France, with its favored position in the great exchange at Cádiz, generally preferred to do its trading with Spanish America through legitimate channels.

The Portuguese, on the other hand, were very much involved. The most important base of Portuguese trade with the Spanish colonies was the little town of Colonia do Sacramento on the estuary of the Rio de la Plata just west of the site of the present city of Montevideo. The Portuguese could undersell the Spanish because of Spain's official system of commerce. Many Spanish colonists crossed the river to trade on their own initiative, and Spanish officials and agents constantly complained that their business was being destroyed by the clandestine Portuguese competition.

All in all, the extralegal trade among the European colonies was a naturalistic sort of free trade which developed to satisfy the needs of the colonists and which to a large extent simply ignored the regulatory systems of the mother countries. For every empire, but especially for Hispanoamerica, this trade was a major determining factor in the decline of their mercantilistic policies.

Economic Reforms

During the reign of Carlos III in the second half of the eighteenth century, the economic administration of the Spanish colonial empire was drastically revised. The reforms that took place resulted in large measure from the fact that in actuality the old, rigid, exclusive system was breaking down; at the same time they were powerfully influenced by the appearance of a new philosophy of national wealth, a set of ideas that centered on the basic principles of freedom of trade.

Thus, in Spain, there now appeared a group of thinkers, all of them influenced by the Enlightenment, some of them foreigners, some of them native Spaniards, whose ideas gradually supplanted the old mercantilist doctrines of Jerónimo Uztáriz and Bernardo de Ulloa. Among these men the works of José Campillo y Cossío, written in the 1740s, had a considerable influence. Campillo favored, among other liberalizing internal reforms in the colonies, a reduction of import duties on foreign goods and a removal of restrictions on intercolonial trade — a sort of freedom of commerce within the empire. Bernardo Ward, an Irishman who rose high in the economic administration of Spain and was probably the most outstanding Spanish economist of the period, pursued Campillo's line of thinking and advocated " 'looking at free trade as the soul of commerce, . . . the fundamental principle of all other interests of the monarchy.'"[7]

Among the ministers, the Count of Aranda, José Gálvez, the Count of Floridablanca, the Count of Campomanes, and Gaspar Melchor de Jovellanos were all men of the Enlightenment; all to a greater or lesser extent agreed with Ward's liberal ideas regarding colonial trade, and all supported reform in the colonial system. They had not, however, moved completely to a philosophy of international free trade. Although

[7] Quoted by Roland D. Hussey, *The Caracas Company, 1728–1784* (Cambridge, Mass.: Harvard University Press, 1934), p. 227.

in one way or another they desired a relaxation of the old system, their interest in free trade was directed chiefly toward greater autonomy for Spaniards and Hispanoamericans within the empire. For example, Campomanes, like William Wood in England, favored almost complete commercial freedom among the members of the empire, but he still adhered to the old mercantilist doctrine of the closed and exclusive economic empire in international relations.

It was thinking such as this, coupled with the de facto confusion and decline in imperial trade, that led to the practical reforms. A special commission appointed to study the situation reported in 1765 that the Cádiz monopoly and its cumbersome system of administration were responsible for much of the decline, and it recommended a relaxation of the system. As a result, the more important Caribbean colonies were freed from the monopoly and were allowed to trade with certain towns in Spain other than Cádiz. In addition, a number of the old, onerous duties on trade were removed. The results were salutary, and the new system of relative freedom was extended to other parts of America, including Rio de la Plata, Chile, and Peru (1778). As has been noted, the Caracas Company along with its monopoly was dissolved in 1784, and five years later the Cádiz monopoly with its convoy system of trade was suppressed. At the same time, limited relaxations, even in trade with foreign colonies, were authorized, and an edict of 1789 permitted the Spanish colonists to buy black slaves directly from foreign traders — which, of course, opened the door for substantial trade in other commodities as well.

The practical results of these liberalizing measures were highly gratifying. The volume of trade increased everywhere; prices in America were reduced; above all, contraband trade was actually discouraged and lowered. Furthermore, the new freedom and prosperity were an impetus to the growth of a new class of American, or creole, merchants, who achieved a position of great power and influence in the economics and politics of their native colonies; later they would contribute significantly to the movements of the first decades of the nineteenth century toward autonomy and, eventually, independence. Indeed, the exigencies of the wars of the French Revolution would stimulate the spiraling growth of economic nationalisms in the various new regional societies of the hemisphere.

Francoamerica

The economic administration of the French empire in America centered in the French Ministry of the Marine, the head of which, the minister of the marine, was under the direct supervision of the chief minister of France and, through him, of the king. Assisting the minister were several assistant ministers, or *commis*, one of whom had charge of colonial affairs. In general, the de facto authority of this *commis* was well-nigh absolute.

The economic theory governing French colonial policy was, as in all the other colonial empires, mercantilism. The colonies, according to this principle, had been founded for the economic benefit of the mother country. They were essentially profit-making enterprises, established to produce commodities for the mother country that it could not produce for itself. In the last half of the seventeenth century, Colbert had applied the ideas of mercantilism to the French colonies in the West Indies and to New France (Canada): he had used the power of the French crown to encourage immigration to both Canada and the French West Indies and to develop the economic life of all the colonies. He had created the Company of New France (1664) and the Company of the West Indies (1667), only to override them by directing colonial affairs personally or through the Ministry of the Marine.

During the War of the Spanish Succession and after the accession of a Bourbon prince to the Spanish throne, France enjoyed a favorable position in the commerce of the Spanish colonies, even sending its merchant ships to Rio de la Plata and around Cape Horn into the South Pacific to trade with Chile and Peru. But France's own colonies suffered as the tides of war and the influence of Charles of Austria (the allied-sponsored king of Spain) opened the commerce of the French colonies to the ships of England and its allies. After the Peace of Utrecht, which stipulated that France had to withdraw from the trade of the Spanish empire and the English and the Dutch (legally, at least) from that of the French colonies, the French colonial administration pulled itself together and reorganized the "System."

After the War of the League of Augsburg but before the War of the Spanish Succession and its demoralization of colonial commerce, the Code of Colonial Commerce was reenacted in 1698. Certain specific edicts of the code laid the legal framework for colonial commerce. Thus, an ordinance of 1717 provided that commerce to and from the colonies must be carried only in French ships, using exclusively fourteen specified ports in France; commodities shipped to, and imported from, the colonies were given preferential duty rates; the colonies, however, were granted permission to import salted meat directly from Ireland and to trade directly with the Spanish colonies.

An edict of October 1727 established the so-called *Exclusif* regarding trade with foreign nations. By it, the importation of foreign commodities, whether by foreign or French ships, was strictly forbidden, as was the exportation of goods of any kind to any foreign country. Foreign ships were prohibited from even approaching the shores of the French colonies; a sort of perpetual privateering war against foreign interlopers was proclaimed.

Such was the French colonial commercial policy of the *Exclusif*: the colonies existed only by and for the metropolis; all their industry, all their commerce, must be regulated solely in accord with the convenience and the self-interest of the mother country; all their economic relations with the outside world must be conducted under the flag and in the ships of France; similarly, the colonies must not engage in industries that would compete with those of the mother country.

However, far from being a system of suppression, the *Exclusif* — logically enough — was meant to encourage and promote the productivity and the prosperity of the colonies; the white population was to be built up to an optimum level; the importation of slaves must be fostered to provide the colonies with a plentiful labor supply. Nevertheless, despite all this paternalism, certain local forces contributed to a growing self-consciousness and even to the erosion of, and resistance to, the "System."

As early as 1715, the minister Pontchartrain requested the colonies to formulate a system of self-taxation to defray the expenses of their own administration and promised that the funds thus raised would always be superintended by the colonial governments themselves. The colonies agreed, and from that time on it was an established principle that taxation should be raised by councils established in the colonies for the purpose, thereby achieving a degree of financial autonomy.

Production

The economic life of the French colonies was characterized by the same sort of regional differences that existed in all the other colonial areas. The economy of Canada centered on the fur trade with the Indians of the interior of North America; Louisiana had little economic life that was worthy of note except trade; the French West Indies, very much like their English, Dutch, Portuguese, and Spanish neighbors, concentrated their economic activities on the cultivation of sugar and the manufacture of rum on large plantations worked by slave labor. Canada and Louisiana were never very profitable to France, although a few private individuals made fortunes in the Canadian fur trade; the French West Indies, on the other hand, were highly profitable because of the sugar, tobacco, cacao, dyewoods, and other semitropical products they were able to ship to the mother country. Not only were these islands profitable: they sent to France so many new, exotic American products that the French way of life, as Voltaire said, was substantially modified and enriched. It has been estimated that the total trade between France and the French West Indies from 1753 to 1755 amounted to thirty million livres per year. This fell, during the Seven Years War, to eight million in 1758 and to four million in 1760.

The settlements of Canada were located chiefly in the feudal *seigneuries* along the St. Lawrence River. In these *seigneuries* economic life was largely devoted to the raising of wheat, meats, and other foodstuffs to supply the towns. The chief focal points of the economic life of this colony were the "cities" of Quebec, Three Rivers, and Montreal, which became prosperous through the trading in, and the shipping of, furs.

There were two basic ways of conducting the fur trade. The first, and perhaps most primitive, involved long canoe trips or pack trips by French traders into the Indian country. Licensed fur traders, the voyageurs (travelers) went up the rivers and lakes to established posts such as Detroit or Michilimackinac, where they met the Indians with the skins they had collected during their winter's hunting. At the posts the voyageurs traded with the Indians under the supervision of the agents of the crown. Other traders, often without license or supervision, the so-called *coureurs de bois* (bushrangers) traveled far out into the Indian country, to the very villages of the Indians themselves, and there they did their trading. All the traders, but especially the *coureurs de bois*, mingled with the Indians and with the Indian women to produce a race of half-breeds, called the métis, comparable to the mestizos of Spanish

America. Many of these métis became fur traders themselves and constituted a significant factor in the economic and sociological development of the colony.

The fur trade was also conducted at the great "fairs," the most famous of which was at Montreal. Early each summer fleets of Indian canoes, laden with furs, would come down the lakes and rivers, converging upon the city. Once there, the Indians traded their furs for the European-manufactured goods the French merchants had to offer — such things as blankets, pots and pans, hats, scalping knives, and, most essential of all, guns and ammunition.

In an age when European buildings were poorly heated and clothing, coats, and hats made of fur were fashionable, Europe provided a ready market for Canadian and other American furs — bearskins, deerskins, and, most important of all, the soft, warm skins of the American beaver. These skins, brought to Canada from the interior, were loaded on ships at Montreal, Three Rivers, or Quebec and exported to France. There they were manufactured into clothing or hats, and either sold in the domestic market or sent to a foreign market.

The value of the Canadian fur trade steadily increased during the eighteenth century. The value of the furs shipped to France was 262,000 livres in 1718, 2,096,000 livres in 1727, and 3,932,000 livres in 1754. From then on it declined precipitately until after the Seven Years War, when, under English rule, the value of the trade gradually rose again. It reached nearly £ 150,000 sterling (1,800,000 livres) in 1782. After the War for United States Independence the area and the profitability of the Canadian and Hudson Bay fur trade again steadily increased; the opening of the northern Pacific coast signaled another dramatic expansion, which included both inland furs from the Columbia River basin and Rocky Mountain highlands and pelts from the fabulously rich seal fisheries along the Pacific coast.

Canada's productivity and commerce were not limited, however, to the fur trade. The Canadian forest industries were already of considerable importance toward the end of the eighteenth century; Canadian-based fisheries were even more so. In addition, Canada had always traded with the English colonies to the south and with the French and British West Indies; after 1763 that intercolonial commerce steadily grew.

The economic life of the French Caribbean colonies presented a sharp contrast with that of Canada. There, in the colonies of Martinique, Saint-

Domingue (Haiti), and Guadeloupe, the predominant economic activities were the cultivation of sugar and the manufacture of rum. Some indigo, cacao, dyewoods, and, late in the century, coffee and cotton were also raised. The sugar plantations were operated by methods similar to those used in the other European colonies in the Caribbean area.

The great plantations of the French West Indies, like those throughout the Caribbean, were essentially capitalistic enterprises; the plantation owners were the magnates of French West Indian capitalism. Of course, the exportation of commodities from these colonies was legally directed exclusively to the merchants and factors of the mother country, and the processing of commodities such as sugar and the redistribution of products such as sugar and tobacco in the European markets were in the hands of the great merchant-capitalists of France. In 1777, for example, there were eighteen sugar refineries in the city of Orléans alone.

Black slavery furnished the labor supply for the productive industries of the French West Indies, as in the other, non-French islands. It was estimated that 500 slaves were required to operate a plantation of thirty-two hectares if the plantation engaged in the entire production of sugar, from growing the cane to the shipment of the crude sugar. Since the slave population failed to reproduce itself, a constant importation of new slaves was necessary: in the period between 1728 and 1760 an estimated 203,522 blacks were shipped to the French islands in 723 slave ships operating out of Nantes, La Rochelle, Bordeaux, and St.-Malo.

The French islands were generally prosperous. In addition to sugar, they exported cotton, indigo, cacao, leather, dyewoods, and coffee to the metropolis; they imported from France such things as manufactured goods, luxury items, and wines. From Canada they bought flour, salt, beef, fish, textiles, and lumber.

In addition to this licit commerce the French islands also enjoyed a great clandestine trade with foreigners, especially the English, Dutch, and Angloamericans. In clear violation of the official "System" of the *Exclusif*, these foreigners, often with the connivance of the French inhabitants and even officials, brought in much needed foodstuffs — fish, salt meat, flour — lumber, barrel staves, and mules, and took in return the sugar, molasses, rum (which could not be exported to France because of the feared competition with French brandy), and other commodities that the islands offered. This "illicit" trade was beneficial to both sides and manifested a tendency on the part of the French colonists toward economic autonomy — a factor which, in reality, introduced an international development toward free trade that arose, as elsewhere in America and despite all restrictions, out of the economic self-interests of the colonists.

Economic Reforms

International trade, deriving as it did from the actual self-interests of the colonists, gave rise to a growing restiveness under the restrictions of the "System" and to suggestions, even demands, that those restrictions be eased. It is apparently true, too, that many statesmen in France, for example, Turgot and Minister Choiseul, were influenced toward a partial freedom of trade for the colonies by the writings of the physiocrats, led by the economic philosopher François Quesnay.

In any case, a self-conscious movement of ideas which was directed toward a greater economic autonomy developed among the colonists in the third quarter of the eighteenth century. All attempts to modify the *Exclusif* were vigorously opposed in France by the monopolistic entrepreneurs of colonial trade, and reform was blocked for decades. Little by little, nevertheless, the colonists were able to bring about a mitigation of the rigors of the "System," and these reforms steadily expanded the economic freedom of the colonies during the second half of the century.

The more or less deliberately liberal reforms of the French colonial system really began when Choiseul appointed Jean Dubuc as commissioner in charge of colonial affairs in the Ministry of the Marine in October 1764, about a year after the Peace of Paris.

Dubuc, a native of Martinique who had been serving as a "deputy" (agent) for that colony in France and who was probably the first colonial to become administrator of the colonial system of any Euroamerican empire, understood, probably better than any Frenchman, the problems of the colonies and the true nature of their relationships with the metropolis. More than anyone in France he realized the colonies' need for a certain amount of free foreign trade.

Confronted by the conservative mercantilistic outlook of the great vested interests of France Dubuc had to proceed cautiously. He succeeded, however, in convincing his opponents that an increase in the productivity of the colonies depended upon the freedom to import food for the labor force, the slaves, from outside the empire. With this object in view, he prevailed upon the Council of Commerce to issue an edict on July 29, 1767, which permitted for the first time trade with foreigners, but in two ports only, Le Carénage on St. Lucia and the Mole-St. Nicolas on Saint-Domingue (Haiti). Foreign ships might now freely come to these two ports; likewise, colonists who wished to buy from them or sell to them had to go to these ports.

This was the opening wedge, and it was a great success. Presently, foreigners were granted entry to other ports on other islands. After the recognition of the independence of the United States, which had been deprived entirely of trade with the British West Indies during the war, the new country demanded of its old ally the opening of the French West Indies to its merchant ships, and in the edict of August 30, 1784, the request was met. For the French West Indies this was a long step toward economic liberation. The trade was not entirely free, but the number of free ports was increased to seven; the list of permitted imports (mostly foodstuffs) was significantly extended, and the number of exportable articles was practically unlimited.

The advent of the French Revolution brought with it a new and more liberal, though vacillating, economic policy, which was underscored by the needs and the military fortunes of the colonies in an era of warfare that lasted, with one short break, from 1792 to 1815. The end of the period found the French colonies relatively free and entering into a new era in their history.

Angloamerica

The economic hub of the British empire in the eighteenth century was London. Not only did the great merchant-bankers of London control most of the daily ebb and flow of imperial commerce, but the official economic policy of the empire was determined and put into effect by the British Privy Council, Parliament, and the Board of Trade.

As already mentioned, the core of the imperial government in economic as well as political matters was the Privy Council. This somewhat inchoate body, composed of the most outstanding politicians and statesmen of the realm, members of the Cabinet, and advisers of the king, occupied a place in imperial affairs not unlike that of the Portuguese Overseas Council or the Spanish Council of the Indies. However, there was a profound difference: whereas those councils were organized and existed for the specialized and almost exclusive purpose of administering colonial affairs, the British Privy Council was granted all the powers of government concerning everything that government was supposed to do, for the "realm" as well as for the empire.

Technically presided over by the king of England, the Privy Council and its affairs were really directed by the prime minister, who (along with the other ministers in the Cabinet) was a member of Parliament. Often occupying the post of secretary of state for the Southern Department (who was also the chief executive for colonial affairs), he was assisted in the administration of the imperial government by the other ministers — the lord chief justice, the secretary of state for the Northern Department, the first lord of the admiralty, the first lord of the treasury, and the secretary for war. Each of these ministers was assisted by a committee of lords members of the Privy Council, and most of the daily business of the council was done by these committees. In the management of the economic affairs of the empire, including the colonies, the everyday duties were performed by the Committee of Trade or the Committee for Plantation Affairs.

But the brain of the colonial system, economic, political, and international, was the Board of Trade. The economic philosophy underlying the formation of the Board of Trade had been and still was, in the eighteenth century, the nationalistic philosophy of mercantilism: its function, like that of the Portuguese Overseas Council, the Spanish Council of the Indies, and the Bureau of the Colonies in the French Ministry of the Marine (except that it had no power to make law), was to make the national monopoly of the economic profits derived from the colonies effective. The basic ideology here, as described above, was practically identical with that which dominated Portuguese, Spanish, and French colonial outlooks: colonies were basically business ventures, initiated and capitalized by the mother country for financial profit. In the case of England, Chambers, in his *Cyclopedia*, said in 1728 that modern "Colonies of Commerce, are those established by the English, French, Spaniards, Portuguese, and other Nations within the two last centuries . . . either to keep up a regular Commerce with the natives, or to cultivate the Ground, by planting Sugar-Canes, Indigo, Tobacco, and other Commodities."[8]

[8] Quoted by Richard Koebner, *Empire* (Cambridge: At the University Press, 1961), p. 41. The same words are repeated in E. Chambers, *Cyclopedia: Or an Universal Dictionary of Arts and Sciences*, 4 vols. (London, 1786), s.v. "Colony."

William Wood had voiced the same sentiment in 1722: "Therefore I may safely advance, that our Trade and Navigation are greatly encreased by our Colonies and Plantations, and that they are a Spring of Wealth to this Nation, since they work for us, and their Treasure centers all here: And as the Laws have ty'd them fast to us, it must be through our own Fault and Misgovernment if they do not ever continue to enrich Great Britian; or any, or all of them become independent of it."[9]

Thus, the Board of Trade was consulted on the issues that led to the passage by Parliament of the Woolens Act (1699), the Hat Act (1732), and the Iron Act (1750), all intended to limit colonial manufacturing for the protection of English manufactures against colonial competition. It deliberated on the problem presented by the continental colonies' trading with the French, Spanish, and Dutch colonies in the Caribbean area — a problem resolved by the so-called parliamentary Molasses Act of 1733. Its advice was also sought on questions pertaining to such matters as colonial currency, customs, and post-office affairs.

Already, in the seventeenth century, the basic complex of laws regulating imperial economic life had been instituted. Under a series of so-called Navigation Acts, commodities going to or from the colonies could be carried only in ships of British (English or American) registry. The act of 1660 had enumerated a list of articles, staple commodities of the colonies, that could not be exported from the colonies directly to foreign markets but must first be shipped to an English or a colonial port. By the terms of an act of 1663 only England could ship manufactured goods to the colonies; in 1673 stringent regulations were laid down in an attempt to make the preceding laws effective. In 1696 the so-called Great Navigation Act was passed which consolidated the stipulations of the previous acts and included provisions to tighten up the enforcement of the system, especially by the colonial governors. In the next year viceadmiralty courts were established in the colonies for better enforcement of the Navigation Laws.

The high point of the effectiveness of the Board of Trade was reached in the 1750s, under the presidency of the Earl of Halifax. Halifax, like Pombal in Portugal and Aranda in Spain, initiated a series of imperial reforms calculated to strengthen the mother country's control over the colonies. Most of his reforms were political, centering on the effort to strengthen the crown's prerogative in the colonial governments, but he

---

[9] William Wood, *A Survey of Trade* (London, 1722), pp. 135–136.

tried very hard to make the system of imperial economic control more efficient. Thus, after Halifax became its president in 1748, the board embarked upon a program to broaden its powers, and they were extended in several ways.[10] The board also initiated a program of economic experimentation in the colonies calculated to encourage the production of commodities such as wine and silk, which England could not produce. No significant results came out of this program, however; the most notable achievement of the board in this period was that it increased the effectiveness of collecting customs duties.

Although the basic economic policy of the British empire was still mercantilism, the British system of economic control was on the whole less rigorous and less effective than the systems of the Portuguese, Spanish, and French empires. For whereas those systems, in theory, were hermetically sealed against commerce with foreigners, the British system allowed the colonists to trade with any country in the Atlantic community, so long as they did so without violating the Navigation Acts. Foodstuffs, for example, could be shipped anywhere, provided they were carried in English or American ships and manned by English or American sailors.

Production

The economic productivity of the Angloamerican colonies was highly sectional. For the most part agricultural production in New England, the middle colonies, the southern continental colonies, and the West Indies varied sharply. The farms of New England provided wheat, Indian corn, horses, apples, etc., mostly for home consumption, while the lands of the middle colonies reaped great quantities of wheat and other grains, salt meat, and breadstuffs for export. In the southern colonies, agriculture was devoted mainly to the production of tobacco, indigo, and rice. The chief commodity of the British West Indies was sugar and its by-products, although the islands also exported cacao, coffee, and dyewoods.

But the productivity of the British colonies was by no means limited to agriculture: several extractive industries were of vast importance in the total British imperial economy. Fishing, for example, constituted a solid base for the commercial economy of New England. In one form or another, the fur trade with the Indians was vital to practically all

[10] See above, chapter 2.

the colonies from New Hampshire to Georgia, but most especially to New York. New England and North Carolina benefited from the naval stores industry, and the harvesting of dyewoods was an active business, particularly along the coasts of Honduras and Central America.

Although manufacturers in Angloamerica were relatively few, such industries as silver working, woolens manufactures, hat manufactures, ironworks, and furniture making had grown, chiefly in the colonies from Pennsylvania northward, to a place of real significance in the total colonial economy. Colonial manufactures existed primarily for the satisfaction of internal colonial needs. Even so, their existence and their activity gave the Board of Trade and English manufacturers considerable concern.

The productivity of the British American colonies increased steadily during the eighteenth century. In 1743, Robert Dinwiddie, surveyor general of the customs for the southern part of America, estimated that the overall production of the colonies amounted to £4,980,000. The bulk of the colonial products, with the exception of the relatively small amount of manufactures, was crude, raw materials that were consumed or processed in England, some other European country, or other colonies in America.

Commerce

The significant increase in the total productivity of the British colonies was in large measure caused by the constant enlargement and improvement of the area of land devoted to agriculture. This, in turn, was the result of the phenomenal increase in immigration, which provided a steadily growing labor force, composed of free workers, indentured servants, and black slaves. Basically, however, colonial productivity increased because the commodities produced in Angloamerica commanded such profitable markets all over the Western world. In other words, the expansion of the capital wealth of the colonies was due to commerce — to the export of the colonial product and its sale abroad at a profit.

The British West Indies exported to England in 1768 commodities (mostly sugar and its collateral products, rum and molasses) worth about £4,000,000; in the same year they imported from England goods worth only about £1,125,000. Their commerce with the mother country was heavily favorable and profitable to them, although it was also highly profitable to the mother country, for a large percentage of the West Indian goods sent to England was reexported to the markets on the continent of Europe.

At the same time, the British West Indies enjoyed a highly active intraimperial trade with the northern continental colonies, in the course of which they shipped sugar, molasses, and rum to the continent and took in return fish, breadstuffs, salt beef, and apples. The balance of this trade was against the islands and favorable to the northern colonies, but the islands more than made up the loss by their shipments to the mother country.

The trade of the southern continental colonies was more evenly balanced. In 1768 goods (tobacco, naval stores, rice, indigo, deerskins) valued at £ 956,000 were shipped to England from Maryland, Virginia, North Carolina, South Carolina, and Georgia. These same colonies imported from England, in that year, goods worth £ 820,000. The balance was more nearly equalized by the "invisible" imports to England of interest on debts, services, etc. The southern colonies were able to post a more favorable balance, however, by exporting such commodities as tobacco, rice, naval stores, onions, and Indian corn to the West Indies.

The direct trade of the middle colonies (Delaware, Pennsylvania, New Jersey, and New York) with England in 1768 was distinctly unfavorable to the colonies. For while they exported some £ 150,000 worth of goods to England, they received from the mother country commodities (mostly manufactured goods) valued at some £ 900,000. The unfavorable balance was paid off by receipts from trades with other areas, such as the British and foreign West Indies, Spain, Portugal, Italy, and the Canary and Madeira islands. These exports, which were exchanged for the products of those areas and bills of exchange upon London, usually consisted of wheat and flour, Indian corn, salt meat, and lumber. The favorable balance of these non-English trades resulted in a large margin of profit for these colonies and contributed to their great expansion of capital wealth.

The overall picture of the economy of New England in the eighteenth century is perhaps the most dramatic of all. Although its trade with the mother country was not as large as that of the middle colonies and was highly "unfavorable" (exports to England, 1768, £ 150,000; imports from England, £ 420,000), its non-English commercial dealings were enormous. In 1768 New England shipped an estimated £ 431,000 worth of fish to southern Europe and £ 206,000 worth to the British West Indies — to which must be added the vast (probably larger) amount shipped to the French, Spanish, and Dutch West Indies. Along with the fish went candles, lumber and barrels, grain and flour, horses and mules, rum, and beeswax.

This non-English trade was augmented by the African slave trade, in which New England rum and foodstuffs and English "gewgaws" were shipped to Africa to be given in exchange for "black ivory," which was then taken to Jamaica, Charleston, or some other slave entrepôt for sale at another substantial profit.

The basic export staple of New England was fish, which was supplemented by such items as lumber, rum, horses, and mules. But the New England merchants also made handsome profits in the carrying trade — that is, carrying cargoes of commodities such as tobacco, rice, or sugar for the colonies that did not have shipping of their own.

All these non-English trades added up to a highly profitable commercial balance for New England, which, in turn, resulted in a steady and rapid increase in the capital wealth of this section, as elsewhere.

The merchants of the Angloamerican colonies, whether in the British West Indies, the middle continental colonies, or New England, enjoyed a large and profitable share of that eminent international commerce called "illicit" or "clandestine." This trade, for the Angloamericans, was not illegal so long as it did not violate any of the English Navigation Acts (which, of course, it often did). It was clearly unlawful only when it violated the Spanish or Portuguese monopolistic regulations of trade or the French system of the *Exclusif*. This unsanctioned commerce did violate these laws, and it was therefore liable to attack and suppression by the coast-guard services of Spain, Portugal, or France; but it was so profitable that the loss of an occasional ship, with its cargo and its crew, could be comfortably written off.

For the Angloamericans, this trade was carried on in clandestine visits of American ships to the ports of Spanish, French, or Portuguese colonies. There the cargoes (fish, other foodstuffs, English manufactured goods, lumber) were exchanged for products of the foreign colonies, which might be hides, sugar, molasses, rum, dyewoods, or, most precious of all, gold and silver coins that went back to North America partly to make up the serious shortage of specie.

The visits of the Angloamerican ships to a foreign empire were usually made without the knowledge or consent of the officials and were in direct violation of the laws of that empire. But they were usually welcomed by the foreign colonists who needed the northern products; often they were actually ignored by the officials, whether because they realized the genuine need of their colonists for the Yankees' goods or because the Yankees found means to make it worth the officials' while to look the other way. In any case, this commerce was a large portion of the overall commercial activity of the Angloamerican colonies. At the same time it was completely international, and it was free in the sense that it paid little attention to the mercantilistic regulatory systems of the various empires. So far as the Angloamericans participated in it, it must be viewed as one of the commercial activities that contributed mightily to the expansion of their capital wealth.

Economic Reforms

All in all, the phenomenal economic expansion of the Angloamerican empire in the eighteenth century derived from the expansion of the production of unprocessed commodities for the markets of the North Atlantic Basin and from the favorable balances of trade, whether in the direct trade of the West Indies with the mother country or in the non-English trades of the continental colonies with other parts of the North Atlantic community. These non-English trades built up the wealth that made economic growth possible. Of great significance, too, was the fact that such a large part of the commerce of the continental colonies was international in character. It was no accident, therefore, that there was developing in the colonies a powerful reaction against, and nullification of, the British system of regulation and control and toward a demand for a greater degree of economic autonomy and freedom of commerce. As Thomas Jefferson was to write in 1774, on the eve of the American Revolution, "That the exercise of a free trade with all parts of the world, possessed by the American colonists as of natural right, and which no law of their own had taken away or abridged, was next the object of unjust incroachment [by Parliament]. [The Navigation Acts were actions of parliamentary tyranny.] . . . The true ground on which we declare these acts void is that the British parliament has no right to exercise authority over us."[11]

[11] Thomas Jefferson, "Draft of Instructions to the Virginia Delegates in the Continental

About the middle of the eighteenth century, the economic value of the American colonies to England was immense. Malachy Postlethwayt, writing about 1755, estimated that the value of the tobacco imported into England was approximately £ 600,000 annually; of this amount, about two-thirds was reexported. Sugar, indigo, ginger, and cotton to the value of £ 1,300,000 were imported, and about one-third of these commodities was reexported. Postlethwayt estimated that Great Britain exported to the royal colonies goods valued at £ 850,000, and that imports from all of them, including silver and gold coins, were worth some £ 2,600,000. So that "we have a ballance, in return thereof, to the value of £ 1,750,000 [before reexport] which centers and remains among us, and is not like such a ballance in foreign trade, as must be carried out again directly in money, or in bills of exchange, to any other port of the world." [12]

Postlethwayt, although intellectually a mercantilist, unconsciously heralded the naturalistic decline of mercantilism and the rise of the basic doctrines of free trade.

It is true, indeed, if a breach of the act of navigation, or any other beneficial act relating to our plantations, should be connived at, or broke through in any particular that would prove injurious to the kingdom, even our own plantations may become more profitable to other nations than to this; but, while the governors, and the other officers under the crown, whose business it is to take care thereof, do their duty, they can never prove detrimental to the nation.

By insisting that no breach in the navigation, or other act of the legislature, should be made, which has been enacted for the mutual benefit of England and her colonies, I would not have it inferred, that I am against permitting the inhabitants of our colonies to trade with each other, or that they should be prohibited to trade to the colonies of foreign nations, or carry their product, according as the law at present tolerates, directly to foreign countries. For, by our colonies trading with those other nations, we, in some measure, render foreign colonies and plantations the colonies and plantations of Great Britain; which brings me to observe, that all laws in our foreign plantation which lay high duties on sugar, indigo, ginger, and other West-India commodities, imported into them, when impartially considered, will be found not only prejudicial to them, but to the general trade and navigation of this kingdom; and therefore

Congress [July 1774]," *The Papers of Thomas Jefferson*, ed. Julian P. Boyd, 19 vols. to date (Princeton, N.J.: Princeton University Press, 1950–), I, 123–124.

[12] Savary, *The Universal Dictionary of Trade and Commerce*, trans. from the French and expanded by Malachy Postlethwayt, 2 vols. in 4 (2nd ed.; London, 1757) I, pt. 1, p. 532.

it is our interest, and should be our care, that no laws laying such duties should remain in force, or be passed for the future.

For, the inhabitants [of our colonies], by carrying on a trade with their foreign neighbors, do not only occasion a greater quantity of the goods and merchandises of Europe being sent from hence to them, and a greater quantity of the product of America to be sent from them hither, which would otherwise be carried from, and brought to Europe by foreigners, but an increase of the seamen, and navigation in those parts; which is of great strength and security, as well as of great advantage, to our plantations in general.[13]

British commercial thinking was already moving toward definite concessions to the principles of free trade clearly enumerated in 1776 by Adam Smith. This is seen, for example, in the series of steps taken after the Peace of Paris of 1763 by which England acquired several new islands in the Caribbean and in the course of which several of the islands were opened as free ports to the commerce of the world.

In 1765 Denmark opened its islands of St. Thomas and St. John as free ports. They immediately became centers of great commercial activity, and therefore England was faced with the problem of channeling the active international trade of the area into British hands without undermining the old navigation system. The government concluded that some modification of the old system was necessary in order to permit French and Spanish ships to bring bullion and products of the Spanish colonies into British territory. The result was the creation of Dominica as a free port. The purpose was to draw to it the great contraband trade then centered at Dutch St. Eustatius and Danish St. Thomas. Eventually, Jamaica was also made a free port.

The Free Ports Act, passed by Parliament on June 6, 1766, symbolized a drastic revision of the old British navigation system, for it provided that foreign ships might bring unmanufactured American products into the ports of Dominica and Jamaica. Similarly, foreign ships could carry out of those ports, with some exceptions, commodities produced in England or in the other English-American colonies. Certain limitations were placed on the imports and exports of these free-port colonies, but the action of the mother country in opening them marked the first significant breach in the old navigation system and a step in the direction of admitting in practice the principles of free trade.

[13] *Ibid.*

As has been seen, this acceptance of the "free-port" system by the British paralleled programs undertaken by the Portuguese, Spanish, French, and Danish empires. The Dutch, of course, had already profited from the benefits of free commerce in all their colonies, especially those in the West Indies. The British free ports in the West Indies were not an immediate success, largely because of the outbreak of the War of United States Independence; their chief significance lay in the fact that the adoption of this policy was a de facto breach in, and reform of, the old mercantilistic policy of colonial administration represented by the Navigation Acts and the Acts of Trade. The new policy signified a new international mood, which the British empire shared with its imperial competitors.

Dutch America

The economic life of the Dutch colonies in the eighteenth century was concentrated in the Dutch West India Company, originally organized in 1621. The company had been reorganized in 1670, as already related, but it did not enjoy a monopoly. Postlethwayt estimated that the company controlled one-third of the trade of the Dutch empire, while the remainder was divided equally between the city of Amsterdam and the heirs of Mynheer van Somersdyk, operating privately. In any case, it is to be remembered that the company was closely linked to the States-General, which exercised a considerable degree of political control over the company's activities.

There were several segments of Dutch imperial commerce. The "legal" commerce of the empire, centered in the colonies of the Caribbean (Curaçao, St. Eustatius, Surinam), was a trade in colonial products purchased with European-manufactured goods. This was augmented by the very active trade of the Dutch in black slaves. But it is impossible to distinguish clearly between "legal" trade and "illegal" trade, for the Dutch were the "clandestine" traders (smugglers) par excellence. Curaçao was the base of the most extensive operation of this immense, new international network, while both St. Eustatius and Surinam were also important entrepôts for the Yankee seamen from continental Angloamerica.

The Dutch carried to Europe sugar, indigo, cotton, dyewoods, hides, salt, cochineal, cacao, vanilla, tobacco, quinine, sarsaparilla, and gold and silver, all drawn from every part of the hemisphere with a high degree of impartiality. In return they delivered manufactured goods from Europe and fish and foodstuffs brought from North America by way of Surinam, for example.

Since the Dutch had little or nothing of their own production to sell to the world except herring, they were the world's great barterers and carriers. Practically everything they imported into Europe from America was reexported to other European markets; almost everything they sold in America was produced in other European states or in other American colonies.

In the eighteenth century there were still some mercantilistic hangovers in the regulatory system of Dutch imperial commerce. But it is obvious that the people of Hugo Grotius had far more to gain from international freedom of commerce and freedom of the seas than from a mercantilist monopoly. It was no accident, therefore, that the Dutch were the de facto leaders in the growing realization, among the economic thinkers of the eighteenth century, that freedom of trade must take the place of the old mercantilism.

CHAPTER 5

American Society and the New American Societies

Population

It is utterly impossible to find accurate figures for the population of the American hemisphere at the beginning of the eighteenth century. It is possible, however, to estimate the population in round figures that may be reasonably close to reality.[1] Table 1 shows the total population in round numbers and its approximate distribution among racial groups and within each empire.[2]

If these figures are reasonably close to the truth, the Indians still constituted by far the greatest single ethnic group in the hemisphere. The whites were a minority whose cultural, economic, religious, and political dominance was out of all proportion to their numbers. The black population, as well as that of the mixed breeds, was still relatively small.

[1] For the studies upon which these figures are based, see the bibliography for this chapter.

[2] It is to be remembered that, as of the year 1700, the Angloamerican empire included only the land east of the Allegheny Mountains on the continent of North America and a handful of small islands in the Caribbean where the number of Indians was negligible. Similarly, the Francoamerican empire included little more than the settlements in the St. Lawrence River Valley, a sparse scattering of posts in the Great Lakes Basin, and — if La Salle's claim is accepted — the Mississippi River Valley, as well as a few islands in the Caribbean. If the larger concept of the Francoamerican empire is used, the number of Indians estimated to be living in that empire must be increased.

Angel Rosenblatt, *La población indígena y el mestizaje en América, 1492–1950*, 2 vols. in 1 (Buenos Aires: Editorial Nova, 1954), estimates that in 1750 there were 1,004,500 Indians in "North America north of Mexico" (p. 57). Of that enormous area, however, by far the major part lay outside both Angloamerica and Francoamerica.

Table 1. Population of the American Hemisphere about 1700

Empire	Whites	Indians	Blacks	Mestizos	Mulattoes	Total
Brazil	200,000	600,000	100,000	30,000	70,000	1,000,000
Hispanoamerica	700,000	9,000,000	500,000	40,000	60,000	10,300,000
Francoamerica	80,000	20,000	50,000	20,000	30,000	200,000
Angloamerica	300,000	30,000	100,000	10,000	10,000	450,000
Dutch and Danish	50,000	?	30,000	?	20,000	100,000
Total	1,330,000	9,650,000	780,000	100,000	190,000	12,050,000
Percentage of total population	11%	80%	6.5%	.85%	1.6%	

Table 2. Population of the American Hemisphere about 1820

Empire	Whites	Indians	Blacks	Mestizos	Mulattoes	Total
Brazil	920,000	400,000	1,950,000	200,000	500,000	3,970,000
Hispanoamerica	3,400,000	8,000,000	2,100,000	4,000,000	1,500,000	19,000,000
Angloamerica and the U.S.	9,000,000	600,000	1,900,000	?	100,000	11,600,000
French West Indies (including Haiti)	110,000	?	400,000	?	100,000	610,000
Dutch and Danish	70,000	?	50,000	?	?	120,000
Total	13,500,000	9,000,000	6,400,000	4,200,000	2,200,000	35,300,000
Percentage of total population	39%	25%	18%	11.8%	6.2%	

Above all, it should be noted that the population of America was already highly conglomerate and that the vastly preponderant numbers of the inhabitants were of non-European origin.

With the exception of Spanish Peru and Chile, which faced upon the Pacific, and New Spain, whose shores were washed by both the Atlantic and the Pacific, the European establishments in the American hemisphere faced upon the Atlantic Ocean. Although by 1700 they had demonstrated both their capacity to survive and their economic and strategic worth to the mother countries, the umbilical relationship between all the colonies and their European metropolises was still very strong, even vital to their continued existence.

In the course of the eighteenth century the population of the hemisphere rapidly increased, and in all probability was three times as great as the figures suggested for 1700. By the end of the colonial era or, say, about 1820, the population of the hemisphere may have totaled some 35,000,000 persons (see Table 2).[3]

The increases shown in Table 2 can in large measure be explained biologically. But they are also the result of two great waves of immigration: one of Europeans, which directed itself chiefly (but far from exclusively) to Angloamerica; the other of African blacks, which flowed into all the Euroamerican colonies.

At the end of the century, perhaps 100,000 of the whites were of European birth; the rest were creoles, that is, they were born in America of European ancestry. Although the Europeans and creoles still dominated society, government, culture, and religion, they actually numbered fewer than 40 percent of the total population. About 60 percent of the population was composed of non-whites. On the other hand, the Indian population, if it had not actually decreased, had apparently remained stable; in 1700 Indians accounted for approximately 80 percent of the population, whereas their number had declined to some 25 percent in 1820. During the same time, the number of blacks had increased phenomenally from about three-quarters of a million, or 6.5 percent, in 1700 to 6,400,000, or 18 percent, in 1820. The population of people of mixed blood had increased during the same period from under 300,000, or some 2.4 percent, to 6,400,000, or about 18 percent.

[3] Cf. Bailey Diffie, *Latin-American Civilization: The Colonial Period* (New York: Octagon Books, 1967), pp. 455–459, and Silvio Zavala, *El mundo Americano en la época colonial*, 2 vols. (Mexico: Editorial Porrua, 1967), I, 331.

Obviously, the two major trends noted above had moved at an accelerated rate: the Euroamericans were still a dominant minority, but a much larger one than in 1700; of these, however, the European-born whites were now hardly more than a handful, while the vast majority of whites was American-born and America-oriented. Thus, the other major trend, that toward a preponderantly non-European population, was a striking reality: America was more than ever cosmopolitan; it was more than ever American.

The Ethnographic Factor

The entire American society during the eighteenth century was a conglomerate of ethnic types. The dominant group, despite the fact that it was a numerical minority, was the whites, composed of persons born in Europe and the pure white American descendants of Europeans, the creoles. In the twilight zone between this group and the native Indians, the imported African blacks, and their descendants stood the mestizos, the offspring of Europeans and the native Indians, and the mulattoes, who were products of the mixture of whites with blacks. There were also a considerable number of so-called "zambos," the result of matings between blacks and Indians. Below the whites and the mestizos in the sociological structure of things were the blacks, who had been brought to America as slaves, and the Indians, the indigenous native peoples of the continent. In general, with some exceptions, the blacks lived within the white man's culture. The Indians usually lived apart, even when gathered in the communities of the missions.

These ethnic groups existed in all the societies of the continent. Culturally, socially, economically, and intellectually they maintained a certain separation from one another, although the lines between were often blurred or crossed in the process of miscegenation. The proportions of these groups to the total population varied, however, from area to area. For example the number of half-breeds in relation to the total population was smaller in Angloamerica than, say, in Brazil; the ratio of métis to the total population of Canada was somewhat smaller than the proportion of mestizos in the society of Mexico.

The American societies were highly stratified, generally on the basis of biological descent. The whites enjoyed the highest social status, the mulattoes and the mestizos stood next, the Indians came below them, and the black slaves constituted the lowest stratum of the structure. There were many subdivisions within each of these ethnic divisions, the social statuses of which were determined by factors other than biological. For example, the European whites were generally considered higher in status than the American-born creoles; the wealthy creoles stood higher on the social ladder than small farmers, cattlemen, small shopkeepers, and free white laborers. Among the "colored," the mulattoes preceded free blacks on the social scale, and they in turn stood higher than the black slaves.

Among the creole aristocracy a distinction was frequently made between the landed aristocracy and the mercantile aristocracy of the cities; the former generally enjoyed a higher social rank than the latter. Thus the aristocracies of America were almost exclusively composed of whites. These aristocracies, whose social status was based on wealth, whether derived from land and agriculture, commerce, or mines, existed in every area of European colonization. Although it cannot be said that there was an interimperial or international aristocracy as such, the aristocrat of Brazil, for example, had much more in common, in his way of living, his culture, and his outlook on life, both with the great landowners of his mother country and with the British sugar planters of Barbados or the tobacco planters of Virginia than he could ever have had with his slaves, with the nearby Indians, or even with his mestizo hangers-on.

Relatively few of the members of this class were members of the European aristocracy, although it is true that many of the officials in the Spanish, French, English, and Portuguese empires were aristocrats in their home countries. Most of the members of the Euroamerican aristocracy were native-born Americans, who had attained their status because their families had possessed large landed estates for long periods of time, perhaps centuries, or because their ancestors had achieved wealth through commerce or mining.

Seigneurial social institutions still existed in some colonies in America, such as French Canada, Maryland, Mexico, Brazil, and Peru, but these institutions were in decline, just as they were in Europe. The breadth of the American frontiers and the plentitude of available land, as well as the corresponding equal opportunities to escape from the feudal systems and to start life anew and economically free, hastened the dissolution of the system throughout the hemisphere; however, it is probably true that the decline was most rapid in Angloamerica and in Dutch

America, since property in those areas was already predominantly possessed in freehold. In the Portuguese and Spanish empires the crowns, in the course of the eighteenth century, recovered direct control of many of the great feudal estates and many of the Indian communities formerly administered by religious orders.

While the American aristocracies everywhere bore a certain similarity to, and tended to imitate, the aristocracies in the mother countries, these aristocracies were essentially American. They were not European; the way of life of the sugar planter on Barbados, for example, probably bore a greater sociological and cultural similarity to that of the creole sugar planter in Cuba than to any great English landlord "at home."

The vast majority of the American population derived their livelihoods from the land. The phenomenal expansion of capital wealth during the eighteenth century, however,[4] and the growth and high social status of the aristocracy that accompanied it could not have been achieved without a parallel increase in the number and size of cities. In most cases, the cities served as entrepôts for the profitable exportation of the products from the land, the mines, or the cattle ranches and for the importation of commodities from the outside world needed by the landed industries. Most, though by no means all, of the important cities, therefore, were seaports, built along the eastern littoral of the continent.

By the middle of the eighteenth century, such great seaport cities as Rio de Janeiro, Bahia, Recife, Buenos Aires, Montevideo, Vera Cruz, Kingston, Havana, Charleston, S.C., Philadelphia, New York, Boston, and Montreal were flourishing in large part from the profits obtained from their export and import business. On the Pacific side there were but few ports: Valparaiso in Chile (the port for Santiago de Chile), Callao (the port for Lima, Peru), and Panama (the port of two-way transshipment of goods between Europe and the Pacific coast of South America across the Isthmus of Panama).

Some major inland cities, such as Mexico City, Quito, Bogotá, Caracas, and Cuzco, had grown up because they were already metropolises of the Indian civilization, because they had been selected by the imperial governments as capitals for the colonial political systems, or for both reasons. Other cities thrived because they were centers of rich mining industries, for example, Zacatecas, Taxco, and Guanajuato in Mexico, Potosí in Peru, and Ouro Preto in Brazil.

[4] See chapter 3.

In every Latin-American city the "plaza" was dominated by the cathedral or the church, the governor's palace, and the buildings of public administration. In the Angloamerican towns, by the middle of the eighteenth century, the "common" was likely to be presided over by a church which often doubled as a town hall, but there were likely to be many churches, of a variety of Protestant sects.

In all the cities the economic basis of life was commerce, which centered around a marketplace. The cities were the ganglia, as it were, through which passed the currents of import and export, of buying and selling, of barter and exchange. It was through these channels that commercial capital wealth accumulated. Although the growth of capital wealth derived in part from the improvement and use of the land in the agricultural or pastoral areas, it is also true that the exchange of the products of the land and the mines for goods from other parts of the world made the expansion of capital wealth, both urban and rural, possible.

Within the cities there existed a social structure that was distinct from that of the land. At the top of the society stood the well-to-do merchant, the entrepreneur who, as buyer and seller, importer and exporter, controlled what fluid capital there was and served as a banker for the other members of society — the small shopkeepers, middle-class farmers, and great plantation owners. It was the merchant prince, too, who, generally in collaboration with the high personages of the officialdom, dominated important social events.

Throughout America the city merchants had built their fortunes on the profits of intraimperial, interimperial, and intercolonial trade. Their social status as urban aristocrats rested upon this commercial wealth. And with social status went education, manners, travel, culture, and political power. In their relations with other social groups, the members of the new commercial aristocracy dealt chiefly with their fellow aristocrats of the land. Through the activities of commerce, they also came in contact with the mercantile aristocracies of other American empires as well as with those of their own metropolises. And along these lines of commerce traveled ideas, culture, and even social exchange.

In some areas a stratum of society evolved that might properly be called a middle class, which was composed of such people as the small farmers and the lesser merchants, tradesmen, and professional men of the Angloamerican cities. Similar groups appeared in other colonies, particularly those of the Dutch; the middle classes of the Portuguese

Rio de Janeiro. From Johann M. Rugendas, *Viagem pitoresca através do Brasil,*
plate 1/7. Courtesy of the University of Washington Library.

TWO CITIES IN EIGHTEENTH-CENTURY AMERICA.

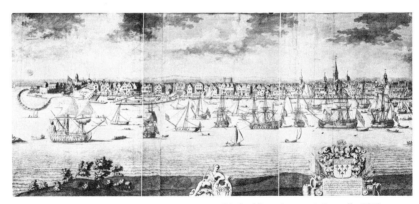

New York. An engraving by I. Harris, published by Thomas Bakewell, 1746.
Courtesy of the Library of Congress.

and Spanish colonies were not proportionally as large, nor was their political and cultural significance as great as in the British colonies.

Similarly, there existed a class of free laborers — artisans, journeymen, freedmen, longshoremen, fishermen — who owned little or no property and whose only capital derived from the labor of their own hands. Closely related to them, and potentially members of this class, were the contract laborers (the British indentured servant, the French *engagé*), who were legally obligated to work for their employers for four, five, or even seven years in return for the cost of their passage to America. At the end of their terms of servitude, they became free laborers. In Angloamerica many of them took up land and entered the class of independent farmers. This practice led to a social fluidity which hardly existed in other areas of colonization.

At the bottom of the urban social pyramid were the slaves, mostly blacks, who served both as servants in the houses of the well-to-do and as bound labor in shops and factories and on the wharves.

A very considerable element in society was the bureaucracy that grew up around the governing officials in the Euroamerican empires. For example, around the viceroy in Brazil or Hispanoamerica there always revolved a "court" of Portuguese or Spanish officials called *peninsulares* (*reinícolas*) in Brazil or *gachupines* in Hispanoamerica, plus a horde of lesser officials, clerks, lawyers, judges, and so on. Some of these bureaucrats bore titles.

Similarly, the colonial governor in each Angloamerican colony was aided by a group of officials, judges, members of the governor's council (usually Americans, however), clerks, and so on. The governors and certain officials, such as customs officials, military officers, and admiralty judges, were usually Englishmen, and the group was called the "court party." The lesser employees were generally Americans. Between the Europeans and the Americans there was a certain tension. The European officials and their hangers-on tended to be haughty, arrogant, and condescending toward the Americans, or creoles; the Americans, on the other hand, resented the presence of the Europeans and were profoundly jealous of their power. This resentment and jealousy constituted one of the basic psychological factors underlying the movements toward independence, and they were also among the roots of later nationalisms.

Wherever the Europeans had penetrated the American continent the social phenomenon known as the frontier had become a significant factor in the growth of the new societies inland from the coast. This phenomenon, as it existed in America, may be defined as a sort of zone between the already well-established society and the wilderness and the native Indian cultures — a zone in which the imported European culture, in the crucible of the total experience of the New World, was being molded into a somewhat new, more American local culture. This process of re-formation evolved in a variety of ways in the different regions in which it appeared. The area between civilization and wilderness in Canada was characterized most typically by fur trading; the frontier in Angloamerica was distinguished by the occupation of the land for farming purposes; that in Mexico by mining, that in northern Brazil by sugar and tobacco plantations, and that in southern Brazil by mining and cattle raising; in Argentina the great frontier was a cattlemen's frontier. In Peru and Chile the frontier, again, was largely reserved for mining; in northern South America the zone of re-formation was, in some areas, mining, in others cattle raising.

In certain places the frontier process not only re-formed society, but actually produced new sociological types, or groups, such as the *coureurs de bois* of Canada, the buccaneers of the Caribbean (who practically disappeared, under international suppression, early in the eighteenth century), the *llaneros* (plainsmen) of internal Venezuela, the gauchos (cowboys) of Argentina, and the *bandeirantes* of Brazil. These frontiersmen, everywhere, were created by America and were peculiar to it.

Throughout America there was a great deal of racial miscegenation. By the middle of the eighteenth century, this biological assimilation had produced a huge and increasing part of the population, composed of three fairly distinct ethnic groups. The first of these were the mestizos (so-called in Hispanoamerica), products of the mating (usually) of white men with Indian women. They were called métis in French Canada, half-breeds in Angloamerica, and *mestiços* in Brazil. Generally repudiated by the whites and often scornful of their Indian forebears, the mestizos constituted a recognizable, separate group, who had more in common with other mixed groups than with either of their parent groups.

The second ethnic group that appeared as a result of racial mixture was the mulattoes, offspring of unions between white men (usually) and black women. Many of them, at the middle of the eighteenth century, were free "persons of color," often liberated by their white fathers. They stood a notch above the mestizos in the hierarchy of social classes, and they commanded a considerable measure of respect, especially among the blacks who were still bound to slavery.

The third group was made up of children of unions between blacks and Indians. The numbers of zambos were never very great or significant, however; the areas where they were numerous were scattered and, generally, small.

The stratification of social classes was generally linked to these ethnic differences. Servile institutions and slavery intervened especially between whites and people of other colors. In Latin America the physical proximity of Iberian colonizers with Indians and blacks was facilitated by Christianity and miscegenation, both of which opened the way to equalitarian progress later on, particularly in Mexico and Brazil.

In Angloamerica contacts between races seem to have been a little more inflexible, more rigidly "racist"[5] than in the Latin countries. The Indians were gradually expelled or destroyed in Angloamerica, as they were, indeed, in some Spanish frontiers such as Argentina and Chile. In French, Dutch, and English America there existed no Indian communities organized by the church and under the rather strict paternalism of the encomienda system. Racial prejudice of whites toward Indians and blacks may have been stronger in Angloamerica and Dutch America than in other empires, but it existed everywhere.

The Blacks and Slavery

The institution of human chattel slavery existed in all the areas of Euroamerican colonization. When the Europeans first landed on the continent, they proceeded, in one degree or another, to enslave the native Indians. Thus Indian slavery existed everywhere. Thousands of Indian slaves were employed in the mines of Santo Domingo, Mexico, and Peru and in the dyewoods industry and the plantations of Brazil, all of which were operated, at the beginning, with Indian slave labor. Indian slavery continued into the eighteenth century, but it had declined, partly because the Indian populations in the mining communities

[5] Winthrop D. Jordan, *White over Black: American Attitudes toward the Negro, 1550–1812* (Chapel Hill: University of North Carolina Press, 1968), *passim*.

decreased, partly as a result of the ameliorating influence of the "Laws of the Indies,"[6] partly — even largely — by reason of the influence of the Roman Catholic church.

In any case, the lack of laborers, whether Indian or other, had created an economic vacuum that was filled by the importation of black slaves from Africa. This importation, in turn, had given rise to the international slave trade.[7] Slavery was itself an international institution, which extended back into the remotest epochs of human history. As established in America, apart from the enslavement of Indians, it involved predominantly the enslavement of African blacks.

As one of the most typical socioeconomic institutions of America, black slavery contributed greatly to the remarkable expansion of capital wealth that took place in the eighteenth century in all the areas of colonization. As a general, international phenomenon, black slaves were geographically distributed in such a way that there were very few in French Canada and not too many more in British New England. As one proceeds southward, the numerical proportion of black slaves to the total population steadily rises: in British Virginia there was one black slave to three whites in 1750; in South Carolina the ratio was about two to three. In the British colony of Jamaica, the proportion was ten blacks to one white; in French Saint-Domingue it was fifteen to one; in northeast Portuguese Brazil it was probably about five to one. In Argentina, however, there were relatively few black slaves.

Evidently the black slave population of America was most dense in the tropical belt, where great plantations were the rule, and least dense at the northern and southern ends, where commerce, fishing, forest industries, or cattle raising were the basic economic occupations. In general, the black population was largest in regions bordering on the Atlantic Ocean.

As a sociological phenomenon, black slavery was a highly significant element in the historical development of the American colonial societies. The slaves usually lived on the plantations of their owners, or, if they worked in the cities, they lived in the homes of their owners. But they were the mudsills of a society that included their white owners, who dominated that society, and the Indians, who were even more isolated than the blacks. Above them, too, on the social ladder was that extensive

---

[6] See volume IV of this series.
[7] See chapter 3 above.

group of mestizos, who lived in a sort of demi-world of their own. Even the mulattoes generally enjoyed a somewhat higher status than the blacks of pure African descent.

Apart from the hard, day-by-day labor of planting, cultivating, and shipping such profitable crops as sugar, tobacco, rice, and indigo, the black men, women, and children constituted a large group in the social microcosms that were the plantation communities. In many areas, for example, in South Carolina, Martinique, or Brazil, the blacks often outnumbered the whites by as many as twenty to one — or even more.

At the same time, there were a good number of black slaves in the cities, from Boston to Buenos Aires. Many of them were the household servants of the mercantile aristocracy. Many others were employed in warehouses, factories, and on the docks. They lived in barracks, or dormitories, of a very primitive sort.

Everywhere the blacks had brought from Africa their culture, their religions, and their social mores. These they were generally allowed to retain. But with the passage of the years the constant influence of the white man's culture and religion, whether through education, "household service," or religion, gradually resulted in at least a partial assimilation of the blacks to the white man's culture and religion. The blacks learned the white men's languages, if slowly and imperfectly; they were taught the rudiments of the white men's religions and morality; most of them, in time, adopted the white men's dress and social customs. Yet, in some areas, most notably Brazil and the French West Indies, the African heritage persisted. This was particularly true of their religions, which took on the various forms of "voodooism," a sort of African witchcraft with a superficial overlay of Christianity. The most extensive and thoroughgoing assimilation resulted from miscegenation; it appears to have been true that cultural assimilation was more profound and effective for the mulattoes than for pure blacks.

The treatment of the slaves varied little from empire to empire and from region to region. In rare cases humanitarian masters treated their slaves with kindness and wisdom; in some areas, such as Brazil, the Catholic church occasionally used its power to humanize the treatment of the blacks; in regions or colonies where there were few slaves the slave codes appear to have been less severe than in areas where the slave population was relatively numerous. But as a social institution slavery was basically and generally the same everywhere. It rested upon the universally accepted assumption that blacks, although human, were inferior to white men, that they could be bought and sold like livestock, and that they could be punished by their masters, by every conceivable means, from whipping to maiming or even execution, without legal recourse. In only some areas were the blacks permitted to marry. They were generally encouraged to multiply, however, because their offspring were slaves from birth, and therefore valuable. In a few places efforts were made to educate them, although, for the most part, education and conversion to Christianity were discouraged, since both enlightenment and a common religion might inspire union and revolt. Slave codes everywhere were harsh, often savagely ruthless; by them the slaves' lives were severely restricted in ways of which the slaves themselves were often totally ignorant and uncomprehending.[8]

Slavery was almost universally taken for granted throughout the Western world, and especially in America. To be sure, a few rationalistic voices among the European and American philosophes — voices such as Voltaire's and Benjamin Franklin's — were raised against the institution, and the Quakers in England and Angloamerica began their own antislavery campaign in approximately 1700. But the actual beginning of the end of the institution had to await the rationalistic and humanitarian application of the doctrine of natural rights in the northern Angloamerican colonies during the American Revolution. The second real advance toward emancipation was made in Haiti, under the leadership of Toussaint L'Ouverture just at the end of the eighteenth century.[9] But the freeing of his race from bondage took place elsewhere in the hemisphere only after the era of independence, well into the nineteenth century.

Legally, slavery had long been established in Spain and Portugal. Yet there had not been many slaves, and the relationships between slaves and masters had often been close and familial. The effects of the institution on the slaves themselves had thus been relatively mild and benevolent. When slavery came to Iberoamerica, therefore, it was not new,

[8] There is a myth among North American historians that slavery was much more humane in Brazil than in Angloamerica, Francoamerica, or Hispanoamerica. For a dissolution of that myth see Charles Boxer, *The Golden Age of Brazil, 1695–1750: Growing Pains of a Colonial Society* (Berkeley: University of California Press, 1964), *passim*. Also see Robert Conrad, *The Destruction of Brazilian Slavery, 1850–1888* (Berkeley: University of California Press, 1972), and Carl N. Degler, *Neither Black nor White: Slavery and Race Relations in Brazil and the United States* (New York: Macmillan, 1971).

[9] See below, chapter 11.

"A negro festival," about 1800. From Bryan Edwards, *The History, Civil and Commercial, of the British Colonies in the West Indies*, 3 vols. (London: J. Stockdale, 1801), II, 184. Courtesy of The Newberry Library, Chicago.

and the attitude of the whites was not heavy with the self-conscious superiority of the Anglo-Saxons or tainted, as with them, with distrust and fear.

With the introduction of black slaves into the Iberian colonies during the colonial centuries, the rulers of both the Spanish and the Portuguese empires had taken a direct interest in the welfare of the blacks, much as they had in the case of the Indians. The king-emperor Carlos I had even ordered slavery abolished, about the middle of the sixteenth century; as late as 1679 and 1693 the king of Spain was still questioning whether the enslavement of blacks was legitimate and whether it was proper for the crown to make contracts for the importation of Africans to the Spanish colonies. But the need of a labor force was thought by the colonists to be compelling, and the institution had grown to be an integral element in the colonial societies.

The Council of the Indies had agreed, in 1685, that slavery was an economic necessity: "There cannot be any doubt as to the necessity of those slaves for the support of the kingdom of the Indies. . . . [The trade may continue] because of the reasons expressed, the authorities cited, and its longlived and general custom in the kingdoms of Castile, America, and Portugal, without any objection on the part of his Holiness or ecclesiastical state, but rather with the tolerance of all of them." [10]

The complex psychological phenomenon known as race consciousness and racial hatred has apparently existed from the beginning of human time. Because the ancient Mediterranean civilizations enslaved white people as well as colored, their institutions of slavery apparently did not give rise to racism. Nor was slavery a necessary base for racism, since racism existed between, say, whites and blacks even where slavery did not exist. After the western commercial nations, Portugal, Spain, France, and England, began to enslave the Africans, the institution, of itself, did not seem to generate racial hatred. It did foster, however, a feeling among the whites that they were superior to the blacks. [11]

This self-conscious sense of difference and of white superiority was, in fact, an important intellectual theme in the sociological thinking of the Western world in the eighteenth century. For all their humanism, the philosophes of the Enlightenment, even though they condemned the institution of slavery, nevertheless thought the black race, as such, was distinctly inferior to the white. Voltaire, for example, was typical of the thinkers of his time when he wrote that "the Negro race is a species of men different from ours [the Europeans] as the race of spaniels is different from that of greyhounds. The mucous membrane, that network that nature has stretched between the muscles and the skin, is white

---

[10] Quoted in Stanley M. Elkins, *Slavery: A Problem in American Institutional and Intellectual Life* (2nd ed.; Chicago: University of Chicago Press, 1968), p. 69.

[11] Jordan, *White over Black*, chapter 1 and *passim*.

among us, black among them, bronze among others. . . . Their black wool resembles our hair not at all, and one may say that if their intelligence is not of another kind from our understanding, it is very inferior." As for slavery, Voltaire says, "We tell them [the blacks] they are men like us, that they are redeemed by the blood of the Lord who died for them, and then we make them work like beasts of burden; if they try to escape, we cut off a leg, and we make them turn with a limb of a tree the sugar mills after we have given them a wooden leg. After that we dare to talk about the law of nations."[12]

In general, the whites originally seem to have held no hatred of the blacks. They felt the blacks were primitive, intellectually undeveloped "children," as Thomas Jefferson called them. Ideally, the treatment of slaves by a master was paternal, humane. Even among the blacks there seems to have been relatively little active hatred of the whites. Of course, many blacks eventually became conscious of the innate inhumanity of the institution and fought fanatically against it, as the numerous slave insurrections in all slaveholding societies attest. Racial hatred, as a historical phenomenon, seems to have been in large measure a product of mutual fear, a fear inspired among the whites by these frequent slave uprisings and among the blacks by their cumulative natural sense of repression as well as the savage and vindictive punishments that always followed the uprisings. And yet, in the years of peace between insurrections, it is equally true, historically, that most blacks appeared to accept their fate; even in their servitude, there were times when they appeared not to be universally unhappy about their condition; even in slavery, as many travelers testified, they displayed a great spirit of lightheartedness, even gaiety, in their moments of relaxation.

A Conglomerate Society

The population of America, then, in the eighteenth-century stage of the "expansion of Europe" was not preponderately European. It was no longer an Indian population — far from it — nor was it predominantly black or predominantly one of mixed blood. It was a conglomerate population, of which the people of European derivation constituted but a distinct minority. The overwhelming fact is that this conglomerate

[12] Voltaire, *Essai sur les moeurs et l'esprit des nations, Oeuvres complètes de Voltaire*, ed. Louis E. D. Moland, 52 vols. (Paris, 1877–85), XII, 357, 417.

population was different from the populations of all the other continents of the world. It was American.

But the population of America was not an evenly consistent mass, even as a conglomerate. Every empire was a society different from every other; and within each major empire there were sectional differentiations sufficiently profound to justify the characterization of the various sections as essentially different societies. In the French empire Canada and the French West Indies were sharply dissimilar; in Angloamerica the northern continental colonies, the southern colonies, and the West Indies had become so acutely different that they were distinct from one another in many ways; in Brazil the northeastern plantation area centering around Bahia and Pernambuco was greatly differentiated from the southwestern mining and cattle-raising areas; in Hispanoamerica Mexico, Colombia, Peru, and the La Plata regions were already profoundly differentiated from one another. At the same time, all of them were significantly different from their mother countries.

Each empire differed from the others, of course, in language and culture. Each was, as indicated earlier, artificially shut off from the others by the mercantilistic colonial policies of the imperial administration, despite which, nevertheless, there was a vast amount of interimperial commerce and cultural exchange. Each empire differed from the others in political institutions and in the forms of imperial administrations. All were emotionally and practically enemies of one another, rivals for the profits of empire and rivals in the process of expanding their territories and building up their own imperial power.

The regional social differences within empires generally originated from the economic specialization that took place as the Europeans adapted themselves to the soil, the climate, and the natural resources of that geographic region. But the differentiation was not merely geographically derived. It also derived in part from cultural factors such as religion — as, for example, the differences between the Puritanism of New England, the Catholicism of Maryland, and the Anglicanism of Virginia. Some regional diversities stemmed from indigenous roots: the unique cultural development of Paraguay, for example, rested largely upon its nature as a predominantly Indian society, molded by the early influence of the Jesuit missions; the development of French Canada was significantly conditioned by the social contacts between the French and the aborigines, whether through the French missionaries, military expeditions, or the fur trade, accompanied, as it was, by the miscegenation of French *coureurs de bois* and voyageurs with Indian women.

One of the most striking sociological phenomena resulting from the growth of these regional societies was that each society became consciously aware of its distinctness and its own separate destiny. They were new societies, no longer European, but different variants of American society. Furthermore, they were not closely bound to one another within the frameworks of the old empires, and by the end of the century they all recognized this fact. In the Spanish empire, these regional differences provided the basis for the separation of the later independent Spanish-American states. In the French empire, French Canada was eventually severed from the French West Indian societies by war. The Dutch colonies, like the French West Indies, maintained their connections with their mother countries; they were too weak to become independent.

In Brazil the regional diversities, great as they were, were not great enough to lead the separate regions to form autonomous nations. The British West Indies, although very unlike the society of England, were too weak to declare their independence. On the other hand, thirteen of the British colonies were led, by their sense of differentness and their inner drive toward autonomy, to secede from the British empire in 1776. Even so, by the end of the era of independence of America (1824), half of the new United States, the so-called southern states, were evolving in the direction of becoming a separate nation, a development which eventually led to the Civil War.

In all of this there is to be seen a sort of socioeconomic cultural process that eventually culminated in the appearance of many new societies, several of which would become, in the last quarter of the eighteenth century and in the first quarter of the nineteenth, the new nations of the modern era.

CHAPTER 6

The International Relations of Rival American Empires

From Utrecht (1713) to Madrid (1721)

The Peace of Utrecht was thought of, both in Europe and in America, as a settlement that would establish a lasting peace in America, based upon the principle of the balance of colonial power.[1] It had provided for certain territorial readjustments between the French and English empires, such as the recognition of Hudson Bay, Acadia, and the island of St. Christopher as British. The Anglo-Spanish Treaty of Peace had stipulated that Spain would grant to England the *asiento*, the contract for supplying black slaves to the Spanish colonies in America. The Anglo-Spanish and Anglo-French treaties had included provisions guaranteeing the maintenance of the territorial status quo in the Spanish colonies: Spain agreed never to alienate its colonies to another foreign power; Louis XIV promised never to try to acquire them, or any part of them; England, in a sort of precursor of the Monroe Doctrine, undertook to guarantee that the territorial status of the Spanish colonies should never be changed. The Hispano-Portuguese Treaty of Peace provided for a return to the territorial *status quo ante bellum* in America. Specifically, Spain gave back to Portugal the Colonia do Sacramento on the estuary of the Rio de la Plata opposite Buenos Aires, thus reextending the southern boundary of Brazil to that river, with the condition that Portugal

[1] See above, chapter 1. See also Max Savelle, *The Origins of American Diplomacy: The International History of Angloamerica, 1492–1763* (New York: Macmillan, 1967), chapter 10.

would not permit any third nation (inferentially the English) to trade there; the mutually exclusive national commercial monopolies in the two empires were explicitly acknowledged and renewed.

But those sections of the Peace pertaining to Europe had not been completed at Utrecht. In particular, Spain and Austria had not made peace between themselves, chiefly because Spain, now ruled by Louis XIV's grandson, Philip of Anjou, as Philip V of Spain, refused to accommodate with Austria its claims to certain parts of Italy.

By a series of alliances intended to preserve the international status quo established at Utrecht, England, France, the Netherlands, Austria, and (later) Sardinia formed between 1716 and 1718 what became known as the "Quadruple Alliance." Spain, still holding out for international, but especially Austrian, recognition of its "rights" in Italy, refused to accede to the Quadruple Alliance and to make the treaty of peace with Austria required by the others as a prerequisite. The other members offered to mediate between Spain and Austria, but Spain rejected their proposal. Instead, it sent a fleet to seize Sicily, which it claimed. Whereupon England sent a fleet to intercept the Spanish fleet, which it did — so successfully, indeed, that it destroyed the Spanish fleet off Cape Passaro in Sicily. In the war that followed, Spain quickly realized it was beaten, agreed to the proposed mediation of England, and acceded to the Quadruple Alliance on February 17, 1721. This event effectively completed the European and American settlement begun at Utrecht.

This war, short as it was, was extended to America. The French seized Pensacola, in Florida, in 1719; there were numerous naval encounters at sea; South Carolina was frightened by a rumored Spanish invasion that never took place; and questions regarding America played important parts in the negotiations between Spain, on the one hand, and France and England, on the other, for a final settlement of their disputes.[2] By the Franco-Spanish Treaty of Madrid (1721), France and Spain mutually agreed to guarantee each other's possessions "in whatever part of the world they may be situated in"; Spain promised France a favored position in the trade with the Spanish colonies by way of Cádiz; and France agreed to restore Pensacola to Spain.

By the Anglo-Spanish Treaty of Madrid (1721), Spain renewed for England the *asiento* of 1713, which was suspended during the war, and England revived its guarantee to uphold the territorial integrity of the Spanish

<hr>

[2] Savelle, *Origins of American Diplomacy*, pp. 309–313.

colonies in America. England also accepted an article vaguely recognizing an undefined right of the Spanish Basques to fish on the Grand Banks of Newfoundland — a provision, be it said, by which the Spanish Basques gained, de facto, exactly nothing.

To the Treaty of Seville (1729)

International questions relative to French, English, Spanish, Dutch, and Austrian colonies and commerce in America ran like a frayed cord through the international Congress of Cambrai (1724) and the Congress of Soissons (1728). The debates were long and the practical outcome nil; final adjustment of the details of American affairs envisaged by the treaties of Madrid in 1721 could not be achieved, largely because they were tied to the continuing wrangling over Austrian and Spanish claims in Italy and the division of the European states into two new rival groups in the balance of power led by, surprisingly enough, Spain and Austria on the one side and England and France on the other.

By this time, too, the increasingly bitter Anglo-Spanish conflict over the conduct of the *asiento* by the English South Sea Company and over the trade of English interlopers from the British West Indies and the English colonies in North America with the Spanish colonies around the Caribbean reached fever heat and precipitated warlike actions on both sides. Since war seemed imminent, England dispatched a fleet under Admiral Hosier in 1726 to intercept the Spanish treasure fleet in order to prevent it from bringing its metallic sinews of war home to Spain. In retaliation for this belligerent action Spanish officials at Vera Cruz seized the South Sea Company's ship the *Prince Frederick*. These actions, coupled with the aggressive stance of the two groups of powers allied under the Austro-Spanish alliance of Vienna (1725) and the Anglo-French-Dutch alliance of Hanover (1725), made war seem imminent and well-nigh inevitable.

The situation was saved, however, by Cardinal Fleury of France, who called for a new congress which met at Soissons on June 18, 1728. Out of this second congress emerged a set of terms that were agreed to by all the powers except Spain and were then submitted to that country for its acceptance.

At the Congress of Soissons American issues were again tied to Spain's interests in Italy. Austria, to cut the Gordian knot (Austria and Spain, after their brief honeymoon under the Alliance of Vienna of 1725, had again become bitter rivals in Italy), agreed to recognize the claim of Spanish Queen Elizabeth Farnese's eldest son, Don Carlos, to certain Italian duchies and Spain's right to send Spanish garrisons to the duchies to support his tenure. England and France agreed to aid and support Spain in this move, in return for which France's privileged position in the trade with Spanish America through Cádiz was to be renewed and the *asiento* was to be again restored to England. The long list of Spain's complaints against England in America and the violations of (English) freedom of the seas in America by Spanish *guarda costas* was to be submitted for peaceful adjudication to an Anglo-Spanish joint commission.

When Spain accepted these terms, they were embodied in the Treaty of Seville, signed by Spain, France, and England on November 9, 1729. Holland acceded to the treaty on November 21, 1729.

From Seville to the War of Jenkins' Ear (1739)

Don Carlos, later to be King Carlos III of Spain, after much wrangling and diplomatic maneuvering among the signatories of the Treaty of Seville, duly entered his Italian dukedoms late in October of 1731. The Anglo-Spanish joint commission for the adjudication of American claims also met, in February of 1732. But it accomplished nothing and found itself bogged down in arguing over the claims of the king of Spain against the South Sea Company as a partner in the company and the unabated continuance of English abuses of its privileges under the *asiento*, especially the Angloamerican traders' smuggling of goods into Spanish America, which led to the seizure of English ships, innocent and otherwise, by the Spanish *guarda costas* upon the high seas. Its deliberations petered out and were informally allowed to cease in 1733. Halfhearted attempts to settle the disputes were continued by direct negotiations, but these also failed. Then, when the attention of Europe's diplomats was diverted from America to Europe by the outbreak of the War of the Polish Succession in 1733, all efforts to settle Anglo-Spanish disputes in America were left entirely in abeyance.

While the Anglo-Spanish joint commission was bickering in Madrid, France and Spain were drawing closer together diplomatically. France needed an ally in the anticipated war over the Polish succession and a strengthened position in the Spanish-American trade by way of Cádiz; Spain needed an ally against England should war break out with that empire, which seemed increasingly probable as the joint commission continued its fruitless wrangling over American affairs. The result of the Franco-Spanish rapprochement was the super-secret Bourbon Family Compact (knowledge of which leaked out almost immediately), signed at the Escorial on November 7, 1733.

This treaty was, in effect, an alliance between France and Spain for the purposes indicated above. It provided for mutual and joint guarantees of the territorial holdings of both the signatories in all parts of the world. France promised its support to Don Carlos should he need it to protect his tenure of his Italian duchies against England, Austria, or any other enemy. Furthermore, should Spain find it necessary to suspend England's commercial privileges in America and should England make war upon Spain or its colonies as a consequence, France would assist Spain in the war against England.

When the War of the Polish Succession broke out in 1733, Spain and France were allies, as stipulated in the Bourbon Family Compact. But a struggle against England was avoided, since England remained neutral during the war, which lasted until 1735. The negotiations between Spain and England over American affairs persisted, halfheartedly and sporadically, as did the disputes and incidents in America that kept the chronic bitterness alive. England, on its side, continued to complain that English ships were being seized by Spanish *guarda costas* on the high seas and that difficulties were being placed in the way of agents of the South Sea Company; Spain complained of the illicit commerce being carried on in the Spanish colonies by English interlopers from England, the British West Indies, and the northern English colonies on the continent of North America. Spain also insisted that no settlement could be made until the South Sea Company paid King Philip V a share of its profits, an accounting of which the company steadfastly evaded giving him.

All these disputes dragged on and were augmented by a new and bitter feud over the British settlement of Georgia. Actually, Georgia was settled in 1733, but Spain had been so preoccupied with the War of the Polish Succession that it had not actively resisted the English or even protested. After the war had ended, Spain made an investigation of the new colony and discovered that it was all too real. Spain protested that this new colony stood as a violation of the treaties of Madrid (1670) and Utrecht (1713), but José Patiño, the Spanish prime minister, was not disposed to go to war over it. It was only when the Spanish governor of Florida, Francisco del Moral Sánchez, made a treaty with Charles Dempsey, acting for James Oglethorpe and Georgia, which recognized the St. John's River as a boundary between the two colonies, that Patiño was driven to make a vehement protest to London over the new English colony. Spain then repudiated the treaty, and its bitterness over Georgia was added to its resentment over the other American issues between the two empires.

The bitterness, however, was not all on one side. Many Englishmen and their representatives in Parliament were becoming increasingly aggressive in the face of what they considered Spain's insults to England and violations of the freedom of the seas in America. The power of the party of "war hawks" in the House of Commons grew rapidly and dangerously, and many harsh things were said that hurt the pride of Spain. The peace-minded government of Robert Walpole welcomed, therefore, Thomas Geraldino's proposal for a mutual settlement of claims, but the suggestion was repudiated by Spain, whereupon the Walpole government instructed its minister in Madrid, Benjamin Keene, to make a final effort to bring about a settlement. This Keene succeeded in doing, and the terms were embodied in the so-called Convention of the Pardo, signed on January 14, 1739. According to this convention, Spain was to pay to the king of England £95,000 sterling to indemnify all outstanding English claims against Spain; all other disputes were to be submitted for adjudication to a new joint commission.

But a new stalemate ensued: the South Sea Company refused to pay its own private debt to the king of Spain, as it was supposed to do, and Philip V refused to ratify the convention unless it did so. There was a furious popular outcry in England against Spain, and even though the convention was narrowly accepted by Parliament, war became almost inevitable. Despite the clamor and tension, war could have been avoided, since both governments wished to do so, had it not been for France's secret goading of Spain. For France, fishing in the troubled waters, wanted to strengthen its own position in the Spanish-American trade by way of Cádiz. It was not really prepared to go to war with England, but when Spain suggested the possibility of a renewal of the Bourbon

Family Compact, France indicated its willingness to assist Spain in return for a new commercial treaty that would give it the economic advantages it desired. Nothing happened, for the time being, but Spain's attitude toward England stiffened, and when England issued a declaration of reprisal against Spanish "depredations" in America on August 20, 1739, Spain responded with a declaration of war on November 28. Thus began the so-called War of Jenkins' Ear.[3]

To the Peace of
Aix-la-Chapelle (1748)

The War of Jenkins' Ear was almost entirely a naval war in America, the most important events of which took place during the first two years of conflict. It started auspiciously for the British with the seizure of Puerto Bello by Admiral Charles Vernon; in 1741 the admiral proceeded against Cartagena with a mighty fleet and extensive land forces, including large contingents from the English continental colonies. This expedition was a colossal failure, after which the war degenerated into a series of naval battles and insignificant maneuvers.

Meanwhile, the attention of the belligerents was diverted from their American fight by the outbreak of the War of the Austrian Succession in 1740. This war revolved around the question of whether Maria Theresa, the daughter of the king of Austria and Holy Roman emperor Charles VI, might succeed him when he died on October 20 of that year. Charles had provided for Maria Theresa's succession in a document he had formulated years before his death called the Pragmatic Sanction; but because it violated the ancient Salic law against women succeeding to the throne, those countries, such as Prussia, that were interested in male heirs whom they had to support sought to set aside the Pragmatic Sanction by war. This war, which sought, among other things, to carve up Austria's states in Europe, promptly involved most of the powers in western Europe, including France, Spain, and England; Holland assisted England and Austria without abandoning its technical neutrality.

During the course of this war France, now desperately in need of help against Austria, again asked Spain to renew the Bourbon Family

---

[3] So-called in honor of the ear of one Captain Jenkins (he was otherwise unknown), said to have been cut off in a fracas on the deck of his ship when it was seized by a Spanish *guarda costa*.

Eighteenth-century warship. From *Encyclopédié*, pt. II, *Planches: Marine*,
plate I. Courtesy of the University of Washington Library.

Compact. Spain, itself in need of assistance against England, agreed;
the result was the so-called Second Bourbon Family Compact, signed
at Fontainebleau, in France, on October 25, 1743. This treaty, like the
Bourbon Family Compact of 1733, was an alliance for the mutual
guarantee of territories "outside of Europe as well as within it"; France
agreed to assist Spain against England in America, and England was
to be forced to abandon the colony of Georgia that had been established
on Spanish soil. Finally, England was to be compelled to surrender the
asiento. Spain now took up its task of assisting France in Europe, and
France declared war on England on April 27, 1744.

In America, the naval war in and about the Caribbean that had begun
in 1739 as the War of Jenkins' Ear now merged with the War of the
Austrian Succession. France sent token naval assistance to Spain in that
area, but the fighting there had little or no impact on the outcome of
the war, which was fought chiefly in Europe and was a stalemate even
there. Elsewhere in America, the English penetrated the Pacific Ocean

and attacked a number of Spanish ports on the west coast of South America without significant effect, and Admiral Lord Anson captured the Manila galleon and its cargo of Mexican silver near the Philippines. In the North Atlantic, an expedition composed of an English fleet and a land force of New Englanders succeeded in capturing the French fortress at Louisbourg, on Cape Breton Island, at the entrance to the Gulf of St. Lawrence in Canada.

By the Peace of Aix-la-Chapelle (1748), which brought to a close the War of the Austrian Succession, the international situation was restored to the status quo that had existed before the war. The Pragmatic Sanction, the chief cause of the war in the first place, was accepted by the signatories, and Maria Theresa became queen of Austria. Louisbourg and Cape Breton were returned to France; the *asiento* was restored to England; other matters in dispute between Spain and England were to be left (by informal agreement not a part of the treaty) to a new joint Anglo-Spanish commission. The Peace of Aix-la-Chapelle settled nothing; so far as America was concerned, it was hardly more than a truce.

England, Spain, and Portugal, 1750–77

Despite the inconclusiveness of the Peace of Aix-la-Chapelle, two genuine achievements in the international affairs of America were accomplished more or less as aftermaths of the treaty. As noted above, it provided that the English *asiento*, interrupted by the war, should be renewed. But the two powers disagreed over the contract's continued duration: England claimed it should run for fifteen years to compensate for the time lost during many interruptions; according to Spain, it should last for only four years, represented by the period between the outbreak of the War of Jenkins' Ear in 1739 and the date of the originally anticipated expiration of the contract in 1743 (that is, thirty years after its original signature in 1713).

Benjamin Keene, the British minister in Madrid, had great difficulty in getting the Spanish government to implement the renewal of the *asiento* because the quarrel of the king of Spain with the English South Sea Company was rekindled along with the renewal of negotiations over the treaty. Furthermore, all the other American disputes between England and Spain over illicit English trade, English logwood cutting on

Spanish soil, and freedom of the seas were also revived. To complicate matters still further, Keene had to take into account the opposition of a pro-French, anti-English party among the statesmen who dominated Spanish politics and international policy, even though a pro-English party was in power at the Spanish court.

In view of these many difficulties, both sides agreed to follow an earlier suggestion that the *asiento* be terminated, once and for all, by a lump sum payment to the South Sea Company. A treaty to this effect was signed on October 5, 1750; Spain agreed to pay the South Sea Company £100,000 sterling, with a mutual cancellation of debts and claims on both sides. Besides its provisions regarding European commerce between the two countries, the treaty also renewed the English privilege of gathering salt on the island of Tortuga; all other disputes between the two empires in America were to be considered as extinguished by the treaty.

For the nonce, England and Spain were at peace with each other in America. Indeed, an atmosphere of goodwill prevailed between them that had not existed during the preceding half-century. Unhappily for them, in view of the events developing in America, this era of good feeling could not last long.

In that same year, 1750, a long-standing quarrel between the Spaniards and Portuguese in the valley of the Rio de la Plata was settled, as it was thought at the time, forever.

The Hispano-Portuguese Treaty of Tordesillas (1494) had drawn a north-south line through the Atlantic which was meant to serve as a boundary between Portuguese and Spanish possessions in the New World.[4] Since the eastern tip of Brazil lay to the east of this line, Portugal's ownership of that region was automatically recognized; by the same token, the line automatically became the western boundary of Brazil. As that colony expanded during the sixteenth century Portugal was under the impression that the western boundary of Brazil lay along the Andes, which would thus be the eastern boundary of Peru, and that the southern boundary was marked by the Rio de la Plata. Portugal also vaguely considered the northern boundary to be the Amazon River.

These uncertain assumptions had caused no difficulty during the period (1580–1640) when Portugal and its empire were annexed to the Spanish

[4] See volume IV of this series.

empire. After their reseparation in 1640, however, their common interest in the Rio de la Plata area brought them into conflict. This clash became intense and violent shortly after the opening of the eighteenth century.

As the Portuguese expanded southward, they eventually settled on the east bank of the Rio de la Plata and founded Colonia do Sacramento (1680) on the shore of the great estuary roughly opposite the growing Spanish commercial and smuggling center of Buenos Aires. The Spaniards sought unsuccessfully to drive the Portuguese out, and there ensued roughly a century of struggle for the control of this area, which would one day become the republic of Uruguay. During the War of the Spanish Succession (in 1702–3), the Spaniards succeeded in seizing Colonia do Sacramento, but by the Hispano-Portuguese Treaty of Utrecht (1713) Spain agreed to give the colony back to Portugal, as has been noted.

The Spaniards, however, dissatisfied with the terms of the Treaty of Utrecht, built the town of San Felipe y Santiago (modern Montevideo) in 1724; not only were they able to maintain their hold there, but they were also able to expand their settlements along the eastern shore to the north of the Portuguese. A minor diplomatic incident in Madrid in 1735 precipitated tension between the Spanish and Portuguese courts and an excuse for a renewal of hostilities along the Rio de la Plata, with the result that the governor of Buenos Aires launched an attack on Colonia do Sacramento. The assault failed, but the Spaniards ravaged the surrounding countryside. The Portuguese retaliated by attempting unsuccessfully to take Montevideo; however, they did proceed to found the town of Rio Grande do Sul, north of Montevideo on the shore of the Atlantic. The tension was mitigated by an agreement arranged under the mediation of England, France, and Holland in 1737, but the rival claims in the Rio de la Plata remained unsettled.

Upon the accession of Ferdinand VI to the Spanish throne in 1746, there ensued an era of good relations between Portugal and Spain, largely because Ferdinand's queen was a Portuguese princess, Maria Barbara da Braganza. The two governments made a genuine effort to settle the dispute in the Rio de la Plata region, and the result was the Treaty of Madrid, signed by the two powers on January 13, 1750.

By the terms of the Treaty of Madrid, the old Treaty of Tordesillas was specifically abrogated and a boundary line was established between

Brazil and the Spanish territory (Uruguay) which moved westward from a point on the Atlantic coast south of Rio Grande do Sul and northward irregularly along certain ridges and rivers of the interior to the Rio Negro, the north branch of the Amazon. The Portuguese settlement of Colonia do Sacramento was awarded to Spain, and seven Spanish missions north of the line were granted to Brazil.

The most noteworthy feature of the Treaty of Madrid, however, was its invocation of the "doctrine of the two spheres" and of American isolation from European wars so that perpetual peace might be established between the subjects of the two crowns in America. In the words of this remarkable declaration,

Since war is the principal cause for abusing or altering established arrangements, His Catholic Majesty and His Most Faithful Majesty wish that if (which may God forfend) a break should take place between the two crowns, the peace between the subjects of both powers in South America shall be maintained, and they shall live at peace with each other just as if there were no such war between their sovereigns. . . . Similarly, neither of the two nations will permit the use of its ports in America . . . by the enemies of the other. . . . The said continuation of perpetual peace and good neighborliness shall have effect not only in the lands and islands of South America . . . but also in the rivers, ports and coasts in the Atlantic from the latitude of the southern tip of the Island of San Antonio, one of the Cape Verde Islands, southward, and from the meridian of longitude that passes through its western extremity toward the west.[5]

Unhappily, this idealistic international gesture could not succeed, since it aroused violent opposition in both Spain and Portugal, including that of José de Carvalho e Melo, the newly appointed Portuguese secretary of state, the future Marquis of Pombal. The two powers did try to implement the treaty's provisions, but the resistance, both in Europe and in America, was too strong. Because of Carvalho's stance, the Portuguese government ignored the provision for the cession of Colonia do Sacramento to Spain, and the Guaraní Indians of the ceded missions, encouraged by their Jesuit tutors, took up arms against both Spain and Portugal in what was called the Guaraní War; the boundary remained unsettled and the Treaty of Madrid remained unexecuted.

[5] Alejandro del Cantillo, ed., *Tratados, convenios y declaraciones de paz y de comercio que han hecho con las potencias extranjeras los monarcos españoles de la Casa de Borbón, desde el año de 1700 hasta el Día* (Madrid, 1843), pp. 406–407.

The Treaty of Madrid was abrogated by both signatories, at the instigation of Carlos III of Spain, by the Convention of the Pardo in 1761. A year later Portugal and Spain entered the Seven Years War, and Colonia do Sacramento was recaptured by the Spanish General Pedro de Cevallos. In 1763 Cevallos invaded the province of Rio Grande. The Treaty of Paris interrupted this Hispano-Portuguese colonial war in America and stipulated, rather ambiguously, that territories conquered during the war (not otherwise specifically provided for) should be restored. Colonia do Sacramento was given back to Portugal once more, but Spain hung on to Rio Grande on the ground that Portugal's possession of that province had never been recognized by treaty.

The quarrel over Rio Grande thus continued the long debate. After a short, uneasy truce (but in a time of peace in Europe), the colonial Portuguese attempted unsuccessfully to recover Rio Grande. This action was disavowed in Lisbon, but in 1776 the Portuguese took the aggressive, again in time of European peace, and with the aid of a British fleet succeeded in recovering Rio Grande. Spain appealed to France for help under the terms of the Bourbon Family Compact of 1761, but the Count of Vergennes, the then French foreign minister, declined on the basis that the Family Compact provided for mutual assistance in Europe only. (This was literally true, although the alliance made early in 1762 did provide for mutual defense in America.) A seesaw series of campaigns followed, during which the Brazilians hung on; not until October of 1777 did Spain and Portugal once more reach an agreement regarding their possessions in the "debatable land" of the Rio de la Plata and Rio Grande areas.

By the Treaty of San Ildefonso, signed October 1, 1777, Spain and Portugal assented to a revised version of the treaty of 1750. Colonia do Sacramento and its hinterlands were turned over to Spain; Rio Grande was recognized as Portuguese. The boundary line between Brazil and Rio de la Plata province was redrawn in a way slightly favorable to Spain.

Another long-lived boundary dispute in America had been resolved. Meanwhile, the War of United States Independence had broken out. France entered it on the side of the British colonies in 1778; Spain joined France against Britain in 1779. With this revival of the old struggle for the balance of power, a new chapter opened in the international history of the hemisphere.

The Anglo-French
Cold War, 1748–54

Although Spain and Portugal and Spain and England had succeeded, about 1750, in resolving their tensions in America, even if only for a few years, such was not the case between the French and British empires in the Caribbean area and on the continent of North America. For the years following the Peace of Aix-la-Chapelle witnessed the accelerating rate of the expansion of these two empires which brought them into well-nigh inevitable conflict — a conflict that had to be decisive for one or the other.

The pace of the expansion of these two empires had been mounting, all around the world, ever since the Peace of Utrecht. In America, the chief arenas of expansion were the Caribbean area and the great interior basin of North America.

In the Caribbean area, territorial expansion centered on the occupation of potentially sugar-raising or strategically located islands that had hitherto not been occupied by any European power. Thus, St. Lucia, with its fine harbor, Dominica, Tobago, and St. Vincent were all claimed by both France and England (Spain also maintained a shadowy right to all of them, on the basis of Columbus's discovery and the Treaty of Tordesillas, but it was no longer in a position to command any respect for its claims, either in the other courts of Europe or in the islands themselves). In the two or three decades following the Peace of Utrecht there was a race between France and England for the occupation and possession of these islands. Tension arose in several places, especially in St. Lucia, but because of the Anglo-French alliance in Europe and other European considerations, the two courts agreed in 1730 to evacuate the islands and to keep them "neutral" until title to them could be determined by negotiation. After the Peace of Aix-la-Chapelle (1748), there was a new rush by both competitors to occupy and exploit the "neutrals," with the result that the conflict over them threatened to precipitate war.

In the north, Acadia had been allotted to England by the Peace of Utrecht, but the Anglo-French Treaty of Peace had failed to define its boundaries. England asserted that Acadia's borders coincided with New England's, while France insisted that it was, at most, only a segment of the peninsula, thereby leaving a vast area from the Isthmus of Chignecto to the Penobscot River, including the valley of the St. John's River, which the French claimed as part of Canada. The Indians in this area, considered as "subjects" by both powers, were wooed by both, and the French encouraged the savages to fight off the English expansion — a disastrous warfare that destroyed many English establishments and compelled the English to use force to bring the Indians to peace.

In the interior of North America, the two empires engaged in yet another race for expansion. Both coveted the fur trade with the Indians of the lands around the Great Lakes and in the Ohio Valley; both sides, but especially the English colonies, with their rapidly expanding population, desired the land. As a strategic measure, the French began to establish a line of forts through the interior of the continent to contain the British expansion, a line of forts that stretched from Fort Frontenac on Lake Ontario along the lakes and down the Ohio, Mississippi, and Alabama river valleys to New Orleans, Biloxi, and Mobile on the Gulf of Mexico.

From Acadia to Louisiana and in the Caribbean, then, the competition for empire had produced tensions. The British colonies on the continent of North America were expanding westward chiefly because their populations were growing at a phenomenal rate. The French colonies were on the defensive: their population was hardly more than static; their chief interests in the interior of North America were directed to the fur trade and the problem of containing the English. Above all, the national prestige of France, *la gloire*, was at stake. As the Marquis de la Galissonière, the governor of Canada, said,

We must not flatter ourselves that our Continental Colonies, that is to say, this [Canada] and Louisiana, can ever compete in wealth with the adjoining English Colonies, nor even carry on any very lucrative trade; for, except peltry, the amount of which is limited, and whose profits are and will be always diminishing, we shall scarcely ever have it in our power to furnish any but similar commodities to those of Europe; we shall not be able to supply them at the same price, though mostly of inferior quality, and though ours is an immense country, we have no outlet except by two rivers equally out of the way, whose navigation is inconvenient and perilous.[6]

No, it was not for material profits that France should maintain and defend

[6] La Galissonière to the Comte de Maurepas, September 1, 1748, in E. B. O'Callaghan, ed., *Documents Relative to the Colonial History of the State of New York*, 15 vols. (Albany, 1853–58), X, 134–136.

its possessions in North America; it was something else: "Motives of honor, glory and religion forbid the abandonment of an established Colony; the surrender . . . to a nation inimical by taste, education and religious principle of the French who have emigrated thither . . . , in fine, the giving up of so salutary a work as that of the conversion of the heathen who inhabit that vast continent."[7]

The two empires stood face to face, in fact, all around the world; in America, the moment of showdown had apparently arrived. But the rivalry of the two European imperialisms was no longer merely one for territorial or material gain: it was now a rivalry that was cultural, ideological, religious, nationalistic; the expansion of Europe, which began as a congeries of commercial enterprises, had now become, in the wilderness of North America and in the Caribbean basin, a competition of nationalistic, imperialistic intangibles.

The Treaty of Aix-la-Chapelle had provided for an Anglo-French joint commission to determine certain questions that were expected to arise out of the fact that the dates for the legal beginning of peace had to be accommodated to the length of time it took for news of the treaty to travel around the world. In view of the tensions in America, and apparently because of a genuine desire to resolve the problems that caused them, the French and English governments in 1750 expanded the functions of this commission to include attempts to settle peaceably the questions of ownership and boundaries, both in the Caribbean and on the continent. The commission met for four years without success, during which time the tensions in the Caribbean, in Acadia, in the Great Lakes area, and in the Gulf Coastal Plain all steadily mounted. Fighting erupted in 1754 when an English expedition from Virginia, under the command of Colonel George Washington, attempted to drive the French out of the Ohio Valley. It continued in Acadia where the two powers had built forts confronting each other across the Isthmus of Chignecto, and in the Caribbean where military and civilian groups from both sides competed for the occupation of the "neutral" islands — a competition won by the French.

Meanwhile, the old Anglo-Spanish tensions over the English logwood cutters in Honduras and Yucatan, illicit English trade with Spanish colonies, and the violation of the freedom of the seas (as the English saw it) by the Spanish *guarda costas* reopened, and the brief period of good

[7] *Ibid.*, p. 222.

feeling between England and Spain initiated by the Anglo-Spanish Treaty of Madrid (1750) came to an abrupt end. Trouble between the Spanish and the Portuguese in the Rio de la Plata region, as already noted, had begun again and actual fighting took place in the area, thus completely nullifying the idealistic provisions of the Treaty of Madrid.

At the beginning of the Seven Years War (1756–63), then, the expanding Euroamerican empires stood with daggers drawn, facing each other along the entire length of the American continent. The French and Spanish empires again united against the British and the Portuguese; the Netherlands, for a century the ally of Britain, remained neutral as did its American empire.

American Impacts on
the Development of International Law

By the mid-eighteenth century the expansion of Europe had stretched the tentacles of European civilization into all the world except Australasia and Antarctica (Australasia would be reached by the end of the century). But by that very extension and by the ensuing contacts with the New World and with each other, the European imperial states had felt a certain reverse impact upon their own cultural and institutional life. This was particularly true in the realm of diplomacy and international law.

The opening of new areas of the world raised the question of the ultimate authority under which conquest and settlement might be justified and by which national title to those lands, and their disposability, might be assured. At first, the exploring and conquering countries turned to the pope, as the highest authority in Christendom, for confirmation of their titles to new lands acquired by conquest and for judgments and rulings regarding their rival claims. The pope, as the international arbiter, had obliged by parceling out the "new world," "discovered and to be discovered," to Portugal and Spain by a long series of bulls, beginning in 1455 and continuing well into the sixteenth century.

In Spain itself a remarkable group of legal theorists, including Francisco de Vittoria, Juan Ginés de Sepúlveda, Francisco Suárez, and others, debated the validity of Spain's title to America. The scholarly product of their debate was a clarification of the rights of conquerors over aborigines, the rights of the aborigines themselves, and the right of the pope to award possession of new ports of the world, with their inhabitants, to Christian monarchs. But these legal philosophers did little more in a practical sense than create a great corpus of brilliant theory in the area of international law and relations; they represented an intellectual movement that arose merely as a European reflex action to European expansion.

On the other hand, the de facto relations of the European powers with the native Indians raised the question of how these peoples were to be treated. Were they sovereign nations, and to be regarded as such, or were they to be dealt with otherwise? The Spanish jurists of the sixteenth century generally, if somewhat vaguely, had contended that the Indians constituted sovereign nations and owned and possessed the land. In the eighteenth century the French and the English, in their epic struggle to gain control of the interior of the North American continent, had taken opposite sides on this question: the French maintained that the Indian tribes were sovereign nations, possessors of the land, and that they must be treated as such; the English generally maintained that the Indians were subject peoples who occupied but did not "own" the land, who had placed themselves under the protection of the British king, and who were therefore subject to that king's orders.

Here, again, there was no international consensus. As in affairs pertaining to the freedom of the seas, an imperial government would be likely to uphold one viewpoint when it suited its convenience to do so and to support the opposite position when it suited the national self-interest better.

In a similar way, the appearance of overseas colonies in the course of the expansion of Europe created the problem of establishing an international rule that would govern the use of the seas for getting to them and returning. Under the papal donations, it was assumed that the grant of the lands of the New World carried with it the ownership of the seas that had to be crossed to get to them. Thus Spain, under the Papal Bull *Inter Caetera* of May 4, 1493, which drew a line through the Atlantic Ocean from pole to pole one hundred leagues west of the Azores Islands, claimed sovereignty over the ocean west of that line (as amended by the Treaty of Tordesillas, 1494) until well into the eighteenth century and even later. Similarly, Portugal claimed sovereignty over the seas to the east of that line and south of the Tropic of Cancer.

Other imperialistically inclined nations — France, England, and the Netherlands, in particular — were not disposed to accept this arrogant and arbitrary seizure of both the lands and the seas "beyond the line" by the two Iberian powers. Francis I of France was an early challenger of the Iberian monopoly and enunciated the doctrine of the openness of the world — including the sea — in his famous remark to the Spanish ambassador in Paris in 1540, "I should like to see the clause in Adam's will that excludes me from the division of the world."[8]

The great pronouncement of the doctrine of the freedom of the seas came from Hugo Grotius, a Dutch lawyer, and arose out of the capture of a Portuguese vessel by a Dutch ship in the Indian Ocean during the Dutch War of Independence. The Portuguese, who had previously seized a number of Dutch ships, claimed that the Dutch had no right to sail in the Indian Ocean since it belonged to Portugal under papal grant and the Treaty of Tordesillas. Grotius replied, on the basis of the concept of natural law, that it was the right of the Dutch to trade with any nation willing to trade with them and that, therefore — by the same natural law — they had a right to traverse the seas that had to be crossed to get to them. All nations must be free to trade with all others. No nation could claim ownership of the sea, since the sea cannot be occupied; the sea and the air are the "common possessions of all men and the private possessions of none."[9]

Relations between the imperialistic powers in the New World, especially in America, also raised the question of freedom of the seas. In the eighteenth century the principle of the freedom of the seas was still moot, however. It was most notably involved in the efforts of the Hispanoamerican *guarda costas* to suppress the clandestine trade of Dutch, French, and English interlopers with the Spanish colonies. The *guarda costas* often captured ships of these nations far out on the open sea on the ground that they were violating waters owned by Spain, in which cases those other states found themselves condemning the Spanish seizures as violations of the freedom of the seas. But this principle did not yet have the status of international law. All the nations appealed to it when it suited their purposes and ignored or rejected it when it did not.

Further commentaries on and modification of the principle of the freedom of the seas came with the interimperial wars in America. For

[8] Quoted by Charles de la Roncière, *Histoire de la marine française*, 8 vols. (Paris: Plon-Nourrit, 1899–1934), III, 300.

[9] Hugo Grotius, *De jure praedae commentarius. The Classics of International Law*, ed. James Brown Scott, no. 22. 2 vols. (Oxford: Oxford University Press, 1950), I, 230, 231.

example, during the course of the Seven Years War, England laid down its famous "Rule of the War of 1756," according to which international trade that was prohibited in time of peace could not be carried on with belligerents by neutrals in time of war; vessels violating this rule could be seized on the high seas. This principle was invoked by Americans of all the Euroamerican empires and, most particularly, by the United States, in the course of the Napoleonic wars. Indeed, this concept was at least one of the causes of the War of 1812 between the United States and England.

Out of the colonial situation, also, arose the "doctrine of the two spheres," that is, the idea that Europe had its own system of international law and custom, while the colonial world beyond the "lines of amity"[10] was a new and distinct sphere of international law and relations in which the international customary laws and international treaties (unless they specifically mentioned the New World) did not apply. As a corollary to this doctrine, the colonizing nations had earlier accepted the assumption that "might makes right beyond the line" and that "there is no peace beyond the line"; in short, seizure of ships or territory of one nation by another in America need not necessarily be a cause of war in Europe. Such, in fact, was the specific sense of the Anglo-French Treaty of American neutrality signed at Whitehall in 1686 and of the Hispano-Portuguese Treaty of Madrid of 1750, which proclaimed, as has been noted, "that should war break out between the two crowns in Europe the subjects of both crowns in America would continue in peace, living as though no such war existed, without committing the least hostilities, by themselves or with their allies." The Treaty of Madrid failed to be executed, however, and was repudiated by both signatories. It was formally abrogated by joint agreement in February 1761.

By the eighteenth century, this old customary doctrine of the two spheres was waning, since all the imperial powers, inspired by the new and self-conscious concept of integral, unitary empires, were actively attempting to bind the colonies more closely to the metropolises, and incidents in the colonies could not be ignored. Actually, the Seven Years War in Europe was in considerable measure caused by conflicts between the French and British and the Spanish and British colonies in America.

Yet the doctrine of the two spheres persisted in other ways in imperial

[10] The "lines of amity" were generally recognized as the north and south line of the Treaty of Tordesillas and the Tropic of Cancer.

ideology. European imperial statesmen generally accepted the notion that the maintenance of a balance of power in the colonial world was absolutely necessary for the stability of the balance of power in Europe: the European imperial states derived much of their economic, military, and naval power from their colonies; a loss or gain of colonies meant a loss or gain of power in Europe. Therefore it was of vital interest to Britain, now the dominant European power, to prevent any disturbance of the status quo in the Spanish empire for the benefit of France. It was on the basis of this consideration that Britain caused to be written into the Anglo-Spanish Treaty of Utrecht (1713) a clause by which Spain promised never to alienate any of its American territories to any other nation and by which Britain promised to protect them from alienation. Similarly, Britain compelled France to abjure, in the Anglo-French Treaty, any further acquisition of Spanish colonies.

Thereafter Britain followed a fairly consistent policy of preserving, in the face of France and other nations, the territorial integrity of the Spanish-American empire. This policy, this British "proto-Monroe Doctrine," was revived during the Napoleonic wars and during the wars of Hispanoamerican independence in British proposals to the United States that led to the pronouncement of the United States Monroe Doctrine in 1823.

It would be a mistake, of course, to imagine that Britain ever thought of applying this doctrine of preserving the territorial integrity of the Hispanoamerican empire against its own ambitions in that area. Quite the contrary, indeed; in the War of Jenkins' Ear and in the Seven Years War, Britain was clearly motivated by the impulse to take territories belonging to both France and Spain.

The "doctrine of the two spheres," then, was a very definite element in the evolution of European "customary" international law in the eighteenth century, the product of another clear, reflexive impact of the colonial situation on European institutions.

The experiences of the European imperialist states in the field of monopolistic economic control of colonies also had an obvious influence on international law and relations. This principle of total cultural and economic exclusiveness in the world of discovery had been invented in the fifteenth century, if not earlier, when Portugal and Spain created the first overseas European empires. As an integral part of the ideology of mercantilism, this idea of the national monopoly of colonial exploitation and development was taken for granted by European statesmen: even though a treaty might provide for freedom of commerce between, say, England and Spain in Europe, the terms of that agreement would never be interpreted as applying to trade between their respective colonies in America.

This mercantilist principle of the "closed door" in the colonial empires persisted into and through the eighteenth century. During that century, as has been pointed out, it began to break down, in considerable measure because it could not be enforced in the face of the actual growth of intercolonial trade, but also because of the impact of the free-trade ideas of a number of Enlightened economic thinkers. Thus, while imperial reforms in several of the Euroamerican empires began to water down the rigor of mercantilistic exclusiveness, an increasing number of international treaties were made, especially after the War for United States Independence and during the Napoleonic wars, which envisaged an opening of the international aspects of the old doctrine of the "closed door." With the era of the independence of the American states and the repeal of the English Navigation Acts in the mid-nineteenth century, that old customary principle of European international relations of the colonial period finally disappeared.

Interimperial Relations in America

Although it is true that the formal diplomatic history of America was made by the statesmen of Europe, it is of the greatest importance to record that the Euroamerican colonies themselves were forming a whole series of direct contacts and relationships out of which germinated colonial — "American" — drives and attitudes toward international affairs that represented the enlightened self-interest of the colonies themselves and that did not always coincide with the international objectives and policies of the mother countries.

For example, the de facto intercolonial and interimperial trades, "licit" and "illicit," that took place despite the strict mercantilistic and monopolistic regulations of the central imperial governments gave rise to an experiential acceptance of the idea and the practice of freedom of trade, even in time of war. In time of peace, there was a network of active trades among all the colonies of all the empires, especially in the Caribbean area, and the efforts of the metropolises to control them were largely ineffective. The self-interests of the colonies demanded it and rationalized it. Even the colonial governors connived at it and on occasion defended it against the rebukes of their home ministries. In time of war, notably during the War of the Austrian Succession and the Seven Years War, there was a significant amount of "trading with the enemy" among the colonies of all the Euroamerican empires. These trades, too, were often excused or even defended by colonial governors who realized the importance of such commerce for the economic survival of the colonies over which they presided.[11]

Similarly, in numerous cases, direct contacts and friendly relations between colonies of rival empires led them to adopt, between themselves, agreements and attitudes of isolation toward European wars. Such, for example, had been the Treaty of Sandys Point (1678) between the English and French colonists on the island of St. Christopher in the Caribbean. Such also was the neutralist stance of the New York Assembly toward the War of the Spanish Succession in 1702, and this attitude, supported by the New York and Albany merchants, was revived during the War of the Austrian Succession.

Even more dramatic as an American rejection of European diplomatic settlements was the Guaraní War, waged against the provisions of the

[11] For a discussion of the interimperial trades of the Angloamericans and their rationalization by the Americans, see Savelle, *Origins of American Diplomacy*, pp. 540–545.

International boundaries in America, 1763–77

Hispano-Portuguese Treaty of Madrid of 1750, or, more particularly, against both the Spanish and the Portuguese governments for having made the treaty. Another example of American rejection of a European settlement was the bitter outcry of New England against the recession of Cape Breton to France by the Treaty of Aix-la-Chapelle (1748).

On the other hand, the territorial expansiveness of the Euroamerican empires gave rise, increasingly in the eighteenth century, to a form of native American territorial imperialism. This can be seen in the give-and-take conflicts between Spanish Argentina and Portuguese Brazil in the Rio de la Plata–Paraguay region in South America, the rival expansions of the island colonies in the Caribbean area, especially the French and the British, the bitter clash between the British of Georgia and the Spanish of Florida, and the antagonism between New England and New York on the English side and Canada on the French. In all these cases the colonial governors, usually backed by their home governments, corresponded directly with each other, and in some cases, such as in the Rio de la Plata–Rio Grande do Sul area, in the Georgia-Florida region, on the Virginia-Canada frontier in the Ohio Valley, and in the Acadia-Canada area, attempts were made to settle the disputes by local agreements or understandings.

More important still, out of these contacts and territorial conflicts arising from the expansion of the rival empires there emerged impulses, emotions, and ideas that tended to be American, that tended to differ from the motivations of the European metropolises, or, at least, tended to be American supplements to European imperialisms. In a number of instances the colonial governors and viceroys, aroused by their contacts with rival colonies along the interimperial frontiers, advocated that their metropolises adopt more aggressive imperialistic policies. For example, the Canadian governor Galissonière urged his home government on to greater and more aggressive expansion in North America, even though New France was a losing venture economically: "If the rapid progress of the English Colonies on the Continent be not arrested, or what amounts to the same thing, if a counterpoise capable of confining them within their limits, and of forcing them to the defensive, be not formed, they will possess, in a short time, such great facilities to construct formidable armaments on the Continent of America, and will require so little time to convey a large force either to St. Domingo or to the island of Cuba, or to our Windward islands, that it will not be possible to hope to preserve these except at an enormous expense."[12] But Canada and Louisiana also constituted a bulwark against the English for the Spanish viceroyalty of Mexico: all the more reason for France and Spain to join forces against the expansive English.

[12] The Marquis de la Galissonière, "Memoir on the French Colonies in America" (December 1750), in O'Callaghan, ed., *Documents Relative to the Colonial History of the State of New York*, X, 222–223.

This Euroamerican imperialism of the governors, a Galissonière for France, an Oglethorpe or a Dinwiddie for Britain, a Lavradio for Portugal, or a José Gálvez for Spain, was intense, rigorous, and active even in time of peace; it certainly had a powerful reverse impact on the policies and the imperialisms of the chancelleries of western Europe. But among the creoles the imperialistic drive was just as intense and at times even more intense. Indeed, the creole imperialists often inspired their European governors. In Angloamerica, for example, a considerable number of American statesmen such as Benjamin Franklin of Pennsylvania, William Livingston of New York, and William Shirley of Massachusetts and religious leaders such as Samuel Davies of Virginia, Aaron Burr, Sr., of New Jersey, and Jonathan Mayhew of Massachusetts expressed extremely imperialistic sentiments. But in the mid-eighteenth century, the imperialistic mood among the preachers was religious as well as political, social and nationalistic as well as territorial. As Mayhew voiced it,

Shall the sword rust? . . . Shall our military garments be moth-eaten for want of use, when such things are doing! It is impossible, Gentlemen [of the Massachusetts legislature], you should be any ways backward, or parsimonious, in such a cause as this, a cause wherein the glory of God, the honour of your King, and the good of your country, are so deeply concerned; I might add, a cause whereon the liberties of Europe depend. For of so great consequence is the empire of North America . . . that it must turn the scale of power greatly in favour of the only Monarch, from whom those [British] liberties are in danger; and against the Prince, who is the grand support and bulwark of them. . . . It is even uncertain, Gentlemen, how long you will have an House to sit in, unless a speedy and vigorous opposition is made to the present [French] encroachments, and to the further designs, of our enemies![13]

Or, as Burr put it,

God has in his sovereign Goodness, chosen the *British Nation* to be the *Bulwark* of the Reformation; to hold up a Standard against those *Superstitions* and *Impostures* [of Rome]. . . . On the one Hand, there is *Poverty, Slavery*, Persecution and Death; on the other, a fruitful Country [Angloamerica], pleasant Habitations, *British* Liberty, and what is dearer than all, undefiled Christianity. . . . I doubt not, by the Smiles of Heaven, we should soon make our Enemies flee before us, and again sit quietly under our Vines and Fig-Trees, and eat the Good of the Land.[14]

[13] Jonathan Mayhew, *A Sermon Preach'd in the Audience of His Excellency William Shirley, Esq . . . May 29th, 1754* (Boston, 1754), pp. 32–47.
[14] Aaron Burr, *A Discourse Delivered in New-Ark, in New Jersey, January 1, 1755* (New York, 1755), pp. 29, 40.

Such was the imperialistic vision: *Canada delenda est*! But it was an Angloamerican who was proclaiming it, and not (for the moment) an Englishman.

This native American imperialism does not appear to have been quite so clearly and distinctly expressed, as yet, in the Iberoamerican empires. Nevertheless, it existed even there, especially between the Lusoamericans and the Hispanoamericans. It also seems apparent that imperialistic sentiments were more intense and powerful among the creole Americans than among their fellow subjects in their European homelands.

The Seven Years War in America

The Seven Years War, which broke upon the Western world in 1756, was a world war that involved not only Europe and its balance of power but also practically every overseas area into which the expansion of Europe had reached — India, Africa, and the American hemisphere. So far as the colonial world was concerned, the war was a universal, life-and-death struggle between two giant empires, the French and the British. The British empire won chiefly because, whereas France had to divide its war efforts, enormous as they were, between its continental European interests and the defense and expansion of its overseas colonies, Britain was able to subsidize its brilliant ally Frederick II of Prussia and direct almost all its military power to the war in the colonies.

The fighting actually began in America, in the Ohio Valley in 1754, the same year in which the French East India Company and the British East India Company had signed a provisional treaty ending for the time being their long war in India. A year later the Seven Years War spread to Nova Scotia and the West Indies. The American conflict triggered the explosive international situation in Europe; war in Europe broke out formally in 1756 and rapidly spread around the world. In America, the English took Louisbourg (Cape Breton) from the French in 1758 and then went on to capture Quebec in 1759 and Montreal in 1760. In the Caribbean area the English seized the French islands, one by one; Martinique fell in 1761 and all the neutral islands and Guadeloupe followed in 1762.

When Spain entered the war on the side of France in 1762, England quickly took Havana and the Philippines. Spanish armies invaded Portugal, and Spanish forces from Buenos Aires once more captured Colonia do Sacramento, as already related. The outcome of the war was a decisive victory for England and its allies, a victory documented by the Treaty of Paris (1763) negotiated by William Pitt for England and the Duke of Choiseul for France.[15]

More American territory changed hands by the Peace of Paris than by any other international settlement before or since. By the Anglo-French Treaty, to which Spain and Portugal assented, all of Canada and the eastern half of the Mississippi Valley were ceded to England. Although British conquests in the French West Indies were restored, England kept all the neutral islands except St. Lucia, which was recognized as French. Cuba was returned to Spain, but England retained Florida; Colonia do Sacramento again was given back to Portugal; however, because of an ambiguity in the treaty Spain hung on to Rio Grande do Sul, which it had taken during the war. By the separate Franco-Spanish Treaty of Fontainebleau, France gave Louisiana to Spain as compensation for the loss of Florida.

The international balance of power in America was thus heavily "rectified" in favor of England and its ally Portugal. But the new balance — or imbalance — was not to last; soon it would be rectified again, not so much by the direct efforts of the losers in the Seven Years War, although they did what they could to accelerate the march of history, but chiefly by the secession of thirteen important British colonies in America from the British empire, an event which opened a new era in the history of the New World, the era of American independence.

---

[15] Pitt resigned in a huff just before the treaty was signed. It was actually signed for England by the Earl of Bute.

CHAPTER 7

Religion in America
in the Eighteenth Century

Religion in the Hemisphere

The Europeans who had emigrated to America in the early centuries of the expansion of Europe were all Christians, except for a small number of Jews. The religious character of their new colonial societies, therefore, was predominately Christian, and in this sense America became a new Christian area. The theology of Christianity, together with its social and ethical outlook, had emigrated to America with the conquerors, the merchants, the politicians, and the humble colonists, so that the Christian culture complex established itself everywhere in the hemisphere.[1]

Religion had been one of the major facets — or, rather, the major cultural facet — of the expansion of Europe and was an integral part of it. The Europeans who had emigrated to America, in addition to their economic and political incentives and their desire for adventure and glory, were powerfully motivated by sincere, often fanatical, religious drives to propagate Christianity. Some of them had simply wished to carry the Cross with them and establish it wherever they went; many were compelled by their hope to convert the heathen pagans of the New World to the true faith; some, like the Spanish or Portuguese Jews, the French Huguenots, and the English Puritans, had fled to America to escape religious discomfort or persecution at home.

Viewed as a whole, the migration of so many Europeans to America,

[1] See volume IV of this series.

150

most of them Christians, appears on the surface to have been a single phenomenon characterized by a basic religious unity. To a large extent this was true of the Roman Catholic migrations, for, despite their national differences, all the Catholics in America looked ultimately to the Holy See in Rome as their highest religious authority. Non-Christians, even Christian non-Catholics, were not permitted to participate in these Roman Catholic migrations. Numerous efforts were made to keep Catholicism pure, and the institution known as the Inquisition, or Holy Office, exercised its functions in the name of religious unity in all the Roman Catholic areas of colonization. Similarly, in the Protestant areas of colonization there was a certain degree of exclusiveness, although it was not nearly as determined, intense, or effective as in the Catholic empires.

Despite the appearance of religious unity, the Christianity that had come to America was by no means a seamless whole. This was especially true in the eighteenth century, and it became more and more so as the century wore on. Even among the hundreds of thousands of Roman Catholics who emigrated to America, there were significant internal differences, as will appear. Among the Protestants, too, there were intranational differences in religion, for example, between the English Anglicans and those of more Calvinist (Puritan or Presbyterian) persuasion. Although many internal differences existed, especially among the Protestants, the expansion of the national religion (or religions) was an integral part of the expanding culture of the colonizing nation. In language, in institutional structure — even, in some cases, in theology — the Christianity of every colonizing nation differed, in one degree or another, from that of the others. Religion, too, was a strong cultural bond between the colonies and their mother countries. In short, religion was one of the major cultural and institutional instrumentalities of national imperial expansion.

Each of the three Catholic empires enjoyed a high degree of national authority in the administration of church affairs. Under the terms of ancient concordats between the kings and the popes, the kings had the power of making appointments to ecclesiastical offices and of formulating laws and ordinances for church matters throughout their realms, both in Europe and in America. The church government in the nation and empire, headed by the king, paralleled the hierarchy of state officials, also headed by the king. There was in every case a formal but not always a clear division of labor between the church and the state because the overlapping functions in many areas caused much bickering, antagonism, and outright rivalry for power. Nevertheless, the national church was a powerful arm of the state for religious, moral, social, missionary, and educational purposes.

The vast majority of Angloamerican colonists were members of the Anglican church, whose doctrinal head was the archbishop of Canterbury and whose secular head under the Act of Supremacy of Queen Elizabeth I was the king. Other Protestants in Angloamerica were independent of the imperial government in religious matters, but some of them created established churches of their own. In the Dutch colonies the Classis of Amsterdam, ruling body of the Dutch Reformed church, cooperated closely with the Dutch West India Company and the States-General.

When the Europeans arrived in America, they organized their religious life around the same religious institutions they had known at home. The Christian churches in America were in effect extensions of the churches of Europe. But under the impact of their experiences in America, the colonists had by the eighteenth century modified the old institutions and even, in some cases, the doctrines. This was true in one degree or another throughout the hemisphere; it was particularly true in those areas where there was a heavy immigration of Africans, with their different religions. In those places, African cults, sometimes tinctured with Christianity, were of profound and lasting significance to the black population. Similar phenomena characterized the areas largely peopled by Indians.

Of course, the churches everywhere ministered to the religious needs of the colonists. Their activities, however, were not limited strictly to the performance of religious ritual and to the salvation of Christian souls. In varying degrees in the different areas of colonization, the churches also engaged in social work, such as charity, the establishment and the operation of hospitals and, above all, education. In all the colonial areas, the churches were little concerned with slavery, generally accepting the institution without question. Many of the churches, religious orders, and even individual members of the clergy held slaves. The first clear religious opposition to slavery as such was expressed by the Quakers in the Angloamerican empire, beginning about 1700.

In the eighteenth century, the purity of the Catholic church, such as it had been in America, had come to be corrupted by the influences

of African and Amerind religions; in the course of the century, this dilu-
tion was furthered by the impact of the Enlightenment. The multiplicity
of Protestant sects in the British and Dutch empires was augmented
by the emigration of more sects from Germany, Switzerland, Scotland,
Sweden, and elsewhere, while the number of Jews slowly but steadily
increased. The result of this combination of circumstances was that the
Christianity of America in the eighteenth century was much more poly-
glot than it was in Europe. Because of this diversity, as well as the liberalizing tendencies of Enlightenment rationalism in America, there
was a notable extension of the principles and the practice of religious
toleration, especially in the Dutch and British colonies.

Besides the churches' ministering to the religious, social, and intellectual needs of their European constituents, the major and most significant aspect of the expansion of Christianity in America was the work
of converting the native Indians to the Christian faith. This missionary
movement reached its apogee in the eighteenth century.

The Indians of Mexico and Mesoamerica — the Toltecs, Aztecs,
Zapotecs, Mayas, and others — already had highly sophisticated religions
when the Europeans arrived, as did the Incas of Peru. These religions
had been subdued by Christianity during the first centuries of colonization.[2]

The Indians in other parts of the hemisphere — in North America,
the valley of the Amazon, etc. — practiced a wide variety of primitive,
essentially animistic, nature cults, which were not significantly
institutionalized and were almost entirely devoid of anything that might
be called theology. The Christians, in the course of the sixteenth and
seventeenth centuries, had made conscious efforts to convert the Indians
to Christianity, and the church in the Catholic empires had made numerous attempts to protect the Indians from enslavement by the white men
as well as from other activities springing from the white men's rapacity,
lust, and greed.

At the beginning of the eighteenth century, there already existed a
line of Christian missions along the frontier from the St. Lawrence–
Great Lakes basin in North America to the valley of the Rio de la Plata
in South America. The missions of Canada were conducted by the French
Jesuits and other orders (Montreal was still a Sulpician mission); those
in Mexico were run by the Spanish Jesuits, Franciscans, Dominicans,

[2] See volume IV of this series.

Indians of Brazil, early nineteenth century. From Johann M. Rugendas,
Viagem pitoresca através do Brasil, plate 3/4. Courtesy of the
University of Washington Library.

and others; the missions of Peru were in the hands of the Jesuits; those
of Brazil were operated by Portuguese Jesuits and others. The famous
missions in the valley of the Rio de la Plata were under the auspices
of the Spanish Jesuits. While other orders did notable missionary work
among the Indians, the operations of the Portuguese, Spanish, and
French Jesuits, although guided by separate national plans, actually constituted a genuine and significant international movement, directed, in
an overall way, by the supreme general of the order in Rome.

The methods of these missions differed somewhat among themselves.
Those of Canada were managed by priests who went out to the Indian
villages and resided there. They erected chapels where they were permitted to do so, they learned the Indian languages, and they preached
Christianity to the Indians; they also did a certain amount of medical
and social work and served as political or diplomatic agents of France
in the eternal struggle of that country against Britain.

The Spanish missions, wherever they were, were religiously organized and governed communities, which regulated every detail of the Indians' daily life. The most famous of the Spanish missionary communities were those established in the upper Rio de la Plata Valley; they were subject to strict religious rule, and here the Indians were taught the skills of the European trades and their native arts were encouraged and cultivated along with those derived from European culture.

This continental system of Spanish missions flourished during the mid-eighteenth century, but, after the expulsion of the Jesuits in the third quarter of the century, it was taken over by other orders. In the 1770s it was extended by the Franciscans northward into California as far as San Francisco Bay. Never again, however, was it to be as effective or as important a spearhead of the advancing European culture as it had been.

The Portuguese missionary system was much like that of the Spaniards. Missionary communities of Indians were founded in the interior of Brazil along the rivers that flowed eastward, especially in the valleys of the San Francisco and the Amazon.

In the Protestant empires the missionary impulse, while not entirely dead in the eighteenth century, was of little historic significance. Among the Dutch and the Danes, the missionary incentive hardly existed at all in the eighteenth century.

When the Jesuits were expelled from Portugal and its colonies (1759), from France and its colonies (1762), and from Spain and its colonies (1767), the missionary work of the Christians in the American hemisphere received a body blow from which it never recovered. The work was continued by other orders, notably the Franciscans, but most of the missions eventually fell into decay and were abandoned.

The religious and intellectual life of America in the eighteenth century was marked — as were the other aspects of life — by a great and brilliant expansion, if by that word is meant a broadening and deepening of man's understanding of the universe and of his own place in it. Not only did this signify a continuing growth of man's knowledge of the geography of the earth, which was the essential intellectual characteristic of the expansion of Europe; it also included a continuation of the scientific revolution that had burst upon Europe in the seventeenth century, with its new insights into the nature of matter and of the laws governing the behavior of matter in the physical universe, into the characteristics of life, into the nature of man and of his knowledge, and into the nature of human society and its institutions.[3]

Inevitably, it would seem, this intellectual revolution had to affect the religious outlook of America. Thus, largely as a consequence of the implications of science, but also in large measure because of the actual daily experiences of the Europeans in the New World, religion in both its theological and its practical aspects was significantly modified. This meant that there appeared in American, as well as in European, Christianity a way of thinking about religion called "rationalism." This philosophy, born of the impact of science upon religious thought, applied to religion the logical implications of science and the concepts of natural law derived from it. The result was a critical questioning, even a rejection, of much of the supernatural element in Christianity and a revolutionary new faith in the dignity of the human being and his rational capacity both to know and use the laws of nature, which were considered to be the laws of God, and to choose rationally between good and evil, thus effecting his own salvation.

This phase of the European Enlightenment, as it migrated to America, also gave birth to a new anticlericalism and a number of modern forms of religion — not merely a rational orthodoxy, but such new creeds as Deism, Unitarianism, and Universalism. The rationalistic mood was strongest and most articulate in Angloamerica, but indirectly through the writing of Voltaire, Diderot, the Encyclopedists, and many others, it infiltrated even the most orthodox areas of Catholic America. Needless to say, it gave the Inquisition in America much work to do; yet its seed took root and grew, to influence and to color religion everywhere in the hemisphere.

Partly out of the Enlightenment's rationalistic approach to religion, partly under the influence of science, but mostly, it seems, out of the sheer expediency of a de facto situation in which many different religions were rubbing elbows with each other, there flowered, in the eighteenth century, in many parts of the Atlantic community, a new international religious and intellectual phenomenon — a genuine and positive theory and practice of religious toleration. The appearance of this phenomenon, accompanied by its concomitant theory of the separation of the church from the state, was most dramatic and clear in Protestant Angloamerica.

[3] For the impact of modern science upon the intellectual life of America, see below, chapter 8.

But it was also evident, in one degree or another, all over the hemisphere. It was discouraged and retarded, to be sure, by the work of the Inquisition and by the political authorities in the Roman Catholic empires; nevertheless, it germinated even there, to bear fruit in the anticlerical movements of the nineteenth and twentieth centuries.

One of the most striking international aspects of the history of religion in America in the eighteenth century was that religion was related to and used as an instrument of the rival imperialistic expansions of the Euroamerican empires. This was true in numerous instances, such as the Hispano-Portuguese confrontation over the valley of the Rio de la Plata; it was most notable, however, in the international conflicts between Protestant and Roman Catholic expansionists. Many of the religious leaders of Protestant Angloamerica, for example, assumed a nationalistic stance against the French in the imperialistic expansion of British North America.

It was in such a religious imperialistic mood that many Angloamerican Protestant leaders proclaimed the superior purity and religious quality of the British empire over the others. Toward the end of the Seven Years War, the "gentle Puritan" Rev. Ezra Stiles sincerely felt that divine Providence, by eliminating the French from North America, was surely

making way for the planting and Erection in this land [of] the best policied Empire that has yet appeared in the World. In which Liberty and property will be secured. . . . Again we are planting an Empire of better Laws and Religion. . . . It is probable that in time there will be found a provincial Confederacy and a common Council standing on free provincial Election. And this may in time some hundred years hence terminate in an imperial Diet. . . .
This Land may be renowned for Science and Arts. . . .[4]

The Reverend Samuel Davies called upon his fellow Virginians to rally to the cause of the interimperial conflict:

and shall these Ravages [of the French and their Indian allies] go on unchecked? Shall *Virginia* incur the Guilt, and the everlasting Shame of tamely exchanging her Liberty, her Religion, and her All, for arbitrary *Gallic* Power, and for Popish Slavery, Tyranny, and Massacre? Alas! Are there none of her Children, that enjoyed all the Blessings of her Peace, that will espouse her Cause, and befriend her now in the Time of her Danger? Are *Britons* utterly degenerated by so short a Remove from

[4] Quoted in Edmund S. Morgan, *The Gentle Puritan: A Life of Ezra Stiles, 1727–1795* (New Haven, Conn.: Yale University Press, 1962), pp. 213–214.

their Mother-Country? Is the Spirit of Patriotism entirely extinguished among us? And must I give thee up for lost, O my Country! and all that is included in that important Word?[5]

In a similar mood, James Sterling of Annapolis, Maryland, "pathetically" urged the Maryland Assembly to take up the course of British expansion:

Let me tell you, my worthy countrymen . . . The eyes of your sister-colonies are upon you. . . . The eyes of your venerable mother-nation will be upon you, who requires and expects, that . . . you will imitate her parliaments in a suitable conduct, when French invasions are threaten'd. . . . Nay, gentlemen, the Argus' eyes of the very French are upon you, who, by their various and conceal'd emissaries, undisguis'd jesuits, pardoned rebels, and traiterous malcontents, will have dispatched to them at Quebec, or even Paris, the accounts of your pro-ceedings. . . . O permit not the zeal of a true public spirit to cool in your breasts; but . . . improve it in yourselves . . . and transmit the hallowed principle to your children's children, to latest posterity; till only the day of Judgment and the Kingdom of Christ put a period to the British dominion in our *new world*; or till time shall be lost in eter-nity.[6]

If Angloamericans were less ardent than their Spanish, Portuguese, and French countrymen in the advancement of Christianity among the Indians, they were, by contrast, more zealous in their use of religion to rationalize their imperialistic impulses toward their Euroamerican rivals.

Religion in the Separate Empires

The Portuguese Empire

Portuguese Brazil, in the eighteenth century, was solidly Roman Catholic, although substantial numbers of blacks worshiped African cults while the Indians not in missions clung to their own indigenous religions. Under the so-called *Padroado*, or ancient concessions from the pope, the king of Portugal appointed the archbishop and the bishops of the church in Brazil as well as the high officials of the regular orders, Jesuits,

[5] Samuel Davies, *Religion and Patriotism the Constituents of a Good Soldier* (Philadelphia, 1758), pp. 4–5.
[6] James Sterling, *Zeal against the Enemies of Our Country Pathetically Recommended* (Annapolis, 1755), pp. 21–22, 30.

Franciscans, Dominicans, Augustinians, Carmelites, and others, all of which were governed by central offices in Portugal. Under the *Padroado*, too, church rules, ordinances, laws, bulls, and other instructions for the church workers in the colony were scrutinized by the Board of Conscience and Orders or by the Overseas Council; any such documents as were disapproved would not be sent.

The king of Portugal's authority in the Brazilian church was not as rigorously or as effectively applied as was the king of Spain's power in the affairs of the church in Hispanoamerica, and there seems to have been little tension between church and state until Pombal became minister. Yet the church was in a very real sense an arm of the state; after Pombal's time it was even more subservient to the state than before.

The church itself was directed in the colony by an archbishop residing in Bahia (later in Rio de Janeiro), under whom there were bishops at Maranhão, Pernambuco, Rio de Janeiro, and other important centers of population. Every bishopric was divided into parishes; in these parishes the secular priests preached and performed the sacraments, conducted schools, did social work, and otherwise ministered to the spiritual and social needs of their parishioners. On the great plantations there were often priests who served as chaplains and who took care of the needs of their patrons and their slaves.

The duties of the "regular" clergy in the religious orders were of a more specific variety. All of them, but especially the Jesuits, the Franciscans, and the Dominicans, participated in missionary enterprises. The Dominicans were particularly interested in education; the Carmelites were noted for establishing and maintaining hospitals. Although the church tolerated slavery (many of the church dignitaries had slaves), it insisted (not always with success) that the human personality of the slave be recognized and that the slaves be given the right to participate in the normal activities of Christians — to attend worship, to marry (though not many did), and to raise families; it also encouraged and facilitated, where it could, the possibility of manumission. Its view of miscegenation was a tolerant one, and it was probably because of this attitude that the mulattoes in Brazil apparently enjoyed a better social status than did those in other colonial areas. It may be true that the Christian church in Brazil was somewhat more humane in its attitudes toward and its treatment of slavery and the slaves than anywhere else in the hemisphere.[7] But the church did little or nothing of a practical sort to ameliorate the conditions of slavery or to weaken the institution, of which, with most of the eighteenth-century world, it approved.

The Brazilian missions were located along the frontiers of the Indian country in the interior. The Indians were gathered together in communities, or *aldeias*, where they were taught the Christian religion and the crafts and arts of European civilization. In these communities they were safe from the exploitative rapacity of the whites (they were exempt from the concerns of the Inquisition), and they were governed well, if in a regimented fashion, by their religious protectors. But the rigorous discipline of the Jesuits, for example, failed to modify significantly the Indian way of life. The *aldeias* were, in effect, "orphanages" or boarding schools "run by prudish if devout priests."[8] By forcing the Indians to wear clothing and to live according to a strict European morality, the Jesuits probably did the Indians more harm than good.

One of the reforms of Minister Pombal was initiated in an effort to absorb the Indians into European society. He therefore invited them to become citizens, on condition that they adopt the white man's way of life. Although some did, the experiment was hardly a success because the Indians found it difficult to adapt themselves to the white man's ways and they tended to remain in the lowest and poorest stratum of society. Others fled to the forest, while many preferred to remain in their old mission communities, which gradually disappeared. From the eighteenth century onward, almost all the Indians in Brazil remained in the jungle, separated by wide forests and by an even broader and deeper cultural gap from the civilization of the whites.

The most striking and picturesque characteristic of the Christian church in Brazil was the degree to which it was influenced by, and even assimilated into its own worship, the mysteries and the practices of the African cults of the black slaves. These cults were permitted, and there were many black brotherhoods and charitable organizations among the blacks. These brotherhoods preserved many African dances and rites which were often performed in the entryways of the Christian

[7] For convincing dissenting discussions of this question, see Carl N. Degler, *Neither White nor Black: Slavery and Race Relations in Brazil and the United States* (New York: Macmillan, 1971), and Robert Conrad, *The Destruction of Brazilian Slavery, 1850–1888* (Berkeley: University of California Press, 1972).

[8] Charles R. Boxer, *The Golden Age of Brazil 1695–1750: Growing Pains of a Colonial Society* (Berkeley: University of California Press, 1964), p. 21.

churches. These brotherhoods also continued to practice the African cults, with their sorcerers, magic, and witchcraft. The blacks engaged in public processions (many under the auspices of the Catholic church) in which fetishes were displayed along with the Christian saints and symbols. Indeed, while most of the blacks rarely had more than the faintest notion of what Christianity really meant, they found it very easy to adopt the saints and the rituals of Christianity as their own. At times there were even black Catholic priests. Thus the impact of Christianity on the blacks, as well as on the Indians, though practically universal, was usually only superficial.

In many of the areas of Brazil where the blacks came in contact with Christianity such Christian institutions as marriage were discouraged among them. Sacramental marriage and the building of a family were prerogatives reserved only for the white masters. Again, there was much concubinage of black women among the white males, including many of the clergy. As a matter of fact, the whites generally encouraged this practice, since its tangible and economically valuable result was the increase of mulatto slaves. Often the children of clerics by their black concubines were given social preferment; a few of them went so far as to enter the university in the footsteps of their fathers.

The role of Christianity in civilizing the non-Christians in Brazil was always significant, but it was especially so during the eighteenth century. As one authority has said,

It is certain that Catholicism, through the influence of Indians and Negroes, had already been considerably altered in the purity of its ethical ideals and philosophy of life. In many other aspects, however, the Catholic Church inculcated everlasting values which has [sic] permitted the dissolution of the slave-system and the integration of the descendants of slaves — Negroes, mulattoes or near-whites — into Brazilian society without deep shocks or intolerable tensions, indeed, with a sense of peaceful convivencia [coexistence] and tolerance which impress upon this society a particular cachet [stamp].[9]

Hispanoamerica

The Christians who emigrated to America from Spain were also Roman Catholics. The titular head of the church in Hispanoamerica was the

[9] René Ribeiro, "Relations of the Negro with Christianity in Portuguese America," *History of Religion in the New World: Studies Presented at the Conference on the History of Religion in the New World during Colonial Times*, ed. Antonio S. Tibesar (Washington, D.C.: Institute of Franciscan History, 1958), pp. 118–148. The passage quoted is on p. 131.

cardinal archbishop of Seville. However, under the terms and the exercise of the *Patronato*, the body of papal concessions to the Spanish kings, the king of Spain nominated the cardinal as well as the bishops of the Sees of Spain and the Indies. The Council of the Indies scrutinized all the ordinances, laws, and instructions sent to the church officials in Hispanoamerica. In effect, then, the Spanish state had a decisive influence — even control — over the most vital institutional activities of the church in America.

In the eighteenth century, the old method of dividing church administration in the colonies into two districts, "northern" and "southern," persisted. The two leading archbishoprics in the northern district were those of Mexico and Santo Domingo; those of the southern district were centered in Bogotá and Lima. Other archbishoprics had been established at Guatemala, Caracas, and elsewhere. Under these archbishoprics were some thirty-five bishoprics which were divided into parishes, each with its own parish church presided over by one or more priests. As in other Catholic countries, the functions of these priests were those of preaching and administering the sacraments, moral supervision of the people, and a certain amount of educational and social work.

The Inquisition was more active in the Spanish colonies than in any other colonial area. This church court, or "Holy Office," directed its activities to the business of maintaining the purity of the Catholic faith, exterminating heretics and heresies, censoring books and learning, etc. It persecuted Jews, "philosophes," Protestants, and even Catholic "Jansenists" and rationalists within the fold of the church itself. It actively sought to suppress all ideas that were critical of or departed from the orthodoxy of Catholicism. The intensity and effectiveness of its work varied, however, from place to place.

Despite the Inquisition, the new ideas of the eighteenth century succeeded in penetrating the Spanish colonies and profoundly influenced not only the Catholic religion itself but also religious and political thought in general.

In another field of endeavor, the church's efforts to Christianize the Indians never quite stamped out the pagan cults of the Indians. The church looked upon the pagan ideas and practices — the nature worship of the Indians, for example — as idolatry. But they continued to be observed in remote areas, and many of their symbolisms, even some of their rituals, were assimilated into the Christian church itself.

View of the Great Square and cathedral of Mexico City, about 1800. From Alexander von Humboldt and A. Bonpland, *Voyage aux regions equinoxiales du Nouveau Continent* . . . 3 vols. and 2 atlas vols. (Paris: F. Schoell, 1814), plate III. Courtesy of The Newberry Library, Chicago.

Like its counterpart in the Portuguese empire the Spanish Catholic religion in Hispanoamerica absorbed certain elements of the African cults of the black slaves. This assimilation, or "voodooism," was not, however, as widespread or as significant a religious phenomenon in Hispanoamerica as it was in Lusoamerica or in the French colonies in the West Indies.

The most dramatic endeavor of the Catholic church in Spanish America during the eighteenth century was the further development of the Indian missions.

Many orders participated in missionary work, but the Jesuits were probably the most active, and the territorial sweep of their missions was certainly the most extensive. In the upper valley of the Rio de la Plata (modern Paraguay and Uruguay), as elsewhere, they gathered the Indians into communities, called *reducciones*, where the natives were taught not only Christianity but trades, agricultural skills, and arts and crafts. The Jesuits governed these communities strictly, effectively, and paternalistically; the Indians became, to all intents and purposes, wards of the white men. Under the Jesuit government the "missionary republic" became rich and powerful, indeed so powerful and haughty that the directors of the missions felt free to defy the orders of the Spanish king — an attitude which eventually led to their banishment from America (as well as Spain) in 1767.

When the Jesuits were expelled, the Dominicans and the Franciscans took over much of their work. The great heyday of the mission system passed, however, with the expulsion of the Jesuits.

Elsewhere, missionary work continued to expand during the last quarter of the eighteenth century. In 1769 Father Junípero Serra, a Franciscan monk, founded a line of missions northward along the west coast of North America into California. By 1776 these missions extended as far north as the modern San Francisco.

As in the other Roman Catholic empires, the church in the Hispanoamerican empire was supported chiefly by tithes paid by the parishioners. The state also assisted the church in many ways and intervened in the administration of its property. The church acquired vast properties everywhere; it built magnificent churches in all the important cities, became the largest landowner in the empire, and possessed much wealth of other kinds — gold and silver, commercial and industrial enterprises, slaves. The relationship between the church and the state was generally very close; in many instances the state even cooperated with the church in the enforcement of religious and intellectual unity.

As the eighteenth century wore on, the role of the church in the life of the Spanish colonies was subjected to the impact of two new forces at work in Hispanoamerican life and society. The first of these was the subtle influence of the European Enlightenment; the second was the growth of nationalism — or, rather, separate local nationalisms — in the various regions of Hispanoamerica.

The Enlightenment was the intellectual mood that characterized the European climate of opinion during the eighteenth century.[10] Among its outstanding exponents were Voltaire, Montesquieu, Vattel, Diderot, Locke, d'Alembert, Rousseau, Hume, Gibbon, d'Holbach, the Abbé Raynal, the American scientist-philosopher Benjamin Franklin, and many others. It was permeated by a faith in science, in the power of human reason, and in the possibility of progress in human affairs. In religion they were often Deists, and many of them were anticlerical, decrying the superstitions, the intolerance, and the corruptions of the churches, but especially the Catholic church.

[10] See below, chapter 8.

Despite the Inquisition and the Index (the list of prohibited books published by the church), the ideologies of the Enlightenment filtered into the thinking and the writing of leading Hispanoamerican intellectuals, even many members of the clergy itself. The science of the Enlightenment found its way into the curriculums of the schools and universities, and many of the Hispanoamerican leaders found it possible to possess and to read the books on the Index.

The other major intellectual or psychological force at work among Hispanoamericans was that of a nascent nationalism. This force, already noted in connection with the evolution of political institutions and thought, also had an impact on religion. For example, as the numbers of *criollos* in holy orders increased, there appeared a distinctly "American" attitude in the administration of religious affairs. Quarrels between *criollos* and *peninsulares* among the clergy were frequent, and the *criollos*, through their extensive and powerful connections with civil affairs, were generally to be found on the side of the regional or national or "American" leaders in their relations with the mother country. When the wars of independence finally burst upon Hispanoamerica, many of the leaders of the independence movements were *criollo* members of the clergy.

Francoamerica

In the French empire the "Gallican Liberties" of the mother country influenced the practices of the church very much as the *Patronato* in the Spanish empire and the *Padroado* in the Portuguese. The government of the Catholic church in Francoamerica was centered in the cardinal archbishop of Paris. Under the "Gallican Liberties," this official, as well as the bishops and other clergy in the colonies, was appointed by the king of France. There were three bishops in the colonies, one resident in Quebec, another in Fort-de-France, Martinique, the capital city of the French Windward Islands, and the third in Port-au-Prince, the capital of Saint-Domingue (Haiti) and the surrounding islands, that is, the French Leeward Islands. In each of the three colonial divisions (Canada, French Windward Islands, and French Leeward Islands) the bishop shared the responsibilities of government with the governor and the intendant. Each bishopric was divided into parishes, and each parish was administered by one or more priests. On the *seigneuries* in Canada and on the plantations of the West Indies there were often chaplains, just as there were on the great plantations of Brazil. In the French empire, too, as in the Portuguese and Spanish empires, the church was in a very real sense an arm of the state. It was responsible for upholding the institutions of marriage, education, and morality and for certain aspects of relations with the Indians.

As in the Portuguese and Spanish colonies, a number of "regular" orders, Jesuits, Franciscans, and Dominicans, were established in the French colonies. Montreal, in Canada, was a fief of the Sulpician order. These orders devoted themselves to education, the erection of hospitals and orphanages, and, especially in Canada, missionary work with the Indians. Each order had its provincial leader and its head in Paris, who worked in considerable independence of the secular clergy.

By the eighteenth century, the Indians of the French West Indies had been well-nigh exterminated. Missionary work there, never very significant, had all but ended. In Canada, however, the French missions to the Indians were still extensive, active, and very important in affairs other than religious. In fact the missions, chiefly Jesuit, constituted one of the spearheads of French expansion into the interior of North America, and the missionaries, mostly Jesuits, were the political agents of the French crown among the Indians.

The methods of the French missionaries in North America differed rather radically from those of their colleagues in Portuguese and Hispanic America. While in those areas the Indians were gathered into *reducciones*, in North America the missionaries went out to the villages of the natives — a hunting people — and lived there, moving with the tribes, improvising altars and chapels, and preaching the Christian doctrine as best they could. They made few converts, but they performed important services as liaison agents between the French and the Indians, not only in religious affairs but also in the political relations of France with the Indians. They were, in truth, far-flung advance agents of European culture and imperialism. This role did not last for the Jesuits, however, for they were expelled from the French empire in 1762. After that, their places were taken by members of the other religious orders, such as the Franciscans.

In the French West Indies the influence of African cults — assimilated, more or less, into the Christian religion — was strong among the black population. The result was the appearance of a powerful and persistent form of "voodooism" that dominated the religious life of the French West Indian blacks.

The Dutch Colonies

Practically all the whites in the Dutch-American colonies were of the Dutch Reformed branch of Christianity, a Dutch brand of Calvinism ruled over by the "Classis" (a form of presbytery) in Amsterdam. The Dutch colonies enjoyed a high degree of religious toleration, however, and the white population included Jews, Anglicans, French Huguenots, and other sects.

Angloamerica

A large majority of the colonists in Angloamerica were members of the Anglican church. The head of this church was the archbishop of Canterbury; American affairs of the church fell under the authority of the bishop of London (there was no Anglican bishop in America). In a number of the northern English colonies in Angloamerica, in the southern continental colonies, and in the British West Indies, the Anglican was the established church. These provinces were divided into parishes, each of which had a church presided over by a pastor, or curate.

In addition to the Anglicans, there were a large number of other Protestant religions in Angloamerica. In the northeastern colonies the predominant forms were Congregational and Presbyterian, both Calvinistic in theology; in the middle colonies there were many Quakers and German sectaries. Throughout the British colonies, but especially in the middle group of colonies on the continent, there were other sects such as Lutherans, Moravians, and Baptists. There were also some Jews and some scattered concentrations of Roman Catholics.

In Angloamerica the spirit of the religious rationalism of the eighteenth century had its most powerful American development. Under the impact of Newtonian science and the rationalistic writings of Anthony Ashley Cooper, Dr. Samuel Clarke, Francis Hutcheson, John Locke, and other English thinkers, a distinguished minority of Angloamerica's religious and intellectual leaders discarded much of the supernaturalism and religious determinism of Calvinism. In the preaching and the writing of such men as Charles Chauncy and Jonathan Mayhew of Boston, Cadwallader

Colden of New York, and Benjamin Franklin of Philadelphia, a whole galaxy of rationalistic religious ideas appeared and became institutionalized. This wave of liberal religious thought gave rise to the beginnings in America of such new religious beliefs as Deism, Unitarianism, Universalism, and even atheism. Above all, the rationalists were characterized by their faith in the power of human reason to know and to choose the good and to behave on the basis of freedom of the will. This belief in the free and capable intellect of the individual led logically to faith in intellectual freedom and religious toleration. As Jonathan Mayhew wrote in 1749, "It is not left to the option of Christians whether they will relinquish their natural liberty in religious matters, or not; they are commanded to assert it. God has given us abilities to *judge even for ourselves what is right*: and requires us to improve them. He forbids us to *call any man master upon earth*. And as he has forbidden us to submit implicitly to the dictates of any man, so he has also explicitly forbid all Christians to assume or usurp any authority over their brethren."[11]

While rationalism was making itself felt in such a revolutionary fashion among the intellectuals and the well-to-do, there swept through the Angloamerican colonies a wave of emotional revivalism, called the Great Awakening. Under the spell of such preachers as George Whitefield, Jonathan Edwards, and Samuel Davies, thousands of people were led to dramatic, emotionally charged religious experiences. Many new sects, emotionally oriented, appeared among the Angloamericans. But the Great Awakening, curiously enough like its opposite, rationalism, placed great emphasis on religious individualism, in this case on the individual's assurance of the value of his soul in the eyes of God and of his capacity to find rapport with God by his own efforts. Whitefield, for example, directed his attention especially to the poor, the uneducated, the "rabble."

For these rabble, my Lord, have precious and immortal Souls, for which the dear Redeemer shed his precious blood, as well as the great and rich. These, my Lord, are the publicans and harlots that enter into the kingdom of heaven, whilst self-righteous professors reject it. To shew such poor sinners the way to God, to preach to them the power of Christ's resurrection; and to pluck them as firebrands out of the burning, the Methodist preachers [he referred to himself as a "Methodist"] go out into the highways and hedges. If this be vile, by the help of my God,

[11] Jonathan Mayhew, *Seven Sermons* (Boston, 1749), p. 56.

I shall be more vile; neither count I my life dear unto myself, so that I may finish my course with joy, and be made instrumental in turning any of this rabble to righteousness.[12]

The Great Awakening did not, however, direct its appeal exclusively to the "rabble." It also excited many who were prosperous — students, businessmen, farmers — and its mood was adopted by many of the preachers and religious leaders of the orthodox churches. As a historical phenomenon, its great significance probably lay in the fact that it aroused a new emotionalism in religion and emphasized the worth and dignity of the individual in the eyes of God. It was, indeed, a stirring of the masses, and this awakening of individualism among the "middling sort" and the "mudsills" of society carried over into politics, as will appear.

Although the conversion of the Indians to Christianity had been a stated objective of colonization from the beginning, missionary enterprise never was as significant in the expansion of Angloamerica as it was in the Catholic empires. There had been a few scattered missionary efforts among the English in the seventeenth century, but nothing of great historical significance had come out of them. In the eighteenth century, the missionary impulse was distinctly weak, even though the Great Awakening did inspire a degree of new vigor in the missionary mood. The Reverend Eleazer Wheelock, for example, opened at Lebanon, Connecticut, a school for Indian boys, the purpose of which was to train the Indians as missionaries to their own people. When Wheelock moved to Hanover, New Hampshire, in 1770, he took his school with him and there inaugurated what would become Dartmouth College.

Similarly, David Brainerd of Connecticut, moved by the Great Awakening, went as a missionary to the Indians in western Massachusetts and, later, to those in New Jersey. Missionaries sent out by the Society for the Promotion of the Gospel in Foreign Parts attempted, without much success, to counter the missionary endeavors of the French among the Iroquois of New York. However, Henry Barclay, one of the missionaries, baptized a number of Mohawks, among whom was the famous Mohawk chieftain Joseph Brant. Another missionary, Samuel Kirkland, established a mission among the Oneidas and founded a school for Indians and whites that would one day become Hamilton College.

In Pennsylvania the Quakers undertook a certain amount of missionary work, but it was the Moravians who were the most active; they trained

---

[12] George Whitefield, *The Works of the Reverend George Whitefield, M.A.*, 4 vols. (London, 1771), IV, 139.

missionaries at the Moravian center in Bethlehem. The most famous of the Moravian missionaries was David Zeisberger, who learned the Mohawk language and ministered among the Iroquois. His most effective work, however, was done among the Delawares, whom he followed into the Ohio Valley in their migration westward.

Elsewhere in the continental colonies missionary activity among the Indians and the blacks was undertaken by missionaries sent out by the Society for the Propagation of the Gospel in Foreign Parts, whose funds came mostly from England. The work of the society, however, was never very successful.

Never among the Protestant Angloamericans were there any systematic and organized missionary efforts like those which characterized the advance of Christianity along the "rim of Christendom" in the French, Spanish, and Portuguese empires. Probably the most significant historic conclusion to emerge from Angloamerican missionary work was the apparent fact that the Indians were allergic to the white man's culture.

While Angloamerica was almost solidly Protestant Christian in religion, the British empire was also distinguished by the conglomerate and rapidly changing nature of its religious life. This heterogeneity had of necessity given a powerful impulse to the growth of religious toleration. This de facto toleration had arisen in part out of expediency, largely because of the necessity for a live-and-let-live attitude among so many dissident sects. But it had developed, in the seventeenth and eighteenth centuries, under the impact of the ideas of such writers as Roger Williams, William Penn and the Quakers, Benjamin Franklin, and Jonathan Mayhew into a positive philosophy of religious and intellectual freedom.

By the end of the eighteenth century, after having been further influenced by science, religious rationalism, and the Enlightenment, the belief in religious and intellectual freedom had become a cardinal tenet in the Angloamerican culture. It is probably true, as Benjamin Franklin said, that Angloamerica, in the third quarter of the eighteenth century, was that part of the world that enjoyed the greatest degree of religious toleration. At the same time, there occurred a slow but sure advance and application of the principle of the separation of church and state. One of the most eloquent expressions of this concept was the preamble to Thomas Jefferson's bill for the disestablishment of the Anglican Church in Virginia, which was introduced into the Virginia legislature in 1779 but was not actually passed until 1786:

Well aware that the opinions and belief of men depend not on their own will, but follow involuntarily the evidence proposed to their minds; that Almighty God hath created the mind free, *and manifested his supreme will that free it shall remain by making it altogether insusceptible of restraint;* that all attempts to influence it by temporal punishments, or burthens, or by civil incapacitations, tend only to beget habits of hypocricy and meanness, and are a departure from the holy author of our religion, . . . *that the opinions of men are not the object of civil government, nor under its jurisdiction;* that to suffer the civil magistrate to intrude his powers into the field of opinion and to restrain the profession or propagation of principles on supposition of their ill tendency is a dangerous fallacy . . . and finally that truth is great and will prevail if left to herself; that she is the proper and sufficient antagonist of error, and has nothing to fear from the conflict unless by human interposition disarmed of her natural weapons, free argument and debate; errors ceasing to be dangerous when it is permitted freely to contradict them.

We, the General Assembly of Virginia do enact that no man shall be compelled to frequent or support any religious worship . . . but that all men shall be free to profess, and by argument to maintain, their opinions in matters of religion, and that the same shall in no wise diminish, enlarge, or affect their civil capacities.

[Furthermore], we are free to declare, and do declare, that the rights hereby asserted are of the natural rights of mankind, and that if any act shall be hereafter passed to repeal the present or to narrow its operation, such act will be an infringement of natural right.[13]

The principle of the separation of church and state, based upon the idea of intellectual freedom as a natural right, thus written into the law of one of the United States, presently became one of the cardinal tenets of the constitutionalism of that country. Presently, also, this same concept would become one of the chief principles in the constitutional ideologies of most of the nations of the hemisphere.

Conclusion

It is clear that the religious life and thought of the peoples of the American hemisphere in the eighteenth century were highly conglomerate. Although the entire hemisphere was basically and ostensibly Christian, the presence of primitive Indian and African religions in all the

---

[13] "A Bill for Establishing Religious Freedom," *The Papers of Thomas Jefferson*, ed. Julian P. Boyd, 19 vols. to date (Princeton, N.J.: Princeton University Press, 1950–), II, 545–547.

Euroamerican empires and the assimilation of these religions with Christianity itself make it obvious that the religion of America was no longer purely European. Both Roman Catholicism and Protestantism had been substantially modified, if not significantly in their basic doctrines at least in their rituals and administrations. There was nothing in Europe, for example, exactly comparable to the missions, or *reducciones*, in the Catholic empires; even among the Protestants there had arisen ideas and practices that differentiated those in America from their brethren in Europe.

As the complexity and the conglomerate nature of religion in America increased, as the differentiation of American religions from European religions became more pronounced, and as the impact of the rationalism of the Enlightenment progressively corroded the purity of ancient religious doctrines, two significant developments took place. First, there appeared a powerful feeling of resentment, even rejection, of the control of American religious life by the European religious capitals. Most of the higher church officials in the Catholic empires, for example, were Europeans and their power and their attitudes were resented by the lower clergy, many of whom, if not most, were native-born Americans. When the mood of independence came into the open, many of the lower clergy stood beside the rebels in the wars of independence.

Similarly, in Protestant Angloamerica there was a considerable measure of discontent with European control, and during the third quarter of the century, there was an almost violent opposition, especially in New England, to the attempt to create in America an Anglican bishopric. It was no accident that, with the advent of the American Revolution and its spirit of independence, the Anglicans and all the dissenting Protestant sects — Dutch Reformed, Presbyterian, Methodist — severed their connections with their European governing bodies.

Not only did the evolution of religion and its institutions result in a self-conscious antagonism between Americans and Europeans, but the various regions within the Euroamerican empires tended to take on distinctly regional characteristics. The American churches tended to identify themselves with the regional groups who were interested in local economic and political concerns. Individual clerics mingled with secular intellectual, political, economic, and social leaders and shared in their nationalistic thinking and feeling. In this way religion became one of the forces making for national feelings among the regional societies.

CHAPTER 8

America
in the Eighteenth-Century
Enlightenment

The European Enlightenment and America

It is to be remembered that the expansion of Europe was not only an expansion of European capital, ships, men, armies, peoples, governments, or even Christianity. It was also a continuous expansion of knowledge and ideas, that is, secular knowledge and secular ideas not directly connected with religion. Such were the corpus of knowledge represented by European science and the body of thought, political, economic, and philosophical, that was formulated in the course of the so-called Enlightenment of the eighteenth century by Locke, Montesquieu, Diderot, d'Alembert, Rousseau, Hume, Voltaire, and many others. Their world view was essentially secular, usually anticlerical, or even, often enough, downright antireligious. Such, too, were the modes, styles, and thought content that prevailed in European literary and aesthetic life during the century.

The "Enlightenment" of the eighteenth century may be defined as that unique mood, or set of moods, ideas, and interests, that characterized European intellectual life during the century, roughly between the publication of Samuel Pufendorf's *Droit des Gens* in 1672 and the appearance of the Marquis de Condorcet's *Esquisse d'un tableau historique des progrès de l'ésprit humain* in 1793. Peter Gay has defined it as "a little flock of philosophes[:] . . . A loose, informal, wholly unorganized coalition of cultural critics, religious skeptics, and political re-

173

formers from Edinburgh to Naples, Paris to Berlin, Boston to Philadelphia. . . . Kant defined it as man's emergence from his self-imposed tutelage, and offered as its motto *Sapere aude* — 'Dare to know.' "[1] In their willingness to "dare to know," the philosophes took every aspect of human existence and every part of the human experience as the "countries" of their intellectual knight-errantry. Basic to the new knowledge, of course, was science, wherein the prophets of all knowledge were Newton and Diderot. In the name of science they explored and analyzed the affairs of men: in politics with Locke, Montesquieu, and Rousseau; in psychology with Locke, Hume, and La Mettrie; in economics with Quesnay, Turgot, and Adam Smith. They were aesthetic rationalists, following the lead of Voltaire and Pope in literature, Hogarth and Goya in art, and such antipodal thinkers as Hume and Kant, Berkeley and d'Holbach in philosophy. As has been mentioned, they were by and large critically skeptical of religion or, at least, anticlerical; nevertheless, while Voltaire would have destroyed the church but not religion and Hume effectively destroyed religion itself, Kant, to his own satisfaction and to that of many generations to come, succeeded in saving it by making it comfortingly rational.

The European Enlightenment, as a historical event, was not confined to any one country. It was truly international among Western peoples. Indeed, among all the aspects of the continuing expansion of Europe during the eighteenth century, it was probably its intellectual aspect that most clearly gave that phenomenon the character of international unity. To be sure, the intellectual center of the Enlightenment was France, but England and its American colonies, Germany, Scotland, Italy, and other countries, including Spain and Portugal and their colonies, produced outstanding intellectual figures who participated in its outlook and contributed to the great corpus of its thought. Its international unity was not monolithic, however, for in every country and in every colony where it appeared it differed in its manifestations.

The Enlightenment made itself felt in the courts of western Europe as well as in intellectual circles, despite the efforts of the churches to suppress it. It even penetrated the leadership of the churches themselves, to become what has been called the "Catholic Enlightenment."

---

[1] Peter Gay, *The Enlightenment: An Interpretation*, vol. I: *The Rise of Western Pragmatism* (New York: Alfred A. Knopf, 1966), p. 3. There are other interpretations, of course. See the titles in the bibliography for this chapter, especially the works by Alfred Cobban and Will and Ariel Durant.

Many of the statesmen governing the destinies of America, especially after the middle of the century, were exponents of Enlightenment thought. The universities also were permeated by this modern view of the world; Montpelier, in southern France, became a favorite place of study for Latin Americans through whom, as well as through other media, the Enlightenment reached out to America. It spread easily and naturally to Angloamerica by way of England to produce such Enlightened thinkers as Benjamin Franklin, John Winthrop IV, John Adams, Cadwallader Colden, and Thomas Jefferson and to Francoamerica to influence such philosophes as Jean Dubuc and Moreau de St. Méry.

The moods and ideas of the Enlightenment did not take root in Iberoamerica as easily as they did in Angloamerica and Francoamerica. It is true, of course, that the intellectual outlook of the Enlightenment, its science, secularism, naturalism, and rationalism, found its way into Spain with the accession of the French Bourbon dynasty to the Spanish throne. These French kings, beginning with Philip V (Philip of Anjou), brought with them many French scientists, writers, and artists and encouraged others to go to Spain and the Spanish colonies. Native Spaniards like Benito Jeronimo Feijóo y Montenegro absorbed the Enlightenment's critical spirit, its interest in science and rationalism, and its concern for America for its own sake. Among such Spanish statesmen as the Count of Aranda, the Count of Campomanes, and Gaspar Melchor de Jovellanos, the critical, anticlerical spirit as well as the basic secular learning of the Enlightenment was strong.

The new intellectual outlook was also introduced to Portugal by the large number of Portuguese and Brazilian students who studied in France or England and then returned to Portugal and thence, many of them, to Brazil, taking the new ideas and attitudes with them. Most notable among these Portuguese men of the Enlightenment was José Carvalho (the later Marquis of Pombal) who became one of the greatest agents of the Enlightenment in Portuguese Brazil.

The expansion and progress of the Enlightenment in the Iberian peninsula and in Iberoamerica were opposed, impeded, and suppressed, as far as possible, by the Roman Catholic church, which used every instrument at its disposal, including the Inquisition, to crush the spirit of the Enlightenment.

Despite all opposition the views and moods of the Enlightenment spread to America, in considerable degree even within the church itself.

To begin with, the philosophical antischolasticism of René Descartes and his followers, which had long since had its revolutionary effects upon the theology of the critics of the Catholic church in Europe, found its way into the thinking of many of the learned men in America, some of them actually members of the clergy. As early as 1771, for example, the University of Lima installed a new curriculum, which included the study of such Enlightenment figures as Descartes, Leibniz, Francis Bacon, and Gassendi. Similar reforms, if less dramatic, took place in other American schools and universities.

The influence of this antischolasticism on theology was significant enough, to be sure, but Cartesian rationalism also seemed to carry with it overtones of rebellion, of resistance to authority exercised for its own sake. As Germán Arciniegas has said, "The spirit of the Enlightenment was a spirit of liberation," and "The fulcrum that turned the lever of the Enlightenment [in America] was Descartes, a prime mover of the seventeenth century."[2]

The doctrines of the Enlightenment reached America even more directly through the books that came in the holds of merchant ships and were distributed despite the somewhat halfhearted efforts of the Inquisition to prevent this traffic in ideas. The private libraries of learned men in Latin America, as well as in Canada, contained copies of the great *Encyclopédie* of Denis Diderot and his associates, not to mention the books of such writers as Montesquieu, d'Alembert, and Voltaire, and, above all, the work of Rousseau.

Rousseau's views, especially those expounded in his *Social Contract* (1763), became a sort of gospel for those thinkers, political and otherwise, who were beginning to see the rents in the seamless fabrics of the Spanish, Portuguese, and French colonial administrative systems. By 1780 Rousseau's concepts of the social contract and the "general will," however misunderstood and misapplied, were widely, if often surreptitiously, accepted throughout Latin America. Moreover, Rousseau's "general will" was interpreted to mean "the sovereignty of the people." Many, defying convention and the Inquisition, preached or wrote about the intellectual revolt; among them were Don Gregorio Funes in Argentina, José Agustín Cabellero in Havana, José Celestino Mutis in Bogotá, Juan Benito Díaz de Gamarra in Mexico, and Luis Vieira da Silva in

---

[2] Germán Arciniegas, *Latin America: A Cultural History*, trans. from the Spanish by Joan McLean (New York: Alfred A. Knopf, 1967), p. 232.

Brazil. Slowly but surely in the second half of the eighteenth century, the ferment of libertarian ideas, both before and after the precedent set by the War for United States Independence, was stirring among the intellectual leaders of Latin America. And nowhere was this agitation more powerful than among the *criollos*, for whom America was their home.

But the Enlightenment's role in the expansion of Europe included much more than the exportation of science, literature, political ideas, and philosophy to America. For America itself had inspired among the philosophes a very considerable body of learning and "philosophy," in science, history, literature, and economic and political thought — a sort of intellectual "backlash" that was an integral part of the Enlightenment "mind." In short, America contributed significantly to the content and the thinking of the Enlightenment in Europe. The Abbé Raynal, Voltaire, Adam Smith, and others saw the expansion of Europe as probably the greatest single event in human history. According to Raynal,

There never was an event so significant for the human race in general and for the peoples of Europe in particular, as the discovery of the Newworld and the passage to the Indies by way of the Cape of Good Hope. For then there began a revolution in the commerce, in the power of nations, in the culture, the industry, and the government of all peoples. It was at this moment that the men of the most distant countries were drawn together by their new relationships and their new needs. The products of tropical climates were consumed in the countries bordering upon the pole; the industry of the North was transported to the South; stuffs from the Orient became the luxuries of the Occidentals; and everywhere men achieved a mutual exchange of their opinions, of their laws, of their customs, of their diseases and their remedies, of their virtues and of their vices.[3]

Nevertheless, the philosophes were not uncritical. Raynal continues by saying that "everything is changed, and must continue to change. But the revolutions that have happened and those that must happen, have they been and will they be of benefit to human nature? Will man, because of them, some day enjoy more of tranquility, of happiness and of pleasures? Will his condition be better, or will it only be changed?"[4]

Voltaire saw the age of expansion as the beginning of a new era: "Here

---

[3] Guillaume-Thomas Raynal, *Histoire philosophique et politique des établissements et du commerce des Européens dans les Deux Indes*, 5 vols. (Geneva, 1780), I, 1–2.
[4] *Ibid.*

[in the Age of Discovery] we have what is doubtless the greatest event in the history of the globe, of which one half had always been ignorant of the other half. It is a sort of new creation."[5] For Voltaire history, including that of the New World, was the history of the human spirit:

The object of our history [including the history of America] was the history of the human spirit, not of nearly-always distorted facts but to see by what steps men have progressed from the barbaric savagery of the times of Charlemagne to the civilization of our own. . . .

One sees in history thus conceived errors and prejudices follow each other and drive out truth and reason. . . . [But] at last men were enlightened a little by the picture of their own misfortunes and stupidities. Societies came, in time, to rectify their ideas; men learned to think.[6]

Adam Smith was similarly impressed and prescient:

The discovery of America, and that of a passage to the East Indies by the Cape of Good Hope, are the two greatest and most important events recorded in the history of mankind. Their consequences have already been very great: but, in the short period of between two and three centuries which has elapsed since the discoveries were made, it is impossible that the whole extent of their consequences can have been seen. What benefits, or what misfortunes to mankind may hereafter result from those great events, no human wisdom can foresee. By uniting, in some measure, the most distant parts of the world, by enabling them to relieve one another's wants, to increase one another's enjoyments, and to encourage one another's industry, their general tendency would seem to be beneficial. To the natives, however, both of the East and West Indies, all the commercial benefits which can have resulted from those events have been sunk and lost in the dreadful misfortunes which they have occasioned. These misfortunes, however, seem to have arisen rather from accident than from any thing in the nature of those events themselves. . . . Hereafter, perhaps, the natives of those countries may grow stronger, or those of Europe may grow weaker, and the inhabitants of all the different quarters of the world may arrive at that equality of courage and force which, by inspiring mutual fear, can alone overawe the injustice of independent nations into some sort of respect for the rights of one another. But nothing seems more likely to establish this equality of force than that mutual communication of knowledge and of

---

[5] Voltaire, *Essai sur les moeurs et l'esprit des nations, Oeuvres complètes de Voltaire*, ed. Louis E. D. Moland, 52 vols. (Paris, 1877–85), XII, 376.

[6] Voltaire, "Remarques pour servir de supplément à l'essai sur les moeurs et l'ésprit des nations . . . " *Oeuvres*, ed. Moland, XXIV, 547–548.

all sorts of improvements which an extensive commerce from all countries to all countries naturally, or rather necessarily, carries along with it.[7]

In another area, too, the expansion of Europe had a profoundly significant effect upon European thought. This was the realm of international law. It was the opening of the New World that had inspired the writings of the great Spanish jurists of the sixteenth century, Francisco de Vittoria, Francisco Suárez, and others. It was also the setting for the pronouncement of the doctrine of the freedom of the seas by Hugo Grotius in 1609. During the eighteenth century the evolution of the principles of international law and diplomacy continued to be influenced by the events in the New World as can be seen in the works of Pufendorf, Vattel, Vico, and others and in the study of such problems as the freedom of the seas, the rights of neutrals, the rights of Indians, the definition of territorial boundaries, and the pacific settlement of international disputes. For the theorists of international law, their discipline was a science of natural law, of international morality, of Vattel's "universal love of humanity" — concepts, incidentally, which only aroused the ridicule and sarcasm of more cynical philosophers like Voltaire.

In any case, despite all their differences and polemical squabbles, the philosophes generally agreed that the expansion of Europe and its impact upon the life-style and the mind of Europe were of supreme historical importance in the evolution of their civilization.

The Enlightened thinkers' interest in America is nowhere better seen than in the realm of science. For there was among them an insatiable desire to know more about the New World of America — its geography, climate, flora and fauna, products, and native populations. This interest was shared by the kings and their courts, as well as by the intellectuals and their societies. Indeed, it was through this channel of scientific interest that the first breaches in the hermetically sealed monopolies of the national empires were made.

The eighteenth century was a time of active popular and official interest in the geography of America. Although basically scientific, this concern was fed and stimulated by the practical needs of commerce and by the demand for geographic knowledge of the Western Hemisphere presented

[7] Adam Smith, *An Inquiry into the Nature and Causes of the Wealth of Nations* (1776), ed. Edwin Cannan, 2 vols. (1776; reprinted London: Methuen, University Paperbacks, 1961), II, 141.

by the almost constant warfare. One response to these various interests was the production of myriads of maps of America and the publication of many, many atlases. Geography became a science in its own right, and distinguished geographers and cartographers such as G. DeLisle, J. B. B. D'Anville, Jacques-Nicolas Bellin, and Robert Vaugondy in France and Dr. John Mitchell in England enjoyed wide acclaim by reason of their maps, which were used extensively in science, commerce, and diplomacy. Descriptive and theoretical geographers like Alexander von Humboldt and Karl Ritter, especially the former, contributed significantly to the theory of geography as applied to America. The great philosopher Immanuel Kant, although he wrote little or nothing about America, placed geography in the great schema of organized knowledge (science), linking it, as the study of phenomena that exist beside each other in space, with history, the study of phenomena that follow each other in time. Geography, according to Kant, is a summary of nature, a philosophy of man's place in nature — mathematical, moral, political, commercial, and theological.

The study of the geography of America was not merely an examination of the continent's physical features, or even, as Kant would have it, a "summary of nature." It was more than that: it was a study of the earth and of man which contributed to one's perspective and to an understanding of humanity and its problems. As Voltaire said,

One of the greatest advantages of geography is, in my opinion, this: your stupid neighbor, and his yet more stupid wife, reproach you endlessly for not thinking as they do in the *rue St. Jacques*. . . . Then take a map of the world, show them Africa, the empires of Japan, of China, of the Indies, of Turkey, of Persia, that of Russia — vaster than that of Rome; . . . finally, you will call to their attention the four parts of the globe, and, in the fifth part, which is as unknown as it is immense, the prodigious number of generations which never heard of the opinions held by your neighbors [of the *rue St. Jacques*] or who have contradicted them, or who have held them in horror; you will set the entire universe opposite the *rue St. Jacques*. . . . Then, perhaps, they may feel a bit of shame for having believed that the organs of St. Severin parish gave the tone to the rest of the world.[8]

Geography was useful: it enabled men to view the world and the human race in their entirety.

[8] Voltaire, s.v. "Géographie," *Dictionnaire philosophique* (*Oeuvres*, ed. Moland), XIX, 256–257.

It was as an expansion of geography that the scientists of Europe carried their investigation of America forward. In the course of the eighteenth century, many scientists and expeditions visited America to study its flora, fauna, geographic features, and people. The scientific curiosity of the Enlightened philosophes and kings about America expressed itself in numerous ways, but in none more clearly than in the long series of scientific expeditions.

The first such expedition subsidized by a European government was that led by two Jesuits, Diogo Soares and Domingos Capassi, sent to Brazil by King João V in 1729. In the first half of the century, however, the most famous of these expeditions was that to Hispanoamericá proposed by the French Academy of Sciences and guided by Charles Marie de la Condamine. Although it received the permission of the Spanish crown, Spain insisted that two young Spanish officers, Jorge Juan and Antonio de Ulloa, both of whom later became renowned in Spanish imperial affairs, accompany it. The chief purpose of this expedition was to determine the exact length of a degree of longitude on the equator; it therefore went to Quito in Peru (now Ecuador). But it observed many things and prepared many reports on the geography of South America, its climate, and its resources (including rubber from the upper Amazon); Juan and Ulloa also wrote an official report on the social, economic, and political conditions in Peru which was so critical that it created an international scandal when it was published in Madrid in 1748. From the reports of this expedition Diderot derived much scientific information about America which was then included in the *Encyclopédie*.

Another international expedition was undertaken by the Dutch botanist Nikolaus Joseph von Jacquin, who, as director of the Austrian Imperial Botanical Gardens of Vienna, received permission to go to the Spanish Caribbean colonies. The Swedish botanist Peter Kalm traveled widely in Angloamerica in 1748 and described the flora and fauna of that empire.

One of the most famous expeditions was that of Louis Antoine de Bougainville, who sailed around the world from 1766 to 1769. Touching at Montevideo in 1767, he sailed through the Strait of Magellan into the Pacific and went on to Tahiti and other islands of the South Pacific. He also visited Alaska. His reports were used by Diderot in his scientific writings about America in the *Encyclopédie*.

A few months after Bougainville reached Montevideo, the English explorer Captain James Cook sailed from England in 1768 on the first

America in European science. Animals of America: Beaver and porcupine. From *Encyclopédié*, pt. II, *Planches: Histoire naturelle*, plate XIII. Courtesy of the University of Washington Library.

of a series of spectacular expeditions into the South Pacific. The primary objective of this voyage, suggested by the Royal Society and subsidized by the British crown, was to observe the transit of Venus from the island of Tahiti in 1769. This and his subsequent voyages enabled Cook to accumulate a great amount of scientific data, including much about America. The third voyage, undertaken from the Pacific side, was a search for the legendary "Northwest Passage"; during the journey Cook visited Alaska and the western coast of North America. It was symbolic of the international nature of scientific study that Cook, on this voyage, carried a safe-conduct issued by Benjamin Franklin, the American minister to France in Paris, protecting him from warships of the United States, then at war with England.

Alejandro Malaspiña, an Italian in the service of Spain, followed Bougainville and Cook in the scientific exploration of the American and Pacific areas of the globe. He formulated a plan to make a great scientific survey of the Spanish empire. Although the Spanish government subsidized him, the group of scientists in his two ships was distinctly international, since it included Frenchmen, Poles, and Italians. The expedition left Cádiz in 1789 and visited the La Plata region, Patagonia, Chile, Peru, Panama, and the Galápagos Islands; in Panama the scientists conceived the idea of an isthmian canal to connect the two oceans. Malaspina visited Mexico and then extended his expedition to the northwest coast of North America. From his expedition came much scientific data — geographical and geological, botanical and zoological, anthropological and sociological — as well as one of the greatest collections of maps of America ever assembled.

Still another Spanish scientist who contributed to the scientific study of America fostered by the Enlightenment was José Celestino Mutis, who was sent to America in intellectual exile from Spain. Mutis's "Botanical Mission" traveled to Bogotá where he undertook the systematic study of the flora and fauna, the land, and the Indians of America; his expedition also built an astronomical observatory at Bogotá. Mutis, who began his scientific life in America as a Spaniard studying the new hemisphere in the name of the Enlightenment, also became one of the brilliant exponents of the Enlightenment in America itself.

The most famous scientific explorer of America in the eighteenth (and early nineteenth) century was the German scholar Alexander von Humboldt, who began his travels in America in company with the French naturalist Aimé-Jacques Alexandre Bonpland in 1799. The two men concentrated most of their work in northern South America (Venezuela, Colombia, Ecuador, Peru). On a second voyage they visited Mexico, Cuba, and the United States. From his observations and his thoughts about America Humboldt produced a monumental set of volumes of both scientific and political data which, taken all together, constitutes the greatest scientific commentary on America and its affairs ever composed. This classic work has had an incalculable influence on scholars from that day to this. It was in a very real sense the culmination and the climax of the scientific study of America stimulated by the European Enlightenment.

The philosophes' scientific interest in America was not, however, confined to the study of its physical geography, resources, flora, and fauna. They were also deeply intrigued by America's people and the "philosophical" problem presented by the discovery in America of a race of men who were obviously different from Europeans and whose culture was profoundly different from European culture. The scientists' inquiry into America was thus anthropological; furthermore, the anthropological theme carried over into literature, and the image of the "noble savage" became one of the hallmarks of the eighteenth century's literary creativity.

In the field of anthropology the *Encyclopédie* had much to say about the American Indians, with articles on the Iroquois, the Incas, the Mexican empire of Montezuma, and so on. Numerous lesser encyclopedias published during the century had similar articles. Individual scientists made many studies of the Indians; the most notable of these was the German Johann Friedrich Blumenbach, a professor at Göttingen and "the father of physical anthropology." Blumenbach classified the races of the world according to skin color and other physical characteristics as Caucasian (white), Mongolian (yellow), Ethiopian (black), Malaysian (brown), and American (red).

Most of the writers on race thought of the Amerinds (and blacks) as innately inferior to the white race. As noted earlier Voltaire felt that "nature has established under this principle [of racial differences] those different degrees of genius and of character that so rarely, if ever, are seen to change. It is according to this principle that the Negroes are the slaves of the other races. . . . Experience has also taught us how superior the Europeans are to the Americans [Indians] who, easily conquered everywhere, have never attempted a real revolution, although they outnumbered the Europeans a thousand to one."[9] In writing thus, Voltaire spoke for his time. As Peter Gay points out, there were many philosophes, and they differed widely from each other in their individual thinking. Nearly every one of them shared this devotion to the grand idea of the progress of the human spirit, despite, as Voltaire says, the stupidity, the savagery, the bigotry, the cruelty, the crimes, and all the other animalistic instincts of men.

The source material for the European studies of the Amerinds was vast, indeed, for many European traders visited America and reported on, among other things, the Indians. The most important source materials for such anthropological study were the reports of missionaries. The Jesuit Pierre François Xavier de Charlevoix, for example, made several voyages to America and wrote histories of French Saint-Domingue, Canada, and Paraguay, which carefully described the lives and customs of the natives in these widely separated parts of America. He was followed by Joseph François Lafitau, another Jesuit, who reported on the plants of Canada as well as on the indigenes, whom he depicted in his widely read book *The Customs of the American Savages Compared to Those of the Earliest Times*, published in 1723. Many of the Jesuits wrote *relations*, or narratives, of their missions. For the students of the eighteenth century, these hundreds of volumes constituted a veritable storehouse of information about the Amerinds — and they still do; they are particularly interesting because, despite national differences in the order, the Jesuits were a truly international organization, working with the Indians in all parts of America. Even though they worked for the Catholic church, their reports were used by many nonchurch, even secular, writers of the Enlightenment.

In the Indians, America had presented to the European philosophes a new and exotic phenomenon, not only of profound interest in its own right, but useful also for their theories on the human race and its problems.

Economic thinkers of the early Enlightenment accepted the assumption that the colonies established in America in the course of the expansion of Europe were in all cases merely extensions of the economies of the mother countries. For example, Veron de Forbonnais, in the article "Colonie" in the *Encyclopédie*, spoke of the colonies in America as having

[9] Voltaire, *Essai sur les moeurs*, XII, 381.

been founded "only for their utility to their metropolises"; therefore, "it follows: (1) that they ought to be under an immediate dependence upon the metropolis, and, consequently under its protection, and (2) that the commerce of the colonies ought to be an exclusive monopoly for the founding nation. . . ."[10] From which result two consequences:

The first is that the colonies could not be more useful if they could get along without the metropolis: thus it is a law inherent in the nature of things, that the industry and agriculture of a colony should be restricted to the production of such objects as serve the needs and the convenience of the possessing country. The second consequence is that if the colony carries on a commerce with foreigners, or if foreign merchandise is consumed there, the sum total of this commerce and of these commodities is by just so much a robbery of the metropolis; it is a robbery that is all too common, but one that is punishable under the laws, and one by which the real and relative power of the mother-state is diminished in direct proportion to everything that is gained by the foreigners.[11]

Montesquieu had said much the same thing. But by the third quarter of the eighteenth century a number of men had come to challenge this assumption and the mercantilist system built upon it. The greatest of the challengers, of course, was Adam Smith, whose *Wealth of Nations*, published in 1776, riddled the economic thinking upon which the mercantilist system was built. As for colonies,

The establishment of the European colonies in America and the West Indies arose from no necessity: and though the utility that has resulted from them has been very great, it is not altogether so clear and evident. It was not understood at their first establishment, and was not the motive either of that establishment or of the discoveries which gave occasion to it; and the nature, extent, and limits of that utility are not, perhaps, well understood at this day. . . .

The colony of a civilized nation which takes possession either of a waste country, or of one so thinly inhabited that the natives easily give place to the new settlers, advances more rapidly to wealth and greatness than any other human society.[12]

It is to be noted that Smith attributes the relatively great prosperity of the British colonies to the fact that they enjoyed freer political institu-

---

[10] *Encyclopédie, ou Dictionnaire raisonné des sciences, des arts el des metiers*, 52 vols. (Paris, 1751–80), s.v. "Colonie," III, 648–650.
[11] *Ibid*.
[12] Smith, *Wealth of Nations*, II, 68, 75.

tions than those of the other colonies. Others, such as the Reverend Josiah Tucker and David Hume, went further and proposed that the colonies be given their independence entirely, even though at the same time they minimized the economic profitableness of the colonies to the mother country. Similarly Quesnay and Turgot, the French leaders of the agrarian, free-trade physiocrats, explicitly or implicitly voiced their agreement with this conception of the colonies as new, inherently autonomous economic societies.

The political nature of the colonies was intrinsically connected with their economic nature. Montesquieu, in his study of the origins of political institutions, considered the government of the colonies to be something apart from the institutions of the mother country, something wisely left to the political expediencies of large commercial companies, something with little relevance to the development of political institutions of the state as a whole:

Several colonizing nations were so wise as to give their empires to companies of merchants, who, governing those distant states uniquely for commercial purposes, created a great accessory [political] power without embarrassing the parent state. . . .

The objective of these colonies is to carry on commerce under better conditions than is possible in commerce with neighboring countries, with whom all the advantages are reciprocal. It has been established that only the metropolis may trade with a colony; and that quite correctly, because the end of the establishment of the colony has always been the extension of commerce, not the foundation of a city or of a new empire.[13]

Here, too, the eighteenth century witnessed the emergence of a new concept of empire. About the middle of the century, the colonies, though still subservient to the metropolises, were considered by imperial statesmen to be integral parts of the empire, social and political units in a kind of national-federative empire with a status much higher than that of mere factories-at-a-distance.

One of the first to express and use this concept was Malachy Postlethwayt, an Englishman writing in the mid-eighteenth century. He recognized the autonomous nature of the colonial governments in Angloamerica, but he also saw them as parts of an integrated political entity.

[13] Montesquieu, *Oeuvres complètes de Montesquieu*, ed. André Masson, 3 vols. (Paris: Éditions Flagel, 1950), I, 518–519.

He even used, again and again, the term "the whole British Empire."[14] In France this idea found its way into the writings of the physiocratic minister Turgot.

In the realm of practical affairs imperial reformers like the Marquis of Pombal, the Count of Aranda, the Duke of Choiseul, and the Earl of Halifax applied the new imperial concept in the management of their respective empires. For them the colonies were no longer factories-at-a-distance, the administration of which had wisely been delegated to private companies or individuals. They were now extensions of the realms of the king, in which he was actively interested and where his will was supreme. The germ of the idea of the federal empire was present, perhaps, in the recognition of the uniqueness of each colonial society (especially in the colonies themselves), but for the statesmen their empires were now integral parts of the imperial realm. Their status had been raised from that of factories-at-a-distance to that of segments of the royal domain, which was directly governed by the monarch, the "benevolent despot," and his ministers.

Nor could thought concerning intraimperial relations avoid consideration of international law and diplomacy. What part did America or the overseas colonies play in the thinking of Pufendorf or Vattel? Inevitably, they were forced to deal with such questions as those involved in the establishment of national title to unoccupied lands overseas: What rights did the Indians have over the lands they occupied? What rights did the trading nations have on the sea that separated America from Europe? What rights, if any, did the European inhabitants of a colony ceded by one imperial state to another have? How were boundaries to be determined? What right did one empire have with regard to visits to, or trade with, the colonies of another?

Vattel, as the brilliant moralistic philosopher of international law, placed his heaviest emphasis on *la loi naturelle* and the moral duty of kings and states to observe that law.

One of the typical characteristics of Enlightenment thought about international affairs was its cosmopolitanism. "I write," asserted the German poet Schiller in 1784, "as a citizen of the world. I have lost my native country at the right time and exchanged it for the wide world.

[14] Malachy Postlethwayt, *Britain's Commercial Interest Explained and Improved*, 2 vols. (London, 1757), *passim*.

Germans, do not attempt to be a nation; be content to be human beings."[15]

Despite its cosmopolitanism, the Enlightenment gave birth to a major intellectual and emotional phenomenon — the rising nationalism. This paradigm of thought and emotion, derived from the historical emergence of the integrated modern state, centered on the concept of a national society as an integral, indivisible whole, bound together by the ties of language, myths, religion, political institutions and ideals, and above all, by a common loyalty to a common monarch. The nation was a mental image of the society; nationalism was a loyalty to that image and to the ideals that the nation stood for in the mind of the citizen. Rousseau gave expression to the ideological basis of nationalism in his *Considerations on the Constitution of Poland*:

It is education that must give to the citizens the national force, and direct their opinions and their tastes in such a way that they will be patriots by inclination, by passion, by necessity. A child upon opening its eyes should see la patrie, and until death he should see nothing but her. Every true republican imbibes with his mother's milk the love of la patrie, that is to say, its laws and its liberty. This love encompasses the whole of his existence; he sees only la patrie, he lives only for her; the moment he is alone, he is nothing: the moment he no longer has a patrie, he no longer exists; and if he is not dead, he is even worse off.[16]

The German philosopher Johann Gottfried von Herder recognized the new phenomenon and considered it, despite the conceits that he knew grew out of it, as part of the human scheme of things. For the individual, in his struggle to achieve the good life, is not entirely sufficient unto himself: he can reach his highest self-realization only in the group; the ideal group is *das Volk*, the nation of which he is a member. But every nation has its own particular genius, its own personality; it is a force for good, for the advancement of human happiness. Each nation makes a unique national contribution to the progress of civilization.

During the eighteenth century, this ideal of supreme loyalty to the nation emerged as one of the major forces in Western history. Although

---

[15] Quoted in Walter Sulzbach, *National Consciousness* (Washington, D.C.: National Council of Foreign Affairs, 1943), p. 17.

[16] Rousseau, *Considérations sur le gouvernement de Pologne et sur la reformation projetée, Oeuvres complètes de Jean-Jacques Rousseau*, ed. Bernard Gagnebin and Marcel Raymond, 4 vols. (Paris: Éditions Gallimard, 1961), III, 966.

it burst upon Europe with all its force during the French Revolution, it had been gestating for a century or longer. An intellectual and emotional rationalization of the de facto integral and absolutely sovereign national state, it lay behind much of the thinking of the imperial statesmen who attempted in the third quarter of the century to bind the colonies to the mother countries more tightly than before and to create the integral national empire centered on the image of the national monarch. It was to this sentiment that statesmen such as Edmund Burke appealed to hold the empires together (in this case, the British empire):

My hold of the colonies is in the close affection which grows from common names, from kindred blood, from similar privileges, and equal protection. These are ties which, though light as air, are as strong as links of iron. . . . As long as you have the wisdom to keep the sovereign authority of this country as the sanctuary of liberty, the sacred temple consecrated to our common faith, wherever the chosen race and sons of England worship freedom, they will turn their faces toward you. . . . It is the spirit of the English Constitution, which, infused through the mighty mass, pervades, feeds, unites, invigorates, vivifies every part of the empire, even down to the minutest member.[17]

This same inchoate sense of imperial and national oneness had become an important psychological factor in the affairs of the Euroamerican empires. It seems to have played a decisive part in the thinking of the imperial reformers — Halifax, Choiseul, Aranda, Pombal. It was shared, too, by the American members of these empires. Benjamin Franklin, for example, as has been noted, wrote in the midst of the Seven Years War while he was in England, "If ever there was a *national war*, this is truly such a one; a war in which the interest of the whole [British] *nation* is directly and fundamentally concerned."[18] This mood also infected the creoles in other Euroamerican empires. For example, Moreau de St. Méry, the *Martiniquais* who became a minister and a voice of the colonies in France, saw the French Caribbean colonies as peculiar societies that were entitled to a high degree of autonomy within the framework of *la patrie*. Moreau's feeling was a form of transatlantic

[17] Edmund Burke, "Speech on Conciliation with America" (1775), *The Writings and Speeches of the Right Honourable Edmund Burke*, 12 vols. (Beaconsfield ed., Boston: Little, Brown, 1901), II, 179.

[18] Benjamin Franklin, "The Interest of Great Britain Considered, with Regard to Her Colonies" (1760), *The Papers of Benjamin Franklin*, ed. Leonard W. Labaree et al., 17 vols. to date (New Haven, Conn.: Yale University Press, 1959–), IX, 75.

nationalism that included the citizens of each empire no matter where they lived.

A sense of national self-consciousness was also being born in the various parts of America, not only in the American half of an empire vis-à-vis the mother country but in different regions in the same empire as well. Distinct beginnings of nationalism were taking root, as will appear, in Hispanoamerica in Mexico, New Granada, Peru, and Rio de la Plata; in Francoamerica in Canada (surrendered to England in 1763), Saint-Domingue, and Martinique; in Lusoamerica in Bahia, São Paulo, and Rio Grande do Sul; in Angloamerica in New England, the southern continental colonies, and the West Indies. The regionalisms of Euroamerica were psychological products of the experiences of those Europeans who had carried the expansion of Europe to America; they were the seeds of later American nationalisms.

In the literature of the Enlightenment, America plays a major role. Among the works of Voltaire, for example, are poems, plays, novelettes, and histories whose themes are derived from the contacts of European civilization with the more primitive culture of the Americans. For Voltaire the great American epic dramatizes the conquest of an inferior Indian culture by the superior civilization of the Europeans; despite the hateful aspects of the conquest, it is the superior civilization that wins. In the play *Alzire, or The Americans*, Voltaire has Alvarez, the leader of the Spanish conquerors, say of Alzire, the Inca princess:

Her heart will give all hearts [of the Peruvians] to the Castillians;
America, on her knees, will adopt our ways;
Faith will put down here it deepest roots;
Her hymen is the tie that joins the two worlds;
These ferocious humans, who detest our laws,
Seeing in your arms the daughter of their world,
With a spirit less proud and with hearts more mild
Will under your happy yoke lower a happy brow;
And I see, my son, thanks to these sweet bonds,
All souls here henceforth Spanish and Christian.[19]

But the Indians also have many qualities that the Europeans might learn to emulate: Alzire says of herself,

I was bred, Emire, in this rude climate,
To follow virtue without seeking fame.

[19] Voltaire, *Alzire, ou Les Américains, Oeuvres*, ed. Moland, III, 390.

Honor is in my heart; it is that which commands
That I save a hero whom Heaven abandons.[20]

This theme of the noble American savage is repeated in the novelette
L'Ingénu. Indeed, the idea of the "noble savage" pervades much of the
literature of the Enlightenment. Dryden sets the theme (without specific
reference to America) in his *Conquest of Granada*:

I am as free as nature first made man,
Ere the base laws of servitude began,
When wild in the woods the noble savage ran.[21]

James Thomson, in his panegyric on British freedom entitled *Liberty*,
glorifies what he feels to be British cultural supremacy and the expansion
of British freedom overseas:

Despairing Gaul her boiling youth restrains,
Dissolv'd her dream of universal sway:
The winds and seas are Britain's wide domain:
And not a sail, but by permission, spreads.
    Lo! swarming southward on rejoicing sons,
Gay colonies extend; the calm retreat
Of undeserv'd distress, the better home
Of those whom bigots chase from foreign lands,
Not built on rapine, servitude, and woe,
And in their turn some petty tyrants prey;
But, bound by social freedom, firm they rise;
Such as, of late, an Oglethorpe has form'd,
And, crowding round, the charm'd Savannah sees.[22]

The infiltration of the concept of America into European literature
— its existence, its mythical and legendary character — was widespread
and profound. Its implications, real and imagined for the values and
the ideals of Europe, were boundless. Here, as everywhere else, America
taught Europe much.

Even in religious ideas and policy the thinking of the Enlightenment
with regard to America made itself articulate. The rationalism of the
Enlightenment found particularly fertile ground in Angloamerica, where

---

[20] *Ibid.*, III, 432.
[21] John Dryden, *The Conquest of Granada by the Spaniards* (London, 1672), Pt. I,
Act I, sc. 1.
[22] James Thomson, *Liberty*, Pt. V, *The Works of the English Poets*, . . . ed. Samuel
Johnson, 21 vols. (London, 1810), XII, 493–500; the passage quoted is in XII, 497–498.

various forms of science-dominated religious thought grew and flourished. Indeed, it bore fruit throughout America, despite the attempts of the Inquisition to render it barren. At the same time, the idea of strengthening the religious authority of the parent states and kings gave impetus to the effort to establish an Anglican bishopric in America and to abolish the Jesuits in all of Latin America.

Most of the Christian religions of Euroamerica had their centers in Europe. The Indian and the African religions, of course, had no European connections. In general, the Christian leaders in Europe assumed that America, in addition to being, in a religious sense, an extension of Europe, was also a rich field for the advancement of the Christian faith among the Indians and the blacks. George Berkeley, the Anglican bishop of Cloyne in Ireland, expressed what seems to have been the generally accepted English attitude when he wrote,

Although there are several excellent persons of the Church of England, whose good intentions and endeavours have not been wanting to propagate the Gospel in foreign parts . . . , it is nevertheless acknowledged that there is at this day but little sense of religion, and a most notorious corruption of manners, in the English colonies settled on the Continent of America, and the Islands. It is also acknowledged that the gospel hath hitherto made but a very inconsiderable progress among the neighboring Americans [Indians], who still continue in much the same ignorance and barbarism in which we found them above a hundred years ago.[23]

But European Christianity itself was being revolutionized by the rationalism of the Enlightenment. From the English rationalists through the naturalism of the Deists to the atheism of such philosophes as Diderot and d'Holbach, the old theology and the old religious institutions were coming under fire. The activities of the Christians in America, whether Catholic or Calvinist, were bitterly attacked by such historical writers as Voltaire, Robertson, and Raynal; the *Encyclopédie* was thoroughly saturated with criticism, explicit or implied, of the religious Establishment.

[23] George Berkeley, "A Proposal for the Better Supplying of Churches in Our Foreign Plantations and For Converting the Savage Americans to Christianity by a College to be Erected in the Summer Islands, Otherwise Called the Isles of Bermudas," *The Works of George Berkeley, D.D.; Formerly Bishop of Cloyne, Including His Posthumous Works*, ed. Alexander Campbell Frazer, 4 vols. (Oxford: Clarendon Press, 1901), IV, 341–364; the passage quoted is in IV, 346.

In America, too, religious thinking tended to become "American," and the "American," localized versions of Christianity tended to align themselves with the other ideological forces, economic, political, and psychological, that were working with increasing clarity, during the middle decades of the century, toward the moods that eventuated in independence. It was strictly in accord with this trend that nearly all the Protestant sects in Angloamerica severed their connections with their European leaders during the War for United States Independence; this same phenomenon, in one way or another, took place in the course of the wars of independence of the emerging Latin-American states.

Eighteenth-century philosophy, strictly speaking, concerned itself little with America directly. For example, in the writings of Immanuel Kant, the greatest of the eighteenth-century philosophers, the student finds few, if any, specific references to the New World.

And yet, in an indirect sense America looms large in the general philosophical outlook of the men of the Enlightenment. John Locke, for instance, was highly regarded for his sensationalism which seemed to justify the thinking of other philosophers relative to America or to anything else; but his important contribution to the Enlightenment philosophy, or "idea," of America derived not so much from what he said about America as from the vast influence he exercised upon the gestating mind of America itself.

David Hume, as a philosopher, wrote little about America as such; in his *History of England*, however, he gives much attention to the development of the Angloamerican colonies and the "noble principles" upon which they were founded. As the tension between the colonies and England increased, Hume became an ardent, often vitriolic, partisan of the Americans, to the point of actually advocating their independence.

On the other hand, Voltaire, as a historian, litterateur, and self-styled philosopher, thought and wrote a great deal about America and its role in the progress of the human spirit. American subjects, for example, receive much notice in his *Dictionnaire philosophique*.

Like Voltaire, the Irish immaterialist George Berkeley perceived in America a stage for the further progress of the human spirit:

> The Muse, disgusted at an age and clime
> Barren of every glorious theme,
> In distant lands now waits a better time,
> Producing subjects worthy fame:

.   .   .   .

There shall be sung another golden age,
  The rise of empire and of arts,
The good and great inspiring epic rage,
  The wisest heads and noblest hearts.

Not such as Europe breeds in her decay;
  Such as she bred when fresh and young,
When heavenly flame did animate her clay,
  By future poets shall be sung.

Westward the course of empire takes its way,
  The four first Acts already past,
A fifth shall close the Drama with the day;
  Time's noblest offspring is the last.[24]

In formal philosophy, as in science, America was indeed an extension of Europe; the American mind was fundamentally an extension of the European mind. In one area of thought alone, the Americans may perhaps be said to have contributed to the development of an original philosophy — a nascent pragmatism that derived from the practical expediencies and the necessity for adaptation that faced them in their effort to find the good life in a "strange new world."

In the course of the Enlightenment, then, Europe "exported" to America knowledge (science), religion, both orthodox and radical, and political and economic theory. But it also imported from America scientific knowledge, both natural and anthropological, new religious concepts, and political and economic ideas based upon the American experience. Out of the European observations of America came themes for European literature and provocative data for the stimulation of European philosophy about the nature of man, his place in the universe, and his future. The Enlightenment was an intellectual climax to the expansion of Europe, and it was also the beneficiary of the reflex action of the expansion of Europe upon Europe itself. Just as Europe had profited from the gold and silver brought from America, just as European standards of living, as Voltaire said, were profoundly and permanently altered by products from America, the European mind of the eighteenth and subsequent centuries was deeply influenced, enriched, and broadened by the impact of its own experiences overseas.

[24] George Berkeley, "Verses on the Prospects of Planting Arts and Learning in America," *ibid.*, IV, 365–366.

The Enlightenment in America

During the eighteenth century, the areas of Western civilization in the North Atlantic became a great international intellectual community. The intellectual achievements of one part of it were soon communicated to the other parts. The creative impulses of the Enlightenment, centering on secular learning, rationalism (as a faith in the viability of human reason, or intelligence), the struggle for intellectual freedom, and the belief in the progress of the human spirit, called into being America's own exponents of the Enlightenment, full-fledged members of the North Atlantic intellectual community who became, as it were, the voices of the New World exchanging ideas with the old. For America produced its own "creole" scientists, religious rationalists, political, economic, and social philosophers, and litterateurs of the American experience.

The science of this, the so-called "Newtonian Era," reached America through the circulation of books. Copies of Sir Isaac Newton's *Principia mathematica; philosophiae naturalis*, first published in 1687, came to America in a steady stream throughout the eighteenth century. It is true that many more copies were shipped to Angloamerica than to the other empires and that its circulation in Lusoamerica and Hispanoamerica was discouraged by the Inquisition and by its inclusion in the Index of Prohibited Books. Numerous condemned books found their way there, nevertheless.

The works of other European scientists, such as Kalm, Buffon, d'Alembert, Condillac, Diderot, and the European doctors of medicine, were read by literate men from one end of America to the other — by many in Angloamerica, by fewer in Francoamerica, by still fewer in Hispanoamerica, and by only a very few in Lusoamerica. Even in Brazil, however, the lists of books in the libraries of learned men toward the end of the century reveal that some of these scientific works were known there.

A large measure of American interest in the science of the Enlightenment was focused on its "useful" or technological aspects. Even the metropolitan governments encouraged the expansion of this facet of scientific knowledge by sending missions to study the resources of the colonies and to disseminate useful or technological information.

Next in importance to the dissemination of science in America was the parallel dissemination of political thought. The actual experiences of the colonies in their political relations with their mother countries, it would seem, prepared the minds of the colonists to receive and adapt the political ideas of Locke, Montesquieu, Rousseau, and the *encyclopédistes*. It is certain that many of these "revolutionary" concepts influenced the thinking of numerous leaders of the American independence movements in the half century between 1775 and 1825.

Similarly, the Americans read and enjoyed and were influenced by the literature of the Enlightenment. The works of such men as Voltaire, Addison and Steele, Thomson, and, toward the turn of the century, Schiller and Goethe (whose writings spanned both late Enlightenment rationalism and early nineteenth-century romanticism — and who, incidentally, also had a lively interest in America) found their way into the libraries of America literati.

Similarly, the ideas of the new rationalistic thinkers in religion and the attacks upon the old religions, especially Roman Catholicism, were dispersed throughout America (again, most effectively in Angloamerica, least effectively in Brazil), and their influence was felt in the discussions of religion everywhere. The expulsion of the Jesuits from Lusoamerica, Hispanoamerica, and Francoamerica was effected in all three areas by European statesmen, notably Pombal, Aranda, and Choiseul, who were themselves men of the Enlightenment.

The European schools of philosophy, too, had their followers in America. One of the deep roots of the Enlightenment was Cartesianism, that is, an attitude of philosophical doubt which Descartes had posed as a challenge to authoritarian Aristotelian scholasticism. This critical attitude was spreading, even among many of the theologians of the Catholic Church itself. Among the philosophes it prepared the way for the more anticlerical religious rationalism that characterized the Enlightenment. Cartesianism, as has been noted, was widespread in America, even in Latin America. Thoroughgoing rationalism, however, was relatively rare in the Latin-American countries, but it had many devotees in Angloamerica.

The communication of Enlightenment interest was not widespread among the various peoples of America before the War for United States Independence. After that event, however, there was an increasing amount of inter-American intellectual exchange and the growth of a "continental idea" — the idea of an "American" intellectual community as opposed to the former European-oriented outlook. The Chilean

Benjamin Franklin, Angloamerican exponent of the Enlightenment in America.
Mezzotint by Edward Fisher after a portrait by Mason Chamberlain.
Courtesy of Benjamin Franklin Collection, Yale University Library.

philosopher Manuel de Salas, for example, propounded what was called
criollismo, a self-conscious sense of American cultural identity by the
American-born of the hemisphere, which rejected the ideas of such European philosophes as the Dutch Jan Cornelius de Pauw, who looked upon
Americans as culturally inferior to the Europeans. According to de Salas,
the work of brilliant Americans, including the Peruvian Pedro Peralta,

the Angloamerican Benjamin Franklin, and the Chilean José Ignacio Molina, demonstrated that Americans were fully as capable as Europeans of scientific and philosophical study. Toward the end of the century this creole point of view was beginning to spread throughout many areas of America.

In the last quarter of the eighteenth century, there also took place an increasing amount of inter-American exchange of scientific information and ideas. Franklin's studies of electricity, for example, were read in the intellectual centers of Latin America; Franklin has been said to have been second only to Newton in popularity and influence there.[25] Latin-American learned societies exchanged proceedings and honorary memberships with such United States organizations as the American Philosophical Society; individual scientists and philosophers corresponded with one another and exchanged their writings; intellectual leaders of all the American countries visited the cultural capitals of the others. On the whole, it seems possible to say that the American hemisphere did indeed constitute an intellectual community, a region, as it were, of the Enlightenment, sharing its work and contributing to it in its own American ways.

There was, of course, opposition to the Enlightenment in all America. In Angloamerica the opposition came mostly from the conservative and the orthodox, who exercised their reactionary influence through their power in government, economic life, the churches, the colleges, and the schools. Still, Harvard College in the heart of Puritan Angloamerica, William and Mary College in patrician Virginia, and King's College in bourgeois New York were lively centers of Enlightenment science, "republican" politics, and naturalistic religion.

In the Latin-American countries opposition to the Enlightenment was of an institutionalized nature. The Holy Office of the Inquisition and the Index of Prohibited Books were both significant instruments in the effort to protect the faithful from the subversive effects of the new ideas, but they were weak and ineffective everywhere. Furthermore, many of the princes and officials of the church itself, being men of lively intellect and committed to the duty of keeping themselves well informed, were themselves well read in the new learning; and there are cases on

[25] Harry Bernstein, "Some Inter-American Aspects of the Enlightenment," *Latin America and the Enlightenment*, ed. Arthur P. Whitaker (2nd ed.; Ithaca, N.Y.: Cornell University Press, 1961), pp. 53–69.

record of officials of the Inquisition reading (and believing) the books they formally condemned and actually selling the forbidden books to the intellectually curious.

Strangely enough, the French Revolution, which in its early phases was a child of the Enlightenment, provoked a series of reactions against many of the influences of the Enlightenment when it became itself more reactionary. It must also be remembered that the majority of the religious leaders and common people everywhere remained orthodox in their religious outlook. As the eighteenth century passed into the nineteenth, the Enlightenment in America, especially in Latin America, was somewhat obscured by the forces of nationalism, conservatism, romanticism, and religious reaction.

The Enlightenment in Angloamerica

The Enlightenment in America shone brightest, until approximately 1800, in Angloamerica. There, intellectual and religious life was relatively free. Science was advanced by such men as John Winthrop IV, a physicist and astronomer at Harvard, Cadwallader Colden of New York, who worked in medicine, botany, and theoretical physics, the botanist John Bartram of Philadelphia, and Benjamin Smith Barton, the anthropologist of the College of Philadelphia who visited Latin America at the turn of the century. Most important of all, perhaps, was Benjamin Franklin, whose work in the field of electricity was unquestionably America's greatest contribution to the development of science in the eighteenth century. At the same time, much work was being done in geography, especially by Lewis Evans of Philadelphia, in medicine by men such as John Morgan and Benjamin Rush of Philadelphia and John Lining of Charleston, and in the anthropology of the American Indian by Colden and Bartram. A considerable number of American scientists were contributing members of the British Royal Society; Benjamin Franklin was a member of the French Academy of Sciences and other European learned societies. In Angloamerica itself, he was chiefly responsible for the establishment of the American Philosophical Society, created in 1743 "for the promotion of useful knowledge among the British Plantations in America." This society was not an immediate success, but it was reorganized in 1769 to become the most distinguished learned society in Angloamerica from that day to the present. During and after the War for United States

Independence many other learned societies, such as the American Medical Society (Philadelphia, 1770) and the American Academy of Arts and Sciences (Boston, 1780), were founded for the "promotion of useful knowledge" in science, art, agriculture, industry, and medicine. In general, the activities of these societies gave a powerful impulse to the spread of the intellectual activities and moods of the Enlightenment in all of Angloamerica.

Enlightenment political and economic doctrines were hardly less powerful in Angloamerica than was science — perhaps they were even more so. The political history of the British colonies made many of them receptive to the ideas of Locke, Pufendorf, Montesquieu, Bolingbroke, Voltaire, Vattel, Rousseau, and others. But the English colonies produced their own outstanding political theorists, among them Richard Bland, John Adams, Alexander Hamilton, Benjamin Franklin, James Wilson, and Thomas Jefferson. All these men were exponents of one or another of the political ideas of the Enlightenment.

As a matter of fact, these American political scientists developed a new and original American concept of sovereignty. This theory, formulated by Bland, Franklin, and others, as opposed to the "indivisible" sovereignty of Jean Jacques Rousseau and William Blackstone, saw the colonies as new bodies politic, each one sovereign within its own boundaries, within a federative empire. As a rationalization of the political relations of the colonies with their mother countries, this theory attempted to harmonize the colonial drive toward self-government with the imperial sovereignty of "Kings, Lords, and Commons," which governed the interests of the "general welfare" and the relations of the empire as a whole with other empires. As Bland expressed it,

Men in a state of Nature are absolutely free and independent of one another as to sovereign Jurisdiction, but when they enter into a Society, and by their own Consent become Members of it, they must submit to the laws of the Society according to which they agree to be governed; . . . But though they must submit to the Laws, so long as they remain Members of the Society, yet they retain so much of their natural Freedom as to have a Right to retire from the Society, to renounce the Benefits of it, to enter into another Society, and to settle in another Country. . . . This natural Right remains with every Man, and he cannot justly be deprived of it by any civil Authority. . . . Now when Men exercise this Right, and withdraw themselves from their Country, they recover their natural Freedom and Independence: The Jurisdiction and

Sovereignty of the State they have quitted ceases; and if they unite, and by common Consent take Possession of a new Country, and form themselves into a political Society, they become a Sovereign State, independent of the State from which they separated.[26]

Benjamin Franklin applied this concept to the structure of the British empire, describing it as a confederation of sovereign societies bound together by their loyalty to a common monarch and by the functional necessity of some central control over the affairs of the whole confederation. In this he anticipated positively the colonial doctrine of sovereignty stated more negatively by Adam Smith. Regarding the "general welfare," Smith maintained:

The colony assemblies . . . cannot be supposed the proper judges of what is necessary for the defense and support of the whole empire. . . . The assembly of a province, like the vestry of a parish, may judge very properly concerning the affairs of its own particular district; but can have no proper means of judging concerning those of the whole empire. It cannot even judge properly concerning the proportion which its own province bears to the whole empire. . . . What is necessary for the defense and support of the whole empire, and in what proportion each part ought to contribute, can be judged of only by that assembly which inspects and superintends the affairs of the whole empire [i.e., Parliament].[27]

Bland's and Franklin's new concept of colonial empires as federations of sovereign states also involved a new idea of sovereignty as being divided between imperial sovereignty, inherent in the monarch, and colonial sovereignty, inherent in the colonial legislature. This concept ran counter to the notion of the indivisible nature of sovereignty as expounded by Rousseau and Blackstone and as adhered to by those statesmen who administered the affairs of the British empire. Significantly there is revealed in these ideologies on the nature of colonial empires the appearance of a new school of thought — an American school — although it is to be recognized that a few Europeans, such as Richard Price in England and Turgot in France, came very close to seeing the growth and the resolution of the political structures of empires in quite similar terms.

In economic and sociological thought the Angloamericans followed the

[26] Richard Bland, *An Inquiry into the Rights of the British Colonies* (1766), ed. Earl B. Swem (reprint ed.; Richmond: Appeals Press, 1922), pp. 9–10, 14.
[27] Smith, *Wealth of Nations*, II, 134.

lead of the European Enlightenment, but they also generated ideas of their own. Thus, when the physiocrats, Turgot, and Adam Smith were opening the era of free-trade ideas, Franklin and others were moving in the same direction in Angloamerica. In his discussions of population problems, for example, Franklin anticipated the thinking of Thomas Malthus. In their social thinking American intellectuals adopted much of the humanitarianism of the Europeans, including a rationalistic, natural-rights condemnation of black slavery which culminated in the emancipation of the slaves in the northern English colonies during the American Revolution.

Religious rationalism, borrowed largely from the English rationalists Clarke, Tillotson, Locke, and Anthony Ashley Cooper, flourished in Angloamerica, ranging from the Unitarianism of such men as Jonathan Mayhew of Boston to the Deism of Thomas Jefferson of Virginia or the English-born Thomas Paine of Philadelphia. The philosophies of the Enlightenment — the empiricism of Locke, the idealism of Berkeley, the realism of Reid, the Deism of Bolingbroke, and the skepticism of Hume — all had their Angloamerican adherents.

The early stirrings of an Angloamerican nationalism, as distinguished from the imperial nationalism of Franklin and Burke, is to be heard in the *Poem on the Rising Glory of America* by Philip Freneau and H. H. Brackenridge.

> This is thy praise America, thy pow'r,
> Thou best of climes by science visited,
> By freedom blest and richly stor'd with all
> The luxuries of life. Hail happy land,
> The seat of empire, the abode of kings. . . .[28]

But the "Americanism" of Angloamerica did not develop immediately into a sense of American national oneness. For the emotional counterpart to the imperial nationalism of Franklin and Burke was a loyalty to one's own colony. Franklin himself spoke of "my country" as Pennsylvania and "my countrymen" as Pennsylvanians. The Reverend Samuel Davies, an ardent Virginia Francophobe, preached emotional patriotism to his fellow Virginians as an allegiance to Virginia. Side by side with Davies, Richard Bland provided a rational philosophical base for the colony- or

---

[28] Philip Freneau and Hugh Henry Brackenridge, "The Rising Colony of America," *The Poems of Philip Freneau, Poet of the American Revolution*, ed. Fred L. Pattee, 3 vols. (Princeton, N.J.: Princeton University Library, 1902). I, 82.

state-focused "nationalism" that prevented the Americans from forming a strong national union until after their War of Independence.

The Enlightenment in Hispanoamerica

The Enlightenment came to Hispanoamerica as an extension of the Spanish Enlightenment that flowered during the reign of Carlos III (1759–89). It reached the colonies through books, scientific missions, and religious leaders and officials who were men of the Enlightenment. The many Hispanoamerican students who studied in French and English universities also introduced Enlightened thinking into the colonies, as did the visits of English, French, German, and North American scientists.[29]

Hispanoamerica, like Angloamerica, made its own contributions to the Enlightenment, although not until later. For example, José Baquijano y Carillo in Lima was at once a scientist, litterateur, and statesman, and frankly sought to apply the principles of natural law to politics. José Hipólito Unánue, also of Lima, an anatomist, botanist, and physicist, made a number of original studies of the cacao plant and published an *Index of Physics* which sought to synthesize all physical phenomena and the basic Newtonian principles. Manuel de Salas of Santiago de Chile was familiar with the work of the contemporary scientists of Europe and proclaimed the doctrine of *criollismo*, mentioned above. José Antonio Alzate y Ramírez of Mexico corresponded with members of the French Academy of Sciences, used and applied the most advanced European mathematics in his studies, and wrote a distinguished study of "natural philosophy" entitled *Observaciones sobre la física, historia natural, y artes útiles* (Mexico, 1787). About the turn of the century the Spanish-born José Celestino Mutis achieved great distinction in the study of botany and astronomy and by building an astronomical observatory in Bogotá in 1803.

These are only a few examples, but they sufficiently illustrate that Hispanoamericans not only participated in the spread of the Enlightenment to America, but also made many original contributions to the advancement of Enlightenment learning.

[29] For a discussion of the Enlightenment in Spain and its contributions to the Enlightenment in Spanish America, see the excellent essay by Arthur Whitaker, "Changing and Unchanging Interpretations of the Enlightenment in Spanish America," in A. Owen Aldridge, ed., *The Ibero-American Enlightenment* (Urbana: University of Illinois Press, 1971), pp. 21–70.

The Enlightenment in Hispanoamerica was not, however, limited to science. On the contrary, there was a great deal of political thought. Rousseau's work, for example, was widely read by the political thinkers of Hispanoamerica almost from the time of the first publication of the *Social Contract* in 1763. For the Latin-American philosophers, Rousseau's "general will" seemed to justify *criollismo*. Not all Hispanoamerican political thought was based on ideas derived from their reading the works of European writers. Much original thinking was being done, in the fashion of Richard Bland or Benjamin Franklin, to rationalize the growing *criollismo* in Hispanoamerica. Thus, José Antonio de Rojas and Manuel José de Orejuela of Chile formulated a plan for an ideal republic: the monarchy would be overthrown and would be replaced by a republic governed by a "sovereign senate" representing the "general will."

At Chuquisaca in upper Peru, the university, called "the Salamanca of the New World," attracted students from all over Hispanoamerica. There they read Montesquieu, Rousseau, Diderot, the *Encyclopédie*, and many others. Here it was that Mariano Moreno, an Argentine scholar, adapted Rousseau's doctrines to America; in his *Memorial de los Hacendados* (1809), published after he returned to Buenos Aires, he expounded a philosophy of American autonomy not unlike Richard Bland's theory of American colonial sovereignty. He also published a translation of Rousseau's *Social Contract* in 1810; in the prologue he stated that "Americans do not consider themselves united with the Spanish monarch through the social pact, which alone can support the legitimacy and decorum of a rule. If the peoples of Spain remain dependents of the prisoner king, waiting for their freedom and remission, all well and good. . . . In no case can America consider herself bound by that obligation; she has not concurred in the celebration of the social pact from which the Spanish monarchs derive their empire's sole title to legitimacy."[30]

Similar views were expressed in Chile, Peru, New Granada, and Mexico. Although based on Rousseau, they all reveal an original American outlook in the sense that they apply the Genevan's political concepts to the nascent impulse of the Hispanoamerican men of the Enlightenment toward national self-determination. In this sense, the Enlightenment in Hispanoamerica provided the seminal ideas that gave birth to Hispanoamerican independence.

[30] Quoted in Arciniegas, *Latin America*, p. 255.

One of the germinal phenomena in the spread of the Enlightenment in Hispanoamerica was the intellectual societies called, in each case, the Society of Friends of the Country, which appeared in the intellectual centers of the colonies. These societies, primarily scientific and literary in purpose, were patterned after the Sociedad Vascongada de Amigos del País (the Basque Society of Friends of the Country), a type of regional academy of sciences organized by Manuel Ignacio Altuna, a friend of Rousseau, in the town of Azcoitia in northern Spain. Societies imitating this one had sprung up all over Spain and had become focuses of Enlightenment ideas. Similarly, the Societies of Friends of the Country became centers for the discussion of Enlightenment ideas throughout Hispanoamerica.

More than that, the Society of Friends of the Country in Vergara, Spain, sent two brothers, Juan José and Fausto Elhuyar, to Germany for training in the latest developments in mineralogy; they were then sent to America by the Spanish government to study the situation in the declining silver mines of Mexico and Peru. Fausto Elhuyar founded the famous Royal School of Mines in Mexico in 1792; he was responsible for a number of significant improvements in the techniques of mining that increased the quantity of silver production in the Mexican mines. He also worked and studied with the Mexican Society of Friends of the Country. Juan José Elhuyar went to Bogotá, where he became associated with the work of Mutis.

The Societies of Friends of the Country did not limit themselves, however, to the study and consideration of purely scientific subjects. For it was almost inevitable that political, economic, and social questions should enter into their discussions. It thus developed that the societies were suspected, with considerable justification, of being centers of criticism of the existing regime and of the nascent creole urge for American emancipation from the Spaniards' administration of the colonies.

Therefore, although the Enlightenment in Hispanoamerica was, first of all, scientific and philosophical, it involved political theory as well. In its broadest aspects it is to be regarded as an intellectual force that tended to free men's minds from ignorance, superstition, intellectual repression, censorship, and persecution. But if it liberated men's minds, it was only natural that it should also free their bodies and their institutions from outside "foreign" control. So the ferment of freedom was political and social too and became a force in the realm of ideas that would grow into the American peoples' fight for emancipation from European control.

The Enlightenment in Francoamerica

Because France was the home of the Enlightenment, it might be expected that the French colonies would be areas for the brilliant expression of its moods. This was hardly the case, however, since intellectual life, both in Canada and in the French West Indies, was almost exclusively guided by the French Catholic church. Schools and colleges, the most notable of which was the Jesuit College in Quebec, were maintained by the Jesuits and other orders. These institutions showed little interest in the experimental, rational, and secular ideas of the philosophes. It was not until the period of the War for United States Independence (long after Canada had been surrendered to England) that the "Voltairian" spirit began to show itself in Canadian publications, with the founding of *La gazette littéraire* in Montreal in 1778 and *Le magazin de Quebec* in 1792. Thus, the Francoamerican colonies contributed little or nothing of major importance to the Enlightenment.

Still, the planters in the French West Indies did send their sons to France to be educated. There they came into contact with the writings of the philosophes, and copies of the *Encyclopédie* and the books of Montesquieu, Diderot, Voltaire, and Rousseau went back to the islands with them as well as with many of the military officers who sailed to the islands with the armed forces. It was in the field of political thought that the islands produced their most prominent intellectual figures, such men as Jean Dubuc and Moreau de St. Méry, both born in Martinique. Both made notable contributions to the political literature of America, especially Moreau with his compilation of the laws of the West Indies colonies and his essays on the societies of the colonies themselves. These men were, indeed, significant contributors to the Enlightenment in America.

The Enlightenment in Lusoamerica

In Lusoamerica the Enlightenment burned with its weakest American flame. Yet, it was not without its manifestations and its exponents, and it was far from being as "retarded" as some historians have supposed. Brazil, in its intellectual life, as otherwise, differed sharply from its mother country and its American neighbors, but it shared with them, if to a somewhat lesser degree, the general intellectual achievements of the century.[31]

The first sparks of the Enlightenment were ignited in the new "academies," or private societies, organized for the study of history and science. A considerable number of these were established in Brazil between 1724 and 1772. Often sponsored by a governor or a viceroy, they were composed chiefly of aristocratic persons with literary, historical, and scientific interests. A number of important studies of the natural history of Brazil were produced by members of these academies.

Other hints of the Enlightenment were to be found in the libraries of educated men, including religious and political leaders; these libraries housed many books that had come from France, even some that were listed on the Index.

The penetration of Brazil by Enlightenment science and thought really began with the founding in 1772 of the Scientific Society of Rio de Janeiro, under the sponsorship of Viceroy Lavradio. This society lasted only until a later viceroy, the Conde de Rezende, suppressed it as a hotbed of revolutionary ideas, but in the two and a half decades of its existence it was responsible for much research in natural history, botany, agriculture, chemistry, physics, and astronomy and for the publication of a number of related studies by its members, which were based on actual scientific observation and experiment.

Its purpose and discussions were apparently not limited to science, however, as the change of its name in 1779 to the Literary Society would indicate. Nor were they unaware, it seems, of politics, for by 1794 the society possessed the finest library in Brazil, a library which included many of the most significant works of European political thinkers published during the century. Elsewhere in Brazil, learned men were also accumulating libraries and studying, thinking, and writing within the framework of Enlightenment thought.

Efforts by the government, the Holy Office of the Inquisition, and the Index of Prohibited Books to check the advance of Enlightenment

---

[31] For studies of the Enlightenment in Portugal and Brazil, see two highly illuminating essays, one by Manoel Cardozo, "The Internationalism of the Portuguese Enlightenment: The Role of the Estrangeirado, c. 1700–c. 1750," and the other by E. Bradford Burns, "Concerning the Transmission and Dissemination of the Enlightenment in Brazil" in Aldridge, ed., *The Ibero-American Enlightenment*, pp. 141–207, and 256–281.

thought met with some success. Liberal-thinking societies were suppressed, private individuals suffered persecution for possessing prohibited books, and some of the more politically liberal-minded men of the Enlightenment suffered arrest and prosecution as enemies of the state.

The work of the Enlightenment in Brazil continued, nevertheless. The flow of books, scientists, students, and officials carrying the virus of ideas continued and managed to spread. Most especially it is to be noted that Brazil was not merely a receptacle for Enlightenment ideas, but that, also, the scientists, scholars, and litterateurs of Brazil, just as their colleagues in the other colonial empires, made significant contributions to the Enlightenment in science, literature, history, and other disciplines.

For example, Cláudio Manuel da Costa wrote and published a series of *Chilean Letters*, following the format of Montesquieu's *Persian Letters*, that trenchantly criticized political and intellectual conditions in Brazil. He also wrote poetry and translated some of Voltaire's works and Adam Smith's *Wealth of Nations*. Luiz Vieira da Silva, a canon of the church and a man of the Enlightenment, possessed a broadly selected library of contemporary European authors covering the secular classics, geography, history, mathematics, physics, astronomy, and medicine; his collection included volumes of the *Encyclopédie* and the works of Montesquieu, Mably, Voltaire, and Condillac. Many Brazilian savants had libraries containing works of the high Enlightenment.

The major achievement of the Enlightenment in Brazil was the quiet, unspectacular accumulation of scientific data, literary pieces, and materials for Brazilian history by societies and individuals. Accused of subversion by both state and church, some of the societies were dissolved to avoid worse fates; some of them, it is certain, were indeed centers for the discussion of growing Brazilian self-consciousness.

Conclusion

The role of America in the Enlightenment was a two-way role. For while the Enlightenment exported to America much learning and many new and revolutionary ideas in science, politics, economics, literature, and philosophy, it also learned a great deal from America. Not only did Europeans sent to America bring back a significant amount of data of all kinds to influence the thinking of the philosophes, but Americans themselves postulated theories and wrote much in science, politics, religion, geography, ethnology, literature, and philosophy. A substantial amount of this thinking and writing was derivative, of course, imitative of the thought and literature of Europe; there were, however, contributions that were new, the first genuine contributions to the ongoing intellectual evolution of the North Atlantic community. The non-European parts of this community, created in the course of the expansion of Europe, had now come, or were beginning, to assume the responsibilities of full-fledged, mature members of it.

Is it possible to make any generalization about the Enlightenment "mind" with regard to America? Were there any ascertainable "common denominators" that ran through most of the thinking of most of the philosophes, or were they but "a family" of thinkers, a host of individual men who did their own thinking individually, each having little in common with the others?

It does appear that there were certain concepts and assumptions that were shared by most of the intellectual leaders of the century, no matter in which fields they worked or in which countries they lived. To suggest only a few, one might refer first to the faith of most of them in science: not only the factual and mathematical knowledge of the universe and man that derived from science, but also the enthusiastic faith that men could know and understand more and that, knowing and understanding, they could influence or control the material universe and its laws for the betterment of the human condition. This epitomized their belief in progress, their faith that man could improve his condition, if he would, by the use of his mind.

It also seems to be clear that the major leitmotiv in the thinking of most philosophes was the "human spirit." This was the essence of their metaphysic. Most of them, from the geographers to the political scientists to the nationalists to the philosophers, held this ideal before them. The bulk of the writing of the philosophes constituted a great morality, even a religion. It was a sort of metaphysic derived from the notions of "nature" and "nature's God," functioning in a system of "natural law" through an ethic based upon scientific knowledge and interpreted by human reason.

So far as the idea of America was a part of this metaphysic, this new world was understood to be at once the scene of terrible aberrations from the moral principles of natural law and a stage upon which might be enacted, at last, the victorious drama of liberty, human rights, and human felicity. In America itself there seems to have appeared a new idea of America, expressing a new concept of what America was and what its destiny, in light of the "human spirit," might be.

CHAPTER 9

The Independence
of the United States

In the half-century between 1775 and 1825 twenty fragments of the Euroamerican empires, that is, twenty of the new national societies formed in the matrix of the expansion of Europe in America, seceded from their old empires and became independent sovereign states.

The fundamental causes of this multiple movement to independence were generally and basically the same in all cases. Sociologically, these movements grew out of the development of regional economic and social interests and societal ambitions that ran counter to those of the mother countries. Psychologically, these fundamental economic and social divergences were exacerbated and intensified by the tensions between the officials and other representatives of the mother countries and the creoles. But these sociological and psychological differences were articulated, ideologically, and encouraged by the ideas of the European Enlightenment, which, by the third quarter of the eighteenth century, had become a common intellectual bond among "liberals" all over the hemisphere. In addition, the psychological phenomenon known as nationalism, itself partly a product of the Enlightenment, had appeared in all the regions of the hemisphere and was a powerful impetus to every one of the American independence movements.

However, although ideologically all the American independence movements may be said to have been among the fruits of the Enlightenment, the fact is that other powerful forces — economic, political, social, and religious — provided the deep-running popular drives that gave each one of the independence movements its own particular and unique incentives and characteristics. Thus, while all these movements shared many

212

common denominators, the basic sociological and emotional forces at work in every "national" region differed from those in others. Consequently, every national movement differed in certain significant local ways from every other. This was notably true in the independence movement in that portion of the Angloamerican empire that became the United States of America.

The birth of a new nation, the United States of America, by the secession of thirteen of the British colonies from the British empire was the first international fruit of the expansion of European civilization into the American hemisphere. The event served to illustrate the famous dictum of Turgot that colonies are like fruit: when they "ripen" — that is, when they mature — they separate themselves from their parent societies to form new ones in accord with their own national geniuses. Turgot's pronouncement seemed to ring true in the case of the Angloamerican Revolution, as well as in those of the other new national societies that, within half a century after the signing of the United States Declaration of Independence, would also separate themselves from their parent states to become autonomous nations in the Western Hemisphere community.

The Angloamerican Revolution, therefore, is of major historical significance not only because its meaning for the new Angloamerican society and its effect upon the structure and the functioning of the British overseas empire were profound, but also because it represented the first great colonial anti-European reaction in the history of the expansion of Europe. These "anticolonial" reactions against the mother states would eventually give birth to the American community of sovereign states and later to the anti-European reactions of colonial peoples all over the world. The expansion of Europe had produced, as it were, its own backlash; ultimately, with the growth of the ideals of nationalism and the self-determination of peoples, it would induce its own end. Indeed, the new states would continue the expansion of the Atlantic community in their own interests: the expansion of Europe would cease to be just "European" and would become "European and American," or "the expansion of Western civilization."

The Happy British Empire, ca. 1750

The Angloamerican independence movement had its roots in a diverse complex of historical developments. Basic to the entire movement was the fact that in their struggle to survive and find the good life in the American environment the English (and non-English) colonists had created new patterns of economic, social, and political life and institutions. Out of these new activities and institutions had grown new self-interests that, in many ways, ran counter to the imperial self-interests of the mother country. The colonies were, indeed, new societies with new life-styles of their own. Autonomy, if not independence, seems to have been logically inherent in this divergence.

About the middle of the eighteenth century, the British empire, or at least the Angloamerican part of it, was a de facto federal entity — much more so than any other Euroamerican empire. The central core of this empire was Great Britain, and the central imperial "federal" government was the British government, institutionalized in "King, Lords, and Commons," that is, "the King in Parliament." The executive functions of this imperial government were concentrated in the king himself and his Privy Council, which was made up of his ministers, members of "the cabinet," who were also usually members of Parliament. As mentioned earlier, executive matters concerned with the overseas colonies were handled by a congeries of committees — the Committee for Plantation Affairs, headed by the secretary of state for the Southern Department, the Committee for War, the Committee for the Treasury, the Committee for Admiralty Affairs, the "Law Lords," and so on, each under the jurisdiction of its own appropriate minister. These ministers, or ministries, could act separately, though theoretically only with the approval of the king; on occasion they acted as a united body, as "the cabinet." It was through these ministries that instructions were directed to imperial officers in the colonies.

This executive division of the British empire included a host of agents, officials, and underlings in the colonies: customs collectors, "naval officers," judges in admiralty, military officers, and the like, all of whom were responsible not to the local colonial governments, but to the ministries in England that supervised their work. The most important imperial officer in the colonies, except in the "corporate" colonies (Connecticut and Rhode Island) and the "proprietary" colonies (Pennsylvania and Maryland), was the royal governor, who was appointed by the king and was responsible to him.

The judicial affairs of the empire focused in the "Law Lords," a committee of distinguished lawyers, members of the Privy Council, presided over by the lord chancellor. This body, as a de facto supreme court of the empire, handled most of the appeals from colonial courts.

In its deliberations upon American affairs the Privy Council and its ministers were assisted by the special institution called the Lords Commissioners for Trade and Plantations, described above. This board, a kind of "think-tank" composed of sixteen men — eight of the ministers of the Privy Council and eight experts who were supposed to know something about the colonies — prepared voluminous reports and recommendations for the ministers and the king. It is probably true that a very high proportion of the details of British colonial policy, in the generation preceding the American Revolution, was the work of this board.

The legislative body of the British empire, of course, was the British Parliament, which was composed of the House of Lords and the House of Commons and made laws both for Britain and for the colonies. Its functions were directed by the ministers of the "cabinet," who were also members of the Privy Council, as noted above. It was this body, for example, which enacted such imperial laws as the Navigation Laws, the Acts of Trade, the Naturalization Act of 1740, the Post Office Act (1710), the New England Currency Act (1751), and many others concerned with what would later be called the "general welfare." Eventually, the American colonies would question the authority of Parliament to legislate their internal affairs, but as of the middle of the eighteenth century the question had never seriously been raised. The theory was, according to such constitutionalists as the distinguished jurist Sir William Blackstone, that in any body politic like the British empire there was one supreme, unchallengeable, and indivisible sovereignty, which resided in the "King in Parliament." Blackstone and most other British statesmen of that era thought of the empire as an integral, indivisible national entity, the symbolic head of which was the king. Actually, the general outlines of this theory of empire — or "imperialism" — paralleled to a surprising degree those of the "imperialists" managing the French, Spanish, and Portuguese empires during these same years.

By contrast, each of the self-governing British colonies enjoyed a high degree of self-direction. Every one of the colonies possessed a great deal of autonomy, both economic and political, within the overall British imperial economic and political system. Each colony had its own representative legislature, and these legislatures, particularly the lower houses, the members of which were elected by the propertied citizens, had gradually and significantly extended their roles in the conduct of government and, through their successful control of the budget, they had gained effective control of government itself, including, to a notable degree, the actions of the colonial governors.

To justify this localization and popularization of government, the colonials of the "Assembly party" in each colony — the colonial "Whigs" — basing their theories largely upon the writings of John Locke and the seventeenth-century English "commonwealthmen," had formulated a set of ideas that defended the assemblies' struggle for power. Colonial leaders such as William Smith and William Livingston of New York, Benjamin Franklin of Pennsylvania, Samuel Adams of Massachusetts, Patrick Henry and Richard Bland of Virginia worked out an Angloamerican political doctrine based upon the concepts of natural right, the social compact, and the British Constitution. In practice this meant an insistence upon the right of government by representatives, the control of the judiciary by the legislature, and a limitation of the prerogative of the crown.

On the other hand, the governors of the colonies, usually Englishmen, supported by the conservatives in the colonial societies — members of the legislative and executive councils, imperial officers, and those who felt a strong emotional attachment to the mother country and its ideals — constituted what was called the "Court party" or colonial "Tory" party. This group, too, had its ideology of colonial government, an ideology that accepted the ultimate authority of the mother country over the colonies, an authority symbolized by the "prerogative" of the crown. This prerogative, while nowhere constitutionally defined, was generally assumed to be independent of and to transcend the powers of the legislature. Instructions issued to the colonial governors in its name were thought to have the force of law (an idea vigorously rejected by the Assembly parties). For the "Court party," the prerogative represented the mystical authority of the kingship and the sovereignty of the entire British empire-nation.

Many efforts were made by British and American theorists to harmonize these two concepts, but there remained a basic, essential conflict between them and between the principles they represented — the Blackstonean notion of indivisible imperial sovereignty on the one side and the increasing autonomy, even sovereignty, of the colonies on the other.

Economically, too, the Angloamerican colonies, although they had grown up within the framework of the mercantilistic British colonial system, had followed the impulses of their own self-interest to the point where they were nullifying the British laws of navigation and trade almost with impunity. They were trading more or less directly — in many cases illegally — with practically all the areas and societies ringing the Atlantic. During the Seven Years War, especially, the British colonies traded with the colonies of the other nations in the hemisphere, even those of France and Spain, with which England was at war.

This wartime trade with the enemy was achieved by the use of neutral ports, particularly those of the Dutch, and by the practice known as the "flag-of-truce" entry into an enemy port. It was prohibited by the mother country, but it continued; the colonists justified it on the ground that the trade with foreign colonies, even those of France and Spain, was necessary in order for them to buy the manufactured goods of England. This trade illustrates the divergence of colonial economic interests from those of the mother country; it was also a clear manifestation of the fact that the commerce of the hemisphere, despite the efforts of the imperial administrations to control it, was becoming a genuinely international phenomenon.

In their social composition the Angloamerican colonies were no longer completely, or even predominantly, English. The large numbers of African blacks who had been forcibly imported into the colonies constituted a huge portion of the population, which fanned out from New England, where there were relatively few blacks, southward through the southern continental colonies, and into the British West Indies, where the blacks significantly outnumbered the whites. This stream of immigration was augmented by hundreds of thousands of Germans, Scots, Scotch-Irish, French Huguenots, Jews, Swiss, Dutch, Swedes, and other non-English minorities, not to mention the American Indians. Government, to be sure, and the larger parts of the economy were dominated by Englishmen or the descendants of Englishmen, but the Angloamerican colonies on the North American continent had become societies that were conglomerate in the extreme; the population was no longer an "English" population; indeed, it is probably safe to say that the creoles of pure English descent in Angloamerica were now a minority of the total population. If this be true, it follows that at least half of the Angloamericans felt little of that loyalty to the mother country that derived from ancestry, blood relationships, or cultural tradition. The Angloamericans, by the middle of the eighteenth century, had begun to call themselves "Americans." This is probably an accurate index of the subtle psychological change in their orientation that was going on among them — even (with the exception of the "Tories") among those of English descent. Although the process of social and cultural assimilation was somewhat slower than has sometimes been assumed, continental Angloamerica was a genuine "melting pot" of races and cultures — much more so, by far, than any other empire in the hemisphere.

In religion, the great majority of the Angloamerican creoles were of the Anglican persuasion; they were ruled, in their religious concerns, by the bishop of London, and their feeling of loyalty to England was relatively strong. But the total panorama of religion in Angloamerica was even more diversified, if possible, than the population. For among those of English descent there were many persons of dissenting sects, Congregationalists, Baptists, Presbyterians, and Quakers, who rejected any English religious control, and many of these sects were rent by divisions among themselves. The Indians had their own indigenous beliefs, and the blacks brought with them a variety of African cults. To all of these religious differences should be added the modifications of religious doctrines and practices introduced by the Great Awakening and the development of religious rationalism, as well as the beliefs and practices of Jews and Roman Catholics, of which there were a few.[1]

The mere presence of so many disparate religious outlooks made for a high degree of religious toleration based on expediency alone. But religious toleration of a more positive listen-and-learn nature was implicit in the intellectual positions of the Quakers and the rationalists; this positive toleration in religion was buttressed by the scientists, who demanded intellectual freedom for the exchange of their findings with one another. Therefore, it is to be noted again that the theory and practice of religious toleration among the Angloamericans made Angloamerica that area of the world where toleration was relatively much more widespread than anywhere else. It provided a rationale and a religious foundation for the intellectual individualism and freedom that were to characterize the emergence of democracy in all America, and it fed the Angloamericans' fear of, say, the establishment of an Anglican bishopric among them, thus further differentiating the Angloamerican societies from their mother country.

[1] See above, chapter 7.

Another religious factor that had a powerful effect on the Angloameri-can Revolution was the strongly moralistic mood of the Angloamerican life-style. Overwhelmingly Protestant, in contrast with the Catholicism of all the other Euroamerican societies except the Dutch, the Angloameri-cans were characterized by an unusual seriousness in their attitudes toward life and politics. From their Puritan, Presbyterian, Baptist, Quaker, and Anglican backgrounds, and from the nearly two centuries of history forcefully activated in the mid-eighteenth century by the Great Awakening, they had inherited a high potential of devotion to what they called "civic virtue"; it seems clear that this attitude morally rein-forced the Angloamericans' fear of being contaminated by the corruption with which they believed English society and politics to be ridden. Cer-tainly this devotion provided a strong motivation, especially among the newly articulate lower classes, for the violent and semiviolent reactions to any reform or disciplinary measures initiated by the British.

In contrast with these religious divergences, the close relationship between the scientists of Angloamerica and those of Great Britain con-stituted one of the strongest intellectual ties binding the colonies to Eng-land before the secession of the United States from the British empire. Perhaps fifty Americans were members of the Royal Society of England before the thirteen colonies separated from the empire. They made many contributions to the *Transactions* of that society, and there was a very extensive exchange of ideas by correspondence between individual American scientists and their colleagues in England. Benjamin Franklin, the most noted Angloamerican scientist, received many awards and hon-orary memberships from the English as well as from the European scien-tific societies.

For the British West Indies, economic dependence upon the markets of England emphasized the feeling of unity with the mother country, as did their need for diplomatic and military protection from the enemies who surrounded them. But in all other relationships, especially between the continental colonies and England, there had developed many differ-ences that tended to separate the "enlightened self-interest" of the col-onies from that of the mother country. In the third quarter of the century, the creole leaders of the Angloamericans were still loyal "Britons," but they had become so accustomed to political, economic, and religious autonomy that any serious effort to limit that freedom or hinder its growth was certain to arouse much antagonism.

The historical fact is that the Angloamerican colonists, during their two centuries of struggle to survive and to find the good life, had developed powerful loyalties toward their own colonial societies — their "countries," they called them — loyalties that were closely akin to nationalism and that competed against the British imperial nationalism for their emotional support. By the mid-century they were self-consciously "Virginians," "Pennsylvanians," or "New Englanders"; each colony was sensitive of its own political, economic, cultural, and religious identity. Samuel Davies called upon his "countrymen" of Virginia to show their patriotism in the fight against the French; Benjamin Franklin urged his "country-men" of Pennsylvania to resist the expansion of the powers of the pro-prietor in that colony; Jonathan Mayhew summoned his "countrymen" of the Massachusetts legislature to appropriate money to drive the French out of North America. This psychological phenomenon, this embryonic nationalism, this "patriotism" for one's colony, was un-questionably one of the forces that lay behind the colonial resistance which was certain to arise in the face of the imperial efforts to limit colonial autonomy.

Imperial Reform and Colonial Resistance

George Montagu Dunk, second Earl of Halifax, became president of the British Board of Trade in 1748. A devoted imperialist, he instituted a series of imperial reforms that were intended to strengthen the hold of the crown on the colonies. His reforms sought to tighten the control of England over the commerce of the colonies, to create a military estab-lishment in the colonies, which would be paid for in part by the colonies under a system of taxation imposed by Parliament, and most of all, to strengthen the power of the royal prerogative exercised in the colonies by the colonial governors.

In 1750 Parliament, at the recommendation of the Board of Trade, passed the so-called Iron Act, which placed limitations on the manufac-ture of hardware in the colonies; a year later it passed the so-called Colonial Currency Act, which prohibited the New England colonies from making their paper currencies legal tender; it undertook a series of efforts to render the Navigation Acts effective; it set up a standing British army in the colonies and established a unified military command for all the colonies; it organized imperial relations with the Indians in North

America into two districts, each directed by an agent appointed by the crown. Above all, the Board of Trade, with its newly won power of writing instructions for the colonial governors, strictly enjoined them to strengthen the power of the prerogative of the crown in their relations with the colonial assemblies.

This program, which was clearly designed to strengthen the central government at the expense of colonial autonomy, was interrupted by the outbreak of the Seven Years War. But it was taken up again in 1763 by the Earl of Grenville, whose plans and projects for the centralization of imperial control precipitated the first outright break between continental Angloamerica and England.

The Seven Years War had a powerful impact on the unself-conscious trend toward the separation of the British American colonies from the empire. Besides the developments that took place during the course of the war itself, the Treaty of Paris, which ended the war, instituted a number of new and puzzling imperial problems, or exacerbated old ones, that both the imperial government and the colonial governments had to face.

In the first place, the Treaty of Paris opened to the imperialistic Angloamericans and Britons an enormous expanse of new territory in North America. Not only was Britain's claim to the eastern half of the Mississippi Valley confirmed, but Canada, Florida, and the islands of Dominica, Grenada, St. Vincent, and Tobago in the Caribbean were opened to British social expansion and "westward movement."

The initial problem confronting the imperial administration, therefore, was that of organizing these vast new acquisitions as parts of the British empire. That would be extremely difficult because all these areas differed from one another in geography, population, government and law, religion, and language. The territories acquired from France were inhabited by French-speaking Roman Catholic Frenchmen, who had been living under the imperial system of France; Florida, acquired from Spain, was peopled by Roman Catholic Spanish-speaking Spaniards; the eastern half of the Mississippi Valley was peopled mainly by Indians with a neolithic culture and primitive tribal governments — if governments they may be called. In the latter area, the task of organization was further complicated by the outbreak of the so-called Pontiac's Rebellion of 1763–66, the most extensive Indian uprising against the white man ever to take place in North America.

The British imperial government, headed by the Earl of Grenville, attacked the problem of organizing the new territories by issuing a royal proclamation, or executive order, on October 7, 1763. According to this proclamation, the westward movement from the old colonies into the Mississippi Valley was to be halted, at least temporarily, near the crest of the Allegheny Mountains. The territories between the Allegheny Mountains and the Mississippi River were to be left to the Indians; trade with them was to be allowed only under license; general relations with them were to be directed by the imperial agents of the northern and southern districts.

Curiously, no provision was made in the proclamation for the government of this new "west." Although the occupation of land was prohibited and trade in the area was to be conducted under license of the governors, it seems to have been assumed that, insofar as government was necessary at all, such government, particularly the management of the military occupation of the area, would be left in the hands of the commanding British general in North America. As for Canada, Florida, and the new Caribbean islands, the proclamation provided that they should be organized as governments under the so-called "royal" plan.

This executive order aroused a considerable outburst of criticism from the colonists, especially the land speculators and the Indian traders. Underlying the outcry, however, was a fear among thoughtful Americans that the great imperial domain of the west, claimed by a number of colonies under their original charters and theoretically administered by them, from now on might become a concern of the central imperial government and would be taken out of the hands of the colonies.

Following the Proclamation of 1763, the Grenville government had Parliament pass a series of laws for the colonies which, by reason of their combined centralizing tendency, could only arouse colonial resistance. It passed the Revenue Act of 1764 to tighten up the administration of the Navigation Acts and to raise money for colonial defense; it extended the Currency Act of 1751 to include all the colonies; it passed the Quartering Act requiring the colonies to assist in quartering the imperial forces stationed in them. But the action that precipitated the most spectacular colonial opposition was the Stamp Act of 1765, which proposed to raise a part of the money for colonial defense by imposing a tax upon all legal paper used in the colonies.

The outcry of the Americans was loud, explicit, and, in some cases, violent. Several of the colonial legislatures, following the lead of Virginia, officially protested the taxation of the colonies by Parliament as a violation of the rights of the Angloamericans as Englishmen, and in the fall of 1765 a congress of representatives of most of the colonies met in New York and drew up a united declaration of grievances against the entire Grenville program. But the most effective part of the colonial protest was the American boycott of goods coming from England. For this hurt the merchants of England: it was their appeal, and not the objections of the colonies, that caused Parliament to repeal the Stamp Act in 1766. At the same time, however, it passed the Declaratory Act, which reasserted in unequivocal terms the principle that the British crown, Lords, and Commons were sovereign over the colonies "in all cases whatsoever" and that this sovereignty could never be challenged.

The Grenville program for a centralized administration of the empire was thus a failure. Another effort, with a similar program, was made by the Pitt-Grafton ministry between 1767 and 1770; in the face of an embattled American resistance, it also failed. The ministry of Lord North aroused the anger of the Americans again by passing the so-called Tea Act in 1773, which continued the policy of parliamentary taxation. The violent resistance to that act by the American radicals precipitated disciplinary measures which in turn led to the use of arms.

The thirteen years between 1763 and 1776 were thus the years of the great split in the Angloamerican empire. The attempts of the Grenville, Pitt-Grafton, and North ministries to impose the principle of the integral and centralized empire on the Angloamerican colonies had stirred and galvanized in the Angloamericans of the continental colonies their nascent sense of maturity, of their natural right to self-government, and of their self-conscious conception of themselves as sovereign or quasi-sovereign societies.[2]

Therefore, it became apparent when representatives of the colonies met in Philadelphia in the fall of 1774 to protest the English disciplinary measures against Massachusetts because of the famous Boston Tea Party that many issues had contributed to the denouement. Economic factors

[2] There was a good deal of sympathy in the British West Indies for the resistance of the continental colonies but the economic and international dependence of the islands upon the mother country, coupled with a much stronger feeling of imperial loyalty among them, made it impossible for them to throw in their lot completely with the continental colonies. It was at this point that the British West Indies parted company with the continental colonies in the history of the Angloamerican empire.

were of basic importance, as were Britain's attempts to impose the will of the crown or Parliament on the colonial governments, the question of the authority of Parliament to tax the colonies contrary to the "rights of Englishmen," the power of the crown to control colonial courts, the colonial fear of the possible establishment in the colonies of an authoritative Anglican church, and so on. The First Continental Congress (1774) represented a genuine crystallization of opinion in all the colonies, but the colonies were not yet ready to secede from the empire. They protested their profound loyalty to the British empire; what they desired above all else was a clarification of the line to be drawn between the rightful constitutional authority of England's government over the colonies and the degree of rightful autonomous constitutional authority possessed by the colonies.

This was the basic issue in the conflict. To the English statesmen, acting on the principles enunciated by Blackstone, the sovereignty of Parliament over all Britons was unlimited, complete, absolute. Sovereignty in the British nation resided in "King, Lords, and Commons"; sovereignty in any nation could not be divided. The resistance of the colonies, therefore, surprised and shocked the English statesmen, for it violated the basic constitutional integrity of the empire.

The Angloamericans, on the other hand, had at last arrived at the reasoned conviction that the colonies were new "British" societies founded on the basis of ancient social compacts (the colonial charters) with the kings of England. The people were Englishmen, with all the rights of Englishmen; nevertheless, the societies were new bodies politic that were by natural right sovereign within their own boundaries. Thus the Angloamerican creole political philosophers introduced into the debate the concept of a divided sovereignty: the "King, Lords, and Commons" were sovereign in matters pertaining to international and intercolonial affairs, but this sovereignty did not extend to matters concerning only the internal affairs of any colony.

The American position, publicized by Richard Bland, Benjamin Franklin, John Adams, James Wilson, and other "Whigs," was a sincere effort to rationalize the autonomy of the colonies within the framework of a federal empire. In the history of the expansion of Europe it was the first articulate formulation of a political theory that recognized and accommodated the emergence of creole societies from the former

Euroamerican colonies. There would be many more such formulations in the next half-century in the history of the American hemisphere.

The Angloamerican concept of a federal empire being governed by the idea of a divided sovereignty was incomprehensible to the English statesmen charged with the administration of the empire. On the basis of their own conviction of the integral, indivisible sovereignty of the British crown, they refused to pay much attention to the Angloamerican petitions and adopted strong military measures to enforce upon the colonies the will of the central government. Both sides resorted to arms, and the "shot heard round the world" was fired in Lexington, a little village in Massachusetts, on April 19, 1775.

The fighting went on for more than a year before the thirteen continental colonies, in desperation over England's refusal to accept their conception of the federal empire, finally resolved to secede from the empire. This action was taken by the Second Continental Congress on July 2, 1776, when the Congress resolved "that these United Colonies are, and of right ought to be, free and independent States, that they are absolved from all allegiance to the British Crown, and that all political connection between them and the State of Great Britain is, and ought to be, totally dissolved."

Two days later, on July 4, 1776, in the famous "Unanimous Declaration [of Independence] of the Thirteen United States of America," the Continental Congress formally announced its action to the world.

The World War for United States Independence

In the formal war with England that followed the signing of the Declaration of Independence, all the odds seemed to be on the side of England. But the Americans, under the leadership of George Washington, hung on despite defeat after defeat and demonstrated to the world that they could not easily be conquered. And when they won a stunning victory over General John Burgoyne at Saratoga, in upper New York, in the fall of 1777, France and other nations decided, for reasons deriving largely from the exigencies of the European balance of power, to throw in their lot with the United States. With the entrance of France (1778), Spain (1779), and Holland (1780) into the conflict, the War for United States

Independence became a world war, and England, instead of subduing thirteen rebellious colonies, now found itself facing a ring of enemies in Europe, Asia, and Africa, as well as in America.

The war in Angloamerica ended with the capture of Lord Cornwallis by Washington and his French allies at Yorktown, Virginia, in 1781. But fighting went on in the Far East and in the Caribbean area, and peace was not finally made until 1783.

By the Anglo-American Treaty of Peace, signed at Versailles in 1783, Great Britain recognized the independency and sovereignty of the thirteen former "continental" colonies, with boundaries that included the Great Lakes on the north, the Mississippi River on the west, and the northern borderline of Florida on the south. Britain retained Canada, but in its treaty with Spain it gave back to that country East and West Florida and the island of Minorca (in the Mediterranean); Spain granted limited freedom to British woodcutters to cut dyewood on the coast of Campeche and Belize (modern British Honduras) and returned to England the island of Providence in the Bahamas, occupied during the war.

In its treaty with France, Britain restored the islands of St. Pierre and Miquelon off Newfoundland and the island of St. Lucia in the Caribbean, and recognized France's title to Tobago; Gorée in Africa was also restored to France, as were the French places in India occupied by British forces. Britain regained possession of Grenada and the Grenadines, St. Vincent, Dominica, St. Christopher, Nevis, and Montserrat, occupied by the French during the war. France surrendered its right to fish along the eastern coasts of Newfoundland from Cape Buenavista to Cape St. John, but Britain conceded to the French the privilege of fishing on the west coast from Cape St. John to Cape Ray in the 47th degree of north latitude. The French fisheries in the Gulf of St. Lawrence were also continued.

The weight of the settlement was thus heavily balanced against England. France had achieved its *revanche*; Spain had somewhat assuaged the humiliation of the Peace of Paris (1763) and now stood as the unchallenged ruler of all the shores of the Gulf of Mexico. But the most significant part of the Peace of Versailles was the recognition by England, France, Spain, and Holland (soon to be followed by other members of the North Atlantic community of states) of the independence of the United States — that is, the birth of a new confederative nation into the world community. The birth of this new state was, again to borrow

Turgot's idea, the first mature "fruit" of the expansion of Europe in the American hemisphere.

The Creation of the
First American Republic

The New States

If the birth of the United States of America was the first fruit of the expansion of Europe, it was also one of the first fruits of the eighteenth-century Enlightenment in world affairs. For the leaders of the American secession from the British empire were all, in one way or another, men of the Enlightenment. The basic principles enumerated in their Declaration of Independence rested upon the thoroughly characteristic political theory of the Enlightenment

that all men are created equal, that they are endowed by their Creator with certain unalienable Rights, that among these are Life, Liberty and the pursuit of Happiness. That to secure these rights, Governments are instituted among Men, deriving their just powers from the consent of the governed, that whenever any Form of Government becomes destructive of these ends, it is the Right of the People to alter or abolish it, and to institute new Government, laying its Foundation on such principles and organizing its powers in such form, as to them shall seem most likely to effect their Safety and Happiness.

Once having declared their independence and sovereignty, the former colonies were faced with the task of establishing new governments that would be more "likely to effect their Safety and Happiness." This they proceeded to do by the adoption of written state constitutions. The most noticeable aspect of these constitutions was that, even though they contained provisions rejecting their allegiance to England and any subservience to outside powers — in other words, asserting their own state sovereignty — they included surprisingly little revolutionary change from the institutions the colonies had enjoyed before independence. Most of the new constitutions, true to the "Whig" aspirations of the colonial period and the representative principle in government, placed the preponderance of political power in the hands of the state legislatures and weakened the power of the executive. Furthermore, they all rejected monarchy in favor of the republican form of government. Their chief objective was the self-government that England, according to the Angloamerican "Whigs," had denied them. The last thing that the makers of these constitutions desired was "revolution" in the modern sense of the word. Therefore, when independence and complete self-government had become realities, the moderate "Whigs" were satisfied.

This was not true, however, of the so-called "radicals." For the civil war that is commonly termed the "American" Revolution was marked, in its political aspects, by the emergence into political power of the hitherto inarticulate and politically powerless lower middle class: the small shopkeepers, "the butchers, the bakers, the candlestick makers," along with some of the laboring class without property — the longshoremen, the "mechanicks," the teamsters, the journeymen, even the apprentices. These were the Sons of Liberty, the activists, the people who constituted the so-called "mobs."

To be sure, this new political force was led, in many instances, by highly able, intelligent, well-educated, and sometimes wealthy men. Such, for example, were Richard Henry Lee and George Mason of Virginia, Christopher Gadsden of South Carolina, Charles Thompson of Pennsylvania, John Morin Scott and Alexander MacDougall of New York, and John Hancock, Paul Revere, and Dr. Joseph Warren of Boston, not to mention Samuel Adams, who was a graduate of Harvard although not affluent. These men were genuinely committed to the Whig principles of representative government. They drew much of their inspiration from the English radicals of the seventeenth century, especially Algernon Sidney, as well as from John Locke. They believed in the natural rights of men, government by social compact, the responsibility of government — all government — to the people, and the right of revolution, by violence if necessary. By and large, they were republicans in their political philosophy. They were conscious of, and rebellious against, the "tyranny" of a Parliament that taxed them without their consent and of a crown that presumed to have a prerogative to suppress their legislatures. But they were also conscious of, and rebellious against, the fact that their own colonial societies were class structures whose economy and government were dominated by the wealthy and the wellborn. They were almost as afraid, therefore, of the possibility that there might appear among them a tyranny of their own aristocratic classes as they were angry at the already present tyranny of Parliament and the crown.

It was for these reasons that these radicals, with the power they were able to command in the bodies that created the new state constitutions, introduced into more than half of these constitutions, in the name of "liberty," "bills of rights" proclaiming the natural rights of men and placing upon the new governments certain limitations in their legal procedures. These were calculated to protect the citizen in the enjoyment of his natural rights against an arbitrary state — such rights as freedom of religion, freedom of the press and of assembly, the right to petition, taxation only by consent given by their representatives, jury trial, and "due process." The radicals were men of principle who would not be satisfied with half measures. It is probably not too much to say that it was chiefly because of the radicals that the movement for United States independence, originally a movement for secession, became a genuine political and social revolution.

The New Confederation

When they turned their attention to the necessity of institutionalizing their union, the new United States adopted a constitution, called the Articles of Confederation, which embodied their old idea of the federative empire. Their union was fundamentally hardly more than a confederation of sovereign states, or republics, in which each state jealously retained its own sovereignty and independence and to which the member states delegated — but did not surrender — certain functions, diplomatic, military, and economic, relative to the prosecution of their common cause. In this constitution there was no hint of the doctrine of natural rights: state sovereignty took precedence, in the affairs of the Confederation, over human rights; indeed, it was assumed that any question of citizens' "rights" was strictly a matter of state concern only.

Under this constitution the affairs of the Confederation, most particularly those concerned with the war, were conducted by the so-called Continental Congress, a congress of representatives of states, not of the people. In the Congress, each state voted as a unit. Neither the Congress nor the Confederation as a whole had any real sovereignty; it could not act in any important matter without the consent of nine of the thirteen states; amendment of the Articles of Confederation could be achieved only by the unanimous vote of all the states. It was a government, if government it was, strictly by "consent"; it had no sanctions; any state could obey or disobey its decisions with impunity.

Within these limitations, the Articles of Confederation delegated to the Continental Congress the authority to raise an army, to carry on relations with other countries, to issue money, and to direct the conduct of the war against the common enemy. It was under this confederative constitution that the War of United States Independence was fought and won.

The "Revolution"

During the war of the United States for independence, a number of significant social changes took place that carried the new society a considerable distance down the road toward democracy.

In a very real sense, the War for United States Independence was a civil war. It was a civil war between a part of the British empire — the colonial part — against the mother society. But it was also a civil war within the colonies. For the society of every colony was divided into two groups, those who clung to their loyalty to the empire, the crown, and the imperial ideals and those who stood with the cause of independence.

The former, the so-called "Tories," were generally conservative of mind and heart, convinced of the logical and traditional supremacy of Britain over the colonies, a supremacy that was typified by the old concept of the "prerogative." Intellectually, they adhered to the ideal of the integral, indivisible empire-nation. When the showdown came, their allegiance to the imperial ideal led them to reject with horror the radical program of independence; many of them left the rebellious colonies altogether and migrated to Nova Scotia, Canada, the West Indies, or England. Socially, this group, while it included persons from all classes of society, was led and dominated by members of the upper classes and the aristocracy. As a social phenomenon, the Tory exodus represented a loss of many of the most wealthy, the best educated, and the most intelligent members of American society.

As opposed to the Tories, the American Whigs of the pro-independence party were more generally of middle-class derivation, and the victory of the American cause was, in effect, a victory for the solid, native American middle class.[3] And yet it is to be remembered that

[3] Although there is a superficial resemblance between the division of the Angloamericans into pro-empire Tories and pro-independence Whigs and the division of Iberoamericans into *gachupines* (*peninsulares*) and *criollos*, or native American leaders, during the wars

the most powerful and aggressive social force in the American Revolution was the newly self-conscious lower classes, the "fourth estate," the so-called "radicals" epitomized by the Sons of Liberty. For the emergence of the lower classes was a social phenomenon, no less than a political one. And if it was these people of the "lower sort" who actually experienced the drudgery and the fighting of the war, it was also they who, in the last years of the war and in the years immediately following it, were chiefly involved in the social and political ferment that gave the American Revolution some of the characteristics of a genuine movement toward social democracy.

In this participation of the lower classes, the revolutionary independence movement that created the United States of America had much in common with the revolutionary independence movements of the other new societies in the hemisphere. Although democracy in the modern sense was neither fully nor permanently achieved, the independence movements in America between 1775 and 1825 did indeed constitute a real advance in the "Age of the Democratic Revolution," both political and social.

Another event of great significance that took place in the United States during the struggle for independence and can be considered one of the fruits of the humanitarianism of the Enlightenment was the rapid growth of the antislavery movement. Many social and religious leaders recognized that if the Declaration of Independence and the bills of rights in the state constitutions proclaimed that "all men are created equal," then that principle of equality logically applied to blacks as well as to whites. As a result of this "contagion of liberty," most of the northern states abolished slavery during the Revolutionary era. Even in the southern states there appeared a considerable body of criticism of the institution.

The beginnings of the movement for the emancipation of women may also be said to date from this period. The same "contagion of liberty"

of Latin-American independence, it would be quite inaccurate to conclude that the two situations exactly parallel each other. The "loyalists" of Angloamerica, while they did include some English-born officials, were mostly native-born Americans. The *gachupines*, on the other hand, were almost all officials sent to the colonies by the imperial governments of Spain or Portugal; they were "foreigners" in the sense that they were not born in the colonies. Among the *criollos*, there was in fact a split between those who led the rebellions and those who remained loyal to their mother countries. The wars for independence were thus also civil wars between "loyalists" and "rebels," much as was the war in the United States. (See below, chapter 11.)

that led to the beginnings of the emancipation of blacks led many thoughtful leaders to the logical extension of the principle to women. The most
distinguished and articulate exponent of this mood was Abigail (Mrs.
John) Adams, and she was ably seconded by Mercy Warren, also of
Boston. The idea of liberation for women began to appear, too, in the
writings of such men as Benjamin Rush. At the same time, a number
of the states passed laws liberalizing the old restrictions on the rights
of women to hold property, to engage in business, and to be the legal
wards of children.

Another by-product of the independence movement in the United
States was the achievement of a twofold independence for the Angloamerican Protestant churches. The Anglicans separated themselves
from the See of London and established their own American Protestant
Episcopal church with its own bishop, Rev. Samuel Seabury of New
York. The Presbyterians divorced themselves from the Scottish Presbytery that had ruled them; the Methodists, a new sect, cut themselves
off from the English Methodists at the end of the war and set up their
own American organization; the Dutch Reformed church withdrew from
the Classis of Amsterdam, which had formerly governed the Dutch
church in America.

Finally, it was during the War for United States Independence that
the psychological phenomenon known as United States nationalism began
to take definite shape.

At the beginning of the movement for United States independence,
there was little in the minds and hearts of the Angloamericans that could
be called a "United States nationalism." The chief loyalty of the Angloamericans in the colonial period was fixed upon the concept and the
ideals of the British empire, the symbol of which was the crown, per-
sonified in the king of England. At the same time, most colonials felt
a great and powerful patriotic allegiance to their own colonies, as has
been noted. This loyalty, coupled with the idea of the best self-interest
of the former colonies, manifested itself in the second article of the Articles of Confederation, which asserts that "each State preserves its
sovereignty and independence." And when the reality of independence
effectually destroyed the old loyalty to the empire, it was this state-
loyalty, or patriotism, which — for all but the Tories — took its place.

To be sure, a few Angloamericans had seen a vision of an American
nation, poets such as Philip Freneau and passionate orators such as Pat-

rick Henry, who proclaimed to the First Continental Congress that "I am an American." But for the most part the loyalty of the former colonists was now fixed upon their former colonies, their states. The old allegiance to Britain and Britain's king was dissolved, for most of them, by the Declaration of Independence; the loyalty to one's state had replaced the old loyalty to one's king.

Now, the fact and the exigencies of the common cause against a common enemy drew men together; the need for common policies and common actions to govern their relations with other states and the new national domain was a great impetus to the growth of a concept of the United States — to which they appropriated the name "America" — as one society, one nation; it also provided a strong incentive to them to think together as an integral society. It was in the course of this evolution that the idea of the United States as a nation was born; once born, it spread rapidly and gradually came to supersede in the affairs of the new republic the power exerted by state-loyalty. The former Angloamericans were seeing and feeling a vision of a new, "American" empire-nation. David Ramsay, in the first recorded "Fourth of July oration," expressed the new idea in 1778:

I appeal, to the experience of all, whether they do not feel an elevation of soul growing out of the emancipation of their country. . . .

We have laid the foundations of a new empire, which promises to enlarge itself into vast dimensions, and to give happiness to a great continent. It is now our turn to figure on the face of the earth, and in the annals of the world. . . .

Generations yet unborn will bless us for the blood-bought inheritance, we are about to bequeath them. Oh happy times! O glorious days! Oh kind, indulgent, beautiful Providence, that we live in this favoured period, and have the honour of helping forward these great events, and of suffering in a cause of such infinite importance.[4]

And Thomas Paine would write, in the last issue of *The Crisis* (1781): "The division of the empire [nation] into states is for our own convenience, but abroad this distinction ceases. . . . In short, we have no other national sovereignty than as United States. . . . Our citizenship in any particular state is only our local distinction. . . . Our great title is Americans — our inferior one varies with the place."[5]

[4] *United States Magazine*, 1:24, 106 (January, March 1779).
[5] Thomas Paine, *The Crisis*, no. 13 (1783), *The Complete Writings of Thomas Paine*, ed. Philip S. Foner, 2 vols. (New York: Citadel Press, 1945), I, 233–34.

A National Constitution

As the War for United States Independence continued, the exigencies of the conflict tended to draw the states together into a closer and closer union. The necessity for united action against a common foe, the maintenance and the direction of a common army and navy, the problems of conducting, in the name of the common good, relations with foreign powers, and, now, after the peace, the problem presented by the possession of a common national domain emphasized and reemphasized the need for an effective central government.

There had always been, indeed, right from the·beginning, a realization in the minds of men such as John Dickinson and Alexander Hamilton that some central authority with power — power even over the states — was needed. Despite the extraordinary successes of the voluntary confederative Continental Congress, the necessity for some centralized authority had become painfully apparent as the war advanced. This need showed itself in many areas, but in none was it so pressing as in finance, that is, in raising money to fund the war. Much aid had come from France, Holland, and Spain in the form of loans or outright gifts, but the Confederation itself had had no power to tax the citizens of the states. It could not even impose an import duty on goods coming into the states. Such money as the Confederation received was in the form of "voluntary" contributions from the states, raised by taxation by the state legislatures. This was a perfectly logical outcome of the colonial rejection of parliamentary taxation; needless to say, the contributions from the states were frustratingly small. The Continental Congress resorted to the device of simply printing paper money, that is, paper which promised to pay the bearers specified sums in the future. But confidence in this paper currency quickly disappeared, and its value declined to almost zero. Financially, the Confederation was practically paralyzed.

In view of such circumstances the nationalists made a number of moves, even before the Articles of Confederation were ratified, to strengthen the central government. As early as 1780 it was proposed in the Continental Congress and elsewhere that George Washington be made a dictator to ensure the financial stability of the Confederation and the support of the army. The suggestion never materialized, but outside of Congress the businessmen and the nationalists combined forces; an interstate conference of businessmen and representatives of the New England states was held at Boston to consider ways and means of strengthening the Confederation. This conference recommended to the states that a number of steps calculated to strengthen interstate cooperation be taken and that "the important national concerns of the United States be under the superintendency and direction of one supreme head." A second meeting, held at Hartford later in the same year (November 1780), urged that Congress be given the power both to tax the citizens of all the states and to coerce the states that failed to pay their quotas.

Meanwhile, the greatest leader of the nationalists, Alexander Hamilton, had formulated his own scheme for a constitution that would concentrate coercive power in the hands of the central government. This government, he said, would be a "solid, coercive union," with "complete sovereignty" over the people of all the states in many matters — civil, military, and economic. In this proposal Hamilton adopted the old Blackstonean doctrine that there is only one sovereignty in the body politic, that that sovereignty resides in the central government, and that it cannot be divided. This was genuine political nationalism: the central authority, and not the old Congress, would be the seat of sovereignty, a sovereignty that would override the states and the "popular" or democratic impulses of the people.

Although these proposals failed to achieve practical results, the nationalists won control of the Continental Congress in 1781 and immediately proposed an amendment to the Articles of Confederation, finally ratified by all the states and put into effect that same year, that empowered the Congress to lay an "impost," or import tax, upon goods brought into the states. The strength of the nationalist sentiment was shown by the fact that all the states ratified the amendment except Rhode Island.

The Continental Congress took other similar steps, such as reorganizing its executive committees of war, foreign affairs, and treasury to give them and it more power, but these moves were also without significant permanent effect. It was not until 1786 that the nationalists were able to prevail upon the Congress to call a convention, to be held in Philadelphia in the summer of 1787, to "revise" the Articles of Confederation. Out of this convention came the second Constitution of the United States.

The debates that took place at the convention were of a three-cornered character. The most pressing practical consideration was the problem of expediency — how to give the central government a sufficient degree of power to operate effectively for the general welfare of the whole confederation of states without crippling the functions of the states in their internal government. This practical problem of the exigency of effectiveness closely infringed upon the realities of state sovereignty as against "imperial" or national sovereignty, and the states vehemently resisted the implied necessity of reducing state sovereignty in favor of an "imperial" sovereignty that would have the power to dominate them. After all, their spokesmen asked, did we not fight our war of independence precisely against this same form of coercion, and must we now accept the very system of subjection that we fought a bitter war to be rid of? It was the question of divided sovereignty all over again. Could there be more than one supreme sovereignty in the "empire"? If so, how was it to be distributed between the central authority and the states?

The final outcome of all these debates and compromises was a proposed constitution that amounted in effect to a total rejection of the old Articles of Confederation and a completely new structuring of the United States government. The constitution of 1787 was notable in two chief ways: it embodied a compromise between the old states-sovereignty idea, institutionalized in a senate composed of two representatives from each state, and the new national idea, institutionalized in a house of representatives based upon the concept of the people-at-large of the nation; it thus incorporated the old, prerevolutionary theory of divided — or shared — sovereignty. The sovereignty of the states, recognized as real, was preserved in the constitution of the Senate; the sovereignty of the nation, perceived as being no less real, was embodied in the stipulation that laws and treaties made under the provisions of the new constitution should be "the supreme law of the land."

This constitution, which was ratified in 1788 and 1789, with the "bill-of-rights" embodied in the first ten amendments to it, adopted in 1791, completed the institutional aspect of the so-called "American Revolution," which was essentially the secession of thirteen colonies from the British empire and their formation as a new national state, the first ex-colonial member of the North Atlantic community of states. It was the first such secession from any of the Euroamerican empires. It would be followed within a few years by the withdrawal of Haiti from the Francoamerican empire and, soon after that, by comparable moves by the Latin-American societies which would presently become members of the American community.

Conclusion

In general, the event known as the United States Revolution not only was both a civil war and a world war, but was characterized by certain social, intellectual, and religious ferments which contributed to the separation of the Angloamerican society from the British empire and significantly liberalized, secularized, and rationalized American society itself. The net outcome of these phenomena was that Angloamerica, in the era of its war for independence, had moved a long way toward the ideal and the practice of democracy. At the same time, the new federal republic was rapidly becoming more and more self-conscious. By the end of the eighteenth century it was a nation in the full sense of the word.

Considered as an event in the history of the expansion of Europe, the emergence of the United States of America out of the old British colonial empire appears to have been the result of the process of the formation of new societies, or new nations, that was one of the more or less conscious natural advances inherent in that expansion in most areas, if not in all. It would culminate in the emergence of other nations (eventually twenty of them) in the other parts of the American hemisphere. Seen in the context of the development of the whole hemisphere, the birth of the United States was in many ways a prototype of the colonial process that was to occur in the other new nations of the hemisphere. As a "creole" reaction against the English metropolis, it provided an ideology, a precedent, and a model for the later reactions of the other embryo American nations against their own metropolises and even a pattern, in a number of cases, for their institutionalization.

CHAPTER 10

The Ferment of Freedom

In the two decades following the War for United States Independence, the feelings and the ideologies leading toward the separation of the new societies of the American hemisphere from their European mother states spread all over the continent. This movement had its roots embedded deep in the colonial experiences of the Euroamerican empires, but it was given special impetus, among the peoples of America in the second half of the eighteenth century, by a series of developments which, taken all together, made the independence of those societies almost inevitable.

Parts of the impulse toward independence derived, to be sure, from outside influences, such as the political ideas of the Enlightenment, the example of the success of the independence movement of the United States, and the complex influences exerted by the French Revolution. But the basic, elemental forces making for the independence of the American societies were internal, derived from the colonial experiences of the American societies themselves.

External Influences

The penetration of American intellectual life by the science and the thought of the Enlightenment has already been reviewed.[1] It has also been indicated that the secession of the United States from the Angloamerican empire was very powerfully motivated by, and eloquently

[1] See above, chapter 8.

rationalized on the basis of, the ideas of Sidney, Locke, Montesquieu, Trenchard and Gordon, and Rousseau.[2] It is to be noted here only that elsewhere in America the same ideological influences were at work and that they constituted a powerful intellectual ferment in the aspirations of Americans all over the hemisphere toward freedom from European control.

In Latin America, the political ideas of the Enlightenment, especially those of Jean Jacques Rousseau, fell upon fertile ground. Already, in the last three decades of the eighteenth century, these concepts were filtering into the universities, the discussions of the Societies of Friends of the Country, and the publications and correspondence of scholars and creole statesmen. Rousseau's *Social Contract* was widely read throughout America, and his explanations of the "general will" and the "sovereign people," adapted to American realities, became ideological bases for the nascent stirrings of American nationalisms among the creole leaders.

Mariano Moreno, an Argentine, discovered Rousseau at the university at Chuquisaca in upper Peru; he became a powerful advocate of the Genevan's principles and laid the ideological foundation for Argentine independence. (He published a translation of Rousseau's *Social Contract* in 1810.) In Peru the ideas of Rousseau found their way into the curriculum of the University of San Marcos in Lima. The priest José María Morelos y Pavón, who later became one of the most outstanding leaders in the Mexican war of independence, also followed Rousseau's ideas in his attempt to bring them to reality in Mexico. Simón Bolívar, the great Venezuelan liberator, was strongly indoctrinated in the ideas of Rousseau by his teachers Simón Rodríguez and Andrés Bello.

With the advent of the French Revolution, the Spanish government enjoined the reading of the subversive French writers in the colonies. The prohibition was futile, of course, for the concepts of the Enlightenment had already taken root in Hispanoamerica, and the ideas disseminated by the French Revolution were of great use to the creole leaders who directed the explosion of the wars of independence.

In Brazil the impact of the political theories of the Enlightenment was less powerful than elsewhere in America. Even there, however, the books of the philosophes were being read, and their ideas were being discussed in the meetings of small learned societies.

The success of the secession of the United States from the Angloameri-

[2] See above, chapter 9.

can empire and the writings of the leaders of that movement provided a powerful example to the Iberoamerican creole leaders who had caught a vision of liberty for their own countries. Not only did the news of the independence of the United States arouse enthusiasm and hope, but the works of Benjamin Franklin, Thomas Jefferson, Alexander Hamilton, and John Adams circulated widely.

The Internal Ferments

In a number of widely separated areas of America during the late eighteenth century, the desperation of the peoples submerged under the yoke of European governments manifested itself in violent rebellions.

It has already been mentioned that the peoples of nearly all the new societies were highly mixed. In most of the American societies, the original inhabitants, the Amerinds, constituted larger or smaller proportions of the total populations, and they had mated with the Europeans to produce very large numbers of persons of mixed blood, who, reared in the environments of their mothers, knew relatively little about the national cultures of their fathers. Their orientation, social, economic, political, religious, and intellectual, was fixed in the society in which they had been born. The Indians and, to a large degree, their half-breed offspring were non-European: they were essentially and practically Americans, not Europeans.

Similarly, literally millions of black Africans had been imported into the hemisphere. These non-Europeans, in most areas, lived apart from their white owners, but a vast amount of miscegenation had taken place between the whites and blacks to produce a veritable race of white-black "half-breeds," or mulattoes. These blacks and mulattoes had little or no consciousness of the fact that they were members of "European" societies. After a few generations they, too, were neither Africans nor Europeans: they were Americans.

A comparable, but less dramatic, event was the immigration of Europeans not of the same nationality as that of the original settlers; this was particularly true in the Angloamerican societies. Even Brazil and the Hispanoamerican societies experienced an infiltration of non-Portuguese and non-Spanish persons — merchants, priests, agents, and others.

By the end of the eighteenth century, even the descendants of the original settlers, the creoles, or *criollos*, reared in American environ-ments and circumstances, had become "Americans" rather than Por-tuguese, Spaniards, Dutchmen, Frenchmen, or Englishmen. Although many of them were still consciously loyal to their mother countries, their supreme allegiance was fixed upon the regional or colonial societies in which they had been reared.

As has been indicated, the overall effect of these internal factors was that the populations of the new American societies were no longer either ethnologically or culturally European. The Americans were culturally different from the Europeans who lived among them and their societies were different from the European societies of their original founders. Furthermore, it was obvious that the different climates, soils, flora, and human populations of the various regions within the empires had given rise to regional differentiations that would eventually become national differentiations.

Ideas and impulses making for liberalizing change — in economic and political life, in social institutions and thought, in religion, and in culture — appeared and developed in all the new American societies. These forces, coupled with an embryonic nationalistic self-consciousness, almost certainly, and quite naturally, would have brought the new societies to self-determination even though the outside impulses had never been felt.

In Brazil and Argentina the Jesuit-Indian missionary communities had been regional societies of a unique, almost purely American, type. The resistance of the Jesuit leaders to the governments of both Portugal and Spain, which (among other things) eventually led to their expulsion, grew out of the fact that these communities had needs and aspirations derived from the peculiarities of their total circumstances that the Portuguese and Spanish governments simply could not comprehend, much less sym-pathize with.

In Peru in the early 1780s, the long oppression of the Indians by the corrupt and tyrannical Spanish government at last induced a dramatic uprising of the native peoples that exploded in the Andean highland from the inland sections of Venezuela to the northern parts of Argentina. The Indians, in their resentment, had developed a racial self-consciousness that could almost be called nationalism. The leader of this uprising was a devoutly religious mestizo named José Gabriel Condor-canqui Noguera, who, because he had acquired land in the region near

Cuzco, called himself the Marquis of Oropesa, a title that could only be borne by a direct descendant of the Inca kings. In the interest of the Indians he protested to the Spanish government against the gross oppression under which they suffered, only to be turned away with scorn. In his desperation, he placed himself at the head of the Indians and proclaimed himself Tupac Amaru II, after the last of the original Inca chieftains who had been executed by the Spaniards in 1571.

In 1780 Tupac Amaru II started a widespread Indian revolt which developed into a genuine race war and which, despite Tupac Amaru's avowals that it was only a confrontation in the interest of reform, had as its ultimate objective the expulsion of the Spaniards from the Inca lands. For a time it seemed that Tupac Amaru might even succeed. Furthermore, a few of the *criollos* who sympathized with the rebellion apparently dreamed of the possibility of using it to drive out the Spaniards and to establish themselves in their place.

But the outcome was never in real doubt. The overwhelming superiority of the Spaniards and the Peruvian whites, who feared the Indians more than they detested the Spaniards, made it inevitable that the uprising would be suppressed. Tupac Amaru was captured and executed, and unchallenged Spanish authority was again in complete control of the Indian country by about 1784.

In New Granada at nearly the same time as Tupac Amaru's rebellion, another uprising occurred among the cattle-raising people allied with the Indians. This was a revolt against oppression and unbearable taxation. Like the one in Peru, it was ruthlessly crushed. But this frantic outburst of the pent-up discontents of the Indians and creole common people was an augury of things to come.

Tupac Amaru II's uprising demonstrated in a fearful manner the power of the Indians in central South America. As an internal force rooted in the racial, social, and political experiences of New Granada, Peru, Ecuador, Argentina, and Chile, that power was indigenous to America. Its influence, if any, on the subsequent independence movements has been debated by historians; most of them, apparently, agree that its direct impact was slight. Yet it provided a precedent — one of many — for uprisings against Spanish power, and it is of course true that Indians and mestizos constituted a large bulk of the armed peoples who eventually did arise, under the leadership of the *criollos*, against the governments of the *peninsulares*.

The French island colonies had long since begun to feel the need for self-determination. Early in the century they had been authorized to send "deputies," or agents, to the French court at Versailles to represent their councils in colonial affairs, somewhat as the English colonies had been doing for nearly a century. Jean Dubuc, mentioned above, had been such an agent for his native Martinique before he entered the Ministry of Marine. During the years immediately following the United States Revolution, the councils had increased their power and influence through these deputies in France, with the result that when the French Revolution occurred they were actually given representation in the French National Assembly.

Unhappily for them, in the years immediately following the War for United States Independence, the French island colonies had fallen under military rule; the former practices of autonomy were severely restricted, and the aspirations of the creoles for self-government were repressed. Despite this fact, however, and in the midst of the prosperity that came to them after the war, the intellectual life of the islands quickened; newspapers appeared, scientific and literary societies — even chapters of freemasons — were organized, and there was a conscious effort to imitate the cultural life of the mother country. This intellectual activity, part and parcel of the French Enlightenment, stimulated thought about the colonies' political relationships with the mother country; out of this intellectual climate were born the works of such men as the *Martiniquais* Moreau de St. Méry. This explosive combination of forces — economic, political, and intellectual — brought with it the threat of civil war. It is not surprising, therefore, that news of the fall of the Bastille on July 14, 1789, was the signal for a flare-up of the long-smoldering colonial discontent. *Vive la revolution* became *Vive la colonie*, and the creoles, who had long been restive under the repression of the military, began to make their bids for power.

Uprisings occurred in several parts of the French islands, and mobs of nonpropertied workers arose against the planters. The French Revolution in the French Windward Islands started as a civil war between the cities and the plantations, between the landless white workers and the landed creole aristocrats; and both sides appealed to the revolutionary government in France. The ultimate crisis took place in Saint-Domingue (Haiti), where in the spring of 1791 a rebellion of the black slaves soon became one of the bloodiest orgies of racial conflict in the history of the hemisphere. Indeed, the "ferment of freedom" was even more power-ful and turbulent in Saint-Domingue than it was in the French Windward Islands. The course of its political history was particularly troubled; the populace continually fought the military governors and a great tension developed between the Council (often called the "National Assembly") and the governors over the imposition of taxes. The problem was exacer-bated by the great increase in the number of "people of color," mulattoes who were free and who joined forces with the "little whites" to resist the payment of taxes and the reorganization of the militia as an instrument of suppression.

Such was the situation in Saint-Domingue at the beginning of the French Revolution in 1789. Here, as elsewhere, the spirit of resistance to imposed government was strong. The first acts of the Revolution, especially those of the French National Assembly, gave hope that the pressure might be eased by statesmanlike colonial policies. But whereas the tensions were resolved in the French Windward Islands, in Saint-Domingue the relations between the French government and the colo-nists broke down. This culminated in a local civil war, which resulted in the emergence of a great native leader in the person of Pierre-Dominique Toussaint L'Ouverture and the independence of Saint-Domingue as the second (after the United States) of the American societies to cast off its subjection to a European power; the island became the new national state of Haiti, as will be related below.

In the course of the centuries the American descendants of the original European colonizers, the creoles, had become differentiated from their still-European cousins. The creoles not only were conscious of the differ-ences between themselves and the European officials sent to govern them, but were resentful of the arrogance and disdain of these officials. The creoles constituted a new generation of native American leaders; in the last quarter of the eighteenth century they were beginning to assume positions of responsibility in the affairs of their peoples which, taken up by a still younger generation, would bring all America to independence.

The great prototype of all the creole — that is, native — exponents of American self-determination was Benjamin Franklin. His early career as a member of the Pennsylvania legislature had conditioned him to be an articulate representative of the Angloamerican colonies in the politi-cal dialogue between them and their mother country regarding the nature of the imperial constitution. He served for many years as an agent of a number of Angloamerican colonies in London and later became one of the chief architects of the independence and the national identity of the United States.

A creole of comparable experience in Francoamerica was Jean Dubuc de St. Pierre (Martinique), who served as a deputy of the Superior Council of his native Martinique at the court of France and later became one of the most successful administrators of the French colonies in the Ministry of Marine. Dubuc wrote much in his effort to adapt the French imperial constitution to the needs of his fellow colonists, and he was highly successful, as has been noted, in doing so.

Rather like Dubuc was the greater Mederic Louis Moreau de St. Méry, also of Martinique. Initially an official at Fort Royal, he eventually became a deputy of the Martinique Superior Council to the Constituent Assembly during the French Revolution and, later, a servant of the French Republic in Europe. Moreau de St. Méry also served his native colony as an intellectual, collecting the laws of the French islands in a colonial code (published in 1785) and writing a classic *Description de l'île de Martinique*.

Another distinguished creole who went to Europe and significantly influenced the life of his mother country was Pablo de Olavide. A Peruvian, Olavide journeyed to Spain and became a friend of the famous Spanish exponent of the Enlightenment Gaspar Melchor de Jovellanos. He instituted liberal reforms in the curriculums of the universities of Seville and Salamanca, disseminated the ideas of Rousseau and others, and sent books and scientific instruments to America. But he was too enlightened for Spain: he was condemned by the Inquisition for atheism and materialism and for reading the works of the French philosophes. Happily, he escaped from prison and went to Paris, where he became one of the leading exponents of the French Enlightenment.

The list of creole leaders in America includes the names of many distinguished American intellectuals. Francisco José de Caldas of Bogotá, for example, wrote treatises on the effect of environment upon society which were strongly nationalistic in outlook. Indeed, his writings so incensed the *peninsulares* that he was executed in 1816. Similarly, Francisco Xavier Espejo of Ecuador penned satirical essays on his contemporary society and openly criticized the failings of the Spanish administrators as well as the falseness and corruption of society itself. Another important creole intellectual and critic of the establishment was Manuel de Lavardén of Buenos Aires, who contributed greatly to the creation of an Argentine national literature. His *Oda al Paraná* (Ode to the Paraná River, 1801) is one of the most famous expressions of early Argentine nationalism.

Another eminent American "precursor" was Francisco de Miranda of Caracas, who became committed to the cause of Hispanoamerican independence at about the time of the War for United States Independence. He served with distinction as a general in the army of France during the Revolution and worked, wrote, and agitated for the cause of American independence, in London and in the United States, from about 1785 onward. His own career ended in a Cádiz prison in 1816, but he prepared the way for the younger and more famous liberator Simón Bolívar.

Yet another of the American leaders was the heroic black Pierre-Dominique Toussaint L'Ouverture, already mentioned, who emerged as the leader of the rebellion of the blacks and the mulattoes in Saint-Domingue in 1791 and went on to become the "father of Haitian independence."

In the 1780s, many Brazilian students attended French universities, notably Montpelier, where they absorbed much of the learning and the radicalism of the Enlightenment. At home, they talked of France and French politics and the expected cataclysm.

It was a still younger generation of Americans, of which "the Liberator" Simón Bolívar was the most famous member, which would eventually lead Latin America to independence. Bolívar, born in 1783 and a member of an old Spanish-Basque family, was taught by Simón Rodríguez, a passionate disciple of Rousseau. Although Rodríguez was implicated in a republican plot in 1797 and was forced to escape the country, he had done his work well, for young Bolívar was both an avid "Rousseau-ite" and an ardent Venezuelan nationalist. He went to Spain, where he became further embittered by the condescending attitude of the court circles toward *criollos* and by his disillusionment with the corruption of royal government. A long stay at the court of Napoleon, who made himself emperor of the French in 1804, increased his apprehension; on a trip to Rome in 1806 with his former tutor, Rodríguez, he swore an oath to liberate his native land from the oppression of Spain.

Hardly less spectacular in his career than Bolívar was the Argentine *criollo* José de San Martín. A child of the Enlightenment and one of the founders of the Lautaro lodge of Masons in Buenos Aires, San Martín also dedicated his life to the liberation of Spanish Americans from Spanish rule, as will appear.

Other distinguished creole leaders were Bernardo O'Higgins of Chile, son of one of the viceroys of Peru, and the priests Miguel Hidalgo y Costilla and José María Morelos y Pavón, who would launch the independence movement in Mexico. There were, of course, many others. The dramatic fact is that among the internal forces that were to break the political ties of the American societies with Europe the most powerful and decisive was a body of native American leaders animated by the drive for freedom, who, in the fifty years between 1775 and 1825, would lead their respective countries to independence.

The Birth of Nationalism

These native Americans who lived and worked for freedom were the voices and the leaders of the ground swell of nationalism that swept through the hemisphere in the years roughly between 1775 and 1825.

Nationalism, surely one of the most powerful psychological determinants in modern history, came into existence during the eighteenth century. As a psychic phenomenon, as a collective self-consciousness, as an emotional commitment by many people to a common societal image called the nation and to its ideals, real or imagined, it has been a force of enormous power. It has served both as a centripetal force holding peoples together as nations and as a centrifugal separative force in the relations among nations.

In the American hemisphere the earliest expressions of nationalism focused largely on loyalty to one's empire, Angloamerican, Hispanoamerican, Lusoamerican, or Francoamerican. To be sure, allegiance to one's empire might usually be centered on one's colony within the empire, and the creole leader might hold to the image of his regional subdivision where he lived, hoping, against the misunderstanding and oppression of his European governors, for a closer and more emotionally satisfying relationship between himself and his "country" on the one side and his king on the other. To the creole this relationship was symbolical of the imperial-national ideal, and it embodied no thought of separation of himself or his society from his empire.

This, indeed, was the kind of nationalism that had characterized the emotional loyalties of the Angloamericans before the advent of the revolutionary era. As time went on, however, the forces in human affairs that gave rise to the formation of distinct and fully self-conscious nations in the American hemisphere became more and more powerful and came ever more and more sharply and dramatically into conflict with those forces which served as bonds holding the empires together.

By the middle of the eighteenth century, the new societies that were the embryonic nations of the future had become distinguished from one another along regional lines. The regions of the Rio de la Plata, Peru, Chile, New Granada, New Spain, the English continental colonies, Brazil, French Canada, and the French West Indies were all different from one another, as well as from their mother countries, in so many ways and so profoundly that each one was in fact unique as a society and in its way of life.

Regional differences also had produced further cultural differentiation. For example, northern Brazil, southern Brazil, and the São Paulo region might very well have separated into three national cultures had not countervailing forces making for continued union prevented it. Similarly, the culture patterns of the French West Indies differed from those of Canada; the northern and southern sections of the British continental colonies were so profoundly different in their ways of life that they eventually did separate into two proto-nations, to be held together only by the tragedy of a long and bloody intersectional war.

The process of nation building in all these proto-national regions was rooted in the land, in the common social experiences of the people, and in their cultural and political conditioning. Each region was the product of a historical evolution that distinguished it from the others.

The American populations, composed of persons who were born in America, could possess no great allegiance to European nations and their kings, of whom they had had no direct experience. What they knew of their "mother" countries, they knew only by hearsay, as it were, from their parents or from their contacts, largely distasteful, with the European officials sent to govern them. This was especially true, of course, among the Indians, the blacks, and their half-breed offspring, to whom Europe or the mother country was only a name, all too often associated with unpleasant exploitation or oppression. But it was almost equally true of the Euroamerican populations, who were now American and no longer European. The loyalties of all these populations were directed toward the land, that is, the region where they had been born, reared, and culturally conditioned, and toward the people among whom they actually lived. These regional societies, usually formed about one or more large cities, such as Quebec or Montreal, Boston, New York, Philadelphia, Charleston, Kingston, Mexico City, Caracas, Bogotá, Lima, Santiago de Chile, Buenos Aires, Montevideo, São Paulo, Rio de Janeiro, and Bahia, were all distinctive, possessing their own culture complex, way of life, and life-style. By the end of the eighteenth century these societies, or at least their culturally and intellectually articulate upper classes, were conscious of themselves and the ways in which they differed from the other societies. In each there existed a certain intellectual and emotional milieu that provided a psychological bond holding the members of the society together. And as consciousness of the society's uniqueness grew, the society was identified with certain symbols, a mythos of its history and its heroes, and a folklore that was thought of as its own. This self-conscious culture complex expressed itself in art, literature, music, folklore, and national historiography.

This process of determining the morphology of nations and of nationalism was going on toward the end of the eighteenth century in most of the regional societies of America. It was the force of nationalism which, motivating such creole leaders as Benjamin Franklin, George Washington, Toussaint L'Ouverture, Simón Bolívar, José de San Martín, and Bernardo O'Higgins, carried the Americans to independence and eventually to the creation of the American states.

One of the clearest and earliest expressions of this budding concept of the nation was the formation, in several of the Latin-American capitals, of the intellectual groups noted above called Societies of Friends of the Country. Largely informal, they were usually recognizable only because they met regularly — often enough in a café. Ostensibly and often primarily established to foster science and technology, these societies also studied literature and the arts and, above all, discussed political writings and — however discreetly — actual political situations.

Thus the Asociación Filarmónica was organized in Lima in 1787 and became the Society of Friends of the Country in 1790; in Havana there was founded the Royal Economic Society of Havana; in Mexico there was a secret society that called itself the Guadalupes, after the patron saint of Mexico; in Buenos Aires a similar society was named the Patriotic and Literary Society; in Bogotá the comparable society was Tertulia Eutrapelica.

Another social force operating against the mother countries was the Society of Jesus, whose members were expelled from the Portuguese, Spanish, and French empires and then went underground and into opposition. Such, for example, was Juan Pablo Viscardo; after his expulsion from Peru, he wrote a *Letter to the American Spaniards* (published in 1799), calling for independence. Many of the Jesuits by the end of the eighteenth century were the natural allies of the *criollos* who had become more and more self-conscious and more and more critical of the mother country.

Newspapers were yet another intellectual force that contributed to the growth of national self-consciousness. They first became important in the American hemisphere in Angloamerica, shortly after 1700. In the English colonies, all of which printed newspapers by about mid-century, these organs were purveyors of foreign and intercolonial news, especially news of international relations. The Angloamerican colonist was extraordinarily well informed about the happenings in England and the course of international relations as reported by the newspapers and the official gazettes of the European courts.

The *Gazeta de Mexico y noticias de Nueva España*, first published in 1722 in Mexico, was the first newspaper to appear in the Spanish colonies. It covered news on economic matters, with reports from Europe and elsewhere, but it carefully avoided discussion of political affairs. In 1768 José Antonio de Alzate y Ramírez began publication of his *Diario literario de México*, but it was suppressed. He did not give up, however, and continued his efforts with a series of papers devoted to literary and artistic matters.

Meanwhile, newspapers began to appear in other colonies. The most notable were the *Mercurio peruano de historia, literatura y noticias públicas* (1791–95) in Lima, the *Papel periódico* in Havana, and the *Papel periódico de Santa Fé de Bogotá* in Bogotá.

All the phenomena just reviewed were manifestations of complex emotions, aspirations, and ideals that focused on the nation. Nationalism was being born as the new nations were emerging out of the old colonies. And if the Enlightenment of the Western world was characterized by ecumenicalism, it was also marked by provincialism; it was characterized by universalism and internationalism, but its very universalism embraced a myriad of nationalisms. This was as true in America as it was in Europe.

The French Revolution and the American Ferment

The bursting of the French Revolution upon the world in 1789 found the "ferment of freedom" already very much alive throughout the American hemisphere. Indeed, the French revolutionaries were themselves interested in America, and they were fully aware of the impact the Revolution was having in the New World. They were, in fact, consciously committed to carrying their proposed reforms to the colonies. Thus, of the *cahiers* submitted to the Estates-General in 1789, 323 mentioned the colonies and called for reform there. Not one of these *cahiers* demanded that the colonies be abandoned, but not one failed, either, to demand more or less extensive reforms. Although the *cahiers* referred only to the French colonies, their colonial philosophy was soon universalized as the French Revolution increasingly became an international movement with repercussions in the colonial policies of the other European powers.

Even before the Revolution, the colonies had become a matter of great and intense public interest. Many books and pamphlets were published to call the colonies into the consciousness and the thinking of the French people. The authors of this literature were usually men who had been educated and conditioned in the colonies themselves, the most extraordinary of whom was Moreau de St. Méry. The writings of Jean Dubuc, Paul Dubuisson, and Hilliard d'Auberteuil were widely read, while the Abbé Raynal's famous *Philosophical History of the Two Indies* went through edition after edition. The mood, the philosophy, of this literature was generally to integrate the colonies into the metropolis, to right any wrongs that had been done, and, presently, to bring to them the joys of "liberty, equality, fraternity."

At the same time, the humanitarianism of the Enlightenment had induced Brissot de Warville, the Abbé Sieyès, and the Marquis de Condorcet to form the Society of the Friends of the Blacks in 1781. This antislavery society was so popular that it achieved a membership of perhaps 500,000 persons; even the king of France proclaimed himself an abolitionist.

The colonists, more specifically the property owners in the colonies, had already organized an equivalent of the English West India Lobby called the Colonial Committee of France (Comité Colonial de France). From the beginning of the Revolution, this group was a powerful lobby against the Estates-General for the promotion of the interests of the island colonies. It was anything but antislavery in sentiment, however; its chief objective was to secure the greatest possible degree of autonomy for the colonies.

The mood in France at the moment of the Revolution was of great interest to the colonies. When the news arrived in the islands that the Estates-General was to meet, the colonial leaders were determined to participate. The colonists (the planters, that is) demanded the right to send delegates, and, when their request was refused and the local superior councils were prohibited from meeting to elect delegates, the councils met, surreptitiously or openly, and elected them anyway. When the delegates arrived in France, the Estates-General considered the question whether they should be admitted; on July 4, 1789, that body agreed to seat ten representatives of the islands, five of whom were already resident in France and five from the islands. These delegates thus became the first official representatives of American colonies in any European parliament. On March 4, 1790, the Estates-General proclaimed the colonies "integral parts of the French Empire." For the moment, at least, the philosophy of integral imperialism was institutionalized.

Unfortunately for the colonies, the disadvantages of this arrangement, long recognized and rejected by the British colonies, soon became apparent: as integral parts of the nation with representatives in the national legislature, they were inexorably bound by any laws passed by that legislature. The ten representatives of the colonies, overwhelmed by the votes of the metropolitan interests, had no hope or means of forestalling legislation that might run catastrophically against the colonial interest. Furthermore, they were utterly without power to resist the implications of the Declaration of the Rights of Man and the Citizen, which logically must involve the eventual freeing of the slaves in the colonies.

The representatives of the colonies, therefore, bound themselves together in the Correspondence Society of the French Colonies, or the Massiac Club (so-called by the name of the hotel where they met). This society used every means in its power to ward off any action by the national legislature counter to its vested interests in the colonies. When the Constituent Assembly passed a navigation act on September 22, 1791, reviving the old "System" of the *Exclusif*, which reserved all the commerce of the colonies to ships sailing under the French flag, the Massiac Club successfully maintained that the Decree of 1784[3] remained in force and "interpreted" this new act in a way that permitted the large extent of free trade with foreigners authorized by the earlier order. Furthermore, the colonial representatives succeeded in getting the Constituent Assembly to rule that "the colonies, [although] integral parts of the Empire, were not included in the Constitution." This meant that the Constituent Assembly would make special laws for the colonies; the Colonial Committee was charged with preparing these laws and in doing so it followed the suggestions of the colonists. As a result, the Colonial Statute of 1791 gave virtually total freedom to the local colonial assemblies. Only the governor and "director general," both named by the king, remained as symbols of the royal authority in every colony. Hence, although the colonies were represented in the national legislature, for all local colonial purposes they were almost completely autonomous.

Since the Constitution provided for universal manhood suffrage throughout the French territories, the question inevitably arose over what should be done about the blacks and mulattoes, especially those who were free, in the colonial elections. As early as October 22, 1789, free "colored people" in the islands had organized themselves and had demanded that their right to vote be recognized. The Constituent Assembly, confronted by the West Indian planters, vacillated; finally on May 15, 1791, it decreed that "the Legislature would never discuss the public status of the colored people not born of free parents without the previous consent of the colonial assemblies; but that people of color born of free parents would be admitted into all the future parochial and colonial assemblies if they otherwise fulfilled the required conditions." Although this official pronouncement evaded the question of slavery, it did admit the free blacks and mulattoes to full citizenship.

This was a partial victory for the white colonists. But the debate, as

[3] See above, chapter 4.

well as the unwillingness of the Constituent Assembly to face the logic of the Declaration of the Rights of Man and the Citizen, antagonized the radicals and led Robespierre to say, "Let the colonies perish if they think by their pressures to force us to take positions favorable to their interests; I declare in the name of the entire nation which demands to be free, that we will not surrender to the deputies of the colonies either the nation, or the colonies, or the whole of humanity."[4]

Nevertheless, most of the colored people of the colonies remained without political power because the colonial assemblies simply would not let them have it. To the assemblies, and to the planters that controlled them, the interest of "the nation" was one thing, while that of the colonies was quite another. Actually, the representatives of the colonies withdrew from the Assembly after Robespierre's declaration; the Assembly, fearful of civil war in the colonies, again delegated the settlement of all local questions to the colonial assemblies. The great landed proprietors had triumphed. The answer to the Revolution was the establishment of a kind of authoritarian dictatorship of the local property owners.

After the National Assembly threw the responsibility for colonial affairs to the planter-dominated assemblies, the "popular" elements in Martinique and Guadeloupe, cooperating with the colored people, seized power, and there ensued a veritable civil war.

The formerly French province of Canada had had its first introduction to quasi-parliamentary institutions under the governance of the English Quebec Act of 1774. To be sure, under this basic constitutional law Canada (Quebec) did not yet fully enjoy representative institutions, for it was governed by an appointed governor and an appointed council. But the council was composed of Canadian citizens, both French and British, and did operate generally on the basis of the interests of the Canadian people as the council understood them. Furthermore, French civil law was restored (although English criminal law remained in force), and the dominant position of the Catholic church was recognized.

Quebec was thus unique in its political and legal institutions. But when some 40,000 Angloamericans immigrated into Canada during and after the American Revolution, they brought with them a lively demand for the type of representative institutions they had known in the older English colonies. At the same time, Canada, now dominated by an An-

---

[4] Quoted in Gabriel Hanotaux and Alfred Martineau, eds., *Histoire des colonies françaises* . . . 6 vols. (Paris: Plon, 1929–34), I, 509.

gloamerican minority, was deeply moved by the emergence of a new self-consciousness of the French Canadians and their demand for the right to control their own political, economic, religious, and intellectual affairs.

In the ensuing confrontation of the two nationalities, the French Canadians, feeling themselves slowly overwhelmed by the Angloamerican tide, fought to preserve their own way of life as regulated by the Quebec Act of 1774. But the Angloamericans, who moved into the area west of the Ottawa River and north of Lake Ontario, exerted an irresistible pressure upon the British Parliament for the establishment in Canada of representative institutions.

As a result of the conflicts in Canada the British Parliament, on June 10, 1790, enacted the Canadian Constitutional Act of 1791 (so-called because it went into effect on December 26, 1791). By this basic constitutional law Canada was divided into two provinces, Lower Canada (Quebec) and Upper Canada (Ontario), separated by the Ottawa River, but with the island and city of Montreal in Lower Canada. (In effect, one province was predominantly French Canadian, the other predominantly Angloamerican.) Each province had its own separate government with a bicameral legislature; the lower house, or House of Representatives, was composed of members elected by the property owners, and the upper house, or Council, was made up of members appointed for life by the crown. A governor and lieutenant-governor, both appointed by the crown, were provided for each of the provinces. These governments were similar to those of the old royal provinces during the colonial period, with this significant exception: the executive arm of each government was provided with an income independent of the control of the House of Representatives. This appears to have been a violation of the age-old British constitutional principle that the representatives of the people control government finances. It was dictated, however, by the disagreeable recollection that the colonial assemblies' gradual seizure of power had led to a de facto autonomy and, in defense of that autonomy, to the eventual secession of thirteen of the old continental colonies from the empire.

Even so, the yoking together of these two radically different provinces could not last. In particular, the British minority in Lower Canada was swamped by the social, intellectual, and folkloric culture of the French Canadians. The differences were aggravated by the fact that the activities of the British minority were devoted chiefly to commerce while those of the French Canadians revolved mainly around agriculture. Further-more, that the executive officials in French Canada (as well as the mem-bers of the Council) were appointed by the British crown and were responsible to it and that they could therefore act with relatively little concern for the interests of the representatives of the people in the assem-bly intensely irritated the French-Canadian people, especially their intel-lectual leaders.

All these tensions were exacerbated by the ideas that drifted into Canada with the news and the influence of the French Revolution. France's effort to enlist the French Canadians in its war against Britain that began in 1792 failed, and French Canada, under the leadership of the Catholic clergy, reacted violently against the republicanism and atheism of the French Revolution and even against France itself. But the French Canadians, under their own religious and intellectual leaders, absorbed so much of the revolutionary mood of "liberté, egalité, frater-nité" that their own defensive and creative self-consciousness — or, as it may more properly be called, nationalism — was intensified.

Eventually the forces making for self-determination in Lower Canada (Quebec) crystallized in a nationalistic movement that demanded more and more autonomy, social, intellectual, and religious as well as economic and political. This drive to self-determination expressed itself in many ways, in literature, in religion, and in folklore; the most dramatic and significant vehicle for its expression was the newspaper Le Canadien, established in 1806, which operated under the motto of the movement, "notre langue, nos institutions et nos lois" (our language, our institutions, and our laws).

This profound cultural movement led, naturally enough, to the forma-tion of a French-Canadian political party, and, as a reaction to it, a Tory party was created which was composed solidly of supporters of the British interest and the crown. A conflict arose between these two parties that was intense, often bitter, and sometimes violent.

A comparable, but not so profound, conflict developed in Upper Canada between the democratic movement that resulted from the steady influx of new American and Scottish immigrants and the politically entrenched "Old Loyalist" clique that controlled the provincial govern-ment.

Although the internal strife within the two provinces was somewhat stilled by the War of 1812 with the United States, it broke out again with renewed virulence after the Treaty of Ghent in 1815 and was exaggerated by a conflict of interests between the two provinces. This combination of conflicts led the British Parliament to make an effort in 1822 to revoke the Constitutional Act of 1791 and to unite the two provinces with the deliberate intention of suppressing the French-Canadian minority. The attempt failed, and the antagonisms persisted and constituted the basis for outright rebellion and civil war in 1837.

The spirits of liberty, nationalism, and even democracy were strong in Canada in the last quarter of the eighteenth century and the first quarter of the nineteenth. The conflicts that they produced would take at least another fifty years to resolve completely. As the "Age of the Democratic Revolution" unfolded on yet another frontier of the great expansion of Europe, events, men, and ideas were working, more or less together, to produce a new society in a new world.

The War of United States Independence and the establishment of the Constitution of 1787 had not brought complete political peace and union to the United States. Although the actual inauguration of government in 1789 had been followed by the incorporation of the Bill of Rights, the natural rights of citizens, into the Constitution in 1791, the administrations of the first two presidents (George Washington and John Adams) witnessed the appearance of a deep division of the people into two political parties, the so-called "Federalists" led by Alexander Hamilton and the so-called "Antifederalists" or Jeffersonian Democrats led by Thomas Jefferson. These parties stood for two sharply opposing sets of principles, those of nationalism and those of federalism.

The conflict between them was intensified by the influence of the French Revolution. The Jeffersonian Democrats and their partisans welcomed the news of the Revolution as a triumph of freedom. When "Citizen" Edmond Charles Genêt arrived in the United States as a diplomatic representative of the new French republic he was enthusiastically hailed by the American "Jacobins." On the other hand, the American nationalists — the "Federalists" who at the moment controlled the government — received him with marked coolness. Genêt himself came to symbolize the deep-running antipathies between the two American parties: the popular faction identified itself with the French Revolution and considered it the cause of humanity and the common man; the nationalists looked upon the doctrines of the French radicals, as echoed by the democratically minded Jeffersonians, as utterly subversive. The presses poured forth a flood of pamphlets and newspaper propaganda on both sides, and the "Federalists," still with a majority in Congress, succeeded in passing the so-called Alien Acts and the Sedition Act which limited the freedom of aliens in the country (meaning, of course, Frenchmen) and the freedom of speech and of the press to publish the "seditious" ideas of "Jacobinism."

The mood of intense anti-Jacobinism subsided with the election of Thomas Jefferson to the presidency in 1800. Thereafter, the impact of the French Revolution on the affairs of the United States was limited to that of the career of Napoleon Bonaparte. Bonaparte's career, indeed, had a tremendous influence on the history of the hemisphere in several different areas and in many different ways, as will appear.

The first reaction of Spanish colonial policy to the French Revolution was an effort to seal off hermetically the colonies against the infiltration of the pervasive French doctrines of "liberty, equality, fraternity." Governors were instructed to suppress all pro-Revolutionary activity, and the publication of news and documents emanating from France, including the Declaration of the Rights of Man, was prohibited.

All to no avail, of course. The literary, economic, and political societies continued their debates, books and propaganda from France circulated widely, and the spirit of Spanish patriotism flared up everywhere. This patriotism arose especially after 1808 in support of the king of Spain against the great conqueror Napoleon. But when Spain fell under his sway and assumed the role of a puppet-country, American nationalism turned against the mother country and, after many years of bitter warfare, found fulfillment by gaining for the new societies of the continent complete national independence.

In the 1780s many Brazilian students attended French universities, as already noted, where they absorbed much of the learning and the radicalism of the Enlightenment. At home, they talked of France and French politics and the expected cataclysm. The Literary Society in Bahia was suppressed in 1794 for discussing the ideas of "liberty, equality, fraternity." One army officer, Joaquín José da Silva Xavier, who came to be called Tiradentes because he had been a tooth puller, spoke indiscreetly of republics and rebellions, but he was not at first molested. However, during the period of *inconfidencia* (uncertainty) from 1789 to 1792, expressions of discontent were numerous and loud in Minas Gerais because of the government's efforts to collect back taxes and impose new ones. The government, disturbed, arrested many of the malcontents, including Tiradentes. Most of them were freed, but Tiradentes, because of his outspoken criticisms and revolutionary talk, was hanged. He left a strong impression on the people and eventually became a national hero.

In time Brazil came to be unique among the new nations of the hemisphere; when Napoleon conquered Portugal in 1808, the monarchy moved in toto to Brazil, and Rio de Janeiro became the capital of the Portuguese empire. It was from this event that the Brazilian movement to independence really started. Yet it was an easy transition: when the Portuguese court moved back to Portugal, Brazil, under Dom Pedro, simply declared itself independent of Portugal, and there was no effort to hold it in the empire,[5] as will be seen in more detail later.

The Independence of Haiti

Meanwhile, the Revolution was taking quite another course in French Saint-Domingue (Haiti). Like the Windward Islands, this colony had elected representatives to the French Estates-General and had resumed its trade with foreigners. But the news of the fall of the Bastille excited a violent spirit of colonialism or local patriotism that had not been as strong in the other islands, and all those who refused to wear the national *cocarde* were massacred. The island was swept by a hysterical liquidation of representatives of the "old regime," and the colonists (the white planters) seized power in the name of self-government. The General Assembly of Saint-Domingue, meeting at St. Marc, established itself as the government for the colony under the decrees of March 8 and 28, 1789, and on May 28 it adopted a constitution which was a veritable declaration of independence: only the approval of the king to the laws passed by the General Assembly should bind the colony to France; laws passed by the National Legislature in France were to have effect in the colony only if ratified by the assembly. The assembly also demanded an oath of allegiance from the French governor and his troops; upon their refusal to take it they were discharged.

The actions of the General Assembly should have guaranteed independence, but the military forces in the island made a vigorous attempt to suppress this incipient colonial revolt. The result was civil war: the

[5] See below, chapter 11.

military forces suppressed the assembly; the assembly embarked en masse for France, where it hoped to win recognition.

The French National Assembly, frightened by the civil wars going on in the colonies, ordered the abolition of all colonial assemblies and the establishment of arbitrary colonial governments to be directed by commissioners endowed with almost absolute authority. These officials were to be supported by a mighty expedition of naval and military power. The Revolution now turned to the suppression of the self-determination of the colonies with forces greater than any the monarchy had ever employed.

This effort, too, was less than successful. All the colonies passed into a condition of anarchy. In Saint-Domingue, in particular, the attempt to dominate the island failed in the face of the strong opposition of the mulattoes.

The most dramatic new element to appear in this situation was the uprising of the black slaves. The mulattoes assumed the leadership of the "coloreds" (blacks and mulattoes) and determined to seize by force the political power that had been denied them by the colonial assemblies. Certain of the leaders were executed, but this only excited the rebellious "coloreds" the more. When news of the decree of May 15, 1791 (giving the mulattoes full political status), arrived, they demanded its effectualization. When this was refused, civil war ensued.

At this point the slaves, who allied themselves with the free "coloreds," by and large deserted their masters, and the French part of the island was swept by roving bands of blacks who massacred the whites standing in their way, destroyed property, and reveled in general pillage. For months Saint-Domingue was a scene of unrestrained carnage, usually with the blacks pitted against the whites, who were no less savage and barbarous in their treatment of the blacks who fell into their hands.

The metropolitan government in France again took steps to bring order to the chaotic island. A decree of April 4, 1792, called for new elections in which the free colored people were to take full part; new commissioners to the island were sent out accompanied by 6000 soldiers. For a moment a semblance of order was established.

The use of force failed again. The troops were decimated by illness, and the commissioners, upon the news of the proclamation of the French Republic on August 10, 1793, were confronted by a new division among the inhabitants themselves. The mulattoes, curiously enough, proclaimed themselves loyal to the king. The commissioners felt obliged to suppress all support of the old regime. In an effort to win the support of the blacks, Commissioner Santonnax, on his own authority, announced on August 29, 1792, that "all the Negroes and mixed-bloods now in slavery are declared to be free, and to enjoy all the rights inherent in the quality of French citizens." Nevertheless, even this extreme measure failed, for the blacks, fully distrustful of all whites in general and the French regime in particular, simply withheld their support.

On February 4, 1794, the Convention in Paris proclaimed the abolition of slavery throughout the French empire. In the French Windward Islands the implementation of this measure was effectively nullified by the white landlords, as has been noted, and slavery there was later reinstituted by Napoleon. In Saint-Domingue, however, the slaves who revolted were never again brought under subjection.

The news of the execution of the king in 1793 split the French army in Saint-Domingue along royalist-revolutionary lines, and many of the royalists joined the Spaniards of Santo Domingo who were at war against the Revolution. British forces invaded the island in September 1793 and were welcomed as saviors by the French planters who stood in mortal terror of being massacred by the blacks. Yet the motives behind the occupation were far from being purely humanitarian; Britain was at war with France, and British strategy called for military occupation, not rescue. Additional British troops were sent to the island, but the English occupation was never really effective; perhaps forty thousand English military men died there of disease within three years. The British also occupied Martinique, Guadeloupe, and St. Lucia in the course of 1794.

Out of this confused and anarchic situation emerged one of the great national leaders of American independence, Pierre-Dominique Toussaint. Toussaint L'Ouverture, as he was called, had been born a slave and had acquired an elementary education in the employ of his white master; now at the age of about fifty, he was the chief leader of the black uprising. He allied his black forces with the Spaniards of Santo Domingo who were fighting against France and received from the Spaniards the military title of marshal. But the nominal French governor, General Laveaux, posing as a defender of the blacks under the emancipation decree of February 4, 1794, asked Toussaint L'Ouverture and his black supporters to join him against the English. Toussaint, sincerely devoted to the principles of the Revolution, calling himself the "Spartacus

Heroes of American independence. Toussaint L'Ouverture. From Ralph Korngold, *Citizen Toussaint* (Boston: Little, Brown, 1944). Courtesy of the University of Washington Library.

of the Blacks," and hoping, both for himself and his followers, to obtain the full status of a French citizen, acceded to Laveaux's invitation. Within a relatively short time, Toussaint and his French allies occupied the northern section of the French part of the island while the English retreated to the area around Port-au-Prince.

Gradually Toussaint succeeded in making himself master of Saint-Domingue, even to the point of reducing his French allies to a subordinate position. When the English wooed him, offering him recognition as an independent sovereign in return for a monopoly of the island's commerce, he refused, preferring to remain within the orbit of the

French empire. Eventually the English retired and gave up most of their holdings in the French islands.

Toussaint, then turning his attention to internal problems, subdued the mulattoes who still resisted him. With the assistance of the black General Dessalines, he carried out this task with ruthless efficacy: at least ten thousand mulattoes were massacred. Toussaint then restored the cultivation of sugar, rebuilt irrigation systems, compelled everyone to work, established a severe regime of "law and order" implemented by a new and efficient police force, and reinstituted the French way of life, which accepted the coexistence and even the mixing of blacks and whites.

On July 8, 1801, Toussaint proclaimed a new colonial constitution, which declared among other things that every person born in the island was ipso facto free and French. The government was concentrated in the hands of a governor general, a position to which Toussaint was named for life. Laws were to be approved but not initiated by an elected assembly. The government of France was recognized as the imperial government of the island, although its powers in the internal affairs of the colony were reduced to nothing. Toussaint then opened the ports of the island to the traders of England, the United States, and other nations, as well as to those of France.

Once again, prosperity returned to Saint-Domingue. The French Revolution, despite its bloody birth pangs, had brought to Saint-Domingue freedom, a new prosperity, and a de facto independence. Independence was not yet legalized, however, and Saint-Domingue, now beginning to be called Haiti, had to fight one more bitter battle to make it so. Despite Toussaint L'Ouverture's proud insistence upon keeping Saint-Domingue French in culture and national identity, Napoleon Bonaparte, now first consul of France, was determined to restore the island to complete and absolute French domination, to reinstitute slavery, and to reestablish in its entirety the order of things that had existed before 1789.

At the moment of the signing of the preliminary articles of the Peace of Amiens (1801), Bonaparte rushed a powerful expedition into Saint-Domingue under the command of General Leclerc, with instructions to crush the independence movement, to annul Toussaint's constitution, and to bring about the complete reestablishment of French authority. The suddenness and the efficacy of the French invasion scattered the

Americans, and Toussaint, facing the reality of defeat, surrendered himself to General Leclerc on May 6, 1802. Then the rains came and with them yellow fever. Eight thousand French soldiers died within a matter of weeks. With death came demoralization, and the effectiveness of the French forces dissolved. The Americans, now under the leadership of General Henri Christophe, took up the fight again in a devastating guerrilla warfare. Leclerc, believing Toussaint L'Ouverture was involved in this renewal of the war, shipped him off to France, where he died in prison on April 1, 1803.

However, the tide was now turning, and the Americans, led by Generals Dessalines and Christophe, steadily whittled away the French troops and their will to win. Napoleon sent reinforcements, but they were incapable of defeating the Americans. In October Leclerc wrote, "My army is destroyed; I have hardly two hundred effectives left." He begged to be relieved, and he died on November 2, 1802.

Leclerc's successor, General Rochambeau, could do no better. He instituted a reign of terror, but it failed because the masses of blacks were already long inured to the excessive barbarisms of the war. They fought on, and successfully. In 1803 the war with England was renewed, and General Rochambeau, to escape annihilation by the blacks, surrendered himself and his army to English Commodore Loring on November 9, 1803. A small remnant of the French armies escaped to the eastern end of the island, which had been ceded to France by Spain in 1795; for the time being, it remained under French domination.

The blacks, however, assumed complete control of the western end of the island. On January 1, 1804, Dessalines and his generals proclaimed the complete independence of Haiti — its pre-Columbian Indian name. All Frenchmen were ordered executed; all French property was confiscated; almost every trace of French influence was utterly destroyed. Dessalines was proclaimed Jean Jacques I, emperor of Haiti, on October 8, 1804. The French made several subsequent attempts to recover the island, but they failed; the independence of Haiti was finally recognized by King Charles X of France in 1824.

Haiti was thus the second new nation of the American hemisphere to proclaim its independence from Europe. Basically, the cause of independence was the same as in the United States: a new society had been born and had grown to maturity, with a compulsive instinct and drive for self-government, self-direction, self-realization. As in the other emerging nations, this evolution toward national identity had gone on without the full awareness or comprehension of the statesmen of the mother country. As in the case of the United States, the international situation had provided a context of conditions that made the realization of independence possible. Haiti, alone among the former French colonies in the Caribbean area, had succeeded in achieving independence and the freedom of its people. In the other islands the fortunes of war and diplomacy had restored the status quo ante 1789, including slavery.

The independent states of America, about 1825 (unshaded areas are those not yet independent)

Conclusion

In the two or three decades following the achievement of independence by the United States, then, there were many forces at work throughout the hemisphere spurring the peoples toward freedom. These forces were of various kinds. The ideologies of freedom coming to America from Europe undoubtedly gave great impact to the stirrings of the American peoples, as did, also, the examples provided by the successful revolutions in the United States and France. But the ferment of freedom among the American peoples was chiefly internal to them and involved the most profound self-interests and aspirations of the Americans themselves. They were at once economic, social, political, religious, intellectual, and, above all, emotional and psychological. The life-style, the mind, the sense of national identity of each of the embryo societies in the New World, long gestating in the course of the historical experiences of those societies, were coming, like wine, to a sort of maturity, and these feelings and ideas were expressing themselves ever more boldly and clearly at the turn of the eighteenth century into the nineteenth. In the case of Haiti, indeed, the cultural and psychological forces contained in the "ferment of freedom" actually burst the bonds of colonialism and succeeded in making Haiti, the old French Saint-Domingue, free. The ferment was the first stirring of anticolonialism (after that of the United States) in the Western world. When the Napoleonic wars swept over western Europe, it was ready to burst into the flame of independence.

CHAPTER 11

The Independence of
Latin America

Although the French Revolution had spread the ideas and emotions associated with the catch phrase "liberty, equality, fraternity" throughout the American hemisphere, it was the phenomenal career of Napoleon Bonaparte that transformed these ideas into the realities of rebellion and independence. Even so, the explosive forces that underlay these realities were internal to the societies of the hemisphere itself as will be seen.

When Napoleon seized power in France on the 18 Brumaire 1799, the French Revolution, per se, was over. France returned to a monarchical form of government (Napoleon crowned himself "emperor of the French" on May 18, 1804), and the French overseas empire, such as it was, came directly under the emperor's control. But revolutionary change continued, both in France and in the colonies, and revolutionary revisions of French institutions like the Napoleonic Code, Napoleon's concordat with the Roman Catholic church, and his alterations of the educational system as well as the structure of government had their effects, even if they were not always fully applied, in the colonies.

For a short period after Napoleon's accession to power, it appeared that he might attempt to restore France's former colonial and imperial grandeur overseas. He retook Louisiana from Spain by the Treaty of San Ildefonso in 1801, and, as has been noted, he made a valiant effort to hold Haiti in the empire. But his attention was soon diverted from America by European developments, and he offered to sell Louisiana

267

to the United States for $15 million, an offer that was promptly accepted by President Thomas Jefferson in 1803. His life-and-death struggle with Great Britain — the death battle of the "tiger and the shark" — led him into a largely paper maritime contest with England. This contest eventually drew the hitherto neutral United States into war with England in 1812, although not as an ally of France.

Hispanoamerica

Napoleon's invasion of Portugal and Spain in 1807–8 opened a new era in the history of America. The Portuguese court promptly fled to Brazil, and Napoleon's forces dethroned Carlos IV, the head of the Bourbon dynasty in Spain, and set up Napoleon's brother Joseph as king. This sparked a chain reaction throughout Hispanoamerica, for the Spanish colonies refused to recognize Joseph Bonaparte as their king. Curiously enough, the *criollos* now joined with the *peninsulares* in reaffirming their loyalty to their rightful king, now Ferdinand VII, against the French impostors. (Carlos, who was Napoleon's prisoner, had abdicated; Ferdinand VII had been named king by a junta of Spanish leaders at Aranjuez although he too was still a prisoner of Napoleon.) Many Hispanoamericans rejoiced when the future Duke of Wellington drove the French armies out of Spain, a movement not completed until the spring of 1813, and they rejoiced at the return of Ferdinand VII to the Spanish throne in 1814. Two years before, they had sent delegates to the Cortes that met in Cádiz to adopt a new and liberal constitution for the Spanish empire. Ferdinand VII had promised to rule according to this constitution, but when he rejected its limitations, imprisoned its liberal authors, and restored a regime of absolutism, the colonies turned against him and the Spain that supported him.

The First Phase:
A Series of Abortive Rebellions

In the six years between the abdication of Carlos IV in 1808 and the return of Ferdinand VII to Spain in 1814, much had happened in Hispanoamerica.

From one end of the continent to the other in several centers of population and government, many common people, directed by their creole leaders, rose against the misrule of the *peninsulares* who represented Ferdinand VII. At the same time, many creoles, like the Angloamerican Tories before them, clung to their supreme loyalty to their mother country. The uprisings were thus civil wars from the very beginning.

Initially there was considerable confusion over the question of who the legal ruler of Hispanoamerica really was. Joseph Bonaparte was universally rejected, but the Junta Suprema Central, a supreme imperial council that replaced the now defunct Council of the Indies and was meeting in Seville in the name of Ferdinand VII, was recognized as, de facto, the supreme authority. It was this junta that carried on the affairs of the empire and that issued instructions to the *peninsulares* who, as imperial officials, managed the affairs of the various viceroyalties.

But the rift between the creoles and the *peninsulares* was rapidly widening and deepening. For, in addition to the traditional antagonisms between the two groups, the near-collapse of authority opened to the creoles a vision of self-government, of power, even of independence and national self-realization, which brought them to the point of action. Since the viceroyalties were the personal domains of the king, they felt justified in assuming control of their affairs in his name, without taking orders from the self-constituted junta in Seville. Moreover, the radicals among them, bitter over the "bad government" of the entire colonial system administered by the *peninsulares*, seized the initiative and started a series of uprisings that were frankly aimed at winning independence.

The first of these outbreaks was a coup d'état at Chuquisaca in upper Peru (which was to become Bolivia), where the university had long been a center of discussion of the subversive political ideas of the Enlightenment. On May 25, 1809, the *peninsular* officials were deposed, and a local junta of creoles, students, and professors, as well as some of the former Spanish officials, seized power in the name of King Ferdinand VII, proclaiming that it more properly had the right to govern the colony than the Junta of Seville. On July 16 a similar coup occurred in La Paz, also in upper Peru, where the government was taken over by the town *cabildo*. Both of these new juntas were suppressed, the first by the viceroy of Buenos Aires, the second by the viceroy of Peru at Lima. But the event aroused an intense interest among the other colonies; the idea of creole self-government spread like wildfire. The conflagration, fanned by the new movement, was supported by many (though not all) members of the downtrodden classes — Indians, blacks, mestizos — who saw in it the dawn of emancipation from their miseries.

Thus it happened that the *cabildo* of Quito, an intellectual center, led by the creole Marqués de Silva Alegre, executed another coup in the name of self-government under King Ferdinand VII in August 1809. This junta, too, was crushed by the viceroy of Peru. Soon after, political power was seized from the *peninsulares* in Bogotá, New Granada, and Valladolid in western Mexico. These actions were also subdued, and the leaders either were arrested or took flight.

Up until the beginning of 1810, then, all the efforts of the creoles to seize power had been suppressed by the *peninsular* viceroys and officials acting under the authority of the Seville Junta which operated in the name of Ferdinand VII although he was in exile. The creole juntas had also acted in the name of the exiled Ferdinand, although they rejected the authority of the Junta of Seville and violently repulsed the *peninsular* officials governing in its name.

But the virus of creole nationalism was not purged. The creoles, now aroused, carried their crusade forward with an increasing degree of organization and effectiveness. They still rallied under the banner of the absentee king, but their real purpose was now clearly to depose the *peninsular* officials and to concentrate power in their own hands. The year 1810, therefore, saw a renewal of the struggle.

The news that Napoleon's troops had conquered all of Spain except Cádiz was a signal for new efforts by the American autonomists. In Spain the Junta of Seville was replaced by the Council of Regency which summoned the colonies to send delegates to a Cortes to be held in Cádiz to write a constitution for the Spanish empire. The creoles in America rejected the call because, for the moment at least, Spain had no king and the empire no government. In a sense "orphaned," they preferred to gather power into their own hands locally — always in the name of Ferdinand VII, to be sure, but autonomously and without any intermediaries. However, the colonies did send delegates to the Cortes of Cádiz which met from 1810 to 1814, but only the *peninsulares* and creoles accepted the authority of the Cortes as the legitimate successor of the Junta of Seville.

In the sense that it was a European parliamentary body which included members representing American colonies, the Cortes of Cádiz was comparable to the French Estates-General at the time of the French

Revolution. Like that body as it had developed, the Cortes of Cádiz also was one of the most radical in modern history up to that time. The American delegates were actually somewhat more conservative than those from the Spanish provinces; their chief concern was to gain greater representation for the American provinces rather than to adopt liberal principles. Bitter debates resulted from the Spaniards' attitude toward the Americans, and the Americans, summoned to the Cortes to help build a common American and Spanish front against Napoleon, were to some degree actually alienated from the Spanish cause.

Yet in 1812 the Cortes of Cádiz instituted a famous constitution for the Spanish empire that was characterized by many of the most advanced liberal principles of the time. Based upon a federal plan, it enunciated the principle of popular sovereignty; the Cortes itself, representing all the parts of the empire, was the seat of sovereignty and power. The constitution also included a bill of rights guaranteeing certain freedoms and immunities to all Spanish and Hispanoamerican subjects. The Inquisition was abolished throughout the empire, and the privileges of the church and the aristocracy were reduced. The constitution reformed the tax system as well and strictly limited the powers of the king.

When Ferdinand VII reentered Spain in 1814, he swore to uphold this constitution, while the viceroys in America endorsed it with reluctance. For a moment it appeared that a new era of liberty and democracy had arrived in the Spanish empire.

As soon as he had reassumed power, however, Ferdinand repudiated his oath to uphold the constitution and proceeded to purge both Spain and Hispanoamerica of the liberals who had formulated it. There then ensued several years of ruthless tyranny; it was not until 1820 that Ferdinand was forced to retake his oath and support the constitution. It was then revived in Hispanoamerica and given a new lease on life, for it served as a model for a number of new constitutions, both in Europe and in America, in the decades following 1820.

Meanwhile, news of Napoleon's conquest of Spain was a signal to the wealthy creoles of Venezuela to try to drive out the *peninsulares* and seize power for themselves. In April 1810 they engineered a coup d'état in Caracas which forced the captain general, a *peninsular*, to resign and which set up the *cabildo* as a junta to exercise local political power in the name of Ferdinand VII. This junta, inspired by the idealism of the Enlightenment and desirous of winning the support of the underprivileged Indians and blacks, abolished the local slave trade and terminated the system of tribute paid by the Indians. A congress of representatives from other towns asserted its own authority in the former captaincy general of Caracas, subject only to the direct sovereignty of Ferdinand VII.

It appeared that the captaincy general might become to all intents and purposes fully independent, under the king. But the revolutionary and republican ideas of the young radicals, led by Simón Bolívar, frightened the more conservative creole leaders, and they called upon the Cortes at Cádiz for help. The Cortes blockaded the coast while the conservatives aroused the interior towns against the revolutionary congress.

The Caracas junta then appealed to Great Britain, which was at war with Napoleon everywhere, for assistance; the most prominent member of the Caracas commission was Bolívar. Although Bolívar's mission to England was a failure, he met the aging Francisco de Miranda in London and persuaded him to return with the mission to Caracas. Upon their arrival they found the revolutionary government in trouble — ineffective, unstable, and tragically split by faction. Miranda and Bolívar seized control of the congress and prevailed upon it to declare, on July 5, 1811, the complete independence of Venezuela from Spain. This was the first declaration of independence among the emergent Hispanoamerican states.

The revolutionaries made Venezuela a federal republic and instituted a whole series of civic reforms based on the ideas of Rousseau. But the pressures of circumstances against them were too strong: a Spanish blockade paralyzed the economy, the departure of the *peninsular* officials incapacitated the government, and the resistance of the interior provinces, led by the conservatives, prevented them from unifying the country. When the Cádiz government sent an expeditionary force to Caracas from Cuba and this expedition won the cooperation of the semicivilized *llaneros* (plainsmen) of the cattle-raising interior, the congress made Miranda a dictator with life-and-death power, but to no avail. Miranda and Bolívar failed to arrest the invasion, and their government collapsed in July of 1812. Miranda, betrayed by Bolívar, was sent to Spain where he died in prison; Bolívar escaped to New Granada.

This marked the end of the first independent republic to arise in Hispanoamerica.

Meanwhile, revolutionary movements were erupting in other parts of Hispanoamerica. In New Granada, for example, the creoles had lamented Napoleon's conquest of Spain and had proclaimed Ferdinand VII their king, as had the Hispanoamericans in other areas. But news of the apparently successful completion of the Napoleonic invasion of Spain and of the Caracas "revolution" in 1810 set off a coup d'état, first in Cartagena and then Bogotá where, on July 20, 1810, the *cabildo* seized

The Western Hemisphere, about 1811. From *Cary's New Universal Atlas* (London: J. Cary, 1811), no. 2. Courtesy of The Newberry Library, Chicago.

power and placed the viceroy under arrest. Most of the other municipalities followed suit, and the government of the vice royalty was assumed by creoles.

The creoles of New Granada were no more successful in governing their province than were those of Venezuela. They quarreled among themselves and demonstrated a monumental incapacity for the practical business of governing a country. They called a congress of representatives of the various parts of the country, but the country was too unevenly divided between royalists and creoles to create a congress that would fairly represent all areas and factions. On the contrary, the country split into uncoordinated ideological and institutional fragments. When the congress met, it declared the independence of New Granada from Spain and revived the idea of the federal empire by accepting Ferdinand VII as its king. The congress, however, accomplished nothing more, and the country fell into chaos.

Such was the situation when Bolívar came to Bogotá after the collapse of the revolution in Venezuela in 1812. The Bogotá congress gave him a small army, and he succeeded in driving out the royalists. Then, with his army swelled by Venezuelan refugees and by additional forces from the Bogotá congress, he returned to Venezuela and, after a savage campaign complete with atrocities and terror, entered Caracas in August of 1813. It was this exploit that earned him the title of "El Libertador." The Venezuelan republic was reestablished, although Bolívar governed it as a dictator; it lasted a little more than a year.

The Spanish and royalist army under General Domingo de Monteverde, reinforced, retook the field against the republic. Again assisted by the savage *llaneros*, Monteverde was able to drive Bolívar to the wall; again "the Liberator" fled to New Granada. Once more he was welcomed; once more he was given an army with which to "unify" the country; in this he was in large measure, but not completely, successful.

New Granada could neither be unified nor govern itself successfully. In 1815 Bolívar, confronted by a state of anarchy, gave up and withdrew to the English island of Jamaica, while Spain, now ruled by an absolute Ferdinand VII, sent a great army under the command of Field Marshal Pablo Morillo to recover both Venezuela and New Granada. This it did with terrifying effectiveness: by the spring of 1816 Spanish rule was completely restored in both countries. The creole revolution, originally inaugurated in the name of that same Ferdinand VII, to all appearances was over.

When Napoleon invaded Spain in 1808, the creole-dominated *cabildo* of Mexico City proclaimed Ferdinand VII king. Viceroy José de Iturrigaray vacillated, and the *peninsulares*, fearing that he might sympathize with the creoles, deposed him and installed their own man in his place. By 1810 they were in effective control of Mexico City, which also meant nominal control of most of New Spain.

It was at this moment that Miguel Hidalgo y Costilla, a priest in the village of Dolores situated about one hundred miles west of Mexico City, flashed on the screen of fame. A man of the Enlightenment, educated at the College of San Nicolás in Valladolid and at the University of Mexico, his work with the Indians had awakened in him a profound pity for their condition and an even more intense hatred of the system of government created and perpetuated by the viceroys and the *peninsulares*. His outspoken criticism of the system attracted the attention of the Inquisition, which condemned him and "banished" him to the village of Dolores. There he learned the Indian languages and devoted his life to improving their condition.

When the *cabildo* of Mexico City accepted Ferdinand VII as king and the *peninsulares* recovered power, Padre Hidalgo and other creole liberals formed a conspiracy, led by Ignacio Allende, to oust them. Word came to Hidalgo that the Spanish authorities had learned of the conspiracy and were about to strike. In anticipation of the government's moves, Hidalgo opened the jail in Dolores and freed the prisoners, distributed weapons to his parishioners, and summoned them to the church on Sunday, September 16, 1810. "Would you be free?" he asked them. When they shouted in the affirmative, he proclaimed the motto of the revolution: "Viva Nuestra Señora de Guadalupe! Muera el mal gobierno! Mueran los Gachupines!" (Long live Our Lady of Guadalupe! Death to bad government! Death to the Spaniards!)

This was the famous "grito de Dolores" (shout of Dolores) that marked the beginning of the Mexican revolution. Hidalgo and his fellow priest José María Morelos gathered around them a motley army of about 50,000 Indians and mestizos and swore an oath to destroy the Spaniards. They took the city of Guanajuato and killed every Spaniard in it. They then went on to Guadalajara, where they were welcomed as heroes. When news came to Hidalgo of the Cortes of Cádiz and its offer of amnesty to all revolutionaries, he rejected the idea on the ground that "pardon is for animals, not for the defenders of their country."

Hidalgo, captured by trickery, died before a firing squad on July 31, 1811. His revolutionary movement was carried on by Morelos, who succeeded in getting control of much of western Mexico. He also called a congress at Chilpancingo which declared Mexico independent of Spain and adopted a constitution promulgated in 1814. Nevertheless, the Spanish forces were too strong. Morelos was captured and taken before the Inquisition in Mexico City where he was tried, condemned, defrocked, and executed on December 22, 1815.

The revolution appeared to be extinguished in Mexico, but the revolutionaries resorted to guerrilla warfare and kept the movement alive for five years until the tide began to turn about 1820 when the liberals in Spain staged a revolt against the absolutist Ferdinand VII and forced him to reinstate the Constitution of Cádiz of 1812. By that time the conservative Mexican creoles who had held aloof from the "Dolores revolution" of Hidalgo and Morelos had given up hope of achieving Mexican autonomy under Spanish rule, and threw in their lots with the movement for Mexican independence.

The Completion of Independence in Argentina

Meanwhile, yet another regional revolution had taken place in the Rio de la Plata area. This one was unique, for it was permanently successful.

During the war with Napoleon, England sent a squadron of ships under Sir Home Popham and Colonel William Carr Beresford to Buenos Aires in June 1806. The expedition occupied the city, and the viceroy fled to Córdoba. Beresford proclaimed English sovereignty over the city, named himself governor, and called upon the citizenry to swear allegiance to King George III. He also opened the port to a nearly complete freedom of trade. The people rejected this imposed anglicization, and an Argentine force led by a former French sea captain named Santiago de Liniers ejected Beresford and his army.

The English returned in October, this time to Montevideo, in an expedition commanded by General John Whitelock. The viceroy fled again; the *cabildo* of Buenos Aires declared him deposed and elected

Captain Liniers as their ruler. The English tried desperately to win over the populace of the La Plata area, but the *Platenses* again repudiated them; after an unsuccessful attempt to occupy Buenos Aires, they finally gave up and sailed away. King Carlos IV praised the *porteños* (the people of the port of Buenos Aires) and named Captain Liniers interim viceroy, thereby ratifying the quasi-independent actions of the creoles.

It was out of these circumstances that Argentine independence was born. The creole-dominated *cabildo* of Buenos Aires, encouraged and emboldened by its success in repelling the English invasions without Spanish aid, assumed responsibility for governing the province independently. Thus, when news came to Buenos Aires of the forced abdication of Carlos IV, the *cabildo* proclaimed its loyalty to Ferdinand VII. In 1809 the *peninsulares* attempted to unseat Liniers, but without success, while the Junta of Seville appointed Baltasar Hidalgo de Cisneros permanent viceroy in his place.

Because of the depressed economic conditions and because the *porteños* had so greatly profited from the free trade allowed them during the momentary English occupation, the creoles of the La Plata area were not prepared to return to the old Spanish mercantilist system of national economic monopoly. When Mariano Moreno, an alumnus of the University of Chuquisaca, published a pamphlet denouncing the old system, his ideas inflamed the self-interest and the nationalism of his compatriots, who demanded a reopening of the port, which was tantamount to a rejection of Spain's imperial economic policy. The viceroy hesitantly acceded to the demand, and prosperity quickly returned. The creoles — and Mariano Moreno — seemed justified in their actions.

Such was the situation when news arrived, in 1810, that Spain had fallen to Napoleon. The *cabildo* of Buenos Aires, augmented by a large body of local citizens, met in what was called a *cabildo abierto* (open town council). On May 25, this council proclaimed its right to govern the La Plata viceroyalty in the name of the absentee king, Ferdinand VII. Cisneros, the legal viceroy, was arrested and deported.

The new *cabildo abierto*, controlled by the radicals, now proceeded to govern the province. It succeeded in eliminating the *peninsulares*, and called together a congress representing all the parts of the viceroyalty. When Montevideo refused to send representatives, fighting erupted and did not cease until Buenos Aires conquered Montevideo in 1814. The Paraguay region, too, resisted. An attempt by Buenos Aires to force the Asunción *cabildo* to join failed, but a group of creoles seized control and declared Paraguay's independence. Upper Peru, centering in Chuquisaca and La Paz, also rejected the efforts of Buenos Aires to incorporate it. Other parts of the viceroyalty, however, were gradually subdued and united in the new state of Argentina. The revolution was a success, though the future countries of Uruguay, Paraguay, and Bolivia remained apart and refused to follow the lead of Buenos Aires.

Meanwhile, the government of Buenos Aires floundered through a long history of squabbling, personal and ideological factionalism, and ineffectiveness. It was not until a federal congress met at Tucumán in 1816 and, in fear of the absolutist revival of the restored Ferdinand VII, proclaimed Argentina a fully independent and sovereign state that the revolution was completed. Nevertheless, Argentina's troubles were not over, even though its sovereignty and independence were never again destroyed. It thus became the first of the former Hispanoamerican provinces to establish a permanent independence.

San Martín and the Liberation of Chile

Across the high Andes Mountains from Argentina, in the captaincy general of Chile, the virus of revolution had broken out among the rich creole landowners, as it had in so many other parts of Hispanoamerica. The hatred between creoles and *peninsulares* was just as bitter there as elsewhere, and when news arrived in Santiago de Chile of the abdication of Carlos IV, a junta of creoles proclaimed Ferdinand VII its king. This junta ejected the *peninsular* officials, opened the ports, and then called a congress to rule the captaincy general without interference from the Junta of Seville.

But the revolutionaries were divided. The radicals, led by José Miguel Carrera, a man of Enlightenment ideas, of revolutionary ardor, and with a passion for freedom, demanded that the captaincy general become independent. On the other hand, the conservative creoles, under the leadership of Bernardo O'Higgins, the illegitimate son of the former viceroy Ambrosio O'Higgins of Peru, feared the Jacobin-like ideas of social reform and were not prepared to go so far so quickly. The two sides were about equally balanced, but with the restoration of Ferdinand VII in 1814 and his resumption of absolute government, the *peninsulares* in Chile were able to stage a comeback. In the crisis the weight of public opinion was thrown to O'Higgins, while Spanish forces sent by the viceroy in Lima captured Carrera. Carrera, however, made a deal with the viceroy which put the radical leader back in the field against O'Higgins. The Spaniards crushed O'Higgins, who fled with his followers into Argentina. The rule of the viceroy was restored. Once again, the fires of revolution had been quenched.

By 1816 it appeared that all the Hispanoamerican movements for creole autonomy except those in Argentina and Paraguay had been suppressed and that the authority of Spain, under the reactionary Ferdinand VII, had been restored. The *peninsulares* regained power nearly everywhere and ruled with iron hands. The creoles in Peru had never moved to assert their dominance. It was the events in Europe after 1815 that provided a new opportunity for the American creoles and reawakened the fires of American nationalism and independence. This time they would succeed.

When Napoleon was finally eliminated from the European scene by the battle of Waterloo and the Peace of Vienna, a wave of reaction swept through Europe that revived the old pre-Revolutionary dynasties and initiated a series of efforts, in the name of the principle of "legitimacy," to restore the status quo that had existed before 1789. The so-called Holy Alliance (France, Austria, Spain, and Russia) was formed to provide international backing for the reestablished "old regime," and this association actually entertained a motion, in 1820, to assist Spain in subduing its rebellious American colonies.

In Spain, Ferdinand VII enjoyed his restoration to absolute power and governed the colonies accordingly. Nevertheless, the day was past when the Hispanoamericans would submit to absolute government and a system of economic monopoly. Nor was the king himself a man capable of managing effectively the affairs of such an empire. He did appeal to his American subjects to lay aside their animosities, and there were many Americans who, after the years of civil strife, might have been glad to do so. But the promised reforms did not come, and a vacillating policy of repressing liberalism and liberal leaders in America extinguished the hope that a better time had arrived.

The smoldering fires of creole nationalism now flared up again. The first triumphant manifestation of it was the liberation of Chile by José de San Martín. Born in the Rio de la Plata basin in 1778, San Martín had been educated in Spain and had risen to high military rank in the

Spanish campaigns against Napoleon. In 1811 he went to London and joined the community of Hispanoamerican refugees there; a year later he returned to his native land. He quickly entered politics, got a military command, and organized the Lautaro lodge of Masons. He successfully defended Buenos Aires from a royalist attack from Uruguay, and in 1814 he was given command of the Argentine Army of the North. He resigned from this position, however, to accept the provincial governorship of Cuyo, which faced Chile across the Andes. There, in the capital city of Mendoza, he quietly planned and built a military organization for the liberation of Santiago de Chile. When his "Army of the Andes" was ready, he asked Bernardo O'Higgins to be his chief lieutenant and set out, in the summer of 1817, to march over the 12,000-foot passes into Chile. On February 12, 1817, San Martín's forces defeated the royalist army sent against him at Chacabuco, and within a few days he entered Santiago de Chile.

San Martín was welcomed as a conquering hero, and the *cabildo abierto* of Santiago offered him the presidency of the new state. He declined and nominated O'Higgins for the post; O'Higgins was offered the honor and accepted it. Chile declared its independence from Spain on February 12, 1818. Still, the country was not yet fully liberated, and a Spanish force from Peru defeated O'Higgins at Canaba Rayada, south of Santiago. But on April 5 General San Martín blocked the path of the Spaniards to Santiago at Maipú; in the ensuing battle, one of the bloodiest in the history of American liberation, the Spaniards were finally beaten and Santiago was saved.

The Liberation of Peru

Chile was now safely in the column of the independent Hispanoamerican states. However, San Martín had no inclination to stop his drive toward freedom with Chile, for he realized that the citadel of Spanish power in America was Peru and that that citadel must be taken if America was to be permanently liberated from the Spanish yoke. With characteristic deliberateness, and hindered by Argentina's refusal to help him and the Chileans' only halfhearted support, he succeeded in building up an expedition to go by sea against Lima. His most spectacular achievement in this preparatory stage was the acquisition of the services of Lord Thomas Cochrane, an aristocratic English adventurer with a very shady past but a genuine naval genius nevertheless.

In August 1820 San Martín finally set out for Lima with his fleet, commanded by Lord Cochrane, and a force of about 4000 men. San Martín worked slowly and methodically, as usual, and landed troops at Pisco, south of Lima, and at Huacho to the north.

The most difficult part of San Martín's task was winning over the Peruvian creoles to the cause of independence. Most of them were conservative and distrustful of revolution, and they were reasonably well satisfied with the modus operandi effected by the viceroys. However, San Martín would not move until he felt sure of enough creole support to assure him of success.

Fortunately for him, the people of Spain, worn out by the inefficiency and ruthlessness of Ferdinand VII's government and led by a number of military officers, had risen against their king and had forced him, in March 1820, to promise to restore the liberal Cádiz Constitution of 1812. The viceroys in the colonies were instructed to proclaim the readoption of this constitution.

It was these instructions to Joaquin de la Pezuela, the viceroy of Peru, that turned the tide of opinion in San Martín's favor. For when it was declared that the Constitution of Cádiz would be reinstated, the liberals took heart again. The viceroys were authorized to institute local and provincial representative assemblies, and it was announced, despite the bitter, private appeals of Ferdinand VII to his allies of the Holy Alliance, that no more military expeditions would be sent to the colonies. The frame of Spanish authority was irreparably weakened.

San Martín could not yet move and, when Lord Cochrane seized his funds and sailed away, he found himself stranded. His strategy was working nevertheless, for he had cut off Lima's food supply. He was aided, too, by a revolt of Spanish officers which deposed the viceroy in 1821. The new viceroy, General José de la Serna, attempted to negotiate with San Martín over the food supply, but San Martín, despite his own uncomfortable situation, would accept no compromise: he insisted upon complete independence for Peru. When the negotiations failed, La Serna decided to retire his army from Lima. San Martín then entered the capital, in June of 1821.

Peru was at last free. It was not a spectacular triumph for the cause of independence, nor was the government set up by San Martín distinguished for the brilliance of its success. But the independence held, and after a meeting with Simón Bolívar at Guayaquil late in July 1822,

San Martín retired from the wars, first to Chile, then to Argentina, and finally to Europe, where he spent the last years of his life.

Simón Bolívar and the Independence of Colombia, Venezuela, and Ecuador

In the years during which San Martín was methodically freeing Chile and Peru, the flamboyant Simón Bolívar had succeeded in liberating Venezuela and Colombia. Though he had fled from Bogotá to Jamaica to escape the royalist resurgence in 1815, he had never lost either his faith in the cause of independence or his determination to continue the struggle. Americans and the new American societies were new peoples, ethnologically and culturally different from Europe and the Europeans: they were destined for a glorious life of their own, independent, sovereign, and dedicated to the promotion of human happiness in their own American ways. As he put it in his famous "Jamaica letter," written in 1815,

I desire more than anyone else to see formed in America the greatest nation of the world [— the greatest] not so much by reason of its extent as because of its liberty and glory. Yet although I aspire to the perfection of the government of my country, I cannot persuade myself that the New World should be for the moment organized as one great republic. As it is impossible, I do not dare to desire it; and I desire even less a universal monarchy of America, because that project, without being practicable, is also impossible. . . . The American states must have the care of paternal governments which will heal the scars and the wounds of despotism and war. . . . For one government to bring to life, animate, put into action all the resources of the public prosperity, — correct, illuminate, and perfect the [entire] New World, it would be necessary for it to have all the faculties of a God, not to mention the lights and virtues of all men. . . .

M. de Pradt has wisely divided America into fifteen to seventeen independent states, governed by as many monarchs. I am in agreement with the first idea, because America [really] involves the creation of seventeen nations. As for the second idea, although it would be easier to achieve it, it is less useful, and therefore I am not in favor of American monarchies. . . . [Republics are less aggressive and imperialistic than monarchies; small republics are more desirable than large ones.]

The idea of forming in the New World one single nation, which would have just one tie to bind the parts together and into the whole is a grandiose one. Because [such a great society] would have a single origin, one common language, common customs and one common religion, one might expect, consequently, that it might be ruled by one single government that would hold together the different states that are to be formed. But it is not possible, because remote climates, diverse [geographic] situations, opposing interests, unsimilar characters, divide America. How magnificent would it be if the Isthmus of Panamá were for us what the Isthmus of Corinth was for the Greeks! Oh that some day we may have the happiness of installing there an august congress of the representatives of the republics, kingdoms and empires [of the world] to treat and discuss

Heroes of American independence. Simón Bolívar, "the Liberator." Portrait by Samys Mützner. Courtesy of the University of Washington Library.

the exalted matters of peace and of war with the other nations of the world. This sort of body may take place in some happy epoch of our regeneration. Any other hope, such as that of the Abbé St. Pierre, who conceived the praiseworthy fantasy of bringing together an European congress to decide the fate and the interests of those nations, would be impracticable.[1]

After several unsuccessful landings along the Venezuelan coast, which failed to arouse popular support, Bolívar, with a handful of diehard companions, landed near the mouth of the Orinoco River in 1817. He established his headquarters at the frontier town of Angostura, the present Ciudad Bolívar, and for two years concentrated on the task of building up an efficient, loyal army. He won over the *llaneros* who had been used by the conservatives to destroy him in 1814 and were now led by the legendary José Antonio Paez, and his forces were swelled by the many refugees from the *peninsular* regime who flocked to him. In addition, he was more successful than he had ever been in getting supplies and other assistance from England.

In February of 1819 Bolívar called together at Angostura a "congress" of representatives from the areas he ruled, together with refugees from the Spanish-controlled areas. In a famous oration he urged his hearers to face the bitterness of the struggle for freedom and for the slow building of a national society. He proposed a constitution which in reality envisaged a strong, de facto dictatorial central government; his proposals, at least in principle, were favorably received. In actuality, Bolívar offered himself to his followers as a benevolent dictator, and they accepted him.

In May 1819 he began his campaign. With about four thousand men, he crossed the mountains that separated the Orinoco Valley from Bogotá (Colombia) and, after routing two small Spanish forces, he entered the city in triumph. He appointed Francisco de Paula Santander commander of Bogotá and returned to Angostura to ask his "congress" to create the new and independent state of Colombia. This it did, and it elected Bolívar the president of the new republic.

At this moment Bolívar received news of the revolution of 1820 in Spain. He knew that Spain would send no more armies to America, and he also knew that the displaced viceroy had instructions to negotiate with him. In these negotiations Bolívar insisted that Spain recognize

[1] Vicente Lecuna, ed., *Cartas del libertador*, 10 vols. (Caracas: Lit. y Tip. del Comercio, 1929–30), I, 197, 202.

the independence of his new republic, but the viceroy could not assent to this demand. A truce was agreed upon, however, and the Spanish commander, General Pablo Morillo, resigned his post and returned to Spain. This was a stroke of good fortune for Bolívar, for the Spanish forces, already weakened by desertions, were further demoralized by Morillo's departure.

Bolívar resumed his campaign early in 1821, and at Carabobo, in June, he decisively defeated the royalist army. Within weeks he entered Caracas victoriously.

Meanwhile, the "congress" had adopted a constitution and had reelected Bolívar president of the new state of Colombia. He accepted both the constitution — which was not strong enough to suit him — and the presidency. Then he led his army into the Andes to liberate Peru. Sending young Antonio José Sucre by sea to take Guayaquil, he himself marched through the mountains. Sucre occupied Guayaquil and took his troops into the mountains to meet Bolívar; he routed a Spanish army near Quito on May 21, 1822, and occupied the city to await Bolívar. By this action the province called Ecuador, in which Quito is situated, was joined to Colombia. Bolívar eventually arrived and, as usual, was received in an orgy of celebration.

It was at this time that Bolívar met San Martín. As already related, San Martín had occupied Lima in June of 1821 and had done his best to effect a number of social reforms for the benefit of the Peruvians, including the freeing of the Indians from the hated ancient tribute and the emancipation of children born to black slaves. Although his program was not eminently successful, he did lay the foundations for Peruvian self-government and for a greater degree of social freedom than the country had ever known.

After Bolívar had entered Quito, the two "liberators" mutually agreed to meet. They had long anticipated a meeting, and now it became a reality; the famous event took place at Guayaquil on July 26, 1822. After the meeting San Martín resigned his office as "Protector" of Peru and retired from the American scene. The meeting, in itself, had little significance, though as a symbol of the liberation of most of Hispanoamerica from Spanish rule it was one of the great, dramatic incidents of American history, representing the end of the Hispanoamerican empire established in the course of European expansion.

Iturbide and the Independence of Mexico

Mexico was yet another part of the Hispanoamerican empire that experienced revolution. After the executions of Hidalgo and Morelos, Spanish power had been almost completely restored, and Mexico was actually enjoying a period of prosperity.

When news of the Spanish revolution of 1820 arrived, the viceroy Juan Ruíz de Apodaca, following his instructions, convoked meetings of local assemblies in most of the towns of New Spain which were to elect delegates to the revived imperial Cortes created by the Constitution of Cádiz of 1812. The elections of these delegates set loose a flood of hitherto suppressed liberal and nationalistic ideas. The conservatives were alarmed, and when Augustín de Iturbide, a former creole officer in the Spanish army, offered to subdue the smoldering Hidalgist revolt in the southern provinces, his proposal was accepted and he was given an army of 2500 men. But Iturbide joined forces with the rebel leader Vicente Guerrero, and together they promulgated the famous "Plan of Iguala." The plan called for the independence of Mexico under a monarch, presumably Ferdinand VII, for the recognition of the status quo in religion, which meant an acceptance of the Catholic church and its authority, and for the ambiguous principle of "racial equality."

Iturbide and Guerrero summoned the Mexican people to support them, and they were amazingly successful. They marched out of the mountains, sweeping up the royalists and winning daily accretions to their forces. Within weeks they controlled most of Mexico. Mexico City still held out, but Viceroy Apodaca was recalled, and the new viceroy, General Juan O'Donojú; apparently himself a Spanish liberal, decided to negotiate with Iturbide. He even accepted the "Plan of Iguala." O'Donojú, however, died suddenly, and Mexico was again without a viceroy. In the confusion that resulted, a number of Iturbide's supporters urged him to become the "emperor of Mexico" as stipulated in the "Plan of Iguala," and Iturbide, after a show of unwillingness, acceded to their demand. Many of Iturbide's own liberal followers resisted this act, but by a judicious — and ruthless — use of military force, the "congress" was "persuaded" to accept the new order. Iturbide was declared Emperor Augustín I of Mexico in 1822.

The proclamation of Augustín de Iturbide as emperor of Mexico marked the culmination of the independence movement in Hispanoamerica.

Other regions followed, though Cuba would not become independent until 1898. The process of the separation of the former Spanish colonies from the mother country and of their emergence as new American peoples was now largely complete. To use again Turgot's famous phrase, the colonies, like ripened fruit, had dropped off their parent stems and had taken root, to form their own sovereign national societies. A chapter in the history of the expansion of Europe was finished, another had begun.

Brazil

When Napoleon invaded Portugal in 1807, the insane Queen Maria I, Prince Regent João da Braganza, and perhaps a thousand officials and hangers-on were quickly ferried to Brazil by a British fleet, and Rio de Janeiro became the capital of the Portuguese empire.

This event marked the opening of a new era for Brazil. The presence of the court enlivened the colonial society, and, because the rulers were living in the colony, it became easier for them to see the need for vigorous revisions of the administration. The ports were immediately opened to the ships of all nations, thus demolishing whatever remained of the old national economic monopoly. Immigration was encouraged; the judiciary was reformed and expanded; a national bank was established; the military academy was transferred from Portugal to Brazil; a medical school, a national library, an art museum, and printing presses were founded; and full freedom of religion was permitted the Protestant English. In 1815 the prince regent gave Brazil the status of a dominion within the empire, thus gratifying the nationalistic aspirations of the Brazilian creoles. When Queen Maria died in 1816, the prince regent was crowned King João VI of the United Kingdom of Portugal and Brazil. The Brazilian creole aristocrats mingled with the Portuguese nobility. Never had Brazil seen such brilliance or experienced such national self-gratification.

The honeymoon was of short duration. Dissension mounted between the Portuguese and the creoles. Revolt broke out in Pernambuco in 1817, and a liberal rebellion in Portugal in 1820 unseated the regency and convened a parliament which adopted a constitution patterned after the Spanish Constitution of Cádiz. The new government criticized João's policies in the colony, especially the opening of the ports, and it ordered

Portuguese officials and military officers to ignore his decrees. These incidents set off revolts in Pará and Bahia. On the advice of the English, João decided to return home to pacify his rebellious country, which he eventually managed to do.

When the king departed from Brazil, he left his son, Dom Pedro, to rule as regent in his place. He is said to have remarked to Pedro, "If Brazil demands independence, grant it, but put the crown upon your own head." Pedro was in fact very popular with the Brazilians; the Parliament in Lisbon ordered him home, but he insisted on remaining in the colony. Summoned home again, he again refused, and the Brazilians supported him. In fact, the Brazilians were now demanding independence from Portugal. When Dom Pedro received the second summons from the Parliament, he was at São Paulo; his wife, Leopoldina, an Austrian princess who had imported a number of scientists to study the country, wrote to him, "The apple is ripe; pick it now, or it will rot." He issued a dramatic statement that proclaimed Brazil's independence in the words "Independence or death!" This became known as the "grito de Ipiranga" ("the cry of the Ipiranga River," so-called because of the river that flows near São Paulo). He promised to rule as a constitutional monarch, if the people would have him; a Brazilian parliament, called for the purpose, manifested its enthusiastic acceptance. Pedro was crowned emperor of Brazil on December 1, 1822.

Thus Brazil achieved its independence. There was some resistance from conservatives and leftover Portuguese administrators, but pacification was achieved with little bloodshed — and with the aid of that same flamboyant Lord Cochrane who had deserted San Martín in Peru. In 1824, when the tide in Portugal turned from liberalism to reaction, King João VI summoned his son to lead Brazil back into the empire. The Brazilians would have none of it and Pedro, faced with a dilemma, finally arranged with the aid of the British an agreement with his father whereby he would recognize his father's suzerainty and the king would abdicate his throne in Brazil in favor of his emperor son. It all worked out nicely: everybody saved face, and Brazil was finally and definitely independent.

Conclusion

By the end of the first quarter of the nineteenth century, then, almost all the former colonial societies of the American hemisphere had won their independence. Canada and the British West Indies were still English possessions; Cuba and Puerto Rico were still Spanish; the French Windward Islands were still French; Curaçao, St. Eustatius, and Surinam were still Dutch; the Virgin Islands were still Danish. Otherwise, the expansion of Europe in America was finished. The independence of most of America really marked the end of one era and the beginning of another. Expansion would continue, of course — expansion of one or another American country at the expense of others, in particular the expansion of the United States at the expense of Mexico and the expansion of Chile at the expense of Bolivia and Peru. But it would be American expansion, not European. The processes of history had created a score of new nations in the New World; henceforth, the history of America would be the history of nations, not colonies.

Epilogue

The history of America in the eighteenth century was a history of continuing and continuous expansion. As a chapter in the expansion of Europe it represents the ongoing expansion of Western (now not merely "European") knowledge of the geography of the American hemisphere, Western commerce, Western religion, and Western intellectual life.

The expansion of Western civilization, however, had another, nonspatial dimension. For the expansion of civilization in America was also internal, that is, vertical. For it included, first of all, a phenomenal growth in the population throughout the hemisphere; this increase in the numbers of people carried with it a mixing of ethnic strains that multiplied the genetic combinations among the people, which in turn gave rise to the creation of new social categories. The expansion of civilization in America also meant a vast economic expansion, the appearance of many great and prosperous cities, the further development of the means of communication, and an extension of the establishments and even the theologies of religion. Of enormous significance, moreover, is the fact that, with the spread of politically organized areas, there was an expansion of political institutions which, in the very experience of creating and administering them, generated new political ideas and ideals. With the expansion of society went an expansion of learning; with the expansion of learning went the expansion of education and the broadening and deepening of human understanding about the nature of things, particularly in the realm of science. Finally, the expansion of knowledge was accompanied by the growth of social, political, ethnic, and national self-consciousness: expansion involved the maturation of colonies into self-conscious national societies, of political dependencies into self-governing political states, of "plantations" into nations.

Finally, the expansion of Western civilization in the eighteenth century had a third dimension, represented by the reflex impact of the new American cultures on the civilization of Europe itself. This influence was to be felt in all fields of human activity — in economic, political, and social life and thought, in religion, literature, philosophy, and history, and in the everyday concerns of living such as dress, food, luxuries, medicines, and transportation.

Nor did this three-way expansion end with the independence of the new American societies, anymore than it had begun with the Peace of Utrecht. It was an ongoing process, and it would continue for at least another century. In fact, it is debatable whether the expansion of Western civilization in America has ended even now or whether, indeed, it ever will end.

Selected Bibliography

Selected Bibliography

Bibliographical Note

The expansion of European civilization around the globe was a historical event of monumental proportions and of incalculable significance for the fortunes of the human race. Seen as one event, it carried the culture of Europe, in all its dimensions — economic, social, political, intellectual, and religious — to the farthest corners of the habitable earth and planted it there. Having started in the late medieval centuries, by the eighteenth century of the Christian era it had penetrated eastern Asia, southern Asia, Africa, and America.

By the eighteenth century, this vast process had also come to challenge the historical imaginations of European scholars, and attempts were made to record and interpret it; the most significant efforts, perhaps, were those of Voltaire and the Abbé Raynal. See Voltaire, *Histoire des moeurs et de l'esprit des nations*, in *Ouevres Complètes de Voltaire*, ed. Louis E. D. Moland, 52 vols. (Paris, 1877–85), vols. XI, XII, and XIII; Guillaume-Thomas Raynal, *Histoire philosophique et politique des établissements et du commerce des Européens dans les deux Indes*, 6 vols. (Amsterdam, 1770). America, too, had aroused the interests of historians; histories of the European establishments in America were written by Edmund Burke and William Robertson in England, Juan Bautista Muñoz in Spain (only one volume of whose projected *History of the New World* was ever published), and Arnold Hermann Ludwig Heeren in Germany. See Burke, *An Account of the European Settlements in America*, 2 vols. (London, 1770); Robertson, *The History of America*, 2 vols. (London, 1777); Muñoz, *Historia del nuevo-mundo*, vol. I only (Madrid, 1793); Heeren, *Handbuch der Geschichte des europäischen Staatensystems und seiner Colonien, von der Eutdeckung beyder Indien bis zur Errichtung des Französichen Kayserthums* (2nd ed.; Göttingen, 1811).

During the nineteenth century a number of Latin-American historians devoted their studies to the history of the hemisphere, notably the Chilean Diego Barros Arana. Similarly, the Spanish historian J. Mesa y Leompart wrote a *Compendio de la historia de América desde su descubrimiento hasta nuestros dias* in 1870, but not published until 1911, and Miguel Lobo y Malagamba published a general history of America in 1875. See Arana, *Compendio de historia de América*, 2 vols. (Santiago de Chile, 1865); Mesa y Leompart, *Compendio de la historia de América desde su descubrimiento hasta nuestros dias*, 2 vols. (Paris and Mexico: Librería de la Viuda de Ch. Bouret, 1911); Lobo y Malagamba, *Historia general de las antiguas colonias hispano-americanas desde su descubrimiento hasta el año 1808*, 3 vols. (Madrid, 1875).

295

But historiographical interest in the history of America as a whole declined. Historians, influenced by the rising tides of nationalism, turned their attention to national histories, to the derivations of national origins, and to the development of national societies, both in America and elsewhere. The writing of history tended largely to concentrate on national or regional events. The nation became the favored subject of historical study and, within the nation, smaller and smaller areas, units, or episodes, even single villages, became the case studies for the ever more provincially minded historians. An indirect result of this flight from perspective is that at this time there is no major work in English that surveys the history of America as a whole. Glyndwr Williams's excellent *The Expansion of Europe in the Eighteenth Century* (London: Blandford Press, 1966) is a gratifying exception as is John H. Parry's *Trade and Dominion: The European Overseas Empires in the Eighteenth Century* (New York: Praeger, 1971). Silvio Zavala's magisterial *El mundo americano en la epoca colonial*, 2 vols. (Mexico: Editorial Porrua) appeared in 1967, and Pierre Chaunu's impressive one-volume *L'Amérique et les Amériques* (Paris: A. Colin) appeared in 1964.

During the twentieth century, a number of historians have done notable work in writing the history of the American hemisphere. Such, for example, were Carlos Pereyra in Mexico, Ricardo Levene in Argentina, and Manoel de Oliveira Lima in Brazil. Eugenio Pereira Salas in Chile is presently preparing a master bibliography of the historiography of the American continent. (For a masterly bibliography of American hemisphere history, see Silvio Zavala, *El mundo americano*, II, *passim*, but particularly II, 107–111, n. 16.)

In the United States the first major historian to present the history of the American continent in its entirety was Herbert E. Bolton. As Bolton put it, "There is need of a broader treatment of American history, to supplement the purely nationalistic presentation to which we are accustomed. European history cannot be learned from books dealing alone with England, or France, or Germany, or Italy, or Russia; nor can American history be adequately presented if confined to Brazil, or Chile, or Mexico, or Canada, or the United States. . . . It is time for a change. The increasing importance of inter-American relations makes imperative a better understanding by each of the history and the culture of all. A synthetic view is important not alone for its present day political and commercial implications; it is quite as desirable from the standpoint of correct historiography." ("The Epic of Greater America," *American Historical Review*, 38(no. 2):448–474 (April 1933). The passage quoted is on p. 448.)

Yet historians generally have resisted the idea of seeing the history of America as a single historical phenomenon, arguing that it could not be accomplished in any case, for the history of America is a history of many distinct nations, each different from all the others, with little or no unity in the general pattern. The history of America thus becomes many histories, and the broad perspective of the history of this continent as part of the broader history of the expansion of Europe is lost. See Lewis Hanke, ed., *Do the Americas Have a Common History? A Critique of the Bolton Theory* (New York: Alfred A. Knopf, 1964).

Apropos of the problem, Silvio Zavala has written that "although the task be not easy, it is worth while to return to this concept of the totality, making use of the broader perspectives that are now available to us and profiting by the results of those general and specialized studies that modern historiography has been accumulating with regard to the various periods, places and topics. The critical historical method and the opening of the archives [of the Western world] make possible today a firmer basis of knowledge than that available to the historians of the eighteenth century" (*El mundo americano*, I, xv).

The materials available for such a history are monumental in quantity, and he who attempts it must humbly acknowledge the inadequacy of any one mind to absorb and comprehend it all. He must therefore depend heavily upon the works of other students in his study of segments of the story other than that to which he has devoted his own research. The lists of selected works dealing with the various aspects of the story presented in this volume are organized, therefore, by chapters.

Introduction

Of histories written generally in the framework of the concept of the history of America as a totality within which there must also be diversities, the following modern works are suggested: Antonio Ballesteros y Beretta, gen. ed., *Historia de América y de los pueblos americanos*, 14 vols. (Barcelona: P. Salvat, 1936–56); *Encyclopédie coloniale et maritime*, 10 vols. (Paris: Encyclopédie Coloniale et Maritime, 1944–51); Charles de Lannoy and Herman Van der Linden, *Histoire de l'expansion coloniale des peuples européens*, 3 vols. (Brussels: H. Lamertin, 1907–21), vol. I: *Portugal et Espagne*; vol. II: *Néerlande et Danemark*; vol. III: *Suède*; Alfred Martineau and L. Ph. May, *Tableau de l'expansion européenne à travers le monde, de la fin du XIIe siècle au début du XXe siècle* (Paris: Librairie Leroux, 1935); Francisco Morales Padron, *Historia de América*, 2 vols. (Madrid: Esposa Calpe, 1962); Carlos Pereyra, *Breve historia de América* (Santiago de Chile: Zig-Zag, 1938); M. H. Sánchez-Barba, *Historia universal de América*, 2 vols. (Madrid: Ediciones Guadarrama, 1963); Glyndwr Williams, *The Expansion of Europe in the Eighteenth Century: Overseas Rivalry, Discovery, and Exploitation* (London: Blandford Press, 1966); Frédéric Mauro, *L'expansion européenne, 1600–1870* (Paris: Presses Universitaires de France, 1964); Pierre Chaunu, *L'Amérique et les Amériques* (Paris: A. Colin, 1964); Silvio Zavala, "A General View of the Colonial History of the New World," *American Historical Review*, 66(no. 4):913–929 (July 1961). Silvio Zavala, *El mundo americano en la época colonial*, 2 vols. (Mexico: Editorial Porrua, 1967); Silvio Zavala, *The Colonial Period in the History of the New World*, abridgement in English by Max Savelle (Mexico: Instituto Panamericano de Geografía e Historia, 1962); Leopoldo Zea, *América in la historia* (Mexico: Fondo de Cultura Económica, 1957). Ricardo Levene, ed., *Historia de América* (Buenos Aires: Fondo de Cultura Económica, 1940), is a collection of essays by a number of authors; see also, Manuel de Oliveira Lima, *The Evolution of Brazil Compared with That of Spanish and Anglo-Saxon America*, ed. Percy A. Martin (Stanford, Calif.: Stanford University Press, 1914).

Chapter 1. The Completion of the Occupation of the Continent

For the texts of the treaties composing the Peace of Utrecht, the standard collections are Henri Vast, ed., *Les grand traités du règne de Louis XIV*, 3 vols. (Paris, 1893–99); Jean Dumont, ed., *Corps universel diplomatique du droit des gens; contenant un receuil des traités d'alliance, de paix, de trève, de neutralité, de commerce, d'échange . . . et autres contrats, qui ont été faits en Europe, depuis le règne de l'Empereur Charlemagne jusqu'à present . . .* 8 vols. (Amsterdam, 1726–31); Alejandro del Cantillo, ed., *Tratados, convenios y declaraciones de paz y de comercio que han hecho con las potencias extranjeros los monarcos españoles de la Casa de Borbón, desde el año de 1700 hasta el Día* (Madrid, 1843). A very convenient and well-edited collection of excerpts from these treaties (excerpts that relate to the U.S.) is Frances G. Davenport, ed., *European Treaties Bearing upon the Territory of the United States and Its Dependencies*, 3 vols. (Washington, D.C.: Carnegie Institution, 1917–34). A fourth volume of this work, covering the period 1715–1815, edited by Charles O. Paullin (Washington, D.C.: Carnegie Institution, 1936), is of use in the international history of the Euroamerican empires in the eighteenth century. A definitive modern collection of the principal treaties of this entire period is Fred L. Israel, ed., *Major Peace Treaties of Modern History, 1648–1967*, 4 vols. (McGraw: Chelsea House, 1967).

Vol. I, chapter 1, of Silvio Zavala, *El mundo americano*, cited above, provides a fine survey of the geographic distribution of the Euroamerican empires, the resources, flora, and fauna of the American hemisphere, lines of communication, etc. Chapter 2 surveys the Indian cultures in the hemisphere, the Indian policies of the European empires, and the various degrees of acculturation that took place in the different national areas.

For the continuing exploration and penetration of the unknown parts of the American continent in the eighteenth century, the following works are useful: John B. Brebner, *The Explorers of North America, 1492–1806* (London: A. C. Black, 1933); Antoine Champagne, *Les la vérendrye et le poste de l'ouest* (Quebec: Les Presses de l'Université de Laval, 1968); Walter Prescott Webb, *The Great Plains* (Boston: Ginn, 1931); Frederick Jackson Turner, *The Significance of the Frontier in American History* (New York: Henry Holt, 1932); Nellis M. Crouse, *The Search for the Northwest Passage* (New York: Columbia University Press, 1934); J. L. Burpee, *The Search for the Western Seas: The Story of the Exploration of Northwest America* (Toronto: Mission Book, 1908); G. Bryce, *The Remarkable History of the Hudson's Bay Company . . .* (London: S. Low, Marston, 1900). For a suggestive essay on the international frontier, see Carlton J. H. Hayes, "The American Frontier — Frontier of What?" *American Historical Review*, 51:199–216 (1946). For the exploration and the penetration of the unknown parts of South America, the following books are highly useful: A. de Escragnolle Taunay, *Historia geral das bandeiras paulistas . . .* 11 vols. (São Paulo: Typ. Ideal, 1924–50); Sergio Buarque de Holanda, *Caminhos e fronteiras* (Rio de Janeiro: J. Olympio, 1957); Basilao de Magalhaes, *Expansão geografica do Brasil colonial* (2nd ed.; São Paulo: Companhia Editora Nacional, 1935); José Carlos de Macedo Soares, *Fronteiras do Brasil no regime colonial* (Rio de Janeiro: J. Olympio, 1939); Edward Heawood, *A History of Geographical Discovery in the Seventeenth and Eighteenth Centuries* (New York: Octagon Books, 1965), especially pp. 358–371.

For the exploration of the Pacific shores of America and of the Pacific Ocean, Captain James Cook and James King, *A Voyage to the Pacific Ocean, Undertaken by the Command of His Majesty, for Making Discoveries in the Northern Hemisphere*, 3 vols. (London, 1784), is a classic narrative of Cook's great explorations; J. C. Beaglehole and J. A. Williamson, eds., *The Journals of Captain James Cook on His Voyages of Discovery*, 2 vols. (London: Cambridge University Press for the Hakluyt Society, 1961), is a modern version. L. Berg et al., *Russian Discoveries in the Pacific* (Leningrad: Academy of Sciences, 1926–28), and Carl Ginsberg, *Russian Discoveries in the Pacific and in North America in the Eighteenth and Nineteenth Centuries* (Ann Arbor, Mich.: J. Edwards, 1952), provide the history of the Russian expeditions to the northwest coast of North America. Ernest Dodge, *Beyond the Capes: Pacific Exploration from Captain Cook to the Challenger, 1766–1877* (Boston: Little, Brown, 1971), carries the history of the exploration of the northwest coast of North America to the middle of the nineteenth century. Warren L. Cook's excellent *Flood Tide of Empire: Spain and the Pacific Northwest, 1543–1819* (New Haven, Conn.: Yale University Press, 1973), devotes a good deal of attention to the exploitation of the Northwest and to diplomacy.

Chapter 2. The Political Structure
of the Euroamerican Empires

There is an excellent brief study of the theory and the practice of imperial administration in Silvio Zavala, *El mundo americano*, cited above, vol. I, chapters 7 and 9. Richard Koebner, *Empire* (Cambridge: At the University Press, 1961), is a study of European theories of empire, mostly English. Klaus E. Knorr, *British Colonial Theories, 1570–1850* (Toronto: University of Toronto Press, 1944), is a standard summary of British ideas with regard to colonies. *The New Cambridge Modern History*, 10 vols. (Cambridge: At the University Press, 1957–70), vol. VII: *The Old Regime, 1713–1763*, contains a single chapter on Euroamerican imperial administration.

For the general history of the Lusoamerican empire in the eighteenth century, see Charles R. Boxer, *The Golden Age of Brazil, 1695–1750: Growing Pains of a Colonial Society* (Berkeley: University of California Press, 1964), *Four Centuries of Portuguese Expansion* (Johannesburg: Witwatersrand University Press, 1961), and *The Portuguese Seaborne Empire, 1415–1825* (London: Hutchinson, 1969). A fine one-volume history of Brazil is Caio Prado, Jr., *Formação do Brasil contemporaneo, colonia* (7th ed.; São Paulo:

Editora Brasiliense, 1963), trans. Suzette Macodoas as *The Colonial Background of Modern Brazil* (Berkeley: University of California Press, 1969). An extremely valuable description of Brazil, its institutions, economy, and social and intellectual life during the reign of the first true viceroy, the Marquis of Lavradio, is Dauril Alden, *Royal Government in Colonial Brazil* (Berkeley: University of California Press, 1968), with special reference to the administration of the Marquis of Lavradio, who was viceroy from 1769 to 1779. A major collaborative work is Sergio Buarque de Holanda, gen. ed., *História geral da civilização brasileira*, 5 vols. to date (São Paulo: Difusão Europeia do Livro, 1960–); see Livro Quinto, "A expansão territorial," in vol. I: *A epoca colonial: 1° do descobrimiento a expansão territorial*, and vol. II: *Administração, economia, sociedade*. A highly useful little handbook is José Honório Rodrigues, *Brasil: Periódo colonial*, in Silvio Zavala, gen. ed., *Programa de historia de América* (Mexico: Instituto Panamericano de Geografia e Historia, 1953). José Honório Rodrigues, *Teoria da história do Brasil* (2nd ed.; São Paulo: Companhia Editora Nacional, 1957), is a highly provocative interpretative work. Dauril Alden, ed., *Colonial Roots of Modern Brazil* (Berkeley: University of California Press, 1973), is an up-to-date collection of interpretive essays by contemporary scholars.

For the history of Spain and its role in world history, the great old classic is still Rafael Altamira y Crevea, *Historia de España y de la civilization espanola*, 5 vols. in 6 (Barcelona: J. Gili, 1900–30). A more recent and highly satisfactory collaborative work is Jaime Vicens Vives, ed., *Historia de España y America*, 5 vols. (Editorial Vicens-Vives, 1961). For the Spanish empire in America, Clarence H. Haring, *The Spanish Empire in America* (rev. ed.; New York: Oxford University Press, 1952), is still a basic general work; Charles Gibson, *Spain in America* (New York: Harper & Row, 1966), is a very valuable modern survey of the Spanish empire. José María Ots Capdequi, *El siglo XVIII español en America* (Mexico: Colegio de México, 1945), covers the political institutions of the viceroyalty of Granada; Bernard Moses, *The Spanish Dependencies in South America: An Introduction to the History of Their Civilization*, 2 vols. (London: Smith, Elder, 1914), is an important older general work. A major general work is Carlos Pereyra, *Historia de la América española*, 8 vols. (Madrid: Editorial "Saturnino Colleja," 1920–26). An important collection of essays by various authors is A. C. Wilgus, ed., *Colonial Hispanic America* (Washington, D.C.: George Washington University Press, 1936). D. A. Smith, "The Viceroy of New Spain in the Eighteenth Century," *Annual Report of the American Historical Association*, 1: 169–181 (1908), is a study of the viceroyalties in the era of imperial reform; a more extensive study is John Lynch, *Spanish Colonial Administration, 1782–1810: The Intendant System and the Viceroyalty of the Rio de la Plata* (London: University of London, Athlone Press, 1958). See also Carlos Pereyra, *La obra de España en América* (Madrid: Biblioteca Nueva, 1920). Highly useful handbooks are Mariano Picón Salas, *Suramerica: Periodo colonial*, in Silvio Zavala, *Programa de historia de América*, cited above, and Silvio Zavala, *Hispano América septentrional y media*, in the same series.

For the French empire in America the following books are useful: Gustave Lanctôt, *L'oeuvre de la France en Amérique du nord* (Montreal: Fides, 1951); Émile Lauvrière, *Histoire de la Louisiane française, 1673–1739* (Baton Rouge: Louisiana State University Press, 1940); Herbert I. Priestley, *France Overseas: A Study of European Expansion* (New York: Appleton-Century, 1938); Hubert J. Deschamps, *Les méthodes et les doctrines coloniales de la France du XVIe siècle à nos jours* (Paris: A. Colin, 1953); J. Santoyant, *La colonisation française sous l'ancien régime*, vol. II: *Du Traité d'Utrecht à 1789* (Paris: La Renaissance du Livre, 1929); E. Salone, *La colonisation de la Nouvelle France: Étude sur les origines de la nation canadienne française* (Paris: Guilmato, 1906); George M. Wrong, *The Rise and Fall of New France*, 2 vols. (New York: Macmillan, 1928); Reuben G. Thwaites, *France in America, 1497–1763* (New York: Harper, 1905); Francis Parkman, *The Old Regime in Canada* (Boston: Little, Brown, 1884); M. H. Long, *A History of the Canadian People* (Toronto: Ryerson Press, 1942); Charles A. Julien, *Les Français en Amérique (1713–1748)*, vol. II: *Le Canada, la Louisiane, la Guyane. La politique americaine de Choiseul* (Paris: Presses Universitaires de France, 1955); Gabriel Hanotaux and Alfred

Martineau, eds., *Histoire des colonies françaises et de l'expansion de la France dans le monde*, 6 vols. (Paris: Société de l'Histoire Nationale, La Martin, 1929–34); A. Dessales, *Histoire générale des Antilles*, 5 vols. (Paris, 1847–48); Dantès Bellegarde, *Histoire du peuple Haïtien (1492–1952)* (Port-au-Prince: Collection du Tricinquantenaire de l'Indépendance d'Haiti, 1953); Gustave Lanctôt, *Histoire du Canada*, 3 vols. (Montreal: Librairie Beauchemin, 1960–64); and, by the same author, *L'administration de la Nouvelle France: L'administration générale* (Paris: H. Champion, 1929).

For the Dutch empire in America, the following are useful: Charles de Lannoy and Herman Van der Linden, *Histoire de l'expansion coloniale des peuples européens*, cited above, vol. II; Charles R. Boxer, *The Dutch Seaborne Empire, 1600–1800* (New York: Alfred A. Knopf, 1965); Melvin H. Jackson, *Salt, Sugar, and Slaves: The Dutch in the Caribbean*, James Ford Bell Lectures, no. 2 (Minneapolis: Associates of the James Ford Bell Library, 1965.)

For the Swedish and Danish empires in America, the standard work is Waldemar Westergaard, *The Danish West Indies under Company Rule, 1671–1754* (New York: Macmillan, 1917). Other useful studies of northern European colonization are Manuel Gutierrez de Arce, *La colonización Danesa en las Islas Virgenes* (Seville: Escuela de Estudios Hispanoamericanos, 1945); Amandus Johnson, *The Swedish Settlements on the Delaware . . .* 2 vols. (New York: Appleton, 1911); John Wuorinen, *The Finns on the Delaware, 1638–1655: An Essay in American Colonial History* (New York: Columbia University Press, 1938).

For the British-American colonial empire in the eighteenth century, see E. B. Hertz, *British Imperialism in the Eighteenth Century* (London: Macmillan, 1908); Frank W. Pitman, *The Development of the British West Indies, 1700–1763* (New Haven, Conn.: Yale University Press, 1917); Klaus E. Knorr, *British Colonial Theories*, cited above; J. H. Rose, ed., *The Cambridge History of the British Empire*, 8 vols. (Cambridge: At the University Press, 1929–59), vol. I: *The Old Empire, to 1783*, and vol. VI: *Canada and Newfoundland*. Lawrence H. Gipson, *The British Empire before the American Revolution*, 15 vols. (New York: Alfred A. Knopf, 1946–71), is a magnificent survey. Vincent T. Harlow, *British Colonial Developments, 1774–1834* (Oxford: Clarendon Press, 1903), and, by the same author, *The Founding of the Second British Empire, 1763–1793* (New York: Longmans, Green, 1952), are highly useful. Other important treatments are James A. Williamson, *A Short History of British Expansion* (4th ed.; London: Macmillan, 1961), vol. I: *The Old Empire*; Charles M. Andrews, *The Colonial Period of American History*, 4 vols. (New Haven, Conn.: Yale University Press, 1934–38). See vol. IV for British colonial policy in the early eighteenth century as well as George L. Beer, *British Colonial Policy, 1754–1765* (New York: Macmillan, 1907; reprint, New York: Peter Smith, 1933). For the general history of the British colonies in the eighteenth century, older works are Herbert L. Osgood, *The American Colonies in the Eighteenth Century*, 4 vols. (New York: Columbia University Press, 1924), and Bryan Edwards, *The History, Civil and Commercial, of the British Colonies in the West Indies*, 3 vols. (London, 1801). Alan C. Burns, *History of the British West Indies* (London: Allen & Unwin, 1954), is a brief modern survey. Leonard W. Labaree, *Royal Government in America: A Study of the British Colonial System before 1783* (New Haven, Conn.: Yale University Press, 1930), is a fine study of political institutions in the British colonies.

Chapter 3. International Aspects of the American Economy

There is no general economic history of the American hemisphere. There is, however, an excellent, brief discussion of the general, or international, aspects of the economic history of the hemisphere during the colonial period in Silvio Zavala, *El mundo americano*, cited above, vol. I, chapter 7.

For the European economic theory relative to the Euroamerican colonies, one must go to Eli Heckscher, *Mercantilism*, trans. M. Shapiro, 2 vols. (London: Allen & Unwin,

1935), or to Charles Gide and Charles Rist, *Histoire des doctrines économiques depuis les physiocrates jusqu'à nos jours* (Paris: L. Larose and L. Tenin, 1909). There are some relevant passages in Richard Koebner, *Empire*, cited above, *passim*. A provocative article is Henri Sée, "Les économistes et la question coloniale au XVIIIe siècle," *Revue d'histoire coloniale*, 22:381–392 (1929). Of indispensable value, of course, are such contemporary writings as Adam Smith, *An Inquiry into the Nature and Causes of the Wealth of Nations* (1776), 2 vols. (New York: Dutton, 1954), William Wood, *A Survey of Trade* (London, 1722), François Quesnay, *Tableau économique* (1758) and other essays published conveniently in A. Oncken, ed., *Oeuvres économiques et philosophiques de F. Quesnay* (Paris, 1888), and Gerónimo de Uztáriz, *Teórica y práctica de comercio, y de marina en diferentes discursos, y calificados exemplares, que, con específicas providencias, se procuran adaptar a la monarchía española para su prompta restauración* (2ª impression corregida y enmendada por el autor; Madrid, 1742).

For the international aspects of the commerce of the American hemisphere in the eighteenth century the following are important: David Hannay, *The Great Chartered Companies* (London: Williams and Norgate, 1926); Louis J. P. M. Bonnassieux, *Les grandes compagnies de commerce* (Paris, 1892); Harold A. Innis, *The Cod Fisheries: The History of an International Economy* (New Haven, Conn.: Yale University Press, 1940); E. J. Hamilton, "The Role of Monopoly in the Overseas Expansion and Colonial Trade of Europe before 1800," *American Economic Review*, 38:33–53 (May 1948). Bernard Bailyn, "Communications and Trade: The Atlantic in the Seventeenth Century," *Journal of Economic History*, 13:378–387 (1953), is highly suggestive on the formation of an Atlantic economic community that would continue and grow through the eighteenth and later centuries. Herbert Heaton, *The Economics of Empire*, James Ford Bell Lectures, no. 3 (Minneapolis: Associates of the James Ford Bell Library, 1966), is a brilliant brief synthesis; of particular interest here is Frédéric Mauro, "Toward an Intercontinental Model: European Overseas Expansion between 1500 and 1800," *Economic History Review*, 14:1–17 (1961).

For the international slave trade, the great classic is still Georges Scelle, *La traite négrière aux Indes de Castille, contrats et traités d'asiento. Étude de droit public et d'histoire diplomatique puisée aux sources originales et accompagnée de plusieurs documents inédits*, 2 vols. (Paris: L. Larose and L. Tenin, 1906). Elizabeth Donnan, ed., *Documents Illustrative of the History of the Slave Trade to America*, 4 vols. (Washington, D.C.: Carnegie Institution, 1930–35), is a standard collection of documents. Philip Curtin, *The Atlantic Slave Trade: A Census* (Madison: University of Wisconsin Press, 1969), is a highly valuable statistical study of the slave trade as an international business. Valuable also are Daniel P. Mannix and Malcolm Cowley, *Black Cargoes: A History of the Atlantic Slave Trade, 1518–1865* (London: Longmans, Green, 1963); Hugh A. Wyndham, *The Atlantic and Slavery* (London: Oxford University Press, 1935); Gaston Martin, *L'ère des négriers (1714–1774)* (Paris: Alcan, 1931).

For international aspects of the cattle industry, consult Edward L. Tinker, *The Horsemen of the Americas and the Literature They Inspired* (New York: Hastings House, 1954), Will James, *Cowboys North and South* (New York: Grosset & Dunlap, 1951), and Angel Labrera, *La ballos de América* (Buenos Aires: Editorial Sudamericana, 1965).

For international aspects of the mining industry, the following is a useful standard review: Modesto Bargallo, *La minería y la metalurgia en la América española durante la época colonial* (Mexico and Buenos Aires: Fondo de Cultura Económica, 1955). Arthur P. Whitaker, *The Huencavelica Mercury Mine: A Contribution of the History of the Bourbon Renaissance in the Spanish Empire* (Cambridge, Mass.: Harvard University Press, 1941), is a brilliant case study.

Chapter 4. The Economies
of the Euroamerican Empires

For the economic history of the Hispanoamerican empire in the eighteenth century, see Clarence H. Haring, *The Spanish Empire*, cited above, *passim*; an excellent recent survey is John H. Parry, *The Spanish Seaborne Empire* (New York: Alfred A. Knopf, 1966); there is a good brief treatment in Zavala, *El mundo americano*, cited above, I, 281–292. For the administration of the economic life of the Hispanoamerican empire, *Comercio de Indias: Antecedentes legales (1713–1778)* (Buenos Aires: Sudamerica de Billetes de Banco, 1915), vol. V: *Documentos para la historia Argentina*, is a valuable collection of sources. For the general economic importance of the Hispanoamerican colonies to Spain and Europe, E. J. Hamilton, *American Treasure and the Price Revolution in Spain, 1651–1800* (Cambridge, Mass.: Harvard University Press, 1947), is a classic. For the "company system" of the eighteenth century, the best case study is Roland D. Hussey, *The Caracas Company, 1728–1784* (Cambridge, Mass.: Harvard University Press, 1934). Henri Sée, "Esquisse d'une histoire du commerce français et dans l'Amérique espagnole au XVIIIe siècle," *Revue d'histoire moderne*, 13:13–31 (1928), is a useful study of the French position in the commerce of the Hispanoamerican empire.

For the mining industry in Hispanoamerica, Clarence H. Haring, *The Spanish Empire*, cited above, contains a brief standard account. For the cattle-raising industry, the following studies are useful: Prudencia de la C. Mendoza, *Historia de la ganadería Argentina* (Buenos Aires: L. J. Rosso, 1928); William H. Dusenberry, *The Mexican Mesta: The Administration of Ranching in Colonial Mexico* (Urbana: University of Illinois Press, 1963); Will James, *Cowboys North and South*, cited above; Madeline W. Nichols, *The Gaucho Cattle Hunter, Cavalrymen, Ideal of Romance* (Durham, N.C.: Duke University Press, 1942). For case studies of intercolonial commerce among the American colonies within the Spanish empire, see Woodrow Borah, *Early Colonial Trade and Navigation between Mexico and Peru* (Berkeley: University of California Press, 1954), and W. L. Schurz, *The Manila Galleon* (2nd ed.; New York: Dutton, 1959).

For the economic reforms of the Spanish empire, a good case study is Eduardo Arcila Farías, *El siglo ilustrado en America: Reformas economicas del siglo XVIII en Nueva España* (Caracas: Ministerio de Educación, 1955). Vicente Palacio Atard, *El tercer Pacto de Familia* (Madrid: Escuela de Estudios Hispanoamericanos, 1945), explains French suggestions to Spain for reorganizing the Spanish colonial administration in the direction of free trade. This is also discussed in Arthur S. Aiton, "Spanish Colonial Reorganization under the Family Compact," *Hispanic-American Historical Review*, 12:269–280 (1932). For the intendant system, consult Lilian E. Fisher, *The Intendant System in Spanish America*, and John Lynch, *Spanish Colonial Administration*, both cited above.

Of particular interest are the writings of such Spanish contemporary economists as José del Campillo y Cossio, *Nuevo systema de gobierno económico para la América, con los males y daños que le causa el que hoy tiene, de los que participa caprichosamente España; y remedios universales para que la primera tenga considerables ventajes y la segunda mayores intereses* (Madrid, 1789), and Gerónimo de Uztáriz, *Teórica ya práctica de comercio*, cited above. The work of Uztáriz has been studied in André Mounier, *Les faits et la doctrine économique en Espagne sous Philippe V: Gerónimo de Uztáriz, 1670–1732* (Burdeos: Impr. de l'Université, 1919). For Campomanes see Ricardo Krebs Wikkens, *El pensamiento historico, politico, economico del Conde de Campomanes* (Santiago de Chile: Universidad de Chile, 1960); for Jovellanos, John H. Richard Polt, *Gaspar Melchor de Jovellanos* (New York: Twayne, 1971).

For the economic history of the Lusoamerican empire in the eighteenth century, there is an excellent brief treatment in Silvio Zavala, *El mundo americano*, I, 292–307, and in Caio Prado, Jr., *The Colonial Background of Modern Brazil*, pt. II, both cited above. More detailed studies are Charles R. Boxer, *The Golden Age of Brazil*, and Dauril Alden, *Royal Government in Brazil*, pt. III, both cited above. Other useful works are R. C. Simonsen, *Historia economica do Brasil, 1500–1820*, 2 vols. (São Paulo: Companhia Editora Nacional, 1937); Violet M. Shillington and A. B. Wallis Chapman, *The Commercial Relations of England and Portugal* (London: Routledge, 1907); João Lucio de Azevedo, *Epocas de Portugal economico; esboços de historia* (Lisbon: Livraria Classica Editora de A. M. Teixeira, 1929); Alan K. Manchester, *British Preeminence in Brazil: Its Rise and Decline* (Chapel

Hill: University of North Carolina Press, 1933); Edgar Prestage, *Portugal, Brasil e Gra-Bretagna* (Coimbra: Impr. da Universidade, 1925).

For the economic development of the Francoamerican empire in the eighteenth century, there is a brief account in Silvio Zavala, *El mundo americano*, cited above, I, 308–313. For specific aspects, consult Harold A. Innis, *The Fur Trade in Canada* (2nd ed.; New Haven, Conn.: Yale University Press, 1962); Erik W. Dahlgren, *Les rélations commerciales entre la France et les côtes de l'Ocean Pacifique* (Paris: H. Champion, 1909); Charles W. Cole, *Colbert and a Century of French Mercantilism*, 2 vols. (New York: Columbia University Press, 1939); Charles A. Julien, *Les Français en Amérique (1713–1748)* cited above, vol. I: *Le Traité d'Utrecht, le système de l'exclusif, les isles* (Paris: Presses Universitaires de France, 1955); Donald G. Creighton, *The Commercial Empire of the St. Lawrence, 1760–1850* (New Haven, Conn.: Yale University Press, 1937); Charles W. Cole, *French Mercantilism, 1683–1700* (New York: Columbia University Press, 1943); Nancy M. Miller Surrey, *The Commerce of Louisiana during the French Regime, 1699–1763* (New York: Columbia University Press, 1916); Walter A. Roberts, *The French in the West Indies* (Indianapolis: Bobbs-Merrill, 1942).

For the economic development of the Angloamerican empire in the eighteenth century, Lillian C. A. Knoles, *The Economic Development of the British Overseas Empire*, 3 vols. (London: Routledge, 1924–36), is basic; Stuart Bruchey, *The Roots of American Economic Growth, 1607–1861: An Essay in Social Causation* (New York: Harper & Row, 1965), is a provocative interpretative essay; for the growth of a national economy in the United States after independence, Curtis P. Nettels, *The Emergence of a National Economy, 1775–1815* (New York: Holt, Rinehart & Winston, 1962), is a basic study. For specific aspects of the economic life of colonial Angloamerica, the following are still standard: Emory Johnson, *History of the Domestic and Foreign Commerce of the United States*, 2 vols. (Washington, D.C.: Carnegie Institution, 1915); Percy W. Bidwell and John I. Falconer, *History of Agriculture in the Northeast United States, 1620–1860* (Washington, D.C.: Carnegie Institution, 1925); Lewis C. Gray, *History of Agriculture in the Southern United States to 1860*, 2 vols. (Washington, D.C.: Carnegie Institution, 1933); Victor S. Clark, *History of Manufactures in the United States*, 2 vols. (Washington, D.C.: Carnegie Institution, 1916–28); Frances Armytage, *The Free Port System in the British West Indies: A Study in Commercial Policy, 1766–1822* (London: Longmans, Green, 1953). For the economic history of the British West Indies in the eighteenth century, the following are highly valuable: Frank W. Pitman, *The Development of the British West Indies*, cited above; Richard Pares, *War and Trade in the West Indies, 1739–1763* (Oxford: Clarendon Press, 1936); and, by the same author, *Yankees and Creoles: The Trade between North America and the West Indies before the American Revolution* (London: Longmans, Green, 1956).

For economic thought in Angloamerica, Joseph Dorfman, *The Economic Mind in American Civilization (1606–1865)*, 3 vols. (New York: A. M. Kelley, 1966), vol I, is an encyclopedic review; for the Angloamerican slave trade, consult Philip Curtin, *The Atlantic Slave Trade*, and Elizabeth Donnan, ed., *Documents Illustrative of the History of the Slave Trade to America*, both cited above.

For the Atlantic fisheries, R. G. Lounsbury, *The British Fishery at New Foundland, 1634–1763* (New Haven, Conn.: Yale University Press, 1934), Louis Bronkhorst, *La pesche à la morue* (Paris: Blondel la Rougery, 1927), Raymond MacFarland, *A History of the New England Fisheries* (New York: Appleton, 1911), and Harold A. Innis, *The Cod Fisheries*, cited above, are all standard treatments. For the tobacco industry and trade, Arthur P. Middleton, *The Tobacco Coast, a Maritime History of Chesapeake Bay in the Colonial Era* (Newport News, Va.: Mariners Museum, 1953), is a near-classic. For contemporary statistics, consult David MacPherson, *Annals of Commerce, Manufactures, Fishing and Navigation with Brief Notes on the Arts and Sciences Connected with Them* (London, 1805), and Timothy Pitkin, *Statistical View of the Commerce of the United States* (New Haven, Conn., 1835); for further study, G. N. Clark, *Guide to English Commercial Statis-*

tics, 1696–1782 (London: Royal Historical Society, 1938), and E. B. Schumpeter, *English Overseas Trade Statistics, 1697–1808* (Oxford: Clarendon Press, 1960), are valuable. The importance of the colonies in British overseas commerce is presented in Ralph Davis, *A Commercial Revolution: English Overseas Trade in the Seventeenth and Eighteenth Centuries* (London: Historical Association, 1967). Among the basic works in the history of British imperial economic policy are George L. Beer, *The Old Colonial System, 1660–1754*, 2 vols. (New York: reprint, Peter Smith, 1933); by the same author, *British Colonial Policy*, cited above; Laurence Harper, *The English Navigation Laws: A Seventeenth Century Experiment in Social Engineering* (New York: Columbia University Press, 1939); Charles M. Andrews, *The Colonial Period of American History*, vol. IV, and Klaus M. Knorr, *British Colonial Theories*, both cited above.

For the economic history of the Dutch-American empire in the eighteenth century, Charles R. Boxer, *The Dutch Seaborne Empire*, cited above, is an excellent survey; Charles Wilson, *Anglo-Dutch Commerce and Finance in the Eighteenth Century* (Cambridge: At the University Press, 1941), is a useful special study. Other good treatments are to be found in David Hannay, *The Great Chartered Companies*, cited above; G. J. Renier, *The Dutch Nation: An Historical Study* (London: Allen & Unwin, 1944); and B. H. Maria Vlekke, *Evolution of the Dutch Nation* (New York: Ray Publishers, 1945).

Chapter 5. American Society
and the New American Societies

There is no general history of the growth of the Euroamerican societies. There is, however, a brief survey in Silvio Zavala, *El mundo americano*, cited above, I, chapter 8.

The basic phenomenon, perhaps, in the growth of the American societies in the eighteenth century is the spectacular expansion of population. But of this phenomenon, there is no satisfactory history. The following are useful, each in its own way: Angel Rosenblat, *La población indígena y el mestizaje en América, 1492–1950*, 2 vols. in 1 (Buenos Aires: Editorial Nova, 1954); *América colonial: Población y economica*, Universidad Nacional del Litoral, Facultad de Filosofía y Letras, Instituto de Investigaciones Historicos, *Anuario del Instituto de Investigaciones Historicas*, no. 8 (Rosario: El Instituto, 1965); D. U. Glass and D. E. C. Eversley, eds., *Population in History: Essays in Historical Demography* (London: E. Arnold, 1965); Marcel R. Reinhard and A. Armengard, *Histoire générale de la population mondiale* (Paris: Éditions Montchrestien, 1961).

For the general history of European migration to the American hemisphere, see M. Sorré, *Les migrations des peuples. Essai sur la mobilité géographique* (Paris: Flammarion, 1945); on the international aspects of the stratification of society, Ronald Syme, *Colonial Elites: Rome, Spain and the Americas* (London: Oxford University Press, 1958), is thoughtful and suggestive.

The following are studies of black slavery as an international social phenomenon: Frank Tannenbaum, *Slave and Citizen: The Negro in the Americas* (New York: Albert A. Knopf, 1947); Arnold A. Sio, "Interpretations of Slavery: The Slave Status in the Americas," *Comparative Studies in Society and History*, 7:289–308 (1965); Stanley M. Elkins, *Slavery: A Problem in American Institutional and Intellectual Life* (2nd ed.; Chicago: University of Chicago Press, 1968). A contrasting interpretation to those of the books above appears in Carl N. Degler, *Neither White nor Black: Slavery and Race Relations in Brazil and the United States* (New York: Macmillan, 1971), and in Robert Conrad, *The Destruction of Brazilian Slavery, 1850–1888* (Berkeley: University of California Press, 1972). For slavery in the French colonies see Gaston Martin, *Histoire de l'esclavage dans les colonies françaises* (Paris: Presses Universitaires de France, 1948). Other important studies are W. Zelinsky, "The Historical Geography of the Negro Population in Latin America," *Journal of Negro History*, 34:153–221 (1949); Marvin Harris, *Patterns of Race in the Americas* (New York: Walker, 1964); David B. Davis, *The Problem of Slavery in Western Culture* (Ithaca, N.Y.:

Cornell University Press, 1966); Hugh A. Wyndham, *The Atlantic and Slavery*, cited above; see also Georges Scelle, *La traite Négrière*; Philip Curtin, *The Atlantic Slave Trade*, both cited above; and André Ducasse, *Les négriers ou le trafic des esclaves* (Paris: Hachette, 1948).

For the "great frontier" of European expansion in America as a social process, see Carlton J. H. Hayes, "The American Frontier — Frontier of What?" cited above, and Walter D. Wyman and Clifton B. Kroeber, *The Frontier in Perspective* (Madison: University of Wisconsin Press, 1957). Of value, too, are Ross Hoffman, "Europe and the Atlantic Community," *Thought*, 20:25ff (March 1945); Herbert E. Bolton, "The Mission as a Frontier Institution in the Spanish-American Colonies," in *Wider Horizons of American History* (New York: Appleton-Century, 1939); and Walter Prescott Webb, *The Great Frontier* (Boston: Houghton Mifflin, 1952).

For the growth of the Hispanoamerican colonial societies, there is an excellent summary essay in Silvio Zavala, *El mundo americano*, cited above, I, 344–364. The following present special aspects of the problem: Rodolfo Baron Castro, "El desarrollo de la población hispanoamericano (1492–1950)," *Cuadernos de historia mundial*, 5:325–343 (1959); George Kubler, *The Indian Caste of Perú, 1795–1940: A Population Study Based upon Tax Records and Census Reports* (Washington, D.C.: Smithsonian Institution, 1952); Eugenio Pereira Salas, *El desarrollo historico étnico de la población de Chile* (Santiago de Chile: Impr. Universitaria, 1950). For the history of *mestizaje*, see Angel Rosenblat, *La población indígena y el mestizaje en América*, cited above; Richard Konetzke, "El mestizaje y su importancia en el desarrollo de la población hispanoamericana durante la época colonial," *Revista de Indias*, 7:7–44, 215–237 (1946); Magnus Mörner, *El mestizaje en la historia de Ibero-America: Informe sobre el estado actual de la investigación* (Stockholm: Library and Institute for Ibero-American Studies, 1960), published in English as *Race Mixture in the History of Latin America* (Boston: Little, Brown, 1967).

For the social history of Lusoamerica in the eighteenth century, Caio Prado, Jr., *The Colonial Background of Modern Brazil*, cited above, is a fine one-volume treatment. For the growth of population, see Dauril Alden, "The Population of Brazil in the Late Eighteenth Century: A Preliminary Survey," *Hispanic American Historical Review*, 43:173–205 (May 1963), and, by the same author, *Royal Government in Colonial Brazil*, cited above, appendix I, p. 497. For social history and institutions, the great collaborative work, Sergio Buarque de Holanda, gen. ed., *História geral da civilização brasileira*, cited above, is basic, especially vols. I and II. The works of Gilberto Freyre are classics, especially *Casa Grande e Senzala*, 2 vols. (6th ed.; Rio de Janeiro: J. Olympio, 1950), published (abridged) in English as *The Masters and the Slaves: A Study in the Development of Brazilian Civilization* (New York: Alfred A. Knopf, 1964), and *Sobrados e mucambos: Decadencia do patriarcado rural e desenvolvimiento do urbano*, 3 vols. (2nd ed.; Rio de Janeiro: J. Olympio, 1951). Other useful studies are Charles R. Boxer, *Portuguese Society in the Tropics: The Municipal Councils of Goa, Macao, Bahia, and Luanda, 1510–1800* (Madison: University of Wisconsin Press, 1965), and, by the same author, *The Golden Age of Brazil*, cited above; see also Sergio Buarque de Holanda, *Raizes do Brasil* (Rio de Janeiro: J. Olympio, 1936).

For slavery in Brazil, see the works on slavery already cited. See also Raymundo Nina Rodrigues, *Os Africanos no Brasil* (2nd ed.; São Paulo: Companhia Editora Nacional, 1935); Charles R. Boxer, *Race Relations in the Portuguese Colonial Empire, 1415–1825* (Oxford: Clarendon Press, 1963); Agostinho Marques Perdigão Malheiro, *A escravidão no Brasil: Ensaio historico juridico-social*, 3 vols. (Rio de Janeiro, 1866–67); Mauricio Goulart, *Escravidão africana no Brasil, das origens a extinção do trafico* (São Paulo: Livreria Martins, 1949); Joaquim Nabuco, *O abolicionismo* (London, 1883).

For the social history of the French colonies in America in the eighteenth century, there is a brief survey in Silvio Zavala, *El mundo americano*, cited above, I, 370–375. More extended studies are Gabriel Hanotaux and Alfred Martineau, gen. eds., *Histoire des colonies françaises*, vol. I: *L'Amérique*; Charles A. Julien, *Les Français en Amérique*, both cited above; Jean Hamelin, *Economie et société en Nouvelle-France* (Quebec: Presses de l'Université de Laval, 1960). For the population of Canada, Georges Langlois, *Histoire de la population canadienne-française* (2nd ed.; Montreal: A. Levesque, 1935), is standard. For the Canadian frontier, there is an essay in Walter D. Wyman and Clifton B. Kroeber, eds., *The Frontier in Perspective*, cited above; for the seigneurial system in Canada, William B. Munro, *The Seigneurial System in Canada: A Study in French Colonial Policy* (New York: Longmans, Green, 1907), is standard; Guy Freguit, *La société canadienne sous le régime français* (Ottawa: La Société Historique in Canada, 1954), is highly valuable.

The society of the French West Indies is described in Gabriel Hanotaux and Alfred Martineau, gen. eds., *Histoire de colonies françaises*, cited above, vol. I, and, of Haiti, Pierre de Vaissière, *Saint-Domingue. La société et la vie creoles sous l'ancien régime, 1629–1789* (Paris: Perrin, 1909).

For slavery in the Francoamerican colonies, Gaston Martin, *Histoire de l'esclavage dans les colonies françaises*, cited above, and Lucien Peytraud, *L'esclavage aux Antilles françaises avant 1789* (Paris, 1897), are both useful.

The standard compilation of the population of the continental Angloamerican colonies in the eighteenth century is Evarts B. Greene and Virginia D. Harrington, *American Population before the Federal Census of 1790* (New York: Columbia University Press, 1932); H. R. Friis, "A Series of Population Maps of the Colonies and the United States, 1625–1790," *Geographical Review*, 30:463–470 (1940), gives a graphic presentation of Angloamerican population on the continent of North America. For the population of the British West Indies, see Frank W. Pitman, *The Development of the British West Indies*, especially pp. 369–390; H. A. Wyndham, *The Atlantic and Slavery, passim;* and Lawrence H. Gipson, *The British Empire before the American Revolution*, vols. II and III, *passim*, all cited above.

For the social development of the Angloamerican colonies in the eighteenth century, there is a brief summary in Silvio Zavala, *El mundo americano*, cited above, I, 376–386. Standard works are James T. Adams, *Provincial Society, 1690–1763* (New York: Macmillan, 1927), and Evarts B. Greene, *The Revolutionary Generation, 1763–1790* (New York: Macmillan, 1943); Marcus Lee Hansen, *The Atlantic Migration: A History of the Continuing Settlement of the United States* (Cambridge, Mass.: Harvard University Press, 1940); Abbot G. Smith, *Colonists in Bondage: White Servitude and Convict Labor in America, 1607–1776* (Chapel Hill: University of North Carolina Press, 1947). A classic contemporary essay on the Angloamerican social process is Michael St. John Crèvecœur, *Letters from an American Farmer* . . . (London, 1782). For the British West Indies, see again, Frank W. Pitman, *The Development of the British West Indies*, and Lawrence H. Gipson, *The British Empire before the American Revolution*, both cited above.

For slavery in the Angloamerican colonies, Ulrich B. Phillips, *American Negro Slavery* . . . (New York: Appleton, 1918), is an older account; Stanley M. Elkins, *Slavery*, cited above, is a more recent, morally condemnatory description. Elizabeth Donnan, ed., *Documents Illustrative of a History of the Slave Trade to America*, cited above, is a standard collection of sources. Of special value for an understanding of the attitudes in white-black relations is Winthrop Jordan, *White over Black: American Attitudes toward the Negro, 1550–1812* (Chapel Hill: University of North Carolina Press, 1968).

For the society of the Dutch colonies in the eighteenth century, see Charles R. Boxer, *The Dutch Seaborne Empire*, David Hannoy, *The Great Chartered Companies*, both cited above.

Chapter 6. The International Relations
of Rival American Empires

There is no single study of the international aspects of the history of America in the eighteenth century. There is a good brief survey in Silvio Zavala, *El mundo americano*, cited above, I, chapter 9. The diplomatic history of America is embedded in the general history of Europe and in the histories of European diplomacy. The following books are useful for this history: *The Cambridge Modern History*, cited above, vol. VI; Penfield Roberts, *The Quest For Security, 1715–1740* (New York: Harper, 1947); Walter L. Dorn, *Competition for Empire, 1740–1763* (New York: Harper, 1940); Pierre Gaxotte, *Le siècle de Louis XV*, 2 vols. (Paris: Editions d'Histoire et d'Art, Plon, 1935); Gerald S. Graham, *Empire of the North Atlantic: The Maritime Struggle for North America* (Toronto: University of Toronto Press, 1950); David J. Hill, *A History of Diplomacy in the International Development of Europe*, 3 vols. (New York: Longmans, Green, 1905–14); E. Malcolm Smith, *British Diplomacy in the Eighteenth Century* (London: Williams and Norgate, 1937); Robert B. Mowat, *A History of European Diplomacy, 1451–1789* (London: E. Arnold, 1928); Pierre Muret, *La prépondérance anglaise, 1715–1763* (2nd ed.; Paris: Felix Alcan, 1942); Basil Williams, *The Whig Supremacy, 1714–1760* (2nd ed.; Oxford: Clarendon Press, 1962); Gordon Ireland, *Boundaries, Possessions, and Conflicts in South America* (Cambridge, Mass.: Harvard University Press, 1938); and, by the same author, *Boundaries, Possessions, and Conflicts in Central and North America and the Caribbean* (Cambridge, Mass.: Harvard University Press, 1941).

For America in the diplomacy of the Seven Years War, see Richard Waddington, *La Guerre de Sept Ans: Histoire diplomatique et militaire*, 5 vols. (Paris: Firmin-Didot, 1899–1917); Julian S. Corbett, *England in the Seven Years War*, 2 vols. (London: Longmans, Green, 1907); Lawrence H. Gipson, *The British Empire before the American Revolution*, cited above, vols. VI–VIII: *The Great War for the Empire*; Kate Hotblack, *Chatham's Colonial Policy* (London: Routledge, 1917); Augustin de Peñaranda y de Angulo, *Consideraciones generales sobre el segundo Pacto de Familia . . . 1761, entre Francia y España y las dos Sicilias* (Madrid: Hijos de M. G. Hernandez, 1906); O. P. Renault, *Le Pacte de Famille et l'Amérique: La politique coloniale franco-espagnole de 1760 à 1792* (Paris: Éditions Ernest Leroux, 1922); Albert von Ruville, *William Pitt, Earl of Chatham*, trans. H. J. Chaytor, 3 vols. (London: W. Heineman, 1907); Basil Williams, *The Life of William Pitt, Earl of Chatham*, 2 vols. (London: Longmans, Green, 1913).

For the reverse impact of the expansion of Europe upon European diplomacy and international law, see Max Savelle, *The Origins of American Diplomacy: The International History of Angloamerica, 1492–1763* (New York: Macmillan, 1967), especially chapters 12–19. For the sixteenth-century school of international jurists, see John H. Parry, *The Spanish Theory of Empire in the Sixteenth Century* (Cambridge: At the University Press, 1940), and James Brown Scott, *The Spanish Conception of International Law and of Sanctions* (Washington, D.C.: Carnegie Endowment for International Peace, 1934). For European antecedents of the Monroe Doctrine see Camilo Barcia-Trelles, "La Doctrine de Monroë dans son développement historique . . ." Hague Academy of International Law, *Recueil des cours*, 32:391–405 (pt. 2) (1930). See also Louise F. Brown, *The Freedom of the Seas* (New York: Dutton, 1919); Charles Dupuis, *Le principe d'équilibre et le concert européen de la Paix de Westphalie a l'acte d'Algeciras* (Paris: Perrin, 1909); Gilbert C. Gidel, *Le droit international public de la mer* (Paris: Chateauroux, 1932); William E. Hall, *International Law* (Oxford, 1880); Carl J. Kulsrud, *Maritime Neutrality to 1780* (Boston: Little, Brown, 1936); Renato de Mendonça, *Alexandre de Guzman, el precursor de Monroë y las directrices del Tratado de Madrid* (Mexico: Editorial Cultùra, 1941); Pitman B. Potter, *Freedom of the Seas in History, Law, and Politics* (New York: Longmans, Green, 1924); Max Savelle, "The American Balance of Power and European Diplomacy, 1713–1778," in Richard B. Morris, ed., *The Era of the American Revolution* (New York: Columbia University Press, 1939), pp. 140–213; W. B. Scaife, "The Development of International Law as to Newly Discovered Territory," *Annual Report of the American Historical Association*, IV (no. 3) (1890); Alphons H. Snow, *The Question of Aborigines in the Law and Practice of Nations* (New York: G. P. Putnam's Sons, 1921); Edmund A. Walsh, ed., *The History and Nature of International Relations* (New York: Macmillan, 1922).

The most important contemporary eighteenth-century treatment of international law is

Emmerich de Vattel, *Le droit des gens; ou, Principes de la loi naturelle, appliqués à la conduite aux affaires des nations et des souverains*, 3 vols. (London, 1758). For the international history of the Hispanoamerican empire in the eighteenth century, see Antonio Ballesteros y Beretta, gen. ed., *Historia de España y su influencia en la historia universal*, 9 vols. in 10 (Barcelona: P. Salvat, 1936–56); Alejandro del Cantillo, ed., *Tratados, convenios y declaraciones*, cited above; Jean O. Maclachlan, *Trade and Peace with Old Spain, 1667–1750* (Cambridge: At the University Press, 1940); Alfred Baudrillart, *Philippe V et la cour de France d'après des documents inédits tirés des archives espagnoles de Simancas et d'Alcalá de Henares et des archives du Ministère des Affaires Étrangères à Paris*, 5 vols. (Paris: Firmin-Didot, 1890–1901); Vera Lee Brown, "Anglo-Spanish Relations in America in the Closing Years of the Colonial Era," *Hispanic American Historical Review*, 11:327–483 (1931); by the same author, "Diplomacy of the Louisiana Cession by France to Spain, 1763," *American Historical Review*, 36:701–720 (July 1931); O. P. Renault, *Le Pacte de Famille et l'Amérique*, cited above; François Rousseau, *Le règne de Charles III d'Espagne (1759–1788)*, 2 vols. (Paris: Plon, 1907); Demetrio Ramos Perez, *El tratado de límites de 1750 y la expedición de Iturriaga al Orinoco* (Madrid: Instituto Juan Sebastián Elcano de Geografía, 1946); Vicente Palacio Atard, *El tercer Pacto de Familia*, cited above; Guillermo Kratz, *El tratado hispano-portugués de límites de 1750 y sus consecuencias. Estudio sobre la abolición de la Compañía de Jesús* (Rome: Instituto Historico de la Compañía de Jesús, 1954); Francisco Mateos, *El tratado de límites entre España y Portugal en 1750 y las misiones del Paraguay* (Madrid: Consejo Superior de Investigaciones Científicas, 1952); Henry Folmer, *Franco-Spanish Rivalry in North America, 1524–1763* (Glendale: Arthur H. Clark, 1953); Leon Vignols and Henri Sée, "La fin du commerce interlope dans l'Amérique espagnole," *Revue d'histoire économique et sociale*, 13 (no. 3):300–313 (1925).

For the diplomatic history of Lusoamerica in the eighteenth century the major work is Manoel Francisco de Barros Santarem, ed., *Quadro elementar das relações politicas e diplomaticas de Portugal com as diversas potencias do mundo, desde o principio da monarchia portugueza ate aos nossos dias*, 18 vols. (Paris, 1842–76); Renato de Mendonça, *Historia da politica exterior do Brasil, 1500–1825* (Mexico: Instituto Panamericano de Geografía e Historia, 1945); Eduardo Brazao, *The Anglo-Portuguese Alliance* (London: Sylvan Press, 1957); Luis Ferrand de Almeida, *A diplomatica portuguesa e os limites meridionales do Brasil* (Coimbra: Faculdade de Letras da Universidade de Coimbra, 1957); Artur Cesar Ferrerra Reis, *Limites e demarcações na Amazonia brasileira* (Rio de Janeiro: Impr. Nacional, 1947), vol. I: *A fronteira colonial com a Guiana francesa*; Jose C. de Macedo Soares, *Fronteiras do Brasil no regime colonial* (Rio de Janeiro: J. Olympio, 1939); Jonato da Costa Rego Monteiro, *A Colonia do Sacramento, 1680–1777*, 2 vols. (Porto Alegre: Barcelos, Bertiso, 1937); Guillermo Kratz, *El tratado hispano-portugués de límites de 1750 y sus consecuencias*; Francisco Mateos, *El tratado de límites entre España y Portugal en 1750 y las misiones del Paraguay*, both cited above; Carlos Hermenegildo de Sousa, *O tratado de Methuen no economia nacional* (Aveiro: Grafico Aveirense, 1938).

For the international history of Francoamerica in the eighteenth century, see Arthur McC. Wilson, *French Foreign Policy during the Administration of Cardinal Fleury, 1726–1743* (Cambridge, Mass.: Harvard University Press, 1936); Leon Vignols, "L'asiento français (1701–1713) et le commerce franco-espagnol vers 1700 à 1730. Avec deux mémoires français de 1728 sur ces sujects," *Revue d'histoire économique et sociale*, 13:403–436 (1929); Charles M. Andrews, "Anglo-French Colonial Rivalry, 1700–1756, the Western Phase," *American Historical Review*, 20:539–556, 761–780 (1915); P. Coquelle, *L'Alliance Franco-Hollandaise contre l'Angleterre, 1735–1788* (Paris: Plon, 1902); Gabriel Hanotaux and Alfred Martineau, gen. eds., *Histoire des colonies françaises*, cited above, vol. I; Francis Parkman, *A Half-Century of Conflict*, 2 vols. (Boston, 1892); Max Savelle, *The Diplomatic History of the Canadian Boundary, 1749–1763* (New Haven, Conn.: Yale University Press, 1940); George M. Wrong, *The Rise and Fall of New France*; Francis P. Renault, *Le Pacte de Famille et l'Amérique*, both cited above; Roland Lamontagne, *La Galissonière et le Canada*

(Paris: Presses Universitaires de France, 1962); Charles A. Julien, *Les Français en Amérique*, vol. II; Henry Folmer, *Franco-Spanish Rivalry in North America*, both cited above. There are also chapters relevant to this subject in Max Savelle, *Origins of American Diplomacy*, cited above.

For the international history of Angloamerica in the eighteenth century see Max Savelle, *Origins of American Diplomacy*, cited above, and, by the same author, "The International Approach to Early Angloamerican History," in Ray A. Billington, ed., *The Reinterpretation of Early American History* (San Marino, Calif.: Henry E. Huntington Library and Art Gallery, 1966), pp. 201–229. See also Lawrence H. Gipson, *The British Empire before the American Revolution*, vols. IV–VIII; Gerald Graham, *Empire of the North Atlantic*; Julian S. Corbett, *England in the Seven Years War*; Richard Pares, *War and Trade in the West Indies*, all cited above; and, by the same author, *Colonial Blockade and Neutral Rights, 1739–1963* (Oxford: Clarendon Press, 1938); Vera Lee Brown, "Anglo-Spanish Relations in America in the Closing Years of the Colonial Era," cited above; H. W. U. Temperley, "The Relations of England with Spanish America, 1720–1744," *Annual Report of the American Historical Association*, 1:231–238 (1911); John A. Schutz, "Imperialism in Massachusetts during the Governorship of William Shirley, 1741–1756," *Huntington Library Quarterly*, 3rd ser., 23:217–236 (May 1960); O. A. Sherrard, *Pitt and the Seven Years War* (London: Bodley Head, 1955); Charles G. Robertson, *Chatham and the British Empire* (New York: Collier Books, 1962); Howard H. Peckham, *The Colonial Wars, 1689–1762* (Chicago: University of Chicago Press, 1964); Douglas E. Leach, *Arms for Empire: A Military History of the British Colonies in North America, 1607–1763* (New York: Macmillan, 1973); Albert von Ruville, *William Pitt, Earl of Chatham*; Basil Williams, *The Life of William Pitt, Earl of Chatham*, both cited above; O. A. Sherrard, *Lord Chatham and America* (London: Bodley Head, 1958). The most easily available collection of European treaties and/or excerpts from European treaties bearing upon Angloamerica is Frances G. Davenport and A. O. Paullin, eds., *European Treaties Bearing on the History of the United States and Its Dependencies*, cited above.

For the international aspects of the history of the Dutch-American colonies in the eighteenth century, see Charles R. Boxer, *The Dutch Seaborne Empire*, chapter 10; Charles de Lannoy and Herman Van der Linden, *Histoire de l'expansion coloniale des peuples européens*, vol. II; Louis J. P. M. Bonnassieux, *Les grands compagnies de commerce*; David Hannay, *The Great Chartered Companies*; Charles Wilson, *Anglo-Dutch Commerce and Finance in the Eighteenth Century*; G. J. Renier, *The Dutch Nation*, all cited above; Charles Wilson, *Holland and Britain* (London: Collins, 1946).

There is no complete study of the direct relations between the Euroamerican empires or of the emergence of peculiarly American attitudes toward international affairs. There are, however, a few studies that make a beginning toward an understanding of this history. Such, for example, are Max Savelle, "Colonial Origins of American Diplomatic Principles," *Pacific Historical Review*, 3 (no. 3):334–350 (September 1934), and by the same author, "The Appearance of an American Attitude toward External Affairs, 1750–1775," *American Historical Review*, 52:655–660 (July 1947), and chapters 11, 13, and 20 of the same author's *Colonial Origins of American Diplomacy*, cited above. See also Dauril Alden, *Royal Government in Colonial Brazil*, cited above, chapters 4–10. Other useful studies are A. H. Buffinton, "The Isolationist Policy of Colonial Massachusetts," *New England Quarterly*, 1:158–179 (1928); Verner W. Crane, "The Southern Frontier in Queen Anne's War," *American Historical Review*, 24:379–395 (1919); F. B. Dexter, "Early Relations between New Netherland and New England," *Papers of the New Haven Colony Society*, 3:443–469 (1882); Amandus Johnson, *The Swedish Settlements on the Delaware*; George M. Wrong, *The Rise and Fall of New France*, both cited above; Verner W. Crane, *The Southern Frontier, 1670–1732* (Philadelphia, Pa.: Durham, N.C.: Duke University Press, 1929); W. F. Ganong, "A Monograph of the Evolution of the Boundaries of the Province of New Brunswick," *Transactions of the Royal Society of Canada*, 2nd ser., 7 (sect. 2):139–449 (1901); Francis W. Halsey, *The Old New York Frontier . . . 1614–1800* (New York: Scribner's, 1901);

Herbert E. Bolton and Mary Ross, *The Debatable Land: A Sketch of the Anglo-Spanish Contest for the Georgia Country* (Berkeley: University of California Press, 1925); William B. Dunn, *Spanish and French Rivalry in the Gulf Region of the United States, 1678–1902: The Beginnings of Texas and Pensacola* (Austin: University of Texas Press, 1917); J. Leitch Wright, Jr., *Anglo-Spanish Rivalry in North America* (Athens: University of Georgia Press, 1971); Lawrence H. Gipson, *The British Empire before the American Revolution*, cited above, especially vols. IV and V; John T. Lanning, *The Diplomatic History of Georgia: A Study of the Epoch of Jenkins' Ear* (Chapel Hill: University of North Carolina Press, 1936); Frederick Jackson Turner, "The Diplomatic Contest for the Mississippi Valley," *Atlantic Monthly*, 92:676–691, 807–817 (1904); Felix Gilbert, *To the Farewell Address: Ideas of Early American Foreign Policy* (Princeton, N.J.: Princeton University Press, 1961); J. Fred Rippy and Angie Debo, *The Historical Background of the American Policy of Isolation*, Smith College Studies in History, IX, nos. 3 and 4 (Northampton, Mass., 1924).

Chapter 7. Religion in America in the Eighteenth Century

There is, again, no general history of religion in America in the eighteenth century. Silvio Zavala, *El mundo americano*, cited above, I, 453–493, contains a brief survey. This account is elaborated and supplemented by the collection of papers contained in Antonio Tibesar, ed., *History of Religion in the New World: Studies Presented at a Conference on the History of Religion in the New World during Colonial Times* (Washington, D.C.: Academy of Franciscan History, 1958).

For the history of Christian missions in the American hemisphere, see Kenneth S. Latourette, *A History of the Expansion of Christianity*, 7 vols. (New York: Harper, 1937–45), vol. III: *Three Centuries of Advance, A.D. 1500–A.D. 1800*, chapters I, III–VI, XVI–XVII. S. Delacroix, *Histoire universelle des missions Catholiques*, 3 vols. (Paris: Librairie Grund, 1956–58), vol. II, is an excellent work, but is limited to Catholic missions only. Useful also are Stephen Neill, *Christian Missions* (London: Harmondsworth, 1964), and Thomas Hughes, ed., *History of the Society of Jesus in North America: Colonial and Federal*, 3 vols. (New York: Longmans, Green, 1907–17).

For the Indian religions and their contacts with Christianity, consult the lists of books given for the separate Euroamerican empires. For the African religions, see Melvin J. Herskovits "African Gods and Catholic Saints in New World Negro Belief," *American Anthropologist*, 39:635–643 (1937). Consult also the lists of references given for the separate Euroamerican empires.

For the history of religion in Hispanoamerica, Silvio Zavala, *El mundo americano*, I, 470–475, and Antonio Tibesar, ed., *History of Religion in the New World*, both cited above, are useful. For the history of the Inquisition in the Spanish-American empire, the most important works are Henry C. Lea, *The Inquisition of the Spanish Dependencies* (New York: Macmillan, 1968); José Toribio Medina, *Historia del Tribunal del Santo Oficio de la Inquisición en Lima 1569–1820*, 2 vols. (Santiago de Chile, 1887); Miguel de la Pinta Llorente, *La Inquisición española y los problemas de la cultura y de la intolerancia*, 2 vols. (Madrid: Ediciones Cultura Hispánica, 1953, 1958); Boleslao Lewin, *La Inquisición en Hispanoamerica: Judíos, protestantes, patriotas* (Buenos Aires: Editorial Proyección, 1962). Also useful is Richard E. Greenleaf, *The Mexican Inquisition of the Sixteenth Century* (Albuquerque: University of New Mexico Press, 1969).

The bibliography of the history of the missions in Hispanoamerica is voluminous. The following are especially useful: Herbert E. Bolton, "The Mission as a Frontier Institution in the Spanish-American Colonies," cited above; Pablo Hernandez, *Misiones del Paraguay. Organización social de las doctrinas guaranies de la Compañía de Jesús*, 2 vols. (Barcelona: G. Gili, 1913); J. M. Keys, *Las misiones españolas de California* (Madrid: Consejo Superior de Investigaciones Científicas, 1950). An interesting study of the religious acculturation of Indian and Christian religions in Mexico is Francisco de la Maza, *El Guadalupanismo mexicano* (Mexico: Porrua y Obregon, 1953).

For the history of religion in Lusoamerica in the eighteenth century, Silvio Zavala, *El mundo americano*, cited above, I, 475–480, presents a brief survey. A basic work is Thales de Azavedo, *O Catolicismo no Brasil, um campo para a pesquisa social* (Rio de Janeiro: Ministero da Educação e Cultura, 1955); Roger Bastide, "Religion and the Church in Brazil," in T. Lynn Smith and Alexander Marchant, eds., *Brazil: Portait of Half a Continent* (New York: Dryden Press, 1951), is a useful article. Gilberto Freyre, *Sobrados e mucambos*, cited above, is a near-classic; Charles R. Boxer, *The Golden Age of Brazil*, cited above, Chapters 6 and 11, provides a valuable survey; Sergio Buarque de Holanda, gen. ed., *História geral da civilização brasileira*, cited above, I, pt. 2, sec. II: "La vida espiritual," is an exhaustive, scholarly study.

For the missions of Brazil, Serafim Leite, *Historia da Companhia de Jesús no Brasil*, 10 vols. (Lisbon: Livraria Portugalia, 1938–50), is an exhaustive study of the Jesuit missions there.

For the African cults in colonial Brazil, René Ribeiro, *The Afrobrazilian Cult-Groups of Recife: A Study in Social Adjustment* (Evanston, Ill.: Northwestern University Press, 1969), is especially valuable, as is also his "Relations of the Negro with Christianity in Portuguese America," in Antonio Tibesar, ed., *History of Religion in the New World*, cited above, pp. 118–148. See also Pierre Verger, *Dieux d'Afrique, culte des Oriskas et Vodours à l'ancienne côte des esclaves en Afrique et a Bahía, la Baie de Tous les Saints au Brésil* (Paris: P. Hortman, 1954), and Raymundo Nina Rodrigues, *Os Africanos no Brasil*, cited above.

For the history of religion in Francoamerica in the eighteenth century, the standard work is still Auguste-Honoré Gosselin, *L'église du Canada depuis Monseigneur de Laval jusqu'à la conquête*, 3 vols. (Quebec: Typographie Laflamme-Proulx, 1911–14); Odoric M. Jouve, *Les Franciscains et le Canada*, 4 vols. (Quebec: Convent of the Holy Stigmata, 1915–45), is a study of one order. Joseph Rennard, *Histoire religieuse des Antilles françaises, d'après de documents inédits* (Paris: Larose, 1954), is fundamental for a study of religion in the French West Indies.

For the missions of Canada, Thomas Hughes, ed., *History of the Society of Jesus in North America*, cited above, is basic; Camille de Rochemonteux, *Les Jesuites et la Nouvelle-France au XVIIIe siècle*, 2 vols. (Paris: A. Picard, 1906), covers much the same ground. One of the greatest collections of sources for the work of the Jesuits in the expansion of Christianity is Reuben G. Thwaites, ed., *Jesuit Relations and Allied Documents*, 73 vols. (Cleveland: Arthur H. Clark, 1896–1901).

For the African cults and their contacts with Christianity, consult Eugène Revert, *La magie antillaise* (Paris: Éditions Bellenand, 1951).

For the history of religion in Angloamerica in the eighteenth century, William W. Sweet, *Religion in Colonial America* (New York: Scribner's, 1951), is a general survey. The following special studies are all useful: Elizabeth H. Davidson, *The Establishment of the English Church in Continental American Colonies* (Durham, N.C.: Duke University Press, 1936); Arthur L. Cross, *The Anglican Episcopate and the American Colonies* (New York: Longmans, Green, 1902); Evarts B. Greene, *Religion and the State: The Making and Testing of an American Tradition* (New York: Columbia University Press, 1941); Anson Phelps Stokes, *Church and State in the United States*, 3 vols. (New York: Harper, 1950); Carl Bridenbaugh, *Mitre and Sceptre: Transatlantic Faiths, Ideas, Personalities, and Politics, 1689–1775* (New York: Oxford University Press, 1962); Alan Heimert, *Religion and the American Mind from the Great Awakening to the Revolution* (Cambridge, Mass.: Harvard University Press, 1966); Perry Miller, *Jonathan Edwards* (New York: W. Sloane, 1949); Herbert Morais, *Deism in Colonial America* (New York: Columbia University Press, 1934); Conrad Wright, *The Beginnings of Unitarianism in America* (Boston: Starr King Press, Beacon Press, 1955); Wesley Gewehr, *The Great Awakening in Virginia, 1740–1790* (Durham, N.C.: Duke University Press, 1930); Edwin S. Gaustad, *The Great Awakening in New England* (New York: Harper, 1957); Alfred Caldecott, *The Church in the West Indies* (London: Colonial Church Histories,1898).

For the Christian missions in Angloamerica, see William W. Sweet, *The Story of Religion in America* (2nd ed., rev.; New York: Harper, 1950); Joseph E. Hulton, *A History of Moravian Missions* (London: Moravian Publishing Office, 1923); Robert F. Berhofer, Jr., *Salvation and the Savage: An Analysis of Protestant Missions and American Indian Response, 1787–1862* (Lexington: University of Kentucky Press, 1965); Kenneth S. Latourette, *A History of the Expansion of Christianity*, cited above.

For the carry-over of African religions and religious influences in Angloamerica, see René Ribeiro, *Religião e relações racais* (Rio de Janeiro: Ministerio da Educação e Cultura, 1956); Melvin J. Herskovits, "African Gods and Catholic Saints in New World Negro Belief," cited above; Elsie Clews Parsons, *Folk-lore of the Antilles, French and English*, 3 vols. *Memoirs of the American Folk-lore Society*, 26 (1933, 1936, 1943).

For religion in the Dutch-American empire, Silvio Zavala, *El mundo americano*, cited above, II, 483–486, provides a brief survey. Frederick J. Zwierlein, *Religion in New Netherland* (Rochester: J. P. Smith, 1910), is useful. Charles R. Boxer, *The Dutch Seaborne Empire*, cited above, and Melville J. and Frances S. Herskovits, *Surinam Folklore* (New York: Columbia University Press, 1936), touch upon the subject.

Chapter 8. America in the Eighteenth-Century Enlightenment

The intellectual history of America in the eighteenth century is in large measure a history of the American wing of the eighteenth-century Enlightenment. He who would study the intellectual history of America must, therefore, first acquaint himself with the thought and literature of the Enlightenment in Europe, beginning, presumably, with the works of such philosophes as Montesquieu, Voltaire, Raynal, Diderot and the Encyclopédistes, Hume, Robertson, Kant, Adam Smith, Moreau de St. Méry, Feijóo, Jovellanos, Pombal, Aranda, Burke, and a host of others, all of whom wrote and thought much about America. The general works on the European Enlightenment are legion. Among the most available and useful are the following: Peter Gay, *The Enlightenment: An Interpretation*, 2 vols. (New York: Alfred A. Knopf, 1966, 1969), vol. I: *The Rise of Western Pragmatism*, vol. II: *The Science of Freedom*; Will and Ariel Durant, *The Story of Civilization*, 10 vols. (New York: Simon and Schuster, 1939–67), vols. IX and X. Important also are Alfred Cobban, *In Search of Humanity: The Role of the Enlightenment in Modern History* (New York: George Braziller, 1960), Jean Sarrailh, *L'Espagne éclairée de la seconde moitié du XVIIIᵉ siècle* (Paris: Impr. National, 1954), and Ernst Cassirer, *The Philosophy of the Enlightenment*, trans. Fritz C. A. Kollen and James P. Pettegrove (Princeton, N.J.: Princeton University Press, 1951). A highly valuable collection of studies of the Enlightenment both in Spain and Portugal, on the one hand, and in the Iberoamerican colonies on the other, is A. Owen Aldridge, ed., *The Ibero-American Enlightenment* (Urbana: University of Illinois Press, 1971).

With special reference to America, see Silvio Zavala, *America en el espíritu francés del siglo XVIII* (Mexico: El Colegio Nacional, 1949). Gilbert Chinard, *L'Amérique et le rêve exotique dans la littérature française au XVIIᵉ et au XVIIIᵉ siècle* (Paris: Hachette, 1913), and Hoxie Fairchild, *The Noble Savage; A Study in Romantic Naturalism* (New York: Columbia University Press, 1928), are particularly useful.

There is no general history of the intellectual life of America as a whole. Silvio Zavala, *El mundo americano*, cited above, vol. I, chapter 11, contains an excellent brief survey. There are, however, a number of excellent intellectual and cultural histories of parts of the continent. Among the best is Germán Arciniegas, *Latin America: A Cultural History*, trans. from the Spanish by Joan McLean (New York: Alfred A. Knopf, 1967); Donald E. Worcester and Wendell C. Schaeffer, *The Growth and Culture of Latin America* (New York: Oxford University Press, 1956); H. Bernstein, *Origins of Inter-American Interest*,

1700–1800 (Philadelphia: University of Pennsylvania Press, 1945); by the same author, *Making an Inter-American Mind* (Gainesville: University of Florida Press, 1961); Arthur P. Whitaker, ed., *Latin America and the Enlightenment* (2nd ed.; Ithaca, N.Y.: Cornell University Press, 1961); Angel del Rio, *El mundo hispanico y el mundo anglosajón en América. Choque y atracción de dos culturas* (Buenos Aires: Editorial Bell, 1960); Enrique Anderson Imbert, *Historia de la literatura hispanoamericana* (4th ed.; Mexico: Fondo de Cultura Económica, 1962); Geoffrey Atkinson, *Les rélations des voyages du XVIIIe siècle et l'évolution des idées* (Paris: H. Champion, 1925); Arthur P. Whitaker, *The Western Hemisphere Idea: Its Rise and Decline* (Ithaca, N.Y.: Cornell University Press, 1954); Antonio Tovar, "L'incorporation du Nouveau Monde a la culture occidentale," *Cahiers d'histoire mondiale*, 6:833–856 (1961).

There is also no history of the rise of nationalism in America. The following are standard, however, for the history of nationalism in general: Boyd C. Shafer, *Nationalism, Myths and Realities* (New York: Harcourt, Brace, 1955); Carlton J. H. Hayes, *The Historical Evolution of Modern Nationalism* (New York: R. B. Smith, 1931); Hans Kohn, *The Idea of Nationalism: A Study in Its Origins and Background* (New York: Macmillan, 1944). A recent historical account and interpretive essay of great value is Boyd C. Shafer, *The Faces of Nationalism: New Realities and Old Myths* (New York: Harcourt Brace Jovanovich, 1972). The first two essays in Arthur P. Whitaker, *Nationalism in Latin America, Past and Present* (Gainesville: University of Florida Press, 1962), are relevant to the present study, as is also Max Savelle, "Nationalism and Other Loyalties in the American Revolution," *American Historical Review*, 67:901–923 (July 1962).

For the intellectual history of Hispanoamerica, the following are very useful: Arthur P. Whitaker, "La historia intellectual de Hispanoamérica en el siglo XVIII," *Revista de historia de América*, 40:553–575 (1955); Pedro Henríquez Ureña, *Historia de la cultura en la América hispánica* (Mexico: Fondo de Cultura Económica, 1947); Enrique Anderson Imbert, *Historia de la literatura hispanoamericana*, cited above; Alfonso Reyes, *Resumen de la literatura mexicana (siglos XVI–XIX)* (Mexico: Grafia Panamericana, 1957); Jean Sarrailh, *L'Espagne éclairée de la seconde moitié du XVIIIe siècle*, cited above; Richard Herr, *The Eighteenth Century Revolution in Spain* (Princeton, N.J.: Princeton University Press, 1958); John T. Lanning, *Academic Culture in the Spanish Colonies* (New York: Oxford University Press, 1960); Robert Jonas Shafer, *The Economic Societies in the Spanish World, 1763–1821* (Syracuse, N.Y.: Syracuse University Press, 1958); John T. Lanning, *The Eighteenth-Century Enlightenment in the University of San Carlos de Guatemala* (Ithaca, N.Y.: Cornell University Press, 1956); Bernard Moses, *Spanish Colonial Literature in South America* (New York: Hispanic Society of America, 1922).

For the cultural and intellectual history of Lusoamerica in the eighteenth century, see Germán Arciniegas, *Latin America*, cited above; Alexander Marchant, "Aspects of the Enlightenment in Brazil," in Arthur P. Whitaker, ed., *Latin America and the Enlightenment*, cited above, pp. 95–118; Moreira de Azevedo, "Sociedades fundados no Brazil desde os tempos coloniais até o comenco do actual reinado," *Revista do Instituto Histórico e Geográfico Brasileiro*, 48(no. 2):265–322 (1885); Fernando de Azevedo, ed., *As ciencias no Brasil*, 2 vols. (Rio de Janeiro: Instituição Larragoiti, n.d.); Candido de Mello-Leitão, *Historia das expedições científicas no Brasil* (São Paulo: Companhia Editora Nacional, 1941); João Cruz Costa, *A History of Ideas in Brazil* (Berkeley: University of California Press, 1964); Hernani Cidade, *Ensaio sobre a crise mental do seculo XVIII* (Coimbra: Imprensa da Universidade, 1929); L. Cobral de Moncada, *Un "iluminista" portugués do seculo XVIII: Luis Antonio Vernay* (São Paulo: Saraiva, 1941); João Lucio de Azevedo, *O Marques de Pombal e a sua epoca* (2nd ed.; Rio de Janeiro: Anuario do Brasil, 1922); Fernando de Azevedo, *A cultura brasileira: Introdução ao estudio de cultura no Brasil* (Rio de Janeiro: Instituto Brasileiro Geográfico Estadística, 1943).

For the intellectual history of Francoamerica in the eighteenth century, see Antoine Roy, *Les lettres, les sciences et les arts au Canada sous le régime français: Essai de contribution à l'histoire de la civilization canadienne*, 2 vols. (Paris: Jouve, 1930); August Viatte,

Histoire littéraire de l'Amérique française, des origines à 1950 (Paris: Presses Universitaires de France, 1954); Carl F. Klinck, ed., *Literary History of Canada: Canadian Literature in English* (Toronto: University of Toronto Press, 1965); Marcel Dugas, *Littérature canadienne* (Paris: Firmin-Didot, 1929); Reuben G. Thwaites, ed., *Jesuit Relations and Allied Documents*, cited above; Marcel Trudel, *L'influence de Voltaire au Canada* (Montreal: Fides, 1948); Guy Frégault, *La civilisation de la Nouvelle France (1713–1744)* (Montreal: Société des Éditions Pascal, 1944); Frédéric Louis Elie Morceau de Saint-Méry, *Loix et constitutions des colonies françaises de l'Amérique sous le vent*, 6 vols. (Paris, 1784–90).

For the intellectual life of Angloamerica in the eighteenth century, see Louis B. Wright, *The Cultural Life of the American Colonies, 1607–1763* (New York: New York Press, 1957); Max Savelle, *Seeds of Liberty* (Seattle: University of Washington Press, 1965); Lawrence C. Wroth, *An American Bookshelf, 1755* (Philadelphia: University of Pennsylvania Press, 1934); Michael Kraus, *The Atlantic Civilization: Eighteenth Century Origins* (Ithaca, N.Y.: Cornell University Press, 1949), and, by the same author, *Inter-Colonial Aspects of American Culture on the Eve of the Revolution: With Special Reference to the Northern Towns* (New York: Columbia University Press, 1928); Leonard W. Labaree, *Conservatism in Early American History* (New York: New York University Press, 1948); Perry Miller, *The New England Mind: Colony to Province* (Cambridge, Mass.: Harvard University Press, 1953); Paul M. Spurlin, *Montesquieu in America, 1760–1801* (Baton Rouge: Louisiana State University Press, 1940); Clinton Rossiter, *Seedtime of the Republic: The Origins of the American Tradition of Political Liberty* (New York: Harcourt, Brace, 1953); Gordon S. Wood, *The Creation of the American Republic, 1776–1787* (Chapel Hill: University of North Carolina Press, 1969); Bernard Bailyn, *The Ideological Origins of the American Revolution* (Cambridge, Mass.: Harvard University Press, 1967); Howard M. Jones, *O Strange New World. American Culture: The Formative Years* (New York: Viking, 1964); James T. Adams, *Provincial Society*; Evarts B. Greene, *The Revolutionary Generation*, both cited above; Alice M. Baldwin, *The New England Clergy and the American Revolution* (Durham, N.C.: Duke University Press, 1928); Herbert Schneider, *A History of American Philosophy* (New York: Columbia University Press, 1946); Isaac W. Riley, *American Philosophy: The Early Schools* (New York: Dodd, Mead, 1907); Samuel E. Morison, *Three Centuries of Harvard, 1736–1936* (Cambridge, Mass.: Harvard University Press, 1936); Whitfield Bell, Jr., *Early American Science: Needs and Opportunities for Study* (Williamsburg, Va.: Institute of Early American History and Culture, 1955); Brooke Hindle, *The Pursuit of Science in Revolutionary America* (Chapel Hill: University of North Carolina Press, 1956); Raymond P. Stearns, *Science in the British Colonies of America* (Urbana: University of Illinois Press, 1970); Moses Coit Tyler, *A History of American Literature, 1607–1765* (Ithaca, N.Y.: Cornell University Press, 1949); Robert E. Spiller, ed., *Literary History of the United States*, 3 vols. (New York: Macmillan, 1948), vol. I (see vol. III also for bibliography); Moses Coit Tyler, *Literary History of the American Revolution*, 2 vols. (New York, 1897).

Chapter 9. The Independence of the United States

The achievement of independence by the United States was the first of the movements by which the new societies created by European expansion rejected the dominance of their mother countries and established themselves as sovereign and independent members of the world community of states. The bibliography for the study of this event is vast; the list of suggested titles given below is necessarily brief and highly selective.

There is no satisfactory one-volume history of the American Revolution covering all its aspects from its beginnings (about 1760) to its final completion (about 1791). The following surveys, however, are useful: Esmond Wright, *Fabric of Freedom, 1763–1800* (New York: Hill & Wang, 1961); Edmund Morgan, *The Birth of the Republic, 1763–1789* (Chicago:

University of Chicago Press, 1965); John Alden, *A History of the American Revolution* (New York: Alfred A. Knopf, 1969). For the various modern interpretations of the American Revolution, a series of essays edited by Jack P. Greene, *The Reinterpretation of the American Revolution* (New York: Harper & Row, 1968), is highly thoughtful and provocative; Gordon S. Wood, *The Creation of the American Republic*, cited above, is a brilliant study of the ideological aspects of the Revolution.

Lawrence H. Gipson, *The British Empire before the American Revolution*, cited above, is a magisterial review of the institutions, the wars, and the internal tensions of the British empire in the twenty-five years preceding the American Declaration of Independence. Stephen Watson, *The Reign of George III, 1760–1815* (Oxford: Clarendon Press, 1960), is an excellent survey of the history of England and the empire during George III's reign, including a brief history of the loss of thirteen of the American colonies. John Brooke, *King George III* (New York: McGraw-Hill, 1972) is a first-rate biography.

For the events and the tensions of the years between, say, 1760 and 1776, the following studies are highly useful: Lawrence H. Gipson, *The Coming of the Revolution, 1763–1775* (New York: Harper, 1954); Bernhard Knollenberg, *The Origin of the American Revolution* (New York: Macmillan, 1960); John C. Miller, *Origins of the American Revolution* (Boston: Little, Brown, 1943); Merrill Jensen, *The Founding of a Nation* (New York: Oxford University Press, 1968); Edmund and Helen Morgan, *The Stamp Act Crisis* (Chapel Hill: University of North Carolina Press, 1953); Benjamin Woods Labaree, *The Boston Tea Party* (New York: Oxford University Press, 1964); Jack Sosin, *Whitehall and the Wilderness, 1763–1775* (Lincoln: University of Nebraska Press, 1961); Michael Kammen, *Rope of Sand: The Colonial Agents, British Politics, and the American Revolution* (Ithaca, N.Y.: Cornell University Press, 1968). Of special significance for an understanding of this period is Bernard Bailyn, *The Ideological Origins of the American Revolution*, cited above. See also Charles H. McIlwain, *The American Revolution: A Constitutional Interpretation* (New York: Macmillan, 1923); Randolph G. Adams, *Political Ideas of the American Revolution: Brittanic-American Contributions to the Problem of Imperial Organization, 1765–1775* (Durham, N.C.: Trinity College Press, 1922).

For the military history of the American Revolution as a world war in which Britain stood almost alone against the other states of western Europe as well as the thirteen rebellious colonies, see Piers Mackesy, *The War for America, 1775–1783* (Cambridge, Mass.: Harvard University Press, 1964). For the military history of the Revolutionary War in America, Christopher Ward, *The War of the Revolution* (New York: Macmillan, 1952), is a standard treatment. Don Higginbotham, *The War of American Independence: Military Attitudes, Policies, and Practice, 1763–1789* (New York: Macmillan, 1971), is especially valuable for its sociological approach to the conflict. The following are also useful: George F. Scheer and Hugh F. Rankin, *Rebels and Redcoats* (Cleveland: World Publishing, 1957); Willard M. Wallace, *Appeal to Arms: A Military History of the American Revolution* (New York: Harper, 1951).

The constitutional history of the United States during the Revolution is covered in Allan Nevins, *The American States during and after the Revolution, 1775–1789* (New York: Macmillan, 1927); Merrill Jensen, *The Articles of Confederation: An Interpretation of the Social-Constitutional History of the American Revolution, 1774–1781* (Madison: University of Wisconsin Press, 1940); Clinton Rossiter, *Seedtime of the Republic*; Charles H. McIlwain, *The American Revolution*, both cited above; Edmund C. Burnett, *The Continental Congress* (New York: Macmillan, 1941); Robert E. Brown, *Middle-Class Democracy and the Revolution in Massachusetts, 1691–1780* (Ithaca, N.Y.: Cornell University Press, 1955); Gordon S. Wood, *The Creation of the American Republic*, cited above. A highly valuable work that places the American Revolution in the context of the larger revolutionary movement in the Western world is Robert R. Palmer, *The Age of the Democratic Revolution: A Political History of Europe and America, 1760–1800*, 2 vols. (Princeton, N.J.: Princeton University Press, 1959, 1966).

For the diplomatic history of the American Revolution, see Samuel F. Bemis, *The Diplo-*

macy of the American Revolution (New York: Appleton-Century, 1935); for the history of the final treaty of peace, Richard B. Morris, *The Peacemakers . . .* (New York: Harper & Row, 1965), is indispensable. For the background of revolutionary diplomacy, Gerald Stourzh, *Benjamin Franklin and American Foreign Policy* (Chicago: University of Chicago Press, 1954), Felix Gilbert, *To the Farewell Address*, cited above, and E. S. Corwin, *French Policy and the American Alliance of 1778* (Princeton, N.J.: Princeton University Press, 1916), are useful. Richard W. Van Alstyne, *Empire and Independence: The International History of the American Revolution* (New York: Wiley, 1965), is especially valuable for placing the American Revolution and its diplomatic history in a world context.

For the economic history of the Revolution, Curtis P. Nettels, *The Emergence of the National Economy*, cited above, is now standard. Robert A. East, *Business Enterprise in the Revolutionary Era* (New York: Columbia University Press, 1938), Clarence L. Ver Steeg, *Robert Morris: Revolutionary Financier; with an Analysis of His Earlier Career* (Philadelphia: University of Pennsylvania Press, 1954), and Elmer J. Ferguson, *The Power of the Purse: A History of American Public Finance, 1776–1790* (Chapel Hill: University of North Carolina Press, 1961), are all valuable.

For the social history of the American Revolution, the pioneer work is still J. Franklin Jameson, *The Revolution Considered as a Social Movement* (Princeton, N.J.: Princeton University Press, 1926); Frederick B. Tolles, "The American Revolution Considered as a Social Movement: A Re-evaluation," *American Historical Review*, 60:1–12 (1954), is a valuable critique of the Jameson thesis. Benjamin Quarles, *The Negro in the American Revolution* (Chapel Hill: University of North Carolina Press, 1961), is valuable; R. B. Morris, "Class Struggle and the American Revolution," *William and Mary Quarterly*, 3rd ser., 19:3–29 (1962), is a valuable reevaluation of this problem. Other useful studies include Claude H. Van Tyne, *The Loyalists in the American Revolution* (New York: Macmillan, 1902); Evarts B. Greene, *The Revolutionary Generation*, cited above; William H. Nelson, *The American Tory* (Oxford: Clarendon Press, 1961); Jackson T. Main, *The Social Structure of Revolutionary America* (Princeton, N.J.: Princeton University Press, 1965). Pauline Maier, *From Resistance to Revolution* (New York: Alfred A. Knopf, 1972), is a study of the rise and impact of the common men, the "radicals," on the Revolution.

For the intellectual and religious aspects of the American Revolution, see Moses Coit Tyler, *Literary History of the American Revolution*; Brooke Hindle, *The Pursuit of Science in Revolutionary America*; Gordon S. Wood, *The Creation of the American Republic*, all cited above; Carl L. Becker, *The Declaration of Independence: A Study in the History of Political Ideas* (New York: Harcourt, Brace, 1922); Edmund S. Morgan, "The Revolution Considered as an Intellectual Movement" in Arthur M. Schlesinger and Morton White, eds., *Paths of American Thought* (Boston: Houghton Mifflin, 1963), pp. 11–33; William W. Sweet, *Religion in the Development of American Culture, 1765–1840* (New York: Scribner's, 1952); Anson Phelps Stokes, *Church and State in the United States*, vol. I; Carl Bridenbaugh, *Mitre and Sceptre*, both cited above; Russel B. Nye, *The Cultural Life of the New Nation, 1776–1830* (New York: Harper, 1960). Adrienne Koch, *The American Enlightenment: The Shaping of the American Experiment and a Free Society* (New York: George Braziller, 1965), is a useful collection of writings of the men who made the Revolution.

The emergence of United States nationalism is discussed in Max Savelle, "Nationalism and Other Loyalties in the American Revolution," cited above. Boyd L. Shafer, *Faces of Nationalism*, cited above, and Russel B. Nye, *This Almost Chosen People: Essays in the History of American Ideas* (East Lansing: Michigan State University Press, 1966), are also of value in the study of this phenomenon.

For the completion of the Revolution in the years between 1783 and 1791, see Merrill Jensen, *The New Nation: A History of the United States during the Confederation, 1781–1789* (New York: Alfred A. Knopf, 1950); Forest McDonald, *We the People: The Economic Origins of the Constitution* (Chicago: University of Chicago Press, 1958); by the same author, *E Pluribus Unum: The Formation of the American Republic, 1776–1790*

(Boston: Houghton Mifflin, 1965); Jackson T. Main, *The Anti-Federalists: Critics of the Constitution, 1781-1788* (Chapel Hill: University of North Carolina Press, 1961); Max Farrand, *The Framing of the Constitution of the United States* (New Haven, Conn.: Yale University Press, 1913); Clinton Rossiter, *1787: The Grand Convention* (New York: Macmillan, 1966); Robert A. Rutland, *The Birth of the Bill of Rights, 1776-1791* (Chapel Hill: University of North Carolina Press, 1955); Irving Brant, *The Bill of Rights: Its Origin and Meaning* (Indianapolis: Bobbs-Merrill, 1965).

Chapter 10. The Ferment of Freedom

It is clear that the ferment of ideas and impulses toward "liberty" that had inspired the American Revolution was shared, if in differing degrees of intensity, by all the peoples of the American hemisphere. Indeed, it was not confined to them either, for in the second half of the eighteenth century it was characteristic — again, in varying degrees of intensity — of all the societies in the Atlantic community of nations.

For the European intellectual manifestations of this ferment, Peter Gay, *The Enlightenment*, vol. II, Will and Ariel Durant, *The Story of Civilization*, vol. X: *Rousseau and Revolution*, and Jean Sarrailh, *L'Espagne éclairée de la seconde moitié du XVIIIᵉ siècle*, all cited above, are highly useful. See also Alfred Cobban, *In Search of Humanity*, cited above. Robert R. Palmer, *The Age of the Democratic Revolution*, cited above, is a magisterial synthesis of the fusion of ideas and political change in this era all over the Atlantic world. Jacques Godechot, *France and the Atlantic Revolution of the Eighteenth Century, 1770-1799* (New York: Free Press, 1965), is also highly valuable for the era of Revolution in the "Atlantic world."

For Hispanoamerica the most convenient survey of the intellectual ferment is Germán Arciniegas, *Latin America*, cited above, chapters 11, 12, 13. See also Arthur P. Whitaker, ed., *Latin America and the Enlightenment*, cited above; more recently, by the same author, "Changing and Unchanging Interpretations of the Enlightenment in Spanish America," in A. W. Aldridge, ed., *The Ibero-American Enlightenment*, cited above, pp. 21-57; José de Onís, *The United States as Seen by Spanish-American Writers, 1776-1890* (New York: Columbia University Hispanic Institute, 1952); Ricardo Caillet-Bois, "La America española y la revolución francesca," *Boletín de la Academia Nacional de la Historia*, 13:159-216 (Buenos Aires, 1940); William Spence Robertson, *The Life of Miranda*, 2 vols. (Chapel Hill: University of North Carolina Press, 1929); Jefferson R. Spell, *Rousseau in the Spanish World before 1833: A Study in Franco-Spanish Literary Relations* (Austin: University of Texas Press, 1938); Arturo Ardao, *La filosofía polémico de Feijóo* (Buenos Aires: Editorial Losada, 1962); John H. R. Polt, *Jovellanos and His English Sources, Economic, Philosophical, and Political Writings*, in *Transactions of the American Philosophical Society*, new ser., vol. 54, pt. 7 (Philadelphia: The Society, 1964). Treatments of the idea of an American community are Arthur P. Whitaker, *The Western Hemisphere Idea*, cited above; Leopoldo Zea, *América como consciencia* (Mexico: Ediciones Cuadernos Americanos, 1953); Antonio Gómez Robledo, *Idea y experiencia de América* (Mexico: Fondo de Cultura Económica, 1958). For three of the "precursors" see Edouard Clavery, *Trois précurseurs de l'indépendance des démocraties sud-américaines: Miranda, 1756-1816; Marisco, 1765-1823; Espejo, 1747-1795* (Paris: Impr. Fernand Michel, 1932); for the great "precursors" Pablo de Olavide and Juan Bantisto Viscardo, Marcelin Defourneaux, *Pablo de Olavide ou l'Afrancesado* (Paris: Presses Universitaires de France, 1959, and Miguel Batllori, *El Abate Viscardo; Historia y mito de la intervención de los Jesuites en la independencia de Hispanoamérica* (Caracas: Comité de Origines de la Emancipación, 1953), are of the highest importance. For cultural life in general, see John T. Lanning, *The Eighteenth-Century Enlightenment in the University of San Carlos de Guatemala*; by the same author, *Academic Culture in the Spanish Colonies*; Robert Jonas Shafer, *The Economic Societies in the Spanish World*, all cited above. Of supreme importance for this area are Simón Bolívar, *Obras completas*, 3 vols. (Havana: Editorial Lex, 1950), and Francisco de Miranda, *Archivo del General*

Miranda, 14 vols. (Caracas: Editorial Sur-America, 1929–33). Arthur P. Whitaker, "La historia intellectual de Hispanoamérica en el siglo XVIII," cited above, and Hugo D. Barbagelata, *La Révolution Française et l'Amérique Latine* (Paris: Sirey, 1936), are both valuable.

For a brief account of the ferment of freedom in Lusoamerica, see especially Caio Prado, Jr., *The Colonial Background of Modern Brazil*, cited above, pp. 399–439. See also Germán Arciniegas, *Latin America*, Alexander Marchant, "Aspects of the Enlightenment in Brazil," both cited above, E. Bradford Burns, "Concerning the Transmission and Dissemination of the Enlightenment in Brazil," in A. Owen Aldridge, ed., *The Ibero-American Enlightenment*, cited above, pp. 256–281, and Alfonso Ruy de Souza, *A primeira revolução social brasileira (1798)* (São Paulo: Companhia Editora Nacional, 1942).

For the ferment in the French colonies, see Aimé Césaire, *Toussaint L'Ouverture: La Révolution Française et le problème colonial* (Paris: Présence Africaine, 1961); and Rayford W. Logan, *Haiti and the Dominican Republic* (New York: Oxford University Press, 1968); J. F. Saintogant, *La colonisation française pendant la Révolution, 1789–1799*, 2 vols. (Paris: La Renaissance du Livre, 1930); Ralph Korngold, *Citizen Toussaint* (London: V. Gollancz, 1946); Antoine Roy, *Les lettres, les sciences et les arts au Canada sous le régime français*, cited above; Mason Wade, *The French Canadian, 1760–1945* (London: Macmillan, 1955); Alfred A. Burt, *The Old Province of Quebec* (Toronto: Ryerson Press, 1933); A. Viatte, *Histoire littéraire de l'Amérique française, des origines à 1950*, cited above; Jean Charbonneau, *L'Ecole Littéraire de Montreal: Ses origines, ses animateurs, ses influences* (Montreal: A. Levesque, 1935); C. L. R. James, *The Black Jacobins: Toussaint L'Ouverture and the San Domingo Revolution* (New York: Dial Press, 1938); Mason Wade, "Quebec and the French Revolution of 1799: The Mission of Henri Mezière," *Canadian Historical Review*, 31:345, 368 (1950), and, by the same author, *The French Canadians* (New York: Macmillan, 1955).

For the continuation of revolutionary ferment in the United States, see William N. Chambers, *Political Parties in a New Nation: The American Experience, 1776–1809* (New York: Oxford University Press, 1963); R. L. Ketcham, "France and American Politics, 1763–93," *Political Science Quarterly*, 78:198–223 (1963); John C. Miller, *Crises in Freedom: The Alien and Sedition Acts* (Boston: Little, Brown, 1951); James Morton Smith, *Freedom's Fetters: The Alien and Sedition Laws and American Civil Liberties* (Ithaca, N.Y.: Cornell University Press, 1956); Alexander DeConde, *Entangling Alliances: Politics and Diplomacy under George Washington* (Durham, N.C.: Duke University Press, 1958); Dumas Malone, *Jefferson and the Ordeal of Liberty* (Boston: Little, Brown, 1962).

For the genesis and the growth of nationalism in the American hemisphere during the "Age of the Democratic Revolution," the reader is referred to the bibliographical references for chapter 8.

Chapter 11. The Independence
of Latin America

The literature relevant to the achievement of independence by the Latin-American societies is vast indeed. The list presented here is necessarily brief and highly selective. For a very useful bibliographical essay, see Robin A. Humphreys, "The Historiography of the Spanish-American Revolutions," *Hispanic American Historical Review*, 36:87–93 (1956).

There is a brief general history of the end of the Euroamerican colonial empires in Silvio Zavala, *El mundo americano*, cited above, I, chapter 12. For larger studies, consult Bernard Moses, *The Intellectual Background of the Revolution in South America, 1810–1824* (New York: Hispanic Society of America, 1926); Robin A. Humphreys and John Lynch, "The Emancipation of Latin America," *Reports of the Twelfth International Congress of Historical Sciences*, 4 vols. (Vienna: Verlag Ferdinand Berge & Söhne, 1966), vol. III: *Commissions*, pp. 39–56; also, Robin A. Humphreys and John Lynch, eds., *The Origins of the Latin-American Revolutions* (New York: Alfred A. Knopf, 1965); Arthur P. Whitaker,

The United States and the Independence of Latin America, 1800–1830 (Baltimore: Johns Hopkins University Press, 1941); William S. Robertson, *France and Latin American Independence* (Baltimore: Johns Hopkins University Press, 1939); Enrique de Gandia, *Napoleon y la independencia de América* (Buenos Aires: A. Zamora, 1955); Carlos A. Villanueva, *Historia y diplomacia: Napoleon y la independencia de América* (Paris: Garmier, 1911); Charles K. Webster, ed., *Britain and the Independence of Latin America, 1812–1830* (London: Oxford University Press, 1938), is a useful collection of documents; Arthur P. Whitaker, *The Western Hemisphere Idea*, cited above; Joseph B. Lockey, *Pan-Americanism: Its Beginnings* (New York: Macmillan, 1920); Alfred Schalck de la Fanerie, *Napoleon et l'Amérique, histoire des relations franco-américains specialement envisagée du point de vue de l'influence napoleonien, 1798–1815* (Paris: Payol, 1917); Francisco Cuevas Cancino, *Bolívar: El ideal panamericano del libertador* (Mexico: Fondo de Cultura Económica, 1958). Gerhard Masur, *Nationalism in Latin America: Diversity and Unity* (New York: Macmillan, 1966), discusses the origins and early development of nationalism among the Latin-American nations.

For the independence movements in Hispanoamerica, see Rafael Altamira y Crevea, *Resumen histórico de la independencia de la América española* (Buenos Aires: Menendez y Galli, 1910); Charles P. Griffin, *The United States and the Disruption of the Spanish Empire, 1810–1822* (New York: Columbia University Press, 1937); Marius André, *La fin de l'empire espagnol d'Amérique* (Paris: Nouvelle Librairie Nationale, 1922); Jefferson R. Spell, *Rousseau in the Spanish World before 1833*, cited above; Mariano Cuevas, ed., *El libertador: Documentos selectos de don Augustín de Iturbide* (Mexico: Editorial Patria, 1947); an old standard life of Iturbide is William Spence Robertson, *Iturbide of Mexico* (Durham, N.C.: Duke University Press, 1952); Vicente Lecuna, ed., *Cartas del libertador*, 10 vols. (Caracas: Lit. y Tip. del Comercio, 1929–30); or, in English, Harold A. Bierck, ed., *Selected Writings of Bolívar*, 2 vols. (New York: Colonial Press, 1951). The following biographical studies are useful: Gerhard Masur, *Simón Bolívar* (Albuquerque: University of New Mexico Press, 1948); Caracciolo Parra-Perez, *Bolívar: Contribución al estudio de sus ideas politicas* (Paris: Excelsior, 1928); J. B. Trend, *Bolívar and the Independence of Spanish America* (London: Macmillan, 1946); Victor Andrés Belaúnde, *Bolivar and the Political Thought of the Spanish-American Revolution* (Baltimore: Johns Hopkins University Press, 1938). For Miranda, see William Spence Robertson, *The Life of Miranda*, cited above; for San Martín see Ricardo Rojas, *San Martín, Knight of the Andes*, trans. Herschel Brickell and Carlos Vilela (New York: Cooper Square, 1967); J. C. J. Metford, *San Martín the Liberator* (New York: Philosophical Library, 1950); José Pacifico Otero, *Historia del libertador, Don José de San Martín*, 4 vols. (2nd ed.; Buenos Aires, 1949); Bartolomé Mitre, *Historia de San Martín y de la emancipación sudamericana*, 4 vols. (2nd ed.; Buenos Aires: F. Lajouane, 1890). More general studies are John Rydjord, *Foreign Interest in the Independence of New Spain: An Introduction to the War of Independence* (Durham, N.C.: Duke University Press, 1935); Lorenzo de Zavala, *Ensayo histórico de las revoluciones de México desde 1808 hasta 1830* [1831–32], 2 vols. (3rd ed.; Paris, 1831–32); Luís Castillo Ledón, *Hidalgo. La vida del héroe*, 2 vols. (Mexico: Talleres Gráficos de la Nación, 1949); Juan E. Hernández y Dávalos, ed., *Colección de documentos para la historia de la guerra de independencia de México a 1821*, 6 vols. (Mexico, 1877–82).

For the independence movement in Brazil, see Manuel de Oliveira Lima, *El movimiento de independencia, 1821–1822* (São Paulo: Companhia Melhoramentos de São Paulo, 1922); Tobias do Rego Monteiro, *Historia do imperio. A elaboração da independencia: Quatorze retratos* (Rio de Janeiro: F. Briquiet, 1927); Manuel de Oliveira Lima, *The Evolution of Brazil Compared with That of Spanish and Anglo-Saxon America*, cited above; José Francisco de la Roche Pombo, *Historia do Brasil*, 10 vols. (Rio de Janeiro: Edicão do Annuario do Brasil, 1922); Clarence H. Haring, *Empire in Brazil: A New World Experiment with Monarchy* (Cambridge, Mass.: Harvard University Press, 1958); Gilberto Freyre, *Sobrados e mocambos*, cited above.

Index

Index